D0577686

CHASING LOST TIME

CHASING LOST TIME

The Life of C. K. Scott Moncrieff: Soldier, Spy, and Translator

JEAN FINDLAY

Farrar, Straus and Giroux
New York

Farrar, Straus and Giroux
18 West 18th Street, New York 10011

Printed in the United States of America
Originally published in 2014 by Chatto & Windus, Great Britain
Published in the United States by Farrar, Straus and Giroux
First American edition, 2015

Library of Congress Control Number: 2014959509
ISBN: 978-0-374-11927-0

Farrar, Straus and Giroux books may be purchased for educational, business, or promotional use. For information on bulk purchases, please contact the Macmillan Corporate and Premium Sales Department at 1-800-221-7945, extension 5442, or write to specialmarkets@macmillan.com.

www.fsgbooks.com
www.twitter.com/fsgbooks • www.facebook.com/fsgbooks

1 3 5 7 9 10 8 6 4 2

For Alastair, Theodore, Hugo and Fergus

Happiness is beneficial for the body, but it is grief that develops the powers of the mind.

Marcel Proust, *Remembrance of Things Past, Time Regained*

Let us be grateful to people who make us happy, they are the charming gardeners who make our souls blossom.

Marcel Proust, 'Regrets, Reveries, Changing Skies',
Pleasures and Regrets

Contents

Illustrations

All pictures are from the family collection unless otherwise stated.

Picture section 1:

1: Charles Kenneth Scott Moncrieff, aged 23, taken just before the war.

2: Charles's parents, Jessie Margaret 'Meg' and William George Scott Moncrieff; Weedingshall House, near Polmont, Stirlingshire, where Charles was born in 1889; Charles's mother Meg, as a young woman, with her mother, Katherine, seated.

3: The extended family at their annual seaside gathering at Elie on the Fife coast on the eve of war, 1914; Charles, aged 20, with his father and brother John, in 1910.

4: Charles in his first year at Winchester with other scholars in 1903; Charles aged 16 when he first met Robbie Ross; Christopher Millard, Robbie Ross's secretary, who greatly influenced the young Charles (courtesy of the Master and Fellows of University College, Oxford).

5: Robert Ross, disciple of Oscar Wilde and art critic, photographed by Elliott & Fry, 1914 (© National Portrait Gallery, London); a sketch from the Edgemoor visitors' book of Philip Bainbrigge, a close friend of Charles's from his university days.

6: Charles on a visit to Durie in 1916; Charles surrounded by his first company in the KOSB in 1914, at Portland Bill before they set out for France.

7: Robert Graves in 1920, photographed by Lady Ottoline Morell (© National Portrait Gallery, London); Wilfred Owen in 1916, photographed by John Gunston (© National Portrait Gallery, London); Charles (in spectacles) at the Ducane Road specialist leg hospital.

8: A page from Charles's Bible showing the places and dates he attended mass while in France from 1915 to 1916.

Picture section 2:

1: Portrait of Charles painted in 1922 by Edward Stanley Mercer (© Scottish National Portrait Gallery, Edinburgh).

2: Marcel Proust wearing the uniform of the 76th Infantry Regiment, Orléans, in 1889 (© Mondadori via Getty Images); Charles Prentice with Norman Douglas (© Carl Van Vechten, the Van Vechten Trust).

3: Luigi Pirandello at his desk, Monteluco, in 1924 (© Mondadori via Getty Images); Edward Marsh, civil servant and patron of the arts, painted by Teddy Wolfe (courtesy of RSL); sketch of Charles by Estelle Nathan, in 1925.

4: A cinematic flipbook of Vyvyan Holland and Charles at dinner in Milan, mid-1920s (courtesy of Merlin Holland).

5: Charles (on left) and his friends, sightseeing in Italy, mid-1920s; Oriana Haynes as a young woman, painted by John Collier in 1898; Ruby Melville (second left) in Italy in 1923 (courtesy of Merlin Holland).

6: A postcard of the Hotel Nettuno in Pisa, where Charles often stayed, to his niece, Sita.

7: Charles on holiday with his cousin Louis Christie at Durie in 1926; Claude Dansey, spymaster, caricature by H. F. Crowther Smith; Charles on an Italian mountainside, taken by Vyvyan Holland in 1926 (courtesy of Merlin Holland).

8: A dedication by Charles to his ancestors.

Acknowledgements

This book was suggested in the first place by Euan Cameron, translator and editor, whose unflagging support and lunches at the Havelock have sustained my efforts. The first research I did was in Jamie Fergusson's book collection, at his dining room table. I have to thank many people on the seven-year journey and apologise for leaving anyone out. Suzanne Foster, the Archivist at Winchester College; Sue Usher at the Oxford English Faculty Library; Steve Crook in New York Public Library; Trevor Dunmore at the Royal Automobile Club; Patricia Cox at the Savile Club; Wendy Maynard at the New Club; Susan Thomas and Kira Ferrant in New York; Ulysses Bookshop, WC1; Peter Ellis; Professor James Fawcett at Kings College, Cambridge and Professor Jon Marenbon at Trinity College, Cambridge; Peter Montieth at the Kings College Archives; the Trustees and staff of the London Library; Neville Shack; Theodore Shack; Anisa Malik-Mansell, Librarian, Shrewsbury School; Sandy Christie; Malcolm Gibb; Christina Scott Moncrieff; Georgia Coleridge; Janet Mcgiffen; Maggie and Jamie Fergusson; Madeleine Fergusson; John Hodge from the Olin Library Washington University, St Louis; Lesley Scott Moncrieff; Eileen Scott Moncrieff; Michael Scott Moncrieff; John Scott Moncrieff; Ann Scott Moncrieff; David Lunn Rockliffe; Jaqueline Lunn Rockliffe; Catherine Moberly; the Macdonalds at Alton Burn Hotel, Nairn; S. Stefano at Suites Rome, 67 Via della Croce; Anna Maria Cruciata in Grossetto; Helen Spande at Villa la Pietra, Firenze; Peter Christie at Durie; James Christie; Anthony Mould; Anthony Fraser; Philippa Fraser; Kit Fraser; Sir Michael Holroyd; Sir Crispin Tickell; Keith Jeffry and Rupert Walters. Ian Martin from the KOSB Museum in Berwick-upon-Tweed gave generous time to checking military detail.

I am very grateful for funding from the Hyam Wingate Foundation and the Authors' Foundation. I have had particular advice from my former Professor of French at Edinburgh University, Peter France, and am much indebted to Professor Jon Stallworthy of Wolfson College, Oxford, who has been a princely adviser throughout. I also want to thank my enigmatic and adept agent, Peter Straus; and, most of all, my two brilliant editors: the wise, experienced and patient Jenny Uglow, and the sharp-witted and exacting Juliet Brooke.

CHASING LOST TIME

Introduction

While studying French at university in Edinburgh, I wanted to write my final thesis on Proust. An old uncle whose humour I respected said, 'It killed Proust to write it, it killed CK to translate it; it'll probably kill you to read it . . .' I took his advice and settled for Balzac. The CK to whom he referred was my mother's great-uncle, always known by his initials, as there were a number of Charleses in the family.

I grew up with stories of CK. He was my great-aunt Dorothy's godfather and she would explain with a grave and sad expression, 'He was a chomosecshooal, you know.' In a framed box on the wall in her drawing room she carefully kept his war medals: a Military Cross, the 1914–15 Star, the British War Medal and the Victory Medal, which was the handsomest of all, with a rainbow ribbon and a gold winged figure of Victory. She showed me a fragment of red and yellow stained glass picked up from the ruins of Ypres Cathedral, also a ring made by a French officer out of a shell case. My mother, Lesley Scott Moncrieff, told me that as a child she had slept in an attic beside a dark portrait of Charles with a rip in the canvas, which was later mended and given to the National Portrait Gallery in Edinburgh.

Years later, I was given a battered leather suitcase containing the forgotten letters, diaries, and notebooks of Charles Scott Moncrieff; and I settled down to read his translation of Proust. The general editor of the new translation of Proust's great novel reckons it is now beyond the capability of one single person to translate Proust. The 2002 edition took seven translators seven years. Scott Moncrieff spent eight years from 1921 to 1929 working on this by himself, while also translating Stendhal, Pirandello, *The Letters of Abelard and Heloise*, as well as handling huge amounts of journalism and correspondence. So inspired was his translation that some critics felt he was improving on the original. Joseph Conrad wrote to him in 1922:

> I was much more interested and fascinated by your rendering than by Proust's creation. One has revealed to me something and there is no revelation in the other . . . [You have] a supreme faculty akin to genius . . .

The Scott Moncrieff translation is widely seen as a literary masterpiece in its own right, and he is considered one of the great translators into English of the twentieth century. But there was more to him than the translating genius Conrad discerned. An influential player on the English literary scene, he was a man of contradictions: a dedicated and decorated soldier as well as a poet; an ardent Catholic convert and a lover of men. He explored many of these paradoxes in his own poems, of which he said, 'I am not a good poet and fortunately, I know it.' They are mixed in quality, but are a great insight into his character, and as they are generally unavailable, I have put together all of the poems in my possession, both published and unpublished, in a separate book.

He was not only a man of letters; his war record was outstanding, his attitude to war unusual. His many letters from the front were appreciative and entertaining. Here was a very sensitive, highly intelligent, active poet, who drew enjoyment from being a soldier. His letters threw new light on my view of that time of slaughter.

He was a splendid letter-writer with an habitually irreverent turn of mind. He revealed a complex soul and a dry wit; especially in letters in the Berg Collection in New York Public Library, written to Edward Marsh, civil servant and patron of poets. Charles met him late in life not long before moving to Italy which was an easier climate for his wounds and cheaper on his pocket. There was also an expat colony of English writers. The young Evelyn Waugh wrote to him there in 1923, hoping to become his secretary because he was known by then as a critic and controversial man of letters who had loved Wilfred Owen, was hated by Osbert Sitwell, idealised by Noël Coward, cold-shouldered by Siegfried Sassoon, admired by Joseph Conrad and sniped at by D. H. Lawrence. Waugh dreamt he would spend his time, 'drinking Chianti under olive trees and listening to discussions of all the most iniquitous outcasts of Europe.' However, Charles could not have a secretary who was not privy to his second double life; that of an intelligence agent. When he finally did get one, she also worked in intelligence.

The Society of Authors still awards the annual Scott Moncrieff Prize for translation from French. Conscious of his task of selling Proust to the English-speaking world, he did not make an exact literal translation but a poetic one – one he knew would appeal to the post-Edwardian public – and one that has been the subject of appreciation and controversy ever since.

My research and writing have been a great adventure which took me to the battlefields of Flanders and Picardie; to Florence, Pisa and Rome, staying in the same hotels that Charles did, and finding his exact flat in 67, Via della Croce, Rome, to rent. One autumn I travelled round the Italian Riviera, carrying my baby son's pram up and down the same steps where Charles had limped in the railway stations in the 1920s. He had used the London Library, and so did I; and there, at the foot of the stairs, is a bronze bust of Edmund Gosse, emanating the effortless self-confidence that made me understand his fatherly but cavalier attitude to Charles.

The most startling discovery was that Charles had also been an intelligence agent for the British in Mussolini's Italy. He had learnt early on how to live parallel lives, both of them sincere and believable: the Charles at home, religious, loving and dutiful, as well as the young blood among the homosexual coterie with Robert Ross and his friends in London. The lives did not overlap, nor come into conflict, he just stepped from one parallel to the other. This natural subterfuge made it easy for him to become a spy. (Perhaps a reason so many homosexuals were successful spies.) In fact he enjoyed the sophistication. There is also a connection here to his translating. He translated a work much as an actor took on a character, jumping into someone else's skin and walking around in it. It became effortless; leaving behind one aspect of his character and taking on another.

The role of translator normally requires obedience, almost a shadowy role as a medium for another great mind, but Charles was determined to have the same size of ego as that of any creative writer. No other translator prefaced their works with dedicatory poems to their friends. Likewise his profile in the media thanks to critics like Edmund Gosse was as high as any creative writer. His was an interpretation of a great work, like Casals interpreting Bach, or Olivier enacting Shakespeare. He was compared to Richard Burton, whose translation of the *Arabian Nights* was bold and imaginary, inventing his own vocabulary if necessary.

Having spent the flower of his youth on the war, he felt that he was chasing lost time for the last ten years of his life. This feeling of being hounded by time led to a frenetic work schedule, and him publishing nineteen volumes of difficult translation, writing thousands of letters and neglecting his physical health. It is unlikely he ever cooked himself a meal, relying on black coffee and wine by day and dining out at night where he was celebrated as a first-rate entertainer by his friends. Proust wrote a slow exploration in search of lost time, but Charles was actively chasing time, he was a man never at rest; constantly making unnatural demands on himself, leading an action-packed life. Fuelled by his high ideals:

> To pursue chivalry, to avoid and punish treachery, to rely upon our own resources, and to fight uncomplainingly when support is withheld from us; to live, in fine, honourably and to die gallantly.

He embodied virtues that we have forgotten or are ashamed of, or associate with jingoism and folly. He never ceased from mental strife. This made the quest for the mystery of this man wholly absorbing, taking me through great characters and great literature, walking all over London, Edinburgh, Rome, Pisa and beyond, and dwelling on the Word, the Sentence and its Commas.

After I'd finished writing this book, and set down a tale of a life that was high-minded, abstemious, hardworking and a little lonely, I then discovered 458 pages of letters and postcards to Vyvyan Holland, the translator, and son of Oscar Wilde. These spanned from 1910 to Charles's death, his whole adult life. They are witty and frank: full of Rabelaisian adventures, homosexual badinage, gossip, limericks and the detail of his thoughts and feelings on every activity, especially his sexual affairs. Vyvyan was the one person to whom Charles revealed his sex life; in the absence of these letters I had believed that after the war he was celibate. The letters proved that he practised an exuberant sexuality even until his final illness. To escape being compromised, the letters are in French, Italian, Latin, Greek and German. I felt I ought to ask Vyvyan Holland's son, Merlin Holland, if he would mind my publishing letters that referred so frequently to his father's intimate life. His reply was a relief. 'I don't have a problem with my family because all the skeletons fell out of the cupboard with a gigantic crash in 1895.' The book is now a literary and spiritual journey, recently sown with nuggets of sex.

CHAPTER I

Bloodline

> Every Scottish man has his pedigree. It is a national prerogative, as inalienable as his pride and his poverty.
>
> Walter Scott

Charles Scott Moncrieff lay dying in Rome. Through the arched window of the Convent of St Joseph he could see the cypress trees on the Palatine Hill, while a nun in a white wimple and blue veil entered silently to give him Holy Communion.

In the first volume of Proust's *Remembrance of Things Past* in bed at night the boy remembers longing for his mother to come and kiss him goodnight and he compares the apparition of her face to the white, consecrated host.[1] Charles, a man of forty, was certain that the consecrated host carried by the nun was the body of Christ. His journey to that point was as absorbing to him as his translation of Proust, through which he had lived much of the past nine years.

He knew he was dying. His body was emaciated and his face skull-like. Stomach cancer had been diagnosed only eight weeks before. Morphine muffled his pain. His life lay behind him, coloured and detailed like the view from the window; and beyond that lay his forebears, all gone before him on this final adventure. Except for his mother, still alive and now at his side, visiting, ministering, treating him again like the child he had once been.

Charles's parents were second cousins once removed and shared the family name before as well as after marriage. His father, William George Scott Moncrieff, had died three years before in the same month, February. In childhood Charles had caught his father's passion for the tales of his ancestors. Together they had drawn family trees tracing the line back to the beginning of his name, one of the oldest double barrelled names in Scotland. As was common in Scotland, the name was not hyphenated which distinguished Scots from English double surnames.

In 1740, John Scott of Coats, a doctor, married Madeleine Moncrieffe of Easter Rhynd in Perthshire; their son Robert was the first to register a compound name in 1771. What gave him the idea? Robert Scott Moncrieff was by family reports a liberal, well-travelled man, a friend of Wilberforce, and a founder of the Edinburgh Orphan Hospital. Perhaps one hundred years before the Married Women's Property Act, he wanted to acknowledge his mother's contribution to his estates. Later in life he sold one estate, giving as an excuse to his son, 'I would not wish to see you or any of my children an idle country laird.'[2] The next Robert became a banker and he and his wife were duly painted by Raeburn.

Charles eventually traced his forebears even further back than his father had done. In 1926, his cousin William Moncrieffe came to him for help with a two-volume genealogy of the family.[3] Charles was then translating Proust, Stendhal, the letters of Abelard and Heloise, and the works of Pirandello; his imagination was peopled by crowds of characters, but his own ancestors seemed equally vibrant. It was more than a passion: for a sick man in exile from the land and family he loved, it was an establishing of identity. Now he could go back eight hundred years to the first Moncrieff, called Ramerus. In 1121 he sailed to Scotland from Spain to be Wardrobe Keeper to King Alexander the Fierce, son of Malcolm Canmore and Saint Margaret of Scotland: bringing Spanish silks and feathers to decorate the king among the frozen hills. In 1249, the next King, Alexander II gave lands to Sir Matthew de Moncrieff and his heirs, taking the name from the hills he gave them in what is now Perthshire.

The dying Charles remembered that there was a letter from William Moncrieff and reached sideways to his bedside table, in vain. The nuns were tidy and his secretary, Lucy Lunn, was for the first time filing all his correspondence. It was a necessary task; he had a mountain of letters from his publishers, British and American, from Pirandello, T. S. Eliot, Joseph Conrad, George Moore . . . a long list of distinguished men of letters. Then there were some which he would burn: compromising letters full of sexual detail from Vyvyan Holland, love letters,

letters from Sebastian Sprott, sometime lover of E. M. Forster, Forster who had described Charles as 'entertaining, but unentertainable'.[4] Charles was, by now, celibate.

In *Cities of the Plain* Proust had written of the two angels who are posted at the gates of Sodom to report on the inhabitants' activities. He imagined a citizen excusing himself, 'Father of six – two mistresses', saying that only a man who was a Sodomite himself could detect the fact that the pleader spent his nights with a shepherd on Hebron.[5] At least Charles could not be accused of such hypocrisy: he had never been married.

Charles believed there were three distinct strains in the blood of his ancestors: the warrior spirit, good looks and earnest piety. He had read the diaries of the pious extreme: *The Narrative of James Nimmo*, a Covenanting ancestor, who began writing in 1622.[6] Nimmo's diaries were letters to God about the state of his soul. Nimmo sacrificed his property, was present with the Covenanters at the Battle of Bothwell Bridge, and left his country to keep his own particular Covenant with the Lord. His wife, Elizabeth, wrote heart-rending diaries of their sufferings in exile in Holland. But Nimmo's own diary, though written during such tumultuous times, ignored regicide, civil war, even his daughter's marriage, so busy was Mr Nimmo with the supreme concerns of his own soul. His wife was equally scrupulous, 'I was afraid I had sinned the sin unto death,' she wrote, 'One Sabbath there fell out a strong temptation to *laughter* in the family . . . The challenge seemed to come from the Devil, "O says the enemy you have now sinned the sin unto death."'[7]

In the same century, in 1687, at the luxurious and intriguing French court of Louis XIV, François-Augustin Paradis de Moncrif was born, son of a determined Scots mother who single-mindedly manipulated the way for her son's success at court. As well as a noted satirist and versifier, Paradis became speech writer for the Duc d'Aumont, Ambassador to England in 1713, then to the Comte d'Argenson for whom he famously wrote love letters which were even sent in his own handwriting. He wrote poetry, lectures, pamphlets, plays and in 1735 was elected to the Académie Française as a much-loved wit; on his death the French writer D'Alembert said, '*Paradis de Moncrif sera tout à l'heure Moncrif de Paradis*.'[8] Charles had found a first edition of his fairy stories and resurrected them, translated in 1929 as *Adventures of*

Zeloïde and Amanzarifdine. His long introduction was another excuse to elaborate on the Moncrieff ancestry.

At the turn of the eighteenth century Charles's great-grandfather, Robert Scott Moncrieff of Fossoway in Fife, had felt the same way. He was partly educated in England and had many English friends. 'Yet he was a Scotsman to the backbone rejoicing in the romance, the history, the literature and the beauty of his native land, interested in his own lineage, holding that gentle birth is an incentive to chivalrous action':[9] a conviction held by Charles himself throughout his life. In 1818 Robert Scott Moncrieff married Susan Pringle of Yair, a woman of great beauty who grew up with her ten siblings close to Sir Walter Scott. Her brothers are remembered in *Marmion*,[10] and one of them, Alexander, became Lord of the Treasury under Sir Robert Peel. The Pringle ancestors were famous in Scottish history as standard-bearers to the Douglases by whose side they fought against the English at the great battles of Otterburn, Flodden and Solway Moss from the fourteenth to the sixteenth century. Susan, like her own mother, bore eleven children, and in her short life impressed them with a strong piety. On her death in 1840 she left a letter to them saying, 'The most valuable worldly acquirement you can make is the power of applying your mind vigorously to whatever you have to do, not loitering over it, but doing it with all your might, and finding idleness a burden.'[11] The children were happy and unspoilt, living a simple, frugal, life consisting of, as the eldest, Mary Ann, put it: 'cold bath and lessons, porridge and lessons, a walk and lessons, dinner and lessons'.[12]

This educational rigour, coupled with Susan Pringle's belief that 'We were made for better things than to be wealthy'[13], ensured that her sons went out into the world as the hardworking builders of Empire. The eldest son, Colin Campbell Scott Moncrieff, became an engineer in India, then Director of Irrigation for Egypt, where he was responsible for the Nile Barrages. He was knighted in 1887, returning home as Under-Secretary of State for Scotland. The third child was Charles's grandfather, Robert, who became an East India Company merchant in Calcutta, from 1850 to 1874, cultivating indigo for use as a dye. He was an unusual boss: his papers record a man who refused to beat the natives, let no one work on Sundays, insisted on morning and evening prayers, and would not take bribes.[14] This was rare in the Company, but sadly his enlightened approach didn't make profits. In Calcutta he met and fell in love with a doctor's daughter, the Gaelic-speaking Katherine Mackinnon from Skye. They married happily and had nine children, all of whom lived to adulthood, probably because they were sent home from India aged five to live with Robert's brother David in George Square, Edinburgh.

After 1874, grandfather Robert of Calcutta had a second career. On his return from India he set himself the task of hastening the Zionist cause. At the end of the nineteenth century, in anticipation of the millennium, there was an organised movement of Christians who believed that if the Jews were returned to the land of Israel, it would bring on the Second Coming. Robert was not officially part of this group, but he felt the political pressure, from all over Europe, to establish a Jewish State. He was convinced enough of its necessity to spend twenty years from 1880 till 1900 investigating the Jewish pogroms in Odessa, Constantinople, Romania and Russia, interviewing survivors at first hand. In 1900 he published *The Branches and the Branch* which catalogued every pogrom since AD 33 and set out his own long theological and biblical justification for the Jews having Israel as their homeland. Robert's brother-in-law, John Robertson, Moderator of the Church of Scotland from 1909 till 1910, shared and fed his Zionist zeal; he was minister at Whittinghame, a village in East Lothian, and seat of the Balfour family. He had a direct influence on the young Arthur Balfour, Prime Minister from 1902 till 1905 and architect of the 1917 Balfour Declaration, which supported the establishment of a Jewish State in Palestine.

Charles's mother had always been critical of her father's 'obsession' with the Jews, partly because he abandoned his family to follow it, and as the eldest of nine children she, Jessie Margaret, had early responsibility. As a child, she had a series of governesses who made her read the classics and write daily to her parents in India: she became the first professional writer among the Scott Moncrieffs; and in time made enough money from her writing to put her younger sister Kate through London University. Known as Meg, she was tall and strikingly beautiful with a broad forehead, wide-set eyes and a sensitive, motile mouth, ready with a quip or a laugh. On 9 April 1878, aged twenty, she married her cousin, ten years her senior, William George Scott Moncrieff, known as George, a lawyer with a literary bent. Charles, CKSM, would be the couple's third son, born eleven years after the marriage.

* * *

George was at Edinburgh University in the same year group as Robert Louis Stevenson. In 1870 he contributed to the university magazine edited by Stevenson[15] and also appeared with him in a production of *Twelfth Night*. George later wrote three serial novels for the *Ladies Own* journal. As his father was a cousin of the physicist James Clerk Maxwell, George was a true inheritor of the Scottish Enlightenment, working at a time when lively minds mixed in a country small enough for innovators in the arts and science to know one another.

By the mid-nineteenth century, few of the Scott Moncrieffs were landed gentry, most had migrated to the professional classes and become lawyers, doctors, clergy and explorers. George's great uncle, John Irving, was killed on the Franklin Expedition to the Arctic and his frozen remains were brought back years later to Edinburgh for burial on 8 January 1881.[16] On the night that George went to the funeral in Edinburgh, Meg gave birth to their second son and named him John Irving Scott Moncrieff after the explorer. He was a brother for Colin born in 1879. By then the family were living in Banff Castle on Scotland's north-east coast. George was Sheriff Substitute of Banff: a local judge, he presided over civil and criminal cases. The Sheriff courts in Scotland were above the District Courts and below the Supreme Court and dealt with most of the court work, both civil and criminal. There was always more work than one Sheriff could handle, so the role of Sheriff Substitute was common.

Meg built up her weekly contributions to three Sunday newspapers as well as writing short stories for *Blackwood's Magazine*[17]. She corresponded with R. L. Stevenson and with the novelist Margaret Oliphant. Having read some of her work in *Blackwood's*, Oliphant advised her not to write so much in Scots, or, if she must, to tone it down to a very easy level. However, Meg did not take her advice and continued writing in Scots, sacrificing the larger English audience. This was the dialect that she heard around her and her stories were inspired by George's work in the law courts, among life's real dramas. Literary influence came from both of Charles's parents.

Meg's diaries, written daily for fifty years from 1882 to 1936, chronicle in detail the experience of a liberal Scottish Victorian household.

Reading the visitors' book of Banff Castle, you get the impression life was a succession of plays, parties, fishing and painting expeditions, trips to hear religious preachers and public debates. Most visitors record a trip to the assizes court to hear George's judgments. Scottish high society was a small pool, in which the Scott Moncrieffs were middle-sized fish.

When the Prince of Wales visited Banff in 1883, Meg and George were invited to a ball given for him on 16 November by their neighbours at Duff House. Meg wandered into the drawing room to rest after dancing and the Prince entered. The company stood and chatted with him both in English and French,

> very much in the big voice of Henry V – to whom I always mentally compare him – only he didn't say such clever things. Our loyalty was soon satisfied with standing – but the Prince blocked up the doorway so there was nothing for it but to stand. Count Herbert was behind him – a tall young man with dark hair and moustache and fierce dark eyes – 'A horrid, wild-looking fellow', George called him, 'who would think nothing of calling you out.'[18]

Count Herbert Bismarck, son of Otto, was in 1883 Minister of Foreign Affairs for the First German Empire, which would 'call out' the entire British nation three decades later for the First World War.

Built in the eighteenth century, Banff Castle was one of those old Scottish edifices that are often colder inside than out, like a primitive fridge. Meg, though full of enthusiasm for every aspect of life, developed a bad cough, which wouldn't go away. In 1885 a bad cough in a thin and sensitive lady was mortally suspicious: her friend and neighbour Posie Gordon Duff had TB and would soon die of it. The doctor prescribed Meg opiates to rest her nervous body and amyl nitrate to help dilate her lungs. She asked her sister Mary to come and read to her Tennyson's 'Lotus Eaters', 'which,' she wrote, 'can only be perfectly enjoyed in the drowsiness which follows an opiate!'[19]

The family doctor advised six months in Egypt with Meg's Uncle Colin, who was working there as Director of Irrigation. Leaving the boys was painful, but they had a good nanny and household staff and George would be often at home. Meg and her sister Mary sailed for

Egypt on 5 November 1885. On 13 November they reached Malta, 'I had a bad night and was faint however a few drops of amyl nitrate revived me.'[20] Amyl nitrate has a hallucinogenic effect like LSD. Combined with her prescribed opiates, her tall thin figure, beauty and artistic taste in clothes she looked like a Victorian version of the quintessential glamorous addict.

They reached Cairo on 20 November to stay with Uncle Colin, whose exotic household comprised an English butler, a German female cook, a Nubian male housemaid, and an Arab groom. It was a far cry from Banff – 'oh so hot, a south wind bringing air from the desert'.[21] While there she wrote six extended articles on life in Cairo for the *Scotsman* in Edinburgh, which were signed 'From our Correspondent in Cairo'. From their socio-political content the readers would never guess they came from a pale, thin, coughing lady with a silk parasol. The articles took eight days to reach Edinburgh and she received the printed copy another eight days later.

In Cairo Meg's cultural life was intense and the social life glittered in the heat. Lord Rosebery, who was married to the heiress Hannah de Rothschild and later became Prime Minister, gave the finest parties, and was a friend and colleague of her uncle. To Meg, Colin was a crinkly-eyed, bewhiskered relative; to society he was a man held in high regard as a key player[22] in the abolition of the corvée, the unpaid labour system. He had buried two wives, one in India and the second in Egypt, and was at a low ebb personally. It was a comfort for him to have his two favourite nieces Mary and Meg to stay for six months. He sent for the best doctor available who said she had 'no organic illness',[23] no TB, only weakness, and told Meg to fatten up. But she gained no weight in Egypt and the mental and imaginative effort employed in her writing always took its toll on her energy, as it would years later with her youngest son, Charles.

George came out to join her in March 1888 and they spent a month visiting pyramids in the sunset and seeing the citadel before they sailed back, visiting Europe on the way. Banff is still cold in April and soon Meg's coughing started again. George resolved to search for work further south and was appointed Sheriff Substitute of Falkirk in Stirlingshire.

When they moved for his new job, they found a less daunting home, Weedingshall House between Polmont and Falkirk. Through two slim, pencil-shaped gateposts ran a drive flanked by beech trees, with a valley sloping to the left and open parkland to the right. The house itself was unostentatious: of sandstone, three storeys high with around twenty chimneys and a variety of windows, large, small, curved, bay and square with views to the distant Perthshire hills. It had an unplanned look but was possibly at least partly designed by Robert Adam in 1791.[24] The stable block and laundry lay just beyond the house, hidden from the approach. Today Weedingshall House is a children's home, still untouched as a building within its original grounds and garden, but hidden in a maze of block and tile housing which stretches from Polmont to Falkirk as part of Edinburgh's dormitory suburbia. In 1889, before the advent of cars, it stood alone in rolling farmland.

Behind the house was a walled garden with fruit trees. Meg brought poppy seeds and rose cuttings, which could only grow under glass at Banff, but flourished here outside in the sheltered garden. On 25 September 1889, in a bedroom overlooking this well-nurtured and colourful sanctuary, Charles Kenneth, was born. His father took over his mother's diary at this point and recorded that he arrived quickly at half past eleven and weighed nine pounds, and that Nurse Paton arrived at half past one and 'took possession of us'.[25] Meg's handwriting resumed two days later to note that her latest short story had been accepted by the *Scotsman Weekly*. Throughout her pregnancy she had been turning out three columns a month and many short stories. She did of course have a staff of eight, and never cooked or cleaned. Three weeks after giving birth she noted that she took in the waist of her dress from thirty-five inches to twenty-nine.

Colin and Johnnie, aged twelve and ten, had been sent to boarding school in Edinburgh for the first time that September. Colin sent sad letters home. As soon as the new baby was born, his brothers came home for a week and spent time watching him being fed and bathed by his nurse. Johnnie said, 'He looks like a tea-roll with sugar on him.'[26] The boys were sent back to school but the following Saturday Colin turned up by himself, having got to Waverley Station, boarded the train alone without a ticket and walked from Polmont. He was taken back to school by George, both parents being convinced that boarding was the surest way to foster independence and self-discipline and gain the best in education. A week later, early on a cold October morning Colin was found huddled in the porch of Weedingshall

House. He had arrived at 6 a.m. but had been too afraid of his parents' anger to pull the bell until breakfast time. This time Meg kept him home for a week, allowing him on to the bed with her and the baby, all the while recording in her diary frantic letters and conversations between her and George and the headmistress of his school. Meg, still weak from the birth, copied into her diary, 'Character is formed by compression; emotions and experience that evaporate in expression, contribute little. A pain, a want, a disappointment borne silently strengthens us perceptibly.'[27] At the end of a week at home Colin was sent back again, after much discussion of sacrificing present pleasure for his future, and doing his duty towards his parents who knew what was best for him. He was a tender-hearted child, and although it hurt to be parted from his mother and baby brother, he put on a brave face. Photographs of Colin from then on always look as though he was putting on a brave face.

Boarding school was not only far from loved ones, but far from a loved place. Meg created a beautiful home with pictures and fabrics and furniture from her travels to Europe, to Egypt and from her own childhood in India. She read daily to her children, when they were at home, not only scripture but also fiction. Robert Louis Stevenson, their friend and correspondent, was read and discussed, as were George Eliot, Jane Austen, Milton, Ruskin and all the great poets. Meg was no prude and her tastes often put aesthetics before Victorian morality; by contrast, school for Colin and John must have seemed bare and philistine.

Charlie, as he was known by the family, grew up blithely. With the two older boys at boarding school, Meg concentrated all her efforts on the baby. They had a large, black, shaggy mongrel called Dido and when Charlie reached ten months, Meg wrote 'Baby said *Dido* after me – he grabs her head and squeezes her velvet ears into his mouth.'[28] Meg's diary was filled with exact descriptions of baby developments: his first steps, the first time he left his bed by himself and climbed tentatively downstairs, slipping one stockinged foot before the next.

Until he was three he had a Belgian nanny who only spoke French and he learnt the language fast, like a game. She was however very tough and was dismissed to be replaced by Miss Helen Stephen who became a friend of the whole family and confidante for life. Charlie loved history and at the age of five when learning about Queen Elizabeth I, said enthusiastically, 'Oh aren't you glad Elizabeth's dead?'

'Why?'

'Because she might have killed Victoria as well as Mary.'[29]

On Christmas Day 1883, when Charlie was four, he was initiated into the yearly family ritual. The children came early into their parents' room in their dressing gowns and sang a hymn and opened their stockings. Then George, Colin and John read Milton's 'Ode on the Morning of Christ's Nativity', verse about. Charlie sat on the bed 'looking half robin, half cherub . . . with his ruffled brown features and his red dressing gown'. George said that his favourite lines were 'as when the sun in bed/ Curtained with cloudy red/ Pillows his chin upon an orient ware'. And his youngest son nodded his head: 'Yes, I sink so, I sink so, too.'[30]

As a toddler Charlie saw his mother not only writing daily, but, more unusual still, carving her own oak writing desk. Carving oak is a hefty physical task and Meg's exertions were really a challenging distraction from another temptation: Washington Ray, known as Tony, a schoolmaster from the local boarding school, Blair Lodge, developed a lasting and deep admiration for her. A jealous husband would not have stood for the frequent visits, the many presents of flowers, fruit and books or the intimacy of discussions, nor for the inscription on the bookshelf above her desk, arranged in Latin by Tony.

HIC FLOREAT MI HORTULUS LIBRORUM
AURO CARIOR INDICISQUE GEMMIS
QUI VISUS JUVET ANTEQUAM LEGATUR
QUO LECTO TOLEREM DOMI QUOD ANGAT

Let this little garden of books flower for me
Dearer than gold and Indian gems
May seeing it delight before it is read,
So that after reading, I might bear the torment at home[31]

Passion for a man not her husband would certainly cause torment. But George had a large family of older female advisers, who steered him away from jealousy and towards friendship. He invited Tony to play golf with him, join them for tennis and fishing, and set up a weekly club to discuss the latest books and literary magazines. This discussion was essential to Meg and fed her journalism. George made sure that Meg's sister Mary who taught at the boarding school Johnnie and Colin attended, was invited as often as possible. In 1895, Tony transferred his affections and fell in love with Mary. They married, and together as teachers they would have a profound influence on Charles's life.

CHAPTER 2

Childhood

Les vrais paradis sont les paradis qu'on a perdus.

Marcel Proust, *Le Temps retrouvé,* 1927

On 4 January 1895, when Charlie was five years old, his mother held a New Year party at Weedingshall. The first half of the evening was a production of a play she had written called *The True Lover* for five characters. George, Charlie's father, acted a rich old gentleman who had a niece with three suitors and had to decide which one was 'true' out of a lawyer's clerk, a seedy schoolmaster and a shy gardener. In true fairy-tale tradition, the honest lover turned out to be the gardener. After the performance, complete with lights, costumes, wigs, painted scenery and live music, the audience of forty-two relatives and neighbours had ices in the drawing room and played dancing games. There was a screen across the room between ladies and gentlemen. A lady, unseen, threw a ball and the gentleman who caught it came and led her away to dance. Next each gentleman took two crackers and pulled them with the lady of his choice, then, wearing the hats from the crackers, they danced a cotillion. Midway through the dancing there was a grand supper organised by the new cook. Meg was an exacting mistress, and throughout Charlie's childhood the cooks were always 'new'.

Even though he was the youngest by far, Charlie was allowed to stay up till the end, and savoured every moment. The next day he retold a joke he had heard at the party and when his mother commented on his delivery of the grown-up story, the expression on the faces of the audience and the storyteller's manner, the five-year-old replied, 'Yes, it comes back into my mind like sugar.'[1] He already knew how to recall and embellish a memory and deliver it to entertain.

Two days later the winter set in and the pumps froze just before the annual party given for the family servants. Charlie watched them melting the snow to use as water. These people were an important part of his life: Allison the groom, Mary the cook, Bell the gardener and three housemaids; they also invited the servants from the neighbours' at Parkhill House. Miss Stephen, Charlie's governess, was not at the servants' party, she partied with the family and went wherever the children did. The next evening the boys were dressed in intricate fancy dress to go to the children's party at Parkhill: John as a frog, Colin as a Turk and Charlie as a Japanese doll, carefully negotiating the icy driveway in his tight skirt and looking out at the starry night from behind white face paint and blackened eyebrows.

April that year was hot and Meg went for a break to relatives on the Fife coast. On her return she found that Charlie had taken possession of the attic as a playroom. As she led him to bed he looked fondly at the attic door saying, 'It makes me feel so happy when I see that door.'[2] It was his first real work space. June again was warm and Meg wrote on the 24th, 'The house is all spicy with wafts of honeysuckle from the porch. Lord Rosebery's Government fell.'[3] She remembered going to his parties in Cairo and described them to her five-year-old son, who liked to play behind the carved wooden harem screen which she had brought back from Egypt to decorate her drawing room. Until the age of eight, Charlie's education was all at home: from his governess Miss Stephen and his mother who would read to him from whatever she was reading at the time. As a small child, he grew used to Stevenson, Milton, Wordsworth, Arnold, George Herbert and Ruskin. These were not the usual texts given to small boys to develop an interest.

Each brother had his own speciality. John loved animals, he had ferrets, birds, rabbits, and newts, which escaped from his room and slithered all the way downstairs to the kitchen, making the new cook scream. The cat, Peter, and the dog, Dido, belonged to everyone. One day on a visit to Meg's sisters in Edinburgh, the beloved Dido went missing. After a sleepless night his father put notices in the evening newspapers offering two pounds reward. That evening a very thin young man appeared with Dido, saying the dog had run into his shop, he had taken her home and she had 'gruppit' his children by the sleeve. 'Do you like animals?' he was asked: 'Yes, mum, I like them well enough but I cannae afford tae keep them,'[4] he replied.

Charlie was beginning to recognise how poor the poor were, and how the huge gap between rich and poor allowed even a modest lawyer to employ a number of servants, and feel it was his duty to do so. At the turn of the century the largest single employer was domestic service: a cook's wage was £12 a year while a sheriff earned £1000. In the towns and cities ragged children still begged and some went barefoot even in winter. The family were warned never to give money to the beggar children, but, moved by their plight, a cousin once gave a child a penny and the poor child was instantly set upon by the other barefoot children who hammered him till the penny was taken. In the absence of state welfare, many in the professional classes accepted responsibility and worked hard to alleviate poverty. George was on the board of the local hospital, pushing for reforms; and Meg led the local Girls' Friendly Society – a euphemism for an organisation helping young women fallen pregnant or into prostitution. As well as providing practical supplies, she led it in an educational direction, reading aloud novels by Walter Scott, Elizabeth Gaskell and others which were both entertaining and parables for life.

All summers were spent by the sea and in 1895 they travelled to Tarbert on the Mull of Kintyre, taking a steamer from Greenock and arriving late in the evening. They rented a large house for servants, guests and family on the sea front and the boys swam every day, rain or sun. Charlie won the diving competition for his age group and Johnnie the swimming. They fished and explored coves and islands by boat. The local people spoke Gaelic and sometimes the family would come across a spontaneous Ceilidh on the shore with singing rising into the sunset.

Meg was both relieved and delighted that her sister Mary's wedding to Tony Ray, the schoolmaster and her one time admirer from Blair Lodge School, was during the holiday that year. On 3 September they travelled for the day to Morningside, Edinburgh, to be with the large extended family on this important occasion which kept her dear friend in the close family. While the couple sped south to Normandy for their honeymoon, Charlie's family returned to Tarbert and were still by the sea for his sixth birthday on 25 September. In the evening he appeared with Miss Stephen wearing a necklace of bright red rosehips she had made for him. He opened the six presents which had come by post and cut a bought cake which was a 'triumph of Tarbert confectionery'. His big brothers, aged fifteen and seventeen, toasted his health each with a foot on a chair. 'He looked on with a sort of mystical pride and said "Thanks" with perfect grace.'[5]

Seaside marked the summers of his childhood, and Christmas Day was still celebrated by the reading of Milton's 'Ode on the Morning of Christ's Nativity'. The family met in Meg's room, warmed by the fire and lit by many lamps. When it came to Charlie's turn to read that year, he turned his head away from the book and recited his ten verses by heart. He had learnt them as a surprise present to his mother. (He never forgot them and recited them each year for the rest of his life, even when he was alone.) His present from his parents was a set of wooden boats with magnets to draw them, which he called 'Tarbert Alive' and absorbed his attention totally: his father told him that twenty-five years before, their cousin William Dundas Scott had been partner in the firm that designed the *Cutty Sark*. After breakfast John and Colin skated to Linlithgow, eleven miles away on the river while Charlie played at home on his sledge, tumbling like a black beetle in the snow.

Indoors Charlie was already enjoying reading and writing on his own. In April 1896 a Remington typewriter arrived in the household for the first time. It was used by Meg for her journalism, by Colin for his final school essays and by Charlie aged six to copy the first poem he ever composed:[6]

I

My love lies bleeding in my arms,
My trembling arms are bled with tears,
My love lies bleeding in my arms,
My love my only dear.

II

My child lies kissing in my arms,
My infant here is safe,
From harm,
In my arms.

The influence was clear: Meg read all her stories to her family before sending them off to *Blackwood's*, including a searing melodrama of the death of a child, based on one she had watched while in Egypt.

Charlie's particular sensitivity to the painful scene brought it to life in this first poem.

That summer the whole family took their holiday on the Normandy coast, north of Caen: they stayed at Langrune at the Hôtel du Petit Paradis which consisted of rooms directly off the beach, with white scrubbed wooden floors, sand blowing under the door, and simple furniture. On the feast of the Assumption the streets were filled with processions of girls in white, singing, and there was a fête with dancing in the evening. On Sunday Meg stayed inside and had her private Protestant service with the children while George braved the Catholic church and came home with colourful tales that encouraged the recalcitrant Meg to visit churches throughout the holiday: one day she came upon a woman throwing her crutches on the altar and crowing, '*La Sainte Marie m'a guérie*,'[7] with a dramatic joy incredible to a Scottish Presbyterian. They explored by train the seaside towns of Trouville, Dives-sur-mer, Cabourg, Courcelles and Bernières.

Unknown to them, the young Marcel Proust was on holiday with his grandmother that year at their favourite summer haunt, the Grand Hotel at Cabourg. Proust was twenty-six, as yet unpublished, living the exacting social life of Paris-by-the-sea, meeting the young girls in the bloom of youth that he would later evoke in *Within a Budding Grove,* and exploring the Guermantes genealogy. This was the only time his path crossed unwittingly with that of his future translator. Charlie was now approaching his seventh birthday which was celebrated back in rainy London at Cheyne Walk, the home of Sir Colin Scott Moncrieff, Meg's uncle from her Cairo days, who was now Under-Secretary of State for Scotland.

The following January, 1897, a letter arrived from the Lord Advocate offering George the post of Sheriff of Inverness. It was not happy news; Charles did not want to leave Weedingshall where they had lived peacefully for ten years with friends and close relatives nearby. However, he was strongly advised to take the promotion. With characteristic forethought, he wrote two letters, one accepting and one declining the post, and walked with them both to Falkirk, leaving the ultimate decision to the last minute. He returned with both letters unposted. Dithering was an established Scott Moncrieff trait. However, a decision had to be made and before the end of the month the family had moved to the snowy north, living in rented rooms, while Meg and George looked for a house.

By February they had found a house called Viewmount, just below Inverness Castle which housed the law courts where the Sheriff worked. Perched on a steep hill, it had a charming oval hall decorated with lacy plasterwork with eight doors leading off, and above it an oval gallery with eight bedroom doors. The dining room looked down through a beech wood to the River Ness and the Moray Firth. Their dog, Dido, came with them but Johnnie's pony was left behind. John thought that the steep garden at Viewmount was ideal, however, for grazing a goat. He still collected animals and had some ferrets, which were banned from the house while his cats and birds were allowed inside. Now in Inverness he declared he wanted to keep bats. Soon he had sent off for a parrot from London which arrived in a cardboard box on the train having frustratedly pecked out all its green tail feathers. He spent all his pocket money on pets, but was generous with them. In April he presented Charlie with a cage of two white rats: Colin saw Charlie in the hall with one on his shoulder, 'frightened of John if it fell off and frightened of it if it didn't'.[8] John also told Charlie that the oval hall at Viewmount was an ideal place for keeping 'any Beast that you fear', because you could stay on the upstairs gallery and throw food over the handrail, then retreat quickly behind your bedroom door. Instead of a beast, John next bought a pair of pigeons, but was soon heard bargaining with his mother, trying to sell her the pigeons for the dinner table as they were not good enough for homing. With the money he wanted to buy a real pedigree homer. It was already clear that his love of animals would direct his future life.

Colin, the eldest, was more academic. In March 1897 he won a Classical Scholarship to Queen's College, Oxford with a yearly value of £80. Charlie was impressed with his brother's ability to raise money. When he was at home, Colin would cycle long distances on rough roads, or go to smart parties for boating, tennis and croquet with elegant girls. He seemed a more distant companion to Charlie than John and his lively pets. Left alone often, Charlie liked to read or write poetry, rushing to show his mother when he discovered something he liked in his *Golden Treasury*. He loved and imitated Longfellow. In April 1897 he made himself a bow and arrows, running behind the trees in the garden murmuring scraps of Hiawatha-like verse. When asked to learn Shelley's 'Skylark' by heart by his mother he did it as a labour of love. Then one evening he went to his mother with his latest discovery, Whitman's 'Come up from the Fields, Father' and read it to her with feeling. He kept his own notebook of poems, transcribed in laborious pencil. Aged seven, he read *As You Like It* and declared, 'It's a very good play, so well plotted out. But no real woman would think of doing the things that Rosamond and Celia did.'[9] He was surrounded by ladylike, literary women, and appeared an expert on their gender.

By midsummer 1897, nearly eight years old, he had begun to go to a day school in Inverness run by Herr Waack, an elderly German who believed that seeing beauty in nature, music, and poetry, was as important as arithmetic and grammar. The first day at school entailed a botany lesson, and his homework was to collect 'things' in a tin to study in class. He was also taught astronomy and one entry in his diary of that year read, 'Saw Plough N.W. Must remember Acturus between N.W. and S. Cassiopeia W. To S. W.'[10] He enjoyed living at home and the eccentric Herr Waack, but in October of the following year, aged nine, Charlie left to board at Inverness College. His mother remembered him looking handsome in his new green coat and waistcoat with silver buttons and tartan kilt. With Charlie's departure Meg lost a loving and companionable son – the house seemed empty without him. However, as he was a weekly boarder, he was home at weekends; she could also visit him whenever she liked and would drop in for tea without warning after a wet shopping trip. Both Charlie and Johnnie went to Inverness College: Johnnie eight years Charlie's senior, was finishing his education, while Charlie was starting at school. At the end of that year Charlie brought home his first school prize, coming top of a class of nine of whom he was the youngest.

Religion played a large part in the boys' life. Yet it was a complex relationship: Meg was critical of the Church of Scotland of which her husband was later to become an elder and she wrote a précis of the sermon each week in her diary, finding that the further north they moved, the more the sermons dwelt on punishment for sins and eternal hellfire. She could see that the sensitive Charlie was thoroughly frightened. One bright Sunday in April 1898, Meg didn't go to church but instead sat in the greenhouse reading *Paradise Lost* to her son. The great epic where Hell is also Pandemonium, and Satan a real character with recognisable human qualities, was more suited to their temperaments, not to mention the War of the Angels, which inspired rather than scared them. The following Sunday Charlie was once again at church with his father, who held more orthodox beliefs in Hell. On his return the boy disappeared into the greenhouse and could be found under the plants copying out what Meg called the 'more dubious parts' of the Bible including the Apocrypha. She noticed that he had made a synopsis of them and he told her, 'Ezekiel is such a marvellous book. It tells so much about God.'[11] He then regaled her with the tale of Bel and the Dragon, an addition to the Book of Daniel accepted by Catholics and not Protestants, a criticism of the worship of idols involving sacrifice, secret passages, danger and mass carnage. It was clear he was no longer frightened. Meg was a liberal thinker and felt that the gloomy Calvinism she encountered at the kirk would repel her sons from faith, and she encouraged other approaches to Christianity.

Colin had now gone up to Oxford to study divinity with the intention of joining the Anglican clergy, a choice that even his strict Presbyterian father accepted. Johnnie was also moving on. His uncle Robin, based in South America, had found him a job and he was being kitted out for the journey, parading around the house in his new riding clothes. Charlie went to one last party with him at a nearby grand house with the Misses Gordon who were dressed in high fashion Japanese kimonos; he danced a cotillion as well as reels, reminding him of his appearance as a Japanese doll at his first fancy dress ball at Weedingshall. It was hard for Charlie to say goodbye to his adored big brother, so good at manly activities, shooting and training animals and riding bareback. The family would be very different without him, and Charlie would lose his companion at home.

The rest of the family took a cottage in Kincraig for August and September – with Peter the cat and Dido the dog. Dido was old and sick and George was forced to put her to sleep with chloroform. Charlie, aged nine, was very upset. He organised the funeral, digging a hole in the heather and lining her grave with the purple flowers. He wrote eight perfectly scanned verses for the dog he had loved:

> . . .
> She lived to a tremendous age
> She reached full 13 years
> You may be sure this poet's page
> Is well bedewed with tears.

His scansion did not miss a beat till the last one, which fell intentionally short:

> . . .
> But now we leave her far away
> This is no time to fret
> But surely, til eternity
> We never shall . . .[12]

The following summer Inverness College suddenly closed and Charlie's uncle and aunt, Tony and Mary Ray, set out to fulfil a long-held dream to found their own prep school. They rented a house in Nairn for the start of term and Charlie and eight other boys, all of them ex-Inverness College pupils, took up residence as boarders. Mary had two little girls of her own, Lucy and Mabel, cousins to Charlie and an integral part of the school household. Tony had been a brilliant classics scholar at Oxford and had had fifteen years' experience teaching at boarding schools. His aim was to prepare boys for the great British public schools. There is a portrait of him in ex-pupil David Thompson's childhood memories *Nairn In Darkness and Light*:

> When the formal part of each lesson was over, he read aloud to me, often with passionate excitement, shouting during the dramatic passages, whispering the emotional and sometimes bursting into tears, which embarrassed me greatly although it strengthened my love of him . . . In my reading he treated me as a man, stretching my intellect and emotions far beyond the limits that my previous teachers had set as suited to my age.[13]

Tony Ray was an inspired teacher and treated the boys as equals, believing there was nothing in literature they could not understand. He was not a disciplinarian; Charlie saw him as a second father, not as absent as his own; one who wore plus-four tweeds and smoked a pipe, often seen still smoking from its nest in his jacket pocket. Tony encouraged Charlie's enthusiasm for poetry and at the start of the new century the boy copied these lines from Herbert into his poetry notebook, showing an advanced spiritual understanding for his age:

Whether I fly with angels, fall with dust,
Thy hands made both and I am there.

At school he learnt and recited Gray's *Elegy* so beautifully that his father gave him a copy of William Mason's *The Poems of Mr Gray* – the start of his new library.

Nineteen-hundred was to be a year of changes. In August George applied for the post of Sheriff Substitute of Lanark – which included Glasgow and was the busiest and most important sheriffdom in Scotland – and was appointed in three days. Within the week Meg started packing up the house yet again. Meanwhile a wire had arrived from her brother in Uruguay to suggest Johnnie came home because, 'he hates the country'.[14] Johnnie arrived in August; taller, thicker-set, older in his carriage and more sure of himself. He told Charlie tales of his voyage across the world, 'One day we had quite a fairy breakfast – we got among a lot of flying fish – they came slapping on the deck at your feet and you tossed them down to the cook and he sent them up as fast as they were fried – they were like awfully good herring.'[15] Charlie was so pleased to have Johnnie back among them again that he spent his Christmas shilling on a box of chocolates for his brother's twentieth birthday in January.

By Charlie's eleventh birthday, the family was in lodgings at Lanark, and his father had started his new job. Charlie spent the day making a railway map, joining all the places he had lived and stayed in as far back as he could remember. All his life the family had moved from one rented house to another, painting, papering, refurnishing; in later life Charles never felt the need to own a house or settle, moving from lodging to lodging with equanimity. At the end of September 1900 he went back with his uncle and aunt Ray and cousins to school in Inverness, a second home, as he had known the Rays both separately and together all his life.

One Tuesday evening, just after returning to school in January 1901, Charlie heard the church bells tolling. News spread quickly: Queen Victoria had died. Everyone went into mourning: the teachers, his uncle and aunt and the boys were given black armbands. His mother wore mourning until May that year. He heard eulogies on the character of the late queen, the achievements of her reign, her greatness compared to all other monarchs in history, and her civilising influence on all corners of the globe. Meg wrote to tell him how George, as the Sheriff, had announced the new King at the snowy market cross in Lanark, wearing his wig and gown, standing beside the Provost, and how he had marched on to the steps of the County Hall where he read the proclamation clear and loud, ending with three cheers for the new King. The following year George was invited to the Coronation, but decided not to go because of the expense. At least that was what he told Meg – that it did not warrant an entire new set of court clothes – but George had other reasons for not attending. He strongly disapproved of the shift from Victorian values to Edwardian: a shift from tight-laced to bodice-undone. Victoria had represented self-discipline, work and achievement in Britain and abroad, while Edward VII was known as a libertine. The King would approach the altar to be crowned with Queen Alexandra, but the King's mistresses would all be present in Westminster Abbey, sitting near the front, in stalls that soon became known as the 'horse box'.

Meanwhile George and Meg could find no house in Lanark grand enough for Meg's tastes and were given permission to look as far away as Glasgow; she eventually found a large mansion in Rutherglen called Gallowflat. From May to November 1901 Glasgow held an International Exhibition: it covered seventy-three acres and included an extravagant Oriental Pavilion, as well as numerous other foreign pavilions, one even had a dome topped with an angel wielding an electric torch. Electricity – heating and lighting – in industry and farming was a new excitement. The Exhibition also boasted concert halls, restaurants and cafés. To have such a spacious and comfortable house near Glasgow in the year of this Great Exhibition was a calculated dream. Meg had many guests, not only family, but titled acquaintances who admired her writing and who had been attracted to her exclusive ladies' club in Inverness. But a sheriff's residence was regulated in Scots Law and there were questions in the House of Commons, from the member for Falkirk, about why the Sheriff of Lanark who had traditionally resided in Lanark was now living in Glasgow. The reply from the Lord Advocate was that such matters were at the discretion of the Secretary of State for Scotland – Meg's uncle Colin, knowing his niece's predilection for the grand, allowed her a year of living her fantasy. It was short-lived, however. Not only was the house infested with rats, which

Johnnie enjoyed killing with a shovel, but when the winter of 1902 set in, the water froze and the pipes burst like rivers all over the rambling house. Meg had to cancel many of her house parties and everyone succumbed to illness from damp.

George eventually decided to buy a house in the hope of being finally settled. They found a red sandstone villa on the road leaving Lanark towards Edinburgh, with sweeping open views to the front and a loch and golf course behind for £1650. It was not a country mansion, but had practical benefits, being newly built, with integrated electricity. Still longing for grandeur, Meg decided that they could not move in unless it was extended by a new drawing room, a library and stables. They were to stay at the house they named 'Edgemoor' for sixteen years.

By May 1901, Mary and Tony Ray had almost finished building their new school on the sand dunes by the sea outside Nairn, to be called Alton Burn. Charlie visited it with his mother and the Rays and used his new Brownie camera to take photos of everyone in front of the rising walls including one with his tiny cousin Mabel perched on a window sill. By October the new school was ready for the autumn term and the twelve-year-old Charlie was sent off to Nairn by train, his first journey alone. Mary wired Meg to say he had arrived safely.

Alton Burn was in an ideal situation: one mile east of the town of Nairn, half a mile off the main road, down a sandy track towards the sea. There was a short drive curving between lawns and there stood the large stone school, three storeys high and two rooms deep. The classrooms were on the ground floor, the masters' rooms, matron's department and headmaster's office on the first and, at the top, the huge space was divided into four dormitories, which at the beginning held only three to four boys each. The windows overlooked the gardens, a strip of gorse, the golf links and the sea. It was utterly silent. From his dorm, Charlie could hear each wave of an incoming tide. In the evening there were sunsets that dyed the sea and sky with orange reds and coloured the room with pink. The windows were the same height as the seagulls as they circled in off the sea.

There were fourteen boys to begin with, rising to twenty-eight, but always few enough for the accommodation to be spacious. There were electric lights, and bells for the servants, with two staircases, one at each end of the house, and bathrooms on the stair blocks. The school had its own water tower and, for 1901, was incredibly modern.

Alton Burn exists today very much as Tony and Mary Ray built it. It is a hotel perched on the golf links in front of the sandy beach. The same family that took it over from Tony Ray run it today and there are school photographs in the hallway. The bedroom cupboards are the same as those in which the prep-school boys stowed their games kit, Sunday kilt uniform and second set of weekday uniform: Eton collars, tweed jackets, short woollen trousers. There is an ancient deep sink with brass taps at the end of the stairwell. From the outside there are still twenty chimney pots although no coal fires remain inside. In 1901 twenty fireplaces were stoked by housemaids during the fierce winters, but summertime was generally sunny in Nairn, which was a popular Victorian resort, known as the Brighton of the North.

From his school desk in the bright classroom Charlie could see across the Moray Firth to the Black Isle. On a clear day every detail was crisp and brightly coloured. His translations from Latin and Greek were livened with a vivid sense of nature. On a fine afternoon Tony Ray would take the older boys golfing or swimming in the sea while Mary built sandcastles with the younger boys and her own two girls – ambitious sand buildings imitating the structure of local Scottish castles. On nature walks they would identify trees, flowers and birds. Long-beaked oystercatchers and sandpipers landed on the lawns, and there was a sandy path along the links to Nairn, bordered on the land side by tall Scots pines. Years later, with his war wound limp, Charles would walk a similar path in Viareggio: sand and sea on his left, pines on the right.

The boys wrote and performed their own plays. They were also encouraged to write home often. Charlie's letters show an early descriptive aptitude:

> . . . heavy seas were leaving banks of brown foam two feet deep till the next gust of wind carried them away up the beach to the town. Wild seabirds hanging motionless in the air for a time then dropping swiftly onto the crest of a foaming wave and let themselves be carried in to land. Grimy fishermen wandering aimlessly about and talking together in small groups.[16]

The Rays' small school was inspired by both nature and the curriculum. Charlie also wrote home about a skating party. They took the train from Nairn to Forres and drove by horse-drawn brake to the Loch of Blairs where they skated until lunch on a big circle which had been swept by the servants on the shallow loch. There was lunch in the boathouse – a large pot of soup which had been brought down in a carriage, with lemonade, chicken, potatoes and confectioneries. Someone said it looked like the backwoods of Canada. After lunch they skated until it was snowing too heavily to continue and instead of walking back they drove to his friend Alastair's house, 'one of the finest houses I have ever seen. Altyre is yellow with grey lattice work all over . . . We went to see the ponies and the beavers.'

At night Charlie would think of his own family at home and even invented a family tree to rival in complexity the real ones that George loved drawing up and showing to his son with great seriousness. He wrote to his mother, teasing his father:

> I made out a list of the descendants of Charles Ludmore, and showing how Father might easily become Lord of Ludmore, Welt and Stigham. I sent this to you after making a copy for myself, but what I sent was lost in the post. Another lost letter explains how Grizel Plunkett (daughter of the late Zedekiah Plunkett) a baby, is now in possession of those estates as well as of Loosewave, Fendomit, Glenshowie, and will on his death own Baldido in Fifeshire. However she has died of a fit of catalepsy to which the Stigham family are subject.[17]

In this happy state at the family prep school, Charlie amassed a collection of comic postcards: the first from his father with a picture of a judge in a wig with a hammer saying, 'I have just time for one Sentence . . .'[18] which playfully excused him from further correspondence. George was now exceptionally busy acting as sheriff or judge in the Glasgow courts, and becoming more distant from his son.

Meanwhile his brother John was enrolled at the Glasgow Veterinary School. It was hoped that his passion for animals would give him the determination to overcome the academic challenge – and it did: although he failed Chemistry first time round, he sat the exam again immediately and passed. The train from Glasgow to Lanark took under an hour and this enabled John to be at home as much as possible in order to ride his new horse. But he was not at home for long: before spring, he was packed off to Buenos Aires again to see about getting a job.

In April 1903 Meg and George celebrated their silver wedding anniversary. Charlie woke them at 6 a.m. to congratulate them, then ran up and down the stairs bringing presents from all the relatives: salt cellars, napkin rings, a pen tray, a paper knife, a sweet dish – all made of silver – and from Charlie himself, a silver cream jug with a verse of his own about their anniversary typed out and folded inside. Before he went back to school for his last term at Alton Burn, Charlie and Meg drove out in the dogcart to pay a visit on a neighbour at a house called Harperfield. As soon as they were seated in the drawing room, the governess told them that the children were all suffering from whooping cough: the Scott Moncrieffs fled in terror of anything that might prevent the next phase of Charlie's life – the Winchester scholarship.

CHAPTER 3

Winchester

> Scott Moncrieff is the kind of boy, who is quite happy in bed if he has plenty of literature, only it must *be* literature.
>
> Montague Rendall, housemaster at Winchester, 1904

On a hot Friday in early July 1903, Charlie and his mother caught the train from Glasgow to Euston and took the tube to Earls Court where they stayed the night with his uncle Kenneth, one of Meg's many brothers. Meg was sick from the journey and, more nervous than her son, she suffered from neuralgia for the next few days. On Saturday they arrived in Winchester where Charlie was to take the entrance examination. They drove into the heart of the fine old city, past high walls crowned with drooping snapdragons, yellow, white and red, and under a gateway into the narrow Kingsgate Street, where their lodgings were in the oldest house of all, with an overhanging timbered front wreathed with creepers. While Meg was ill, Joanna Ballard, another aunt on Charlie's father's side, came to entertain Charlie. For the next two days she nursed Meg with military efficiency and explored the ancient town with her nephew.

At Winchester King Alfred, scholar, statesman and lawgiver, began the work of recording Anglo-Saxon history, and his translations from Latin laid the foundations of Anglo-Saxon prose. Winchester was the nursery of the English language. Charles and his aunt visited the cathedral and saw the graves of Saxon kings: Cynegils and Adulphus, Cenulph and Ecgberht. In Winchester in 802 Ecgberht was crowned king of all England and issued his famous edict, abolishing tribal distinctions and decreeing that all within the one nation should be known by one name, English. Charles, however, didn't feel entirely English. He had spent a summer two years previously tracing his own ancestry on a large piece of canvas, back to the half-brother of Mary Queen of Scots, the illegitimate Earl of Murray; not content with that, he had added the descendants of all the kings and queens of England and Scotland around the outside of the canvas with their relationships to each other ending with Queen Victoria and Edward VII. He had placed himself confidently in the history of Britain.

Charlie's entrance exam began with the Latin translation, at which he triumphed. The next was Euclid which he found 'fearfully stiff' although he was back on form for the history exam and Greek translation in the afternoon. There were another three days of exams with candidates from the original hundred being knocked out each day. Names of those still in the competition were shown on a list in the window of Wells bookshop where the last remaining parents gathered on Saturday 11 July – for Charlie a day never to be forgotten. His name was there, among the thirteen scholars, and on seeing it he ran alone to the cathedral to pay homage beside the grave of William of Wykeham, the founder, five centuries before, of one of the oldest public schools in England.

Montague Rendall, who would be his housemaster and a future headmaster, spoke to Charlie's mother. His translations of Latin and Greek gained the highest mark of all the candidates that year. The thirteen-year-old had an instinctive facility of expression. He had translated Ovid's *Metamorphoses* with an almost adult understanding, derived from his absorption and memorising of so much great poetry since a very young age:

> Everything is changed but nothing perishes. The spirit wanders, going hence, thither, coming thence, hither and takes possession of any limbs it pleases. With equal ease it goes from beasts into human bodies and from us into beasts, nor in any length of time does it fail. And as wax is easily moulded in new shapes, nor remains as it had been before, nor keeps the same form, but yet is itself the same; so do I teach that the soul is ever the same, but migrates into different shapes.[1]

Charlie's own metamorphosis would shortly begin.

After a family summer at the beach and shortly before his fourteenth birthday, 25 September 1903, Charles – no longer Charlie – was taken to Winchester by his father to begin his first term. 'I have left him,' George wrote, 'in an earthly paradise which I am glad to think he fully appreciates.'[2] In fact the converse was true: Charles had just left Eden. Winchester was not simply crumbling stone walls and honeysuckle; it had a darker underside. Charles was probably far better off in the homely, creative atmosphere of Alton Burn than at Winchester, where he was expected to conform to hundreds of years of tradition. His individuality would be tested to the full.

Officially known as *Collegium Beatae Mariae Wintoniensis prope Winton,* Winchester College was founded in 1382 by William of Wykeham, Bishop of Winchester and Chancellor to both Edward III and Richard II. The first seventy poor scholars entered the school in 1394. It was founded in conjunction with New College, Oxford, for which it was designed to act as a feeder. Older than Eton, Winchester had a tradition of scholarship and privilege. The nine official public schools recognised in the Public Schools Act of 1868 provided the country with its ruling class, and a scholar at Winchester was deemed the academic cream.

The seventy scholars lived apart from the other students in a medieval stone keep in the central court, called College, or Coll. They ate like courtly knights at ancient oak tables in a stone hall hung with dark portraits of former headmasters and wore gowns to distinguish them from commoners. They lived in the same dormitory that exists today, and slept in communal rooms in mixed age groups. They also studied together, the idea being that the older boys could help the younger ones if necessary and the younger could 'fag' for the older boys – make tea and run errands. Prep time was known as 'toy time'. Desks were known as 'toys', and, to complicate matters, books sent from home were also known as 'toys'. A lot of time was spent erecting bookshelves and arranging toys.

Charles, as a Scot, had an historical prejudice against the English to overcome, while the English boys had an inbuilt indifference to Scots and an assumption of superiority over any other race. Lucky then that Charles Law, another scholar and another Scot, soon became a close friend. The son of Bonar Law, who later briefly became Prime Minister, Charles Law also came from a hard-working Scottish family. At Alton Burn Charles Scott Moncrieff had been the best at every subject, and his father was known as a respected judge, but now he was surrounded by huge academic competition and socially was considered ordinary. His parents, though comfortable, earned their own living, and their wealth was nothing compared to the truly rich of Edwardian England. At Winchester there were members of ruling families like the Asquiths and others admitted to Edward VII's royal set: the frivolous, the witty, the heirs to material and social achievement well beyond the experience of Charles's family. A typical luncheon party for twenty among the very rich could cost £60, when the wages of a maid were £10 a year. The sisters and mothers were debutantes born to a life of leisure; a very different path from Charles's mother.

Charles knew that he was there for reasons primarily of scholarship. Nonethless in his first year 1903–4 he completed all the challenges expected of a fourteen-year-old: ran 'mis maz', climbed 'Hills', learnt Shelley's 'Arethustra'. Among his classmates were Charles Asquith and John Chisholm-Batten. There was A. P. Herbert, later a novelist, whose mother Lady Carnarvon would be known for her humanitarian acts during the war, also James Steuart Wilson, a clergyman's son with a beautiful singing voice, A. G. Hess, George and Tom Gilroy and David Clutterbuck: all of whom he counted as friends. Another classmate, the splendidly named Lyonulphe Tollemache, was in the 'Sick House' when Charles was first ill and sent there,

> Lyon is ripping, he's the only person I've had a good crack wi' yet. He is so intelligent . . . Today is Lyon's birthday, and I was his first-foot as it were. I, as 12 slowly boomed out on Coll. Clock, wished him many happy, etc., before going to sleep. Altogether I think yesterday was one of my happiest days here, for that reason chiefly.[3]

Charles could not see his parents every weekend, but he did write to his dear Mama and his intense, over-excited letters show how he threw himself into the world of books, reading his way through the Moberly Library, an extensive collection donated by its namesake. It was the only place he could read alone, as prep time was communal. His first letter home began, 'Adam Bede *is* good.' Here were the eternal truths of wealth and poverty, vice and virtue that would keep him steady. He went on to describe a visit to local churches in his time off: Otterbourne, Eastleigh, and Golden Common, and drew sketches of details of one of the pillars. He found he was inspired by both literary and visual aesthetics.

He felt the need to do well, but also the desire not to. Sitting in ancient wood-panelled rooms, with the dust of time settling over him, he absorbed the silence, the stones, the carved mantelpieces. He was reading Keats and pondering the oneness of truth with beauty and goodness: a unity which these buildings and this place seemed to sum up for him. Mr Rendall, the College Housemaster, introduced his boys early to Keats's thinking. He was an intrepid bachelor who came from a vicarage family of nine boys, through Classical scholarships at Harrow and Cambridge, and his career had been solely as master at Winchester. Spartan and eccentric, he rarely wore a coat and liked twelve-mile walks or runs as casual exercise. Italian art and architecture were his great loves; he introduced serious lessons on art and was the president of SCROGUS, the Shakespeare reading society. This diversion into the arts was relatively new to Winchester which had, until now, studied undiluted Latin and Greek. The Classics were however still the major part of the syllabus. In a letter to his father, to whom he wrote less often, Charles said, 'We are reading Homer and Plato, Horace and Tacitus this term; at present we are getting into the second Iliad, Laches, Ars Poetica, and Agricola, respectively: in history we are beginning Greek History from the very darkest Ages – In English, Chaucer's Prologue . . .' He went on to mention that he had taken up carpentry: 'The two school carpenters who teach me are very ingenious and much–experienced.'[4] With this new skill he was able to improve his study area, building new bookshelves and fitting them himself, with a small but loud hammer which he inadvertently aimed at the Victorian electric light system, sending the entire college into darkness.

One day in 1903, he wrote home, 'I am getting on quite well in work you will be glad to hear, and am making friends . . .' that bit to please his parents, then the real Charles lost in a reverie . . . 'Everything goes as usual, and will go on, I suppose, as it has for five centuries. I marvel when I think of quaint, long-haired college juniors who sat where my equals and I now sit, and discussed war news, not of Japs and Russians, but of Armigers and Burgundians, or of Yorkists and Lancastrians!'[5]

As well as dreaming of the past, Charles was beginning, less romantically, to look at the people of the present and to compare his own situation with that of others. In his second year he visited a charity school, described in a letter home,

> Pallid girls with their hair over their ears were teaching terribly ugly children. Bright, cheery rooms, with dusty models of giraffes and hippopotami on the mantelpiece in the first room . . . The boys were pent in glass cages around a square hall, where an agnostic with fiery red hair raved to a class of some twenty lifeless shapes. The cleverest and oldest looking were playing rounders in the yard – I suppose they aren't made to learn.[6]

He realised how lucky he was, as a member of the select school, so different from the shabby world around. He also visited an elderly couple, through an introduction from his parents: 'Mrs receives in her bedroom and they up-grub their meals there, but you don't notice it much,' Charles wrote to Meg, who had escaped such a fate through her good marriage and determination to write. 'She wore a white linen robe with a blue cord, like an angelic nun, and lay on a rest couch with a blue cushion. Her face is sweeter than the daughter and very resigned and refined. I wish nice people weren't so poor.'[7]

School gave him an intellectual life and a community, one that he could share, to a certain extent, with his mother. He wasn't good at games and didn't like them much, but he did enjoy the esprit de corps of the Cadet Force.

> Field Day – we took part in a battle royal in a wood, very like the drum scene in *Through the Looking Glass*. The wood was stuffy and musty with the reek of powder and the crash of five great schools firing at each other (Eton and Charterhouse vs. Bradfield, Wellington and Winchester). I don't think anybody won, but you never can tell. We lunched by a roadside with long tables spread with rough and ready delicacies, and motors came slipping along every minute, as it's the Portsmouth to London road, and very important.[8]

When his mother came to the Eton–Winchester Cricket Match in 1904 – the first time Winchester had won since 1897 – Charles was shouting for batsman Gordon who was a College man, a scholar like himself. In celebration Gordon was dragged from the pavilion by force, raised shoulder high and carried round only half-dressed, then up through Meads, the green meadows by the river. 'Did you see us carrying Gordon? I was right under him!'[9] boasted Charles when he joined his family, flushed and happy.

He adored his mother with her beautiful clothing and figure, dramatic height and natural confidence, and was proud to take her round his friends at the match. His school letters to her are addressed 'Dear Lady', 'Dearest Cerissette', 'Dear Homebirdy', 'My dearest One', and he would occasionally sign a guilty 'Yours Lunatically', or 'A Putrescence'.[10] When he became ill with tonsillitis and was put in 'Sick House' for over a week, the housemaster wrote, 'Scott Moncrieff is the kind of boy who is quite happy in bed if he has plenty of literature, only it must *be* literature.'[11] Charles's letters were full of comments on the books he was reading and lending:

> I have a continual drain on my books by people's borrowing and losing them. What a master Trollope is. How can anyone compare *Bleak House* to the *Last Chronicles of Barset*? Toogood is introduced as vulgar and horrid, and turns out so noble, with his ideas of romance and 'blood being thicker than porridge'. My father has not got *Framley Parsonage*, has he? . . . *Memories of Vailima* is very short, but contains some very fine things. It begins with verses written in 1872 by R.L.S. I am so glad you like *Songs of Travel*: though it is a very slim volume yet it contains a lot of gems . . . *Destiny* is glorious. Why is Miss Ferrier not known as well as Miss Edgeworth? she is quite as good. *Destiny* bound in iron would be pleasant, but how much more so if bound in a delightful kind of salmon-coloured cloth . . . Tell Colin to make his book club send him *The Club of Queer Trades* by G.K. Chesterton. A charming, if whimsical, book . . .
>
> Quirk came down here (Sick House) yesterday with a bland look and a set of Aristophanes under his arm, of which he read, or I read to him, some 150 lines before he retired, which was not bad. He returned to me *The Return of the Native*, or rather a fresh

copy: he had become so engrossed in mine as to overwhelm it with private marks which he wanted to keep. I read *A Pair of Blue Eyes* all through yesterday: I had not read it for nearly a year and thought a lot more of it than before. I agree now with you that it is very sad. I had not then seen quite how sad: But none of them could be a patch on *The Return of the Native* . . .[12]

For Christmas 1904, Charles copied out *Music and Moonlight*, the poems and songs of Arthur O'Shaughnessy, for his mother and illustrated them with the inscription, 'embellished by a young man of genteel family, not yet prominent in the world'.[13] The comment was playful, tongue in cheek; on the other hand scholars at Winchester were expected to be successful. He also illustrated his letters home: one in particular when he knew his mother was staining the floors at Edgemoor and working hard on decorating while he sat languidly at school reading literature and writing poetry. 'Much lovelets from your abominable, blear-eyed, cloudy brained, horrid little youngest.'[14]

His family were still integral to his life, despite the distractions of school. He wrote about his eldest brother in 1905, 'I am longing to see Colin again, he is so good and peaceful and quietly humorous.'[15] Colin was now a curate in an impoverished London East End parish and 'whirled around in his black gown hurling soup tickets through widows windows'.[16] Charles invited him to attend his confirmation in 1905, in the comparative luxury of Winchester.

Colin turned up at noon livid with cold, and we warmed at the fire in Second Chamber. I took him to Museum and he glanced at the pictures, but felt like a low-life-high-thought-prophet who has strayed into the Lord Mayor's banquet, who, as his coat and hat have been whipped off by domestics, feels he must go in.[17]

To see the contrast in their lives, Charles went to stay with Colin in April 1905. His brother was not home till after eleven on most nights, but their father George made the trip to London to entertain Charles and took him to the zoo, to lunch at his club, to visit the Irving cousins, to Madame Tussaud's, to Lyons for tea, and to Great

Smith Street baths. They also met a second cousin, Constance Lunn, whose family invited Charles and Colin to tea. Constance greeted them in fine silks and lace and presented Charles with a copy of the *Lyra Sacra*, a book of religious verse, first published in 1895, which he kept to the end of his life. Constance was twenty and Colin twenty-six, and they had plenty in common, as she was a parson's daughter and he an enthusiastic curate. Connie was petite with an hour-glass figure, thick chestnut hair and languorous eyes; Colin was over six foot, big-boned with a high forehead; his serious mission in life gave him an intensity and passion. It didn't take long for love to blossom.

In summer 1906, the Scott Moncrieffs went on their last family holiday before Colin's marriage. They travelled by train to the Swiss Alps and stayed at Gimel and then at Lucerne, walking in the mountains. Colin practised his sermons on the family while Charles was ill in bed with a worryingly high temperature, composing poetry of a very different nature.

> Mark how his body stiffening to the leap
> The cry, the fiery line of flashing limb
> The water rising to the kiss of him[18]

Thinking of the young Wykehamists bathing in Gunners Hole, a part of the nearby river in the summer, he wrote,

> . . . white and cool
> Now he emerges. All the joyful grass,
> Trembling and breaking in flowers at his feet,
> With wondrous fragrance notes where he shall pass,
> While we, his fellow-men, worship, alas
> In silence, whom we dare not run to greet.
> Yea – but to worship him alone – how sweet![19]

While Colin wrote sermons about the adoration of God, Charles, with similar language, was secretly, in his book of private poetry, praising the beauty of living boys.

Two years later on 27 September 1907, Colin married Constance. They shared much of the same philosophy: a humorous and courageous attitude to life and an unquestioning devotion to their faith. Constance was beautiful, profound, dutiful: as a clergyman's daughter, she was perfectly fitted for the role of vicar's wife, bearing Colin eight children, seven of whom survived to adulthood. The wedding took place at her family home, the vicarage at Chillingham, Northumberland. It was still the custom in 1907 to publish lists of wedding presents in the local newspaper and under 'Charles Scott Moncrieff: brother', is listed, 'small table and cheque'. He had made the table in the school carpentry workshop and was proud enough to show it off in public. He also wrote a poem to Colin and Constance on thick vellum paper, wishing their marriage well, and ending with the hope that they would 'inspire our Colony by their Constancy'[20]. They set sail immediately for New Zealand where Colin had been appointed lecturer in Divinity at St John's College in Auckland.

Although Charles admired the transparent goodness of his brother and sister-in-law, his experience at school had already got him into murky waters. At Winchester, Charles wrote that he felt both fearful and superior. Superior because he was a scholar but fearful because of the ragging this invited from commoners; having no brothers and sisters his own age he was not used to teasing. He was also fearful of beatings from prefects. 'Tunding' was a flogging administered with a ground ash stick. To be 'Cut Into' was more severe, meaning to thrash with a ground ash till cuts appeared. No more than a dozen cuts were to be given, but prefects were allowed to administer them. In one of his early letters, he wrote, 'I am happy here now, happy in a quiet, self-respecting, superior-fearing sort of way, but happy all the same.' However, it was evident something was bothering him.

CHAPTER 4

First Love Affairs

A Child – athirst to stand admired:
A Boy – aflame to feel desired:

CKSM, poetry notebook, 1906

Two years after Charles's arrival at Winchester, the Vicar of Compton Rectory invited him to tea. He lent him a book on St Francis of Assisi and kept asking him to sit in different chairs in his drawing room,

> ostensibly for comfort and finally at tea installing me in a chair commanding all the window's lore: a golf course with a sunset on the top, lines of grey and lemon. When the lemon had changed from orange to a dried blood tint, I could no longer refrain from giving tongue. He then explained blandly that that was why he had given me the chair, 'I thought you would notice what other people wouldn't . . .'[1]

The vicar recognised that Charles was different, perhaps guessed how different. Compton Rectory lies three miles south of Winchester, an easy walk for sixteen-year-olds, and it was there in November 1905 that Charles wrote a sonnet dedicated first to David Clutterbuck, then scored out and dedicated to Lyonulphe Tollemache. It begins: 'Alone upon the naked hill we two,' then there is a picture of an erect penis inked over the text,

Am I not brother and more to you, And are you not my brother? . .
Bend over me – lean down, dear love, lean down,
And though it were well that each should quite forget
The other: for the sorrow in my heart.[2]

Both David and Lyonulphe came to stay at Lanark for holidays and had their names recorded in the visitors' book. At Edgemoor during the Easter Holiday of 1906, they climbed hills, visited Edinburgh and Glasgow, played golf, and went to church with the Scott Moncrieffs. Charles dedicated some of his other early poems to David and Lyonulph. These were published (without the dedications, which were only written in pencil in his poetry notebook) in the school magazine, *The Wykehamist*. From the age of fifteen Charles had poems published regularly in the magazine and a year later in the journals the *Westminster Gazette* and the *Academy*. His parents were proud of his poetry, and the school magazine recognised it as accomplished and entertaining. However for Charles it reflected the profound unrest he felt at his desire for fellow boys. The title of one poem seemed to justify it all 'God and one Man – Make a Majority', so long as God forgave him, everyone else was irrelevant.

> . . . I will fight for Thee if I may fight with Thee
> Against our strength what mortal might endure?
> Make me thine armour-bearer, Lord, but prithee
> Let none reproach me that I am not pure.
>
> What God hath cleansed may no man call common
> Then cleanse me Lord that I be clean and fair,
> So may Thy Son who scorned not Birth of Woman
> Enter my Heart and make His Temple there.[3]

This religious verse, inspired by the metaphysical poets, with its strong awareness of sin and desire for cleansing, was dedicated to his friend David Clutterbuck. His letters home, as well as listing his voracious reading of everything high and low, sacred and profane, begged his mother, 'Please pray for me to be good.' 'Pray that I may be good, I want to be good.'[4] Among these letters, torn from a jotter is the beginning of a short story about a little pale boy in the heavy black gown of a scholar sitting at the back of the classroom. He has a weak mind, added to and controlled by an abnormally weak body which makes him too slack to join with any spirit in games. 'He was in short what is ably termed a wreck.'

> . . . for are we not each a part of a great fleet, to which that of Xerxes would be as a rowing-boat to a man-of-war; so we sail forth, all alike, at the start, all with equal hopes of a fair voyage? Yet how few come back. Some, shattered at an early age by sickness, others, as the boy in question, disabled owing to incompetency in facing the earliest difficulties of life. Others, later still, sunk in battle, or driven ashore by the gale of their own passions.[5]

It could have been autobiography, with the last description, driven by the gale of his passions, fitting him well. In his poetry, his classical education and the high ideals of chivalrous and romantic love allowed him to transform his longings. Love could justify the occasional failings of the flesh; the golden conversion of lust into love, and the triumph of virtue over vice:

> Were you but vain, your vanity
> To read my love might move you:
> But were you vain, that could not be
> For then I should not love you:
> Strange cozenage, that I cannot gain
> You humble, nor desire you, vain.[6]

Ralph Wright, a fellow scholar, later a second master at College, remembered that in his first year Charles had a rough time. He was different from the 'healthy barbarians' of his year, even the scholars, and he was teased heartily when they found a poem beginning, 'God built a worm'. The following year, Ralph and Charles got on better and Ralph became more interested in Charles's unique taste in books, also through mutual friends 'such as that amazingly attractive boy Guy Lawrence, for whom we both had a deep sentimental admiration'.[7] Two years older than Charles, Guy Lawrence was prefect of chapel and captain of fives, handsome and good at sports, and he was to play a part later in his life.

Meanwhile Charles's reading matter widened, with him often devouring ten books a week and writing a commentary to his mother. Aged fifteen he read *The Challoners* by E. F. Benson, a novel that described a familiar view over a hazy valley to the grey towers of Winchester, 'Old Challoner is the Puritanic rector. His son becomes a Romanist from a love of beauty, shocked by the crudities of the father's church; the daughter reads George Eliot to her father's horror and then marries an atheist.'[8] These were actions that struck a chord with Charles's own life. In the same batch came Henry James, F. T. Bullen, Geikie's *Scottish Reminiscences*, G. K. Chesterton's *Heretics*, *The Road in Tuscany* by Maurice Hewlett, *The Sacred Cup* by Vincent Brown, Laurence Housman's *Cloak of Friendship*, and *The Hill* by Horace Annesley Vachell.

He read novels, travel, history, theology, poetry and journalism. Vachell's *The Hill* is a romantic story about the passionate love of two Harrow schoolboys. Laurence Housman, (the brother of A. E.), was a Uranian poet. 'At its most pure,' wrote historian Paul Fussell, 'the program of the Uranians favoured an ideal of Greek love' – in other words the worship of young male beauty without sex. But more often than not the model was impossible to sustain 'and earnest ideal paedophilia found itself descending to ordinary pederastic sodomy'.[9]

James Steuart Wilson, another schoolboy friend, sang as a soloist in the choral society to which Charles belonged and where boys were encouraged to write songs and compose music to be performed by themselves. Charles dedicated a poem to him which described a pure, idealised and untouchable love that verges on cruelty. In his private notebook he dated and recorded each time he fell in love by writing a poem. Sometimes there was joy, but not without pain, as in 'The Prince's Page':

Down the street the young Prince rode
Very fair for the eye to see
My head was bowed to my heart's grave load
No woman turned to smile at me
I was but the Prince's page: and he
The cause of all my misery.

Charles's sexuality was something he would by turns embrace joyfully, then regard as an affliction which heralded great anguish. Charles realised that his father would never be understanding about his homosexuality. A lifetime as a judge in the criminal sector meant no one could fool him about his son's activity. He had looked into the eyes of the sodomites and the sodomised at the saddest, most degrading end of the human scale. For him there was no literary, spiritual or positive emotional aspect to homosexuality. Meg, on the other hand, without knowing anything about the physical details, had been reading Charles the poetry of Walt Whitman since he was eight. He grew up loving the literature of those outside conventional morality. He told his mother he had found a first edition of *Hadrian the Seventh* by Baron Corvo,[10] a comedy about an Englishman who becomes Pope and reforms the Vatican by getting rid of its wealth, in Wells Bookshop, and he treasured it all his life. He was also drawn to the writing of the *fin-de-siècle* sensualists. He read Walter Pater whose *Renaissance* is suggested as one of the books that corrupts Dorian Grey in Wilde's novel about the man who never ages no matter what his transgressions, while his portrait, which reflects his soul, rots in the attic. Oscar Wilde, playwright, novelist, essayist, was recently dead, but his reputation would never die, and his spirit was kept alive by his friends. Charles knew all about the drama of Wilde's life and the court case of 1895 where he had been tried for gross indecency and condemned to two years' hard labor, breaking his health and confidence; although he had written one of his most poignant pieces, *De Profundis*, in prison and been inspired while there to compose the *Ballad of Reading Gaol*.

Robert Ross was a dedicated friend of Oscar Wilde, who continued to campaign for the rehabilitation of his reputation long after Wilde's death.[11] His house at 40 Half Moon Street, just off Piccadilly, acted as a salon for poets, writers and critics. He was also an art connoisseur who collected fine old paintings and furniture, papered his walls with gold wallpaper and liberally gave out Turkish delight and expensive cigars.

The date and circumstances of Charles's first meeting with Ross are unclear, although it certainly happened when Charles was sixteen. It is possible that the first meeting was a casual conversation in a second-hand bookshop on the Charing Cross Road, where Charles used to pass time on trips to London to visit Colin, who only had time for him in the very late evening. There was a poem dedicated to Robert Ross in Charles's poetry notebook called 'Hylas', which was published in *The Wykehamist* in November 1906, without the dedication, and a year later in the *Academy*.

Charles wanted to impress Ross with his poetic ability and his knowledge of the Greek myth, which told that Heracles took on the young Hylas as an armour-bearer and taught him to become a warrior, whereupon Hylas left him for female Naiads and stayed with them, while Heracles cried in vain for his loved one.

> . . . Yet he came not.
> Lies he on some green bed
> Mute trophy of their fruitless victory
> That round him mourn? Perhaps he is not dead
> But rules their region, and is fancied free
> While lank-stemmed lilies, wreathed about his head,
> Rise to the air, and plead for liberty.[12]

Charles's poem spoke of the loss of any loved one, and the loss of Wilde to Ross; the longing for the dead lover who still 'rules their region'. Wilde would have approved of the 'lank-stemmed lilies, wreathed about his head' especially as they plead for liberty. Charles felt close to the religious inspiration of Wilde's work, and he was told by Robert Ross of the author's deathbed conversion to Catholicism and of Wilde's description of the Roman Catholic Church as being 'for saints and sinners alone – for respectable people, the Anglican Church will do'. During his time at Trinity College, Dublin, and later in prison, Wilde had pored over the works of Augustine, Dante and Cardinal Newman.[13]

The character Algernon in Wilde's *Importance of Being Earnest* has the surname Moncrieff. That must have lent Charles an amusing aura with Wilde devotees; in the letters which discuss Charles, Robert Ross always called him 'Moncrieff'. It is clear that Charles made trips to London from Winchester and visited Ross at Half Moon Street, a haunt of the literary homosexual coterie. Robert Ross wrote in a letter in May 1907, 'Scott Moncrieff is due to come here Monday or Tuesday. He has told me the hour of his arrival and the method of his arrival: indeed everything except the date. He is obviously a real poet . . .'[14] Charles was nervous over his initial invitation, something he could not share with any of his family or friends. It was only thirteen years after the Wilde trial and the idea of a schoolboy going to London to meet Wilde's associates would have been met with horror from school and home alike. On the other hand, it appealed to his pride to be accepted by an elite minority with exclusive intellectual tastes. Ross wrote again that month, 'Moncrieff came here as he will have told you, and was as charming as ever. But he is very very shy, except when he is talking about books and he writes delightful letters full of racy criticisms about literature.'[15] Charles's fears were allayed when his mother came to London in August and Charles brought Ross to tea with her and the Rays at the Lyceum Club. Meg's intellectual snobbery and her own naivety far outstripped any suspicions she might have that her teenage son would be seduced.

At that time Ross had engaged Christopher Sclater Millard, a charismatic and seductive bookseller, as his secretary. Charles was soon invited to visit Millard's house, which had a large garden with a hammock slung between apple trees. Here all the birds and squirrels of the area were fed by Millard who collected first editions and looked after his books with as much care as his birds. Millard was reluctant to give away books, but for the fine-looking and poetic Charles he would part with anything. It was he who gave him the first edition of *Hadrian the Seventh* by Baron Corvo. Charles had told his mother he had found it in Wells bookshop in Winchester: the first of many lies. Anything to do with his visits to London was obscured. The more he lied, the more separate he became from his parents and the principles of his upbringing. Like Corvo, Millard was a Catholic convert of a decadent type. Ten years Charles's senior, with an MA in Theology, Millard was a disciple of Wilde and was currently engaged in his impressive and thorough lifework, a bibliography of Wilde's writings – which he dedicated, 'To CSM from CSM'. This dedication was against the advice of Ross who wrote to Millard in May 1907, 'Try like a good fellow and leave Moncrieff out of the bibliography. You are nearly as bad as Mr Dick.'[16]

The writer A. J. A. Symons gave a vivid description of Millard as a tall, striking figure and a 'natural philosopher'. Always hatless, with thick, curly, greying hair, he wore a blue shirt, green jacket and grey trousers, which he patched and mended himself, but there was a great dignity about him, 'he was perhaps the most self-possessed man I have ever known.'[17]

To add to this, Millard was described by one of the editors of the *Burlington Magazine*[18] as 'the sort who couldn't resist, when out on a country walk, leaping the hedge and raping a ploughboy'.[19] In March 1907 he also gave the sixteen-year-old Charles a small leather-bound copy of the *Little Office of the Blessed Virgin Mary*,[20] and beside his dedication in Latin stuck a halfpenny postage stamp from the British Virgin Islands; two allusions to virginity. He was imprisoned twice for homosexual offences: the first time just before he met Charles, for three months from June 1906,[21] for gross indecency[22]. Undoubtedly his influence on Charles was more than literary, aesthetic and religious. Moreover, his chosen Catholicism was a religion which offered the forgiveness that society could not provide. In April 1907 Charles spent the first week of his 'Easter holiday with Millard at Coulsdon and Worthing, and was afterwards deposited by him at 15 Vicarage Gardens, before going home to my astonished parents in Scotland'.[23] His mother commented in her diary, 'Charlie has had a pleasant week going about with various literary friends.'[24] Charles wrote much later about the holiday, 'There has been hardly any single thing in my life since that is not affected by his influence and teaching at that time.'[25]

Millard impressed Charles with the ancient Greek tradition of pederasty where an older man would take a youth as a disciple and lover and instruct him both in knowledge and in the ways of eros. However this was not a Greek city state, this was London in 1907 where the punishment for boy love was prison; a life to which these lovers of beauty and ideals were entirely unsuited. Millard was imprisoned with other sexual offenders: paedophiles, rapists and suspected sodomites charged with indecency were categorised in the same group. Prisons in 1907 were grim places where squalor, neglect and moral depravity ruled. Food was basic, heating minimal, tobacco was banned; access to books, letters and visits had to be earned. Prison terms were not long, but few who sampled them wished to do so again. The Half Moon Street atmosphere was both liberating and frightening; no wonder Charles was halting and shy with Ross: he was being brave just being there at all. But that was his outward behaviour; internally, he felt he was living the drama of Milton's Fall. 'Do you know Richard de Castre's prayer in Lyra Sacra page 4-6? How "Jesus snapped sin's fetters and burst the gates of Hell",' he wrote in a letter to his mother in 1907.

Charles tried to turn his attention to a young lady he had met. 'Miss Daphne, driven by hunger like a winter wolf, has come to room in Winchester. *She walks 8 miles a day*. Rain or snow. To teach two thankless boys. Thus fame is made.'[26] Miss Daphne was an impoverished governess who was befriended by the whole family. She came home to stay at Lanark when Charles was seventeen and Meg noted that she was very good and kind and pretty. She was also educated and useful, unlike the society girls who were sisters of Charles's school friends. Any hoped-for romance with Charles did not flourish, but he liked her as a friend and she accompanied the Scott Moncrieffs to the Belgian seaside on their summer holiday. While there Charles wrote and dedicated to her a poem called, 'Sunset in Flanders':

> . . . Harshly a Flemish mother speaks;
> Two Flemish infants wail
> While, heaving high each warped and rusted sail
> To be hurled down again,
> The mill, convulsed by age-long pain,
> Shudders and shrieks . . .[27]

The poem is hardly romantic. The terrific noise and pain of the mill suggests a fear of womanhood, childbirth and all that family life entails. But Charles did contemplate the sort of future his parents so obviously hoped for when they encouraged friendships with girls. He dedicated poems to other women including one called 'A Ghost Story' to Gladys Dalyell, sister of a schoolfriend. This was written in 1906 and published a year later. These dedications were in some ways to reflect what was expected of him, but he also charmed girls and had lively friendships with them.

Charles wrote copious amounts of poetry and there were not enough outlets. In 1907 he and his closest friends, A. G. Hess, George Gilroy and John Chisholm-Batten founded their own literary magazine at Winchester called the *New Field*. It was sold by subscription stating, 'A Subscription implies that the Paper will be sent to the Subscriber until one of the three expires.'[28] 'A Ghost Story' appeared there – a short poem about the Ghost of Bishop Hugh. A long poem written in the same year, 'Agnes Dead in Martolm', another ghost story, in the form of an ancient ballad, was dedicated to Janet Robinson, a family friend, and also published in the *New Field*. None of the poems to women have a sensual or erotic element. 'Agnes Dead in Martolm' is a tragic ballad about impossible love and a ghastly, unearthly haunting.

The attraction of the sweet, hardworking Miss Daphne was nothing compared to the charisma, the erudition, the sheer drama of Millard, who had endured imprisonment for the love that dare not speak its name. For Charles, whose chief influence was literature and the scope of heroism, Millard's stature, maturity and passion represented a fulfilment he had never come across before. And while Miss Daphne was innocently flirtatious, Millard was practised in the art of seduction.

Charles read Latin and Greek poetry. He translated pieces from the *Iliad* taking as his example the powerful and loving relationship of Achilles and Patroclus, brother warriors who would die side by side if necessary and who groomed each other prior to battle. He read the *Symposium* where Socrates said great 'was the reward of the true love of Achilles towards his lover Patroclus'.[29] On the other hand weighed the importance of his own culture and religion and the accepted codes and punishments of society. Over and above all this was his devotion and obedience to his mother. 'A Mother's Prayer', published in the *New Field* in April 1908, is perhaps thinking of his own mother and demonstrates the power of his awareness of transgression.

A Mother's Prayer

Beautiful James Alison,
What thing have you done?
I am your mother and
You are my son.
Is it nought to you
My days in fasting pass,
My nights in prayer and weeping
For you my son, alas.
You never loved your mother
As she you, James;
But kindled in another
Unhallowed flames. –
Who can tell for certain
The death that he shall die
Drawing fate's close curtain?
Neither you nor I!
But you have kindled flames
And in flames your ghost will burn,
And all your vaunted beauty, James,
To leprous ashes turn.[30]

Charles's conscience had been formed as an eight-year-old, reading Milton with his mother in the greenhouse: he was acutely aware of the Fall. His youthful poems are full of references to his knowledge of his own wrongdoing. He believed he was offending more than the average teenager and every return to the regular Sunday services with his father at the local Church of Scotland on visits home reinforced the teaching that the wages of sin were death. His imagination was full of angels on the one hand and the devil on the other; the elevated and the damned. However, it was not enough to stop him. In his final year at Winchester, as editor of the *New Field*, which circulated among the parents, masters and old boys, Charles published under his own name an ambitious story called *Evensong and Morwe Song*. The title was taken from the General Prologue of Chaucer's *Canterbury Tales*, line 830, 'If evensong and morwesong accord'. It began:

> . . . 'And if we are found out?' asked Maurice. He was still on his knees in the thicket, and, as he looked up to where his companion stood in an awkward fumbling attitude, his face seemed even more than unusually pale and meagre in the grey broken light. It was with rather forced nonchalance that Carruthers answered 'O, the sack, I suppose' – and he stopped aghast at the other's expression. Then as only at one other time in a long and well-rewarded life did he feel that a millstone around his neck might perhaps be less offensive than the picture of those small, startled features hung for all eternity before his eyes.[31]

The story is not erotic; it is about snobbery, hypocrisy, the public school system and the fact that, among adolescent boys, homosexual acts were not uncommon. The older boy becomes a headmaster and is just about to punish a child for a sexual offence when he remembers he did the same as a boy and into his mind 'floated a picture of two boys in a thicket; of the one's charming nonchalance; of terror sickening the other, a child that had just lost his soul'. He discovers that the boy he is about to punish is the son of the boy he himself seduced at school and remembers a letter from him of how he had been lowered as a result, how his children would be barred from the great public schools and would have to attend a minor school such as this one. Instead of being understanding, he violently condemns the boys in his care for similar acts – 'his flaying sarcasm and his pessimistic prophecies drew great salt tears from the younger boy's eyes' – expels them and ruins their lives.

Charles had shared the experience of both children. The younger, aged fourteen, was terrified, for all the reasons he knew; for the punishment of 'tunding' and being cut into if he didn't do as the older boy asked. Later, as the older boy, he was frightened of the spiritual consequences of seducing a younger boy. He knew his New Testament, Luke 17: 'It would be better for him if a millstone were hung round his neck and he were cast into the sea, than that he should cause one of these little ones to sin.' He was in physical shock at the knowledge of temptation, the desire, the need for affection; all were consummated in this one act on his knees in the bushes. On the other hand the portrait of the headmaster's bad conscience was all too acutely observed,

> Before his ordination he had prayed for spiritual armour, and had received a coat of self-satisfaction which had so far held out against all assaults of man or woman. Now it felt rusty . . . Then he picked up the sheet of tremendously coat-armoured school notepaper . . . On it he drew obscene figures for half-an-hour.

He had painted a recognisable picture of a Winchester master. What was seen as Charles's arrogance and insolence had its consequences. He hoped to go up to Oxford to try for a scholarship to Magdalen or Exeter, just as his older brother Colin had won a scholarship to Queen's. The Oxford scholarships depended on both the competitive entrance examination in March and the report from the headmaster at Winchester. J. M. Burge, the headmaster, still smarting from the scandalous story circulated among parents, wrote to Charles's father in April 1908 saying that the competition in the Oxford Scholarship Exam was, 'too "hot" for him at this stage . . . He must not let his taste and style become too wayward – or his pen run away with him into the waste places of "Journalese".'[32] The patronising tone masked real anger: Charles' 'Journalese' was far too 'hot' for the headmaster. Even one hundred years later, a school magazine would hesitate before publishing such a story.

In March Charles sat both exams: the scholarship for Exeter College and a Magdalen College Demyship. In April Dr Burge wrote the letter. We do not know whether he failed to get in because of the exams or because of the headmaster's report. But his failure was a blow: as a scholar he had expected to follow his brother, all his good friends were Oxford bound, and it was undoubtably where he would have met the most like-minded of colleagues.

The last Domum Day for those who were leaving school came at the end of July. The band played in the Meads until dusk. The school sang again and again, until everyone left except the scholars and their parents, who went into the chapel for prayers.

Too much time spent indoors writing poetry and reading romantic novels was not considered healthy for a young man of eighteen. Sheriff George Scott Moncrieff no doubt blamed this for Charles's final error in expending his energies on risky journalese. Charles was therefore encouraged by parents and masters to join the School Cadet Unit which left for Aldershot immediately after the final service at Winchester, to join the Public Schools Brigade in camp for a week's training. He enjoyed outdoor exercise in the company of other youths, being gradually trained for responsibility and leadership. He could put behind him the bitter disappointment of failing to get into Oxford and the humiliation of having his magazine abruptly stopped, withdrawn from circulation and pulped.

It was with mixed feelings then that he left the school he had entered five years before with so much promise, which had helped form his literary and aesthetic tastes. It really did mean *Domum*, home, to him, with the companionship of his friends, the stimulation from the masters and the dreamy beauty of the buildings, fields and river. Later he would write longing poems from the Western Front, of nostalgia for this boyhood idyll.

CHAPTER 5

To Edinburgh

Ask Satan, please, to be my friend:
He would do anything for you.

CKSM, 'To a Public Man', 1909

Named after Joseph Lister, the father of modern surgery, Lister House was an eighteenth-century tenement, five storeys tall with a dormer attic peeking out on to the slate rooftops. Off the top of the Royal Mile near Edinburgh Castle, an arched entrance to a narrow passage opened out into a courtyard, where ragged children were playing hopscotch and skipping. Charles had to climb three storeys to his room, up a stone stairway with no light, but his twelve-paned window looked out on to the highest view in all Edinburgh: from the top of the Mound across the Firth of Forth to the Island of May and the Kingdom of Fife.

Charles and Meg had visited this student residence during the summer and 'liked it' as she recorded. But as the winter closed in Charles scribbled notes on the back of envelopes about freezing among piles of bleak, unforgiving stones. After a brisk Scottish childhood, he had experienced teenage warmth and companionship in an English public school – and now he had come back to study in the cold winds among the smoke-blackened stone of Auld Reekie. He found one other Wykehamist at Lister House, 'Young Maconochie, who is in his tenth year of Law,' he quipped to his parents in his first letter home. 'Also there is a pianist who plays the same polka, or at least stops in the same place every time on the floor below . . .'[1]

He was not enrolled in any faculty when he first moved to Edinburgh in 1908. He had begged his parents to be allowed to try once more for the Oxford and Cambridge Entrance Examinations and to have this year to study for them. Convinced that he could win the same honours as Colin, his parents agreed to pay his way, not having had to pay full school fees during his years as a Winchester scholar.

He often went home for house parties at Lanark when he would invite a guest, or meet family friends of his and his brother John's age. His mother made sure there were plenty of young women invited. Among these were Amy, Gladys and Lily Dalyell, sisters of his friend Theodore from Winchester. Also three of the seven Wood sisters Anna, Rita and Molly from Edinburgh; Anna would eventually marry his brother John. John was still studying and failing veterinary exams at Glasgow, which he had been doing since 1902; his attempt to pass as a vet would go on for another five years during which time he gave up and was sent to the Colonies twice, hated it and returned home. He was the least academic boy in the family but his understanding of animals and his determination saw him through. He finally qualified, to everyone's relief, in July 1913. Lanark was equidistant from Edinburgh and Glasgow and the brothers saw a lot of each other. Colin, however, was far away in New Zealand, teaching and starting a family with Connie.

That Christmas John and Charles read Milton's 'Ode' in front of the fire before breakfast with their parents as they had done for as long as they could remember. They also acted, as they always had, in their mother's play *The True Lover*, first for family and friends and then as a New Year entertainment, for the Convalescent Home in Lanark, Charles playing the lead male part and their friend Norah Bayley Jones the leading lady. The Bayley Joneses had their own New Year pantomime in Edinburgh where Charles played the part of Prince Charming before family and friends and local charitable organisations. Ideal for the part, Charles at nineteen was strikingly handsome and was invited to balls and house parties around Scotland, partnered by the prettiest and most interesting of women. Sadly for his mother, his letters hardly ever mentioned these girls. If romance was on his mind it was with men, and he could only share that with his book of private poems. In March 1909 Charles brought a new friend, Alec Tonnochy, back to Lanark for the week. Meg wrote that he sang beautifully and was a tall, delicate and gentlemanly lad – 'Like a swan'.[2] They went to church on Sunday where 'Charlie read the lessons with so much feeling – I do wish he were going to be ordained.'[3] Meg then travelled to Edinburgh leaving Charlie and Alec at Edgemoor. On her return she noted that Tonnachy was gone and, alone 'Charlie swam in the Mouse [a freezing hill loch] which seemed risky.'[4]

In Charles's book of poems is a sonnet entitled 'My Mistake' dated April 1909:

> Thinking Love's Empire lay along that way
> Where the new-duggen grave of friendship gaped,
> We fell therein, and, weary, slept till day.
> But with the sun you rose, and clean escaped,
> Strode honourably homewards. Slowly I
> Crept out upon the crumbling other side.
> And thither held my way where love should lie
> But scorn set hedges rent my cloke of Pride
> And stones my feet – that yet no nearer came.
> I looked to you – but you were gone from sight
> To honour in an honest house of shame:–
> Should I press on, hills hide the road, and night.
> And should I turn the bitter pathway lies
> Across that grave; where, smothered, friendship dies.[5]

It was St Augustine who wrote that his own homosexuality was primarily a sin against friendship. Charles's 'new-duggen grave' suggests that he had pushed friendship too far. It did not bother him for long; a month later he was in love once more, writing to a friend in the south;

> Dear man!
> Those birds remembered first to sing
> That saw together you and me and Spring;
> And I <u>was</u> happiest.[6]

That May he went to Winchester for the Eton match, visited old schoolfriends in Cambridge and then dropped in on Robert Ross in London. Later that summer his experiences moved from happy to bitter. On his visit to Oxford in August to resit entrance exams, he thought he would take up an invitation from Frank Benson, an actor he had shown round Winchester in his last year there. Inserted into his poetry book at this date is a letter from Benson of 15 July 1908

– the year before – thanking him for his kind hospitality to his wife and himself on Pageant Sunday at Winchester and inviting him to visit him when next in Oxford. Charles's poem 'To a Public Man' was probably the result of his meeting with Benson:

> I have admired so your life,
> So watcht you on your curious way!
> I am too male to be your wife
> And most I look towards the day
> When, slightly leaner in the loin,
> Strippt of your pretty pants and paints,
> Death shall dispatch you, dear, to join
> A cunning company of saints.
> Then will my prayers like smoke descend
> And melt like well-developed dew.
> Ask Satan, please, to be my friend: –
> He would do anything for you.[7]

Benson was famous: later, in 1916, his performance in *Julius Caesar* pleased King George V so much that the monarch summoned him after he came off stage at Drury Lane and promptly knighted him. (At that time very few actors were knighted, the first being Henry Irving in 1895.) 'Strippt of your pretty pants and paints' – who wears paints but an actor? The final damning lines of the poem invoking Satan with a Faustian invitation imply that this encounter with Benson was one where Charles felt exploited and begs the question of his actual sexual experience to date. Perhaps it was not the romantic Millard who took his virginity, but the hurried, and married, Benson. This is the only really angry poem he wrote until after the war.

When Charles sat the Oxford entrance exam again, of the five subjects, he received high marks only in Latin, passes in English and French and low marks in Greek and Mathematics. With such results he gave up all hope of Oxford and began in 1909, as had his father, grandfather and great-grandfather before him, to read for a Law degree at Edinburgh. In his first academic year he attended the lectures of Professor Hardie in Latin and of Professor Millar on Constitutional Law; the following year, he studied logic and metaphysics under Professor Andrew Seth Pringle Pattison and took Honours in the class of Public Law. This blast of rigour and rote learning in a cold climate was refreshing but he missed his schoolfriends and the exotic company of Ross, Millard and the Wilde group with whom he kept in contact: Ross wrote to Millard in January 1909 asking, 'I wish you would tell me what has happened to Moncrieff. Is he reformed?'[8] 'Reform' was always an option for any attractive but serious young man who had finished with homosexual experimenting, and was constantly offered to Charles in the form of introductions to young women.

His travelling from Edinburgh to the south in search of congenial company and old friends continued throughout his time at university. But he did make one great friend at Edinburgh. His name was Richard Reynolds Ball – referred to as Ball by Meg in her diaries where she described him as a designer of metal and glass who shared an interest in her carving, painting and design. Ten years older than Charles, Richard was the only son of a clergyman, an old Wykehamist, and a graduate of Trinity College, Cambridge. He became almost a fixture at Edgemoor, and Meg sometimes visited his Edinburgh workshop to see his designs. By 1910 he was sharing rooms with Charles at Lister House. A family story told how Charles and Ball found a crate of rotten oranges; the two students took them to their rooms, set up a catapult with pieces of rubber and fired the oranges out over the Mound across to Princes Street below. We do not know if in the dark, they hit anyone, but citizens were amazed next day to see oranges lying beneath the trees in Princes Street Gardens.

During this friendship with Richard, Charles wrote his best and most carefree love sonnet:

The Beechwood, 5th Feb 1910

Tired we are of people and the waving town –
While on every beech bough hot buds burst and grow
To a radiant wonder of greenness: we will go
Now into the green woods and lie lightly down,
Lie down and watch the sun fluttering through green leaves;
I will lie still and just gaze on you where you lie,
And you will smile to see the delicate new sky
Pierce those silken curtains that the green beech weaves.
Happy, happy dreamers! But before evening:–

While gentle, like the spirit of some slain young thing
A white moon creeps up where little clouds go racing;–
We will rise and shake off last year's brown leaves that cling,
And cross the valley slowly, slowly climb the hill
Then laugh to hear our respectable streets so still.[9]

Richard was a gentle soul who understood him. There is a diffuse eroticism in the hot buds bursting, the delicate new sky piercing the silken curtains, and the slain young thing. But the gap between wishful poetic imagery and actual physical love is unclear and we will never know the full nature of their relationship. However, the lovers in the poem do laugh at respectability – the avoidance of which seemed easier on visits to the more populous south where he could be anonymous. Here he was to meet Philip Bainbrigge, a man who did become his lover.

Charles did not discuss politics in his letters, but 1910 was an unusual year. In July Charles went to Cambridge 'with Bainbrigge and a man Spring Rice who is a Nationalist from Kerry. We had tea with Francis Birrell, the son of the man who runs Ireland.'[10] The first general election that year brought in a Liberal Government with the Irish nationalists holding the balance of power. In return for their support the liberals promised to bring in a Home Rule Bill. It seemed to many that Home Rule for Ireland was inevitable. Charles was merely a ringside spectator, 'When we got back I routed out Bewley . . . from the Euston Hotel, and we set the two Nationalists to converse one with the other. Bainbrigge and I sat awestruck watching them, and supped.'[11]

Philip Bainbrigge was at Trinity College with Charles's old schoolfriend Ralph Wright. He was the elder son of a London clergyman, had been a King's scholar at Eton, before going up to Cambridge as a classical scholar. Philip later came to Edgemoor for visits and fitted in well with the family as his mother had come from Lanark herself. He gave Charles an edition of *The Oxford Book of English Verse* and a manuscript copy of his explicit version of Plato's *Symposium*, both of which Charles treasured. Philip was an exceptional Classicist, but despite his 'incalculable breadth and depth of classical and modern reading', as Charles wrote years later, he was 'creative only in correspondence, in light verse, parodies and ballads of a topical and private kind'. Being too racy for publication, not many have survived. However, one of his clerihews was judged by the inventor of the form, E. C. Bentley, to be a perfect example,

> The Emperor Pertinax
> Kept a certain axe
> With which he used to strike
> Men whom he did not like.[12]

Striking men with axes was far from Philip's own nature. He was described as 'a tall, delicate weedy man with very thick glasses in his spectacles without which he was as blind as a bat'.[13] His forehead was large, with a thin receding hairline; a Greek nose in profile, delicate straight lips, ears that stuck out noticeably from his rounded head, steady brown eyes and a clear complexion. He later taught at Shrewsbury and was remembered as a brilliant young sixth-form schoolmaster, though a natural reserve and diffidence caused him to hide his erudition. Philip became more than a friend, as Charles wrote in a poem much later,

> . . . Friend – nay, friend were a name too common, rather
> Mind of my intimate mind, I claim thee lover . . .[14]

When he was in London, Charles continued to visit the Ross stronghold at 40 Half Moon Street, with its central table littered with the latest books signed by their authors. Here he met a young man who was to become a lifelong, intimate friend. Vyvyan Holland was the son of Oscar Wilde and had been eight at the time of his father's trial. He had been sent by his relatives to school in Germany and Monaco, where he had become a Catholic, and then to the Jesuit school at Stoneyhurst in England. His brother Cyril, a year older, went to Radley. Vyvyan was advised not to go to Oxford because of the association with his father, so went to Cambridge to study Law. Vyvyan always remembered his father as 'the kindest and gentlest of men, a smiling giant, who crawled about the nursery floor with us and lived in an aura of cigarette smoke and eau de cologne'.[15] Ross had only met Vyvyan in 1908 and from then had become his and Cyril's protector and provider – tracking down royalties from Wilde's plays abroad. Charles and Vyvyan started a correspondence that was to last Charles's lifetime. It was based on witty sexual badinage, gossip about mutual friends, criticism of Vyvyan's poetry, and in-depth description of their private lives. Vyvyan was always in need of money; Charles bought his law books from him and lent him both his own and Ball's money. Charles flirted and longed for Vyvyan to visit: during 1910 he signed off one letter 'your friend and (olim) bedfellow (at 44 Bramerton Street, Kings Rd, Chelsea)'[16], and another 'you are seldolm absent sacramentally from the bosom of . . .'[17], and 'this ought to convey the impression that I am really – and unaccountably fond of you: not from sodomistic snobbery . . .' meaning that many of Wilde's followers fell in love with Vyvyan simply because he was Wilde's son. Knowing this and in order to counteract it, Vyvyan and Cyril both became promiscuously heterosexual and Vyvyan accrued a number of female conquests. Although Charles was three years younger and had no experience to speak of he found himself giving advice to Vyvyan on how to deal with his mistresses: 'you will be bankrupt before you are thirty . . . I am afraid you are only detentor not possessor of your mistresses.'[18] Then he would tease him: 'Papa's nurse died and left me £20 . . . would you like some of it to buy some horse-hair night robes wherewithal to frissonise your new mistress?'[19] Vyvyan knew Millard and Charles discussed him in their letters, saying that Christopher, or 'Xptofer' as he referred to him in his half-Greek cipher, would write every month. Charles also sent Vyvyan a critical set of verses on Millard including,

A man lover, madman, and Millard,
A spoiler of youth and the young
A most fatuous fellow and furious
Unacquainted with girls and with gods
He is heated, his household is whoreous
A flatful of sods.[20]

Charles would beg Vyvyan to visit, and on holiday that summer in Argyll wrote, 'I shall have to wait until there is a mistress strike before visiting you (and not even then as a substitute).'[21] They exchanged photographs and Vyvyan chided Charles for having photographs of other young men, which Charles denied, but insinuated that Vyvyan had been visiting a clergyman recently who was known for misbehaving with young boys. About this seemingly perennial problem, Charles wrote a piece of dirty doggerel.

> The Dean of St Pauls talks absolute balls,
> The Dean of Westminster showed his to a spinster
> The Dean of Oswestry frisks girls in the vestry
> The Bishop of Birmingham buggers boys while confirming 'em,
> The Bishop of Norwich makes them come in his porridge,
> The Dean of West Ham smears their bottoms with jam.

With Vyvyan, Charles's adolescent schoolboy humour never changed. Their correspondence kept alive the witty, clever talk of the Ross set, with in-house criticisms and in-house jokes: it was a far cry from his next experience.

In December Charles motored through a blinding snowstorm to serve as a presiding officer at a polling booth set up in Biggar High School, near Lanark, for the second general election of 1910. The presiding officer was charged with checking that no one had cheated or voted twice; and also with the counting of votes; it was a duty for which his father put him forward, hoping to stimulate an interest in politics. After nine hours he had polled 346 people and claimed to have made 'very few mistakes' in a letter to his parents. Charles revealed little interest in politics but a great deal in people, describing how the Tories were proud to reveal their votes, while the Radicals hid theirs. One man explained, 'I cudna vera well vote against my own laird, cud I?'

> . . . We had a horrible old man from Symington with a bright blue face, like a distempered wall, and a fishbasket-bearing man who said, like a miracle play: 'This old man is John Ritchie of Whitecastle.' I suppose he was. Anyhow we gave him a vote and he went quavering away, roaring and beating his stick on the ground.[22]

In May 1911 Charles went to Ireland as best man to Theodore Dalyell, his schoolfriend from Midlothian who was marrying an Irish girl. Again he made no comment on Irish politics in his letters but he enjoyed the wedding and journey and said that he would go over again in the summer as it was nearer to Edinburgh and cheaper than London. 'Also it was a very good opportunity of obliging the girls,' he wrote to Meg. 'They all looked delightfully pretty: Amy in diaphanous bright blue, very young and sweet: Gladys was a bridesmaid in silver net, and Lily was dashing in a grey frock, enormous black hat and eyes, and fluffy feathers.'[23]

Two incidents during his student days reminded Charles that his youth and beauty were not eternal. Having discovered that he had an astigmatism, he got his first spectacles although he often preferred not to wear them. Also in early 1909 he was at home at Lanark with a large, painful abscess on his jaw. A doctor was called, extracted three molars without painkillers and promptly sent Charles back to study in Edinburgh the following day. He was fitted with a plate. He now had glasses and false teeth before the age of twenty. Musing on his own mortality, he visited a dissecting room in Edinburgh with a medical student and wrote some verse to the bodies on the slab, which he suggested would go well to the hymn tune of 'Jerusalem the Golden':

. . .
If I can't earn my living
Gloved hands will lay me low
And hew me small for giving
To boys I'll never know
Who'll find me firm and yellow
And pare me with a knife
As I this quaint dead fellow
That may have led my life.[24]

The idea of not being able to earn his living was a real spectre to Charles. He was not going to inherit anything. Not only was he the youngest son, but his mother loved spending his father's ample though hard-earned income on clothes, house decorating and travel. He had earned no scholarship for university as Colin had, and this shamed him, although his other brother, John, had always been dependent on his parents.

Now, though, there was a crisis involving Colin. Colin wrote from New Zealand about his interest in theosophy; meaning literally, 'god-wisdom', theosophy had interested Meg since the 1880s, when she had read Madame Blavatsky's inscrutable books, *Isis Unveiled* and *The Secret Doctrine*. Theosophy was a relatively new attempt at an amalgamation of all world religions into one. By 1910 the movement was led by the charismatic Annie Besant who had been a successful writer and trade unionist in London. Now as President of the Theosophical Society she had moved to India, thinking Hinduism was closer to the spirit of Theosophy. A year before, Besant's mystical colleague, Charles Leadbeater, had met the adolescent Krishnamurti on the beach and had declared him to be the vessel for the new Enlightened Being – a Christ or Buddha figure. Besant became his legal guardian and surrogate mother, replacing his own parents. Gandhi and Nehru were both closely associated with theosophy, though neither formally accepted Krishnamurti's status. Colin Scott Moncrieff, however, did.

With the zeal of youth, Colin became interested in the mystical aspects of theosophy including clairvoyance and communicating with the dead. His involvement had started when the brothers' grandfather, Robert Scott Moncrieff, the merchant of Calcutta, died in Edinburgh at the age of eighty on 25 May 1908. Missing his family, and unable to share in their grief directly, Colin employed the services of a clairvoyant who wrote what Colin considered to be the most astonishingly accurate future for himself and Connie: births, deaths and how his boss at the Theological College would object to his theosophical investigations. That final forecast would have taken no clairvoyant skill – the Rector of St John's College was outraged at Colin suddenly teaching Theosophy instead of Theology, calling it 'Anti-Christian'. Yet the more Colin was criticised, the more entrenched his beliefs became. On 14 September 1909 he resigned the wardenship of the College and sent Connie home ahead of him, heavily pregnant with twins. With her sailed their nanny and the two-year-old Colin. His father decided to take a detour to India to meet Annie Besant. He had the charisma, intellect and social skills to rise to the higher ranks of the English clergy, but he would never compromise his beliefs for advancement. Devoted Connie went home to her own mother at Merchiston Crescent in Edinburgh, and on 9 April 1910 she gave birth to twins. The second twin came half an hour after the first and 'breathed and died'.[25] The surviving baby, a boy named George, born with a cleft palate, grew up to become the writer of the next generation of Scott Moncrieffs.

Colin arrived in Edinburgh more than a month later having met the teenage Krishnamurti and been convinced that he was indeed the incarnation of a new enlightened being. He met Canon Erskine Hill of Glasgow who was prepared to find him a job, although he had to accept that he could not preach theosophy from the pulpit of an established church. At this stage, a compromise had to be made bearing in mind a living was required for a wife and two small children, the young Colin and newborn George. By October 1911 he was accepted as curate at Gatehouse of Fleet, Dumfriesshire, a poor living in an Episcopalian Church granted by a private patron Lady Maxwell, who was charmed by Colin and his passionate beliefs. He began to set up his own version of Christianity, an experiment that lasted for a number of years, although it didn't succeed due to a lack of followers.

In the following year Charles spent a lot of time with his mother, Connie, Colin and their children. In February his mother started painting a portrait of him from behind, seeing only a quarter-profile with long, dark eyelashes and a strong upper lip – a strange angle to paint, but oddly fitting for a man used to keeping secrets to be only partially visible. Sitting for it gave him time to think. Charles was aware of Colin's dilemmas; personal freedom versus the need to earn a living – and he himself had tried hard to like the law. He passed Honours in Public Law in 1912 and then begged to be able to study for a degree in English Language and Literature. He could not see himself as a lawyer and the only activity that he was consistently pursuing, almost as naturally as breathing itself, was writing. His parents, liberal and indulgent to all three boys, agreed to support Charles for his further degree at Edinburgh.

His new director of studies was George Saintsbury, Regius Professor of Rhetoric and English Literature, a department established in 1762 – the first such department in Britain. Saintsbury, a stooped, white-haired man in his sixties, wrote copious books of literary criticism, always wore a skull cap and it was said that he had read everything ever written in almost every language. He had begun as a critic of French literature; his first essay, on Baudelaire, was published in 1875 in the *Fortnightly Review* and he went on to contribute thirty articles on French Literature to the *Encycopaedia Britannica*. Moving on to English Literature he wrote on Dryden, Scott and then a *History of Elizabethan Literature* followed while also overseeing a forty-volume translation of Balzac and writing the introductions. He admitted that in his career he must have written the equivalent of a hundred volumes of criticism. Charles was impressed and inspired by him and had already started attending his lectures informally while he was finishing his Law degree. As a critic, Charles was later clearly influenced by Saintsbury's view that, 'Criticism is the endeavour to find, to know, to love, to recommend, not only the best, but all the good, that has been known and thought and written in the world.'[26] Saintsbury believed that the true and only test of literary greatness was the 'transport', the absorption, of the reader. He was more a man of letters than an academic and clearly inspired in Charles a love of French literature.

Since his last years at school, Charles had kept up his interest in the army cadet force and spent three weeks every summer on Lanark Moor in cadet training. In October 1912, before he started his literature degree, he was chosen to escort a dozen cadets from his summer battalion of the Royal Scots to the National Exhibition in Canada. Eight months after the sinking of the *Titanic* this was seen as a risky trip; it was a real adventure and exercise in responsibility, representing Britain in the New World. It would be the only time Charles ventured beyond Europe. 'Under Captain and Adjutant W. B. J. Reid, comes Second Lieutenant C. Scott Moncrieff' ran the *Scotsman* article, with a photograph. The boys attracted crowds as they marched down Princes Street to Waverley Station in their Highland uniforms: scarlet doublets, black ostrich feather bonnets, red and white hackle plumes, kilts, full horsehair sporrans, swords, shouldered rifles, and led by their own piper. They sailed from Liverpool on the RMS *Virginian*. Introduced into the first-class smoking room, he met the Canadian Minister of Justice, who had been in Britain visiting Lloyd George and been very impressed by him. Charles was not cowed by rank or authority and had recently become more interested in politics. They had a lengthy discussion and Charles lent him his copy of the political and literary periodical, *The Eye Witness*.

The journey to Montreal took six days and Charles and Reid exercised their cadets regularly on deck by getting them to dance eightsome and foursome reels to the piper in full regalia. However they soon had to give up as the other passengers crowded round and giggled so much. The spectacle of kilts swinging high was distracting for passengers at close quarters. For the Royal Scots there was nothing unusual in the wearing of the kilt in the traditional manner, without underwear, but they soon realised that it made the other passengers uncomfortable.

The heat of the late August weather made the ship's dining room odorous and there was no escape from crowded decks with only two places onboard to spend money and while away leisure time – the barber's shop and the smoking room. After a trip up the St Lawrence River they arrived in Montreal on 24 August 1912. 'Everything', Charles wrote, was bigger and brighter than Scotland: the grass 'a more sage green than ours', the vast Quebec railway hotel, 'The biggest in the world, I think'. 'It seems a splendid country,' he declared. From Quebec the cadets travelled overnight on an uncomfortable train, Charles precariously gripping an upper berth, with his great coat for a pillow, scared of falling off in his sleep, to arrive in Toronto, hot and dirty, on a bright Sunday morning. At the hastily constructed exhibition grounds, subject to heavy rains that turned the walks into mud paths, the camp was prettily perched above the lake. He and the Scottish cadets began to make friends among the two Canadian Battalions representing Western and Eastern Canada.

'We march in to the arena and get on to the stage at 9, where we form a big semi-circle facing some twenty thousand people nightly,' Charles wrote home. 'Twenty-four rather seedy actor fellows walk in from behind and form a living flag by opening their robes and spreading themselves on an espalier. Then we sing (twice) the chorus of Rule Britannia. Reid has been put on the staff, so I have to do everything.' This went on for eight days with heavy rain and careless visitors making the grounds increasingly muddy. 'There is nothing lacking except tidiness. Things are left about here in the most appalling way. An army of men goes about sweeping up paper and candy boxes in the grounds.'[27]

After a sightseeing trip across Canada, the cadets returned to Montreal and embarked on the voyage back home. Wiser through experience, Charles and his fellow officers insisted on taking the return trip comfortably in first class – and they avoided any form of dancing exercise.

* * *

Family life, his degree and the army were absorbing enough, but Charles also continued trying to publish his poetry. He managed it sporadically in the *Wykehamist* and the *Academy*, and sent poems to competitions run in the *Westminster Gazette* and the *Saturday Westminster*. Two years older than Charles, Rupert Brooke entered his first poems in these competitions and won twice in 1908 for poems under the name of Mnemon. Charles won once that year for a sonnet called 'The Grammairian's Wedding'[28] and twice got a commended. Famed both for his looks and his talent, Brooke published his first collection of poems in 1911. Charles was well aware of new poetry through his visits to and continuing friendship with Robert Ross. London was the hub of the serious poets and in January 1913, the poet Harold Monro opened the Poetry Bookshop in a narrow slum street near the British Museum. The tiny room was crowded with poets for the first reading. Monro published anthologies, often at his own expense, with the assistance of the civil servant and patron of the arts, Edward Marsh, and was responsible for the first anthology of *Georgian Poetry*. These poets saw themselves as modern, moving beyond Victorian poetry and its accepted form. The 'Georgians' included Robert Graves, Walter De la Mare, D. H. Lawrence, James E. Flecker, Walter Turner, J. C. Squire, Siegfried Sassoon, Wilfrid Gibson, Robert Nichols and Rupert Brooke. Five volumes of *Georgian Poetry* appeared between 1911 and 1922. Had Charles lived in London, or had more confidence in his own poetry, he would certainly have been involved.

In Edinburgh, he decided to compile an edition of poetry by the sixteenth-century Scots poet Gavin Douglas, with the hope of finding a publisher. Douglas, who was also a bishop and a translator, had written his dream allegory *The Palice of Honour* in 1501. There were no surviving manuscript copies. It had been published twice, once in London in 1553 and once in Edinburgh in 1579: concessions had obviously been made for anglicisation in the London edition and it palpably lost some of its humour. Charles typed out both versions and put them in parallel text, with a view to proving that the later text, with more Scots, was probably nearer to the original.[29]

Not finding a publisher, Charles was prompted by the experience to apply for the Patterson Bursary in Anglo-Saxon from Edinburgh University. He sat an exam on the grammar and literary history of Anglo Saxon and translated both verse and prose.

That evening he travelled overnight to London where his old friend Richard Ball, now living near King's Cross, gave him breakfast in his rooms and then accompanied him to Winchester for a few days with friends. They had dinner with Rendall, now headmaster, and were entertained afterwards by singing from a former schoolfriend, the choirboy James Steuart Wilson, with whom Charles had once been in love. He wrote restrainedly to his mother, 'His voice is very much improved in quality, while it has lost none of its character.'[30] Wilson went on to a successful music-hall career. A few days after his visit an article in *The Wykehamist* explained the difficulty of the Patterson Bursary examination and its distinction, and announced Charles as recipient. Suddenly the Dons at Winchester looked on him with more respect – as no longer an undistinguished scholar.

Back in Edinburgh, meanwhile, he was also seen as a useful family member. Aunt Kate, Meg's youngest sister, whom she had funded through university, was very engaged in the burgeoning women's suffrage movement. She invited her sisters and nephews and nieces in Edinburgh to suffragette meetings to hear speakers from London and Glasgow – as well as to hear Kate herself. (Meg noted proudly that Kate spoke effectively to well-attended meetings.) At the seaside at Elie in 1912, they had held a family debate proposing the motion 'Do women need further liberation?'[31] which concluded that the Scott Moncrieff family was overwhelmingly run by its women; they took all the major decisions, and the men were only necessary to provide the money. From his personal experience, women were quite powerful enough. In 1913, Kate, delighted that Charles was living nearby, enlisted her nephew's help with her fundraising. He wrote home, 'I helped at the Suffragette Jumble Sale in Nicolson Street – it was horrible.'[32]

If politics were a chore, there was one activity at university that he enjoyed enormously: acting. He took part in a production of *The Merchant of Venice* and here met Henry R. Pyatt and his wife Fanny who became lifelong friends. Pyatt was a master at Fettes School; he was an amiable optimist who played the cello, wrote light verse and was a genial host. Fanny, the only daughter of the bishop of Edinburgh, was a woman of exquisite taste in clothes, furniture and friendship. Charles spent many evenings with them and they corresponded thoughout his life. Pyatt later wrote of Charles during this period, 'He gave me the impression of being aristocratic by nature in the sense of loving and doing and emulating the best things.' At this point in his life Charles was at his most handsome: heads would turn as he entered a room. He was manly, strong and physically active, with a distinction about his bearing; dark blue eyes, pale skin and a serious expression. His voice was also arresting – soft, clear and deep and he delivered his own witty epigrams using excited, eccentric gestures. There was something tantalisingly elusive about him, remembered Henry Pyatt.

> Impishness is not the word, for that suggests a want of dignity which was never observable in him. I saw him once in his student days at a fancy dress ball attired as a faun, with a leopard skin flapping round bronzed limbs and vine leaves in his hair and said to myself, 'Faun-like, that is it.' . . . Scott Moncrieff was undoubtedly satirical. This attitude was due in fact to his extreme sensitiveness, which tempted him instinctively to whirl a rapier of glittering wit around him to prevent others from getting under his guard, and penetrating to his secret, a thing that few succeeded in doing.[33]

If Pyatt meant by Charles's 'secret', his homosexuality, then it was safe; few save his closest friends discovered it, though others may have suspected. University had been a mixed time, very different from the continuation of school that Oxford would have provided. He came away with two degrees, one in law and one with distinction and a prize in English literature, as well as the experience of having excelled at his cadet training and been chosen to help to lead the group in Canada. The law degree would set him up as an army officer, while the First Class Honours in English would foster his future career in literature. He was aware that he was at his zenith and had a photograph of his profile taken, keeping copies that he gave to friends later in life. All this lent him a certain amount of self-assurance, which could be mistaken for arrogance by some but perhaps was rather an instinct that his life and looks would never be better.

CHAPTER 6

Lightness in War

There is something rather stimulating in being under fire.

CKSM to his mother, 27 October 1914

The urge to glory was too simple a sentiment to describe the impulse that thrust Charles to war, but it was certainly part. The public school ethos glamorised warfare: studying the classics meant engaging in poetry and prose about Greek and Roman warriors, and the team spirit nurtured by sport on the playing fields enhanced partisan feeling. War was the ultimate team game, with the highest stakes. Charles had also been a cadet since leaving school and had spent some of his summer holidays for the last four years training as a lieutenant in the 1st (Highland) Cadet Battalion of the Royal Scots Regiment, under Colonel Holden Mackenzie. In March 1913 he was appointed 2nd Lieutenant in the General Reserve of officers.

The industry for creating soldiers was flourishing all over Europe. With a population of forty million, France had decided in 1913 to match Germany's number of soldiers, though the Germans had a population of sixty million to choose from. All of Europe was well aware of the jostling for military power. The Germans were competing with the size of Britain's navy, egged on by their jealousy of Britain's rule of the waves and the vast British Empire, and Britain, concerned, chose to outbuild their rival in modern battleships. Germany had plans for war and General Schlieffen had begun working on them as far back as 1905. However it was a less organised country that provided the prompt. Not all Serbs lived in Serbia, some boiled resentfully under Habsburg rule in Bosnia, part of the Austro-Hungarian Empire. Franz Ferdinand, nephew to Emperor Franz Josef, was inspecting the

Habsburg army's summer manoeuvres and drove into Sarajevo with his wife Sophie on 28 June 1914. A Bosnian Serb assassination team was planned and in place. They first threw a bomb which killed an officer in the car behind the Archduke who, undeterred, asked to be driven to visit the casualty in hospital. His car took a wrong turning, and out of the crowd stepped Gavrilo Princip who shot both the Archduke and his wife. Then followed a month's silence.

That summer Charles went on the annual camp with his company of Royal Scots cadets, training on Lanark Moor. On 24 July he decided to keep a diary as 'relief from the monotony of half remembered things'.[1] It was a personal record, rather than a run-down of political events in Europe. At camp Douglas Christie was his adjutant, the eldest of the four Christie brothers from the Fife estate of Durie, second cousins with whom Charles had spent many holidays. The Christie boys were unusual characters and regaled Charles with stories of their prep school where they called their lugubrious headmaster 'The Shadow of Death', and his equally sinister manservant, 'The Valet of the Shadow of Death'. Once, as schoolboys at Fettes, they were told they would be beaten by the head boy for a misdemeanour. Their liberal mother, however, who held the advanced view that physical beatings were not the best punishments for small boys at boarding schools, wrote saying that if they were beaten she would remove them. They were beaten and she removed them, taking them with her to Monte Carlo where they lived in a rambling mansion by the coast and were taught, mornings-only, by a personal tutor, while Mrs Christie enjoyed a stylish bohemian life and gambled in the casinos.

On Lanark Moor Douglas and Charles pitched camp in the wind and rain behind the Scottish Rifles mess huts, as there were other regiments there too, and the huts provided some shelter. Charles had brought his typewriter and he and Douglas rigged up rotas on it before walking into Lanark to visit the picturehouse that his father had opened a year before. Then the fledgling officers sat round a fire and drank halfpenny mugs of cocoa out of a Dixie can in the chill evening on the damp moor. Next morning all seventy of the company paraded to Lanark Station to meet the Officer in Command. They had four 'admirable' sergeants. Of one of them Charles wrote: 'The renowned J. M. Davie, such a man as Philip Bainbrigge would say – and such a modest and quiet boy too, for all his authocracy, that one can hardly talk to him.'[2] 'Authocracy' was a rare quality which both he and his friend Bainbrigge found very attractive; a mixture of authority and aristocracy that marked a man as a natural leader.

In the evening the Commanding Officer gave a lecture 'about buttons and duty and the bravery of boys'[3] and asked Charles to organise the drum service for Sunday. Charles stopped the local Minister, whom he knew well, in Lanark High Street and borrowed thirty hymn books, then collected some more from his mother plus a chess board for cousin Douglas and a tin bath for himself, 'in which I bathe every morning at 6.30 outside my tent, as an example to the others'.[4] On the way back to camp he met the CO's adjutant, McHardy, and they passed two nuns from a local convent: 'McHardy and I met two sisters from Smythum and worked up a religious argument. His views are 1843 – mine are 1348, so we don't exactly see eye to eye about it.'[5] McHardy was of the strictly evangelical Free Church which had seceded from the Church of Scotland. Charles had by now a reaction to Protestantism which he saw as unforgiving and puritanical as exemplified by the church he attended with his father and the attitude of some of his masters at Winchester. He was searching for a warmer, less condemnatory approach to faith and in his poetry he harked back idealistically to pre-Reformation times. Perhaps sensing this, one of the nuns from the Smythum Convent kept in contact with him throughout the war.

On Sunday 26 July, inspired by his reaction to McHardy, Charles organised the entire service around his own attitudes to his faith. They had Anglican prayers, including, noted Charles in his diary with an exclamation mark, the absolution – High Anglican prayers, verging on the Catholic. The two lessons were chosen and read by himself. The first was the last two chapters of the Ecclesiastes, which included, 'Rejoice, O young man, in your youth, and let your heart cheer you in the days of your youth; walk in the ways of your heart, and the sight of your eyes.' The second reading was 1 Corinthians 13, the reading about love, concluding, 'So faith, hope and love abide, these three, but the most important of these is love.' They were inspiring texts for any romantically inclined young man. McHardy did not approve of the service nor the hymns, calling it 'Sabbath day entertaining'[6], and he organised a counter service of Psalm singing in the evening without music, beating time with his tobacco pipe on the table. Yet to McHardy's great dismay and Charles's secret triumph, the choir revolted and opted for hymns.

The following day Charles caught the express train to Edinburgh for a break, bought the newspapers and read of a disturbing incident in Dublin where his local regiment, the King's Own Scottish Borderers, (KOSB), was stationed keeping an eye on the ferment for Home Rule. A shipment of arms, including 900 German guns, had arrived at Howth for the Irish Volunteers and the KOSB were ordered to seize the weapons. They were met by an angry crowd throwing stones, and spat on and jeered by the Irish crowd. The KOSB were ordered to fire on the crowd and killed three civilians without managing to capture the arms.

Charles also read with feelings of 'awe and foreboding'[7] of the Austrian Ultimatum to Serbia, Austria's reaction to the Sarajevo shooting. The demands were extreme and even threatened Serbia's existence as a separate nation; the Serbians were given only forty-eight hours to comply. Whilst Great Britain and Russia sympathised with many of the demands, both agreed the timescale was impossibly short. Diplomatic attempts at peace, all too frantic and last-minute, could not stop the mobilisation of troops all over Europe; by now Serbia, Austria, Russia, Germany and France had armies ready to fight.

Charles wrote to the War Office, informing them of a change of address from Lanark to Edinburgh and expressing a hope that he might serve with the 3rd Royal Scots (based at Glencorse in Edinburgh), because he had been to Canada with them. However the regimental system, based on locality, was entrenched, using local officers to command the men. In 1914 a Scottish Border accent would be incomprehensible to someone unused to hearing it. Charles had absorbed Scots; he understood and could also speak it fluently. It was likely he would be called into the King's Own Scottish Borderers – which, as a Lowland Regiment, did not wear the kilt. Charles would have preferred a kilted regiment, like the 3rd Royal Scots – he thought men looked their best in kilts and enjoyed wearing one himself.

When camp was ended on 31 July, Charles and his cousin Douglas returned to Edinburgh. By chance, Philip Bainbrigge reached Edinburgh late that night from Shrewsbury School, amazed to see Charles arriving at the station at the same time. The following day they all went to bathe at the Drumsheugh bath club and then Douglas returned to Durie, his large family home in Fife. Charles, having an obligation to his guest, wrote, 'I stayed and played with Philip.' The friendship was at that point ambivalent as the entry is immediately followed the next day by 'Sat 2nd August – I fled over to Durie also, and spent a very pleasant and quiet weekend, tinged with the excitement of war.'[8] Charles and his cousins awaited their orders. On Monday, Charles travelled to Elie, not far from Durie, where his mother and the extended Scott Moncrieff family were all staying. He posed with them in a photograph in the back garden of Elie Castle, looking handsome, mercurial and mischievous. He was nearly twenty-six and physically and mentally in very good shape. His brothers are both in the picture, John, and Colin with Connie and three children, with numerous cousins, aunts and uncles, while in the centre sit the greying Meg and George Scott Moncrieff, matriarch and patriarch, organisers of the yearly family gathering.

The older faces look more sombre and worried than those of the younger members. Germany had declared war on Russia and France and had announced they would march through Belgium, breaching the Treaty of London of 1839. Britain, expecting invasion from the north French coast and hearing on 4 August that the treaty ensuring Belgian neutrality had been breached, now declared war on Germany.

Cut off in the tiny seaside town of Elie there was nothing to do but wait and discuss and look at the awe and foreboding on the older family members' faces. The banks were shut for three days and the stock exchange closed too. Charles received a friendly letter from one of the cadets' fathers thanking him for allowing his son to fall ill and rest during the training on the moor – but no orders. Charles walked around Elie all day, waiting in frustrated excitement. The orders arrived at his address in Edinburgh where Philip Bainbrigge was staying, and were forwarded to Elie, arriving on Thursday morning in the form of a telegram requesting him to join the King's Own Scottish Borderers at Dumfries.

Charles caught the next train to Edinburgh and rushed about getting his uniform; officers were responsible for buying their own. Andersons, the outfitters, was in a state of siege, but he managed to get a fitting and, best of all, a good second-hand khaki tunic and breeches, which were delivered about 5.30 p.m. to his Edinburgh rooms. Sending Philip over to Elie to stay with his parents for the weekend in his absence, Charles changed and packed in record time and caught the last train to Dumfries at 6 p.m. He fell in with the KOSB on their way from Moffat and had two excited officers in his compartment for the rest of the journey.

Friday was spent meeting other officers, and, after spending that night at the Station Hotel listening to the shunting of endless trains, Charles woke at 6.30 a.m. to start soldiering on the very wet Saturday 8 August – organising the medical inspection for his militia who arrived in twos and threes, then tracking down a Jewish tailor who agreed to buy their cast-off civilian clothing. By 1 a.m. they were ready. They paraded down the muddy and stony streets of Dumfries, lined with 'dimly seen' faces.

> The people turned out marvellously, bless them, to see us off – babies held up to the windows – and crowds all along the way – and then a great overpowering cheer from the bridge over the station as we passed out underneath it. Colonel Dudgeon, Lord Lieutenant of the Stewartry, turned out in cocked hat and feathers to see us off.[9]

The party of King's Own Scottish Borderers left Scotland in the small hours of the following morning, to join the 3rd (Reserve) Battalion at Portland, near Weymouth on the south coast of England, where men were trained up in readiness to be sent to join the 2nd KOSB Battalion in France. They were also positioned for defence against invasion from the sea if necessary. Charles was given command of a battery of 9.2-inch guns perched on the cliff overlooking the west battery and 305 feet above it. He had ninety men: 65 gunners and 25 Borderers. The gunners lived in shelters and the infantry in tents outside. For the first night he slept in the store, on crates of biscuit boxes, in his coat, shirt, breeches and puttees. At 4 a.m. the gunners did their daily parade to uncork and prepare the guns, so he got up and was able to borrow someone else's rug and a coat to sleep under.

Eventually Charles's full kit arrived: his Glengarry bonnet in dark blue wool, with black tails and a band of red, white and dark green dicing, with a red toorie on top. The silver cap badge, set on a black rosette, identified the regiment. The badge bore the Cross of St

Andrew, inscribed 'King's Own Scottish Borderers', and an image of Edinburgh Castle with three turrets, each with flag flying. Above and below, were the mottoes *In Veritate Religionis Confido* ('I put my trust in the truth of religion') and *Nisi Dominus Frustra* ('Without the Lord, everything is in vain') – the motto of the City of Edinburgh. Surrounding the picture was a wreath of thistles. The Regiment was authorised to wear trews of Leslie tartan, the family tartan of the Earl of Leven. Only the pipers wore kilts, of Royal Stewart tartan.

Officers were expected to be gentlemen – aristocrats or men of the upper middle classes, educated at the great public schools, and to be in possession of a private income, buying their own uniform and paying their own meal bills. The pay was nominal – about £250 a year for an officer in the KOSB, which was not considered a smart regiment. Charles never had a private income and lived frugally; he worked out to his relief that he could live off his pay, including mess bills. His diary carries a note for Thursday 20 August, 'My mess bill for these 11 days is only 27/6 for food and 7/6 for a great amount of drink – which is modest and encouraging. At this rate I can live on my pay – as I wear no mufti and have very few outside expenses.'[10]

On realising this he promptly bought some luxury items: a basin and a plate, chocolate and matches. Now that the store where he had slept was closed he rigged himself a tent in a space between a house and the wireless station, and went to bed thinking over the news that the Pope had died, and that the Kaiser would probably have a finger in the conclave and try to set the Italian cardinals in revolt against the Anglophile Italian government. 'May all his schemes perish with him,' he wrote. After going peacefully to bed in his tent he was then hauled up by a telephone message from the colonel telling him to explore the coast and spot any possible landing places. 'I walk up and down the cliffs murmuring to myself "men who march away ere the barncocks say, night is growing grey",' He was annoyed that Thomas Hardy, author of these lines, was so near him, yet he would probably never see him, 'the only living man who has worked out a war almost of these dimensions in *The Dynasts*, to see it all being staged in Europe now'.[11] The next morning he was instructed to attend a court martial to learn how to run one himself. Also attending, to his joy, was Tom Gillespie from school, who was in the 2nd KOSB and had been in Dublin until recently. He sat next to him at lunch and heard that James

Stueart Wilson, the choir boy to whom he had once composed plaintive love poems, was enlisting in the Guards. He also learned that 'Rupert Brooke, the poet, has enlisted in the Artists' Corp.'[12]

On Saturday, a hot, still morning, he got his men to start digging a trench down the side of the enclosure, both for practice and as part of the anti-invasion preparations, and then sat down and wrote to the officer in command recommending a coast patrol and the occupation of an empty lighthouse. He had found this lighthouse with his sergeant and seen several excellent rooms for billeting troops in. He heard that nine years before, when the new lighthouse was finished, it had been rented by a civilian who renovated it, adding rooms, and then shot himself. The stairs were littered with empty champagne bottles, but these were soon cleared up and the place made into comfortable quarters. He could leave the old biscuit box and his rickety tent now that he had a bedroom of his own in the lighthouse; he sent a postcard of it with his room marked to his family.

He also recommended daily bathing parades in the sea. Having spent his life swimming in cold seas all summer long, he was convinced of the benefits, and besides, there were no baths for the men and the officers had only a tin bath to share.

Aware that he had not been to church since his Drum Service on Lanark Moor, he visited one called the Avalanche Church; it was built by Bishop Moberly of Winchester to commemorate a wreck nearby in 1877 when all the crew, the captain and many passengers were lost. Charles thought nothing special of it architecturally, but said it had an arresting quality, as if the souls of the drowned visited it constantly. Sister Benignus of Lanark wrote to say she was praying for him daily and sent thirty medals with Our Lady's image on them to give to Catholics in the Battalion. He took one himself, in gratitude, he said, to the good sister who had thought so well of him.

At the outbreak of war the KOSB had two Regular Battalions (1st and 2nd) and two Territorial (4th and 5th). Later on the 'New Army' Battalions (6th, 7th and 8th) were raised, together with a 9th Battalion, which provided reinforcements for the others. Charles moved from the 3rd to the 2nd to the 7th over the course of the war. The 3rd was the Reserve Battalion and stayed at Portland Bill throughout, providing reinforcements, training and positioning for defence. There were a thousand soldiers in each Infantry battalion, all under the command of a lieutenant-colonel, usually an experienced officer in his forties. His adjutant was his right-hand man, usually a senior captain, though occasionally a major (in time of war, it could be a lieutenant); he was responsible for the administration, organisation and discipline of the battalion; while a quartermaster dealt with stores and supplies. Also part of the team was the regimental sergeant-major, the battalion's senior warrant officer, who ran the battalion headquarters and the orderly room. The fighting strength of the battalion lay in its four rifle companies, each with six officers and 221 infantry men, under the command of a major or a senior captain; each company had four platoons and each platoon had four sections. On his first day of war duty, Charles was a 2nd Lieutenant in charge of a platoon of 22 men. For many officers it was a shock to be confronted for the first time with the men, many of whom came from the lowest social rank and had known extreme poverty. There were men who drank too much and those who gambled, as well as teetotallers and some who used their spare time to improve their education.[13] It was the officer's job to make sure they were bound in the common cause: to serve the regiment which would become their physical and spiritual home.

The regiment was like a family; a tough, fighting unit characterised by loyalty. Each member knew the history of his regiment and fought alongside men from his home area with whom he had grown up and whom he understood. The tribal nature of much of Scottish society, along with the tartans of the uniforms and the bright, feathered bonnets gave the ordinary Scottish soldier more than average pride in his position. No doubt the Highland regiments had the greatest impact: Charles, who had been part of one for his training and had asked to join one when called up, felt nostalgia for the drama, well described by one observer:

> One thing I will never forget is the sight of thousands of rhythmically swinging kilts as a Division of Highlanders swept towards us. Skirling at the head of the column strode the pipers, filling the air with their wild martial music. Beyond glinted a forest of rifle barrels and the flash of brawny knees rising and straightening in rhythm.[14]

At Portland the men were given the new short-magazine Lee-Enfield rifle and an 18-inch bayonet, and spent time every day in what was still called 'Musketry' training, by the end of which they were expected to be capable of firing fifteen bullets a minute, including the loading of new bullets and unloading of spent ones.

After five weeks Charles noted in frustration that there was still no sign of him going off to France. He watched others, including two of his servants, go to war and by 16 September he noticed that he was the senior out of twenty-two 2nd lieutenants and was now put in charge of F company with another 2nd lieutenant under him. By the end of September he was made a 1st lieutenant, in charge of pay and watching the cliffs for invasion, and the court martialling of suspected German spies. But in spite of the speedy promotion and added responsibility, he felt very left behind. After the strained preparation and training of Portland Bill, he was eager to start fighting. Ominously on 25 August he wrote, 'I heard and heard again on reaching here a telephone rumour of 1500 British casualties: why all this cursed secrecy about things of the first importance?'[15]

As autumn approached there was a sudden and desperate need for reinforcements in France. The German invasion of Belgium had doubled the French frontier with the enemy and made it 320 miles instead of 160. The immediate British effort was to stop the enemy from reaching the Channel ports of Zeebrugge, Ostend, Calais, Boulogne, and St Nazaire, which offered the shortest sea routes and the most obvious points for an invasion. Unprecedented numbers of men were being thrown into battle to stop the powerful German army from reaching the coast. They had walked over 'neutral' Belgium without a qualm, so why should they respect Britain? Every soldier could see a reason to fight.

At last Charles was sent to France. He reached St Nazaire on 9 October and joined a detachment of 2 KOSB under Lieutenant Robert Gibson, a Scotsman who had been a don at Oxford for four years. As was customary at school and at war, Charles referred to all his friends by their surnames. They became friends, sharing a tent in dusty old potato fields which Gibson called 'No. 1 Sea View', and taking it in turns to visit the local hotel for a decent meal. One night the waiter asked, *'Est-ce que Monsieur reste dans l'hôtel?' 'Non, je reste dans la poussière, moi.'*[16] They bathed in the sea to wash off the dirt and Charles gashed himself on the rocks, 'to the effusion of much blood which I naturally want to keep for field operations . . .'[17]

All notions of chivalry and honour, deeply embedded in his idealistic spirit, were at last to be tested. On 23 October at 4 a.m. two older captains took over Charles's command and his detatchment arrived at the front by train that evening. Here he was told that Tom Gillespie, fellow Winchester scholar, whom he was looking forward to seeing, had been killed. That was a shock, but there was no time for mourning or reflection. No one had eaten all day and the three officers were glad of a tin of Maconachie for supper, a sort of tinned stew with meat and vegetables which formed a staple at the front. They also got tea and rum, a welcome part of rations in the firing line, and they were under fire as they ate. That night Charles had the luxury of a mattress, though caked in hard mud, and he found a potato sack to put his feet in to keep them warm, but he stayed awake writing home to his mother about Tom Gillespie, for she had once met Tom's mother.

The men were told that they would do forty-eight hours in the front trenches then forty-eight hours behind in support trenches alternately. Trenches at this stage in the war were shallow and rudimentary as they were thought to be temporary, often made under fire with a limited number of tools. The German trenches were far superior: deeper, more fortified with long underground dugouts, electricity and curtained recesses for the officers – it was a great boost to take over a German trench and inhabit it. The Unit Diary kept by the officer in charge of the depleted KOSB ranks recorded on the 24th October that Lieutenant C. Scott Moncrieff of the 3rd KOSB and a draft of 83 men joined them making their 'Strength in trenches A 14+10, B 133+10, C 170, D170'.[18] Still a lot less than a thousand men.

Two days later Charles was heading his letters 'in the Field, France', and getting his first taste of trench warfare. As he wrote and told his family of three friends who had died already, bullets sang overhead and a man was lying at his feet unconscious with a temple wound, breathing heavily. A doctor arrived to say the man would die, but 'the rest of us are cheery in spite of the rain last night,'[19] which filled the trench with slippery mud. That night they were on the move again and Belgian soldiers on the railway told him of the utter ruin and desolation of the towns along the line. Next night at midnight, he got a turn in the front line,

> We shot pretty hard for half an hour or so. Everyone had been very sleepy, but there is something rather stimulating in being

> under fire. I sat up on an ammunition box in one of the traverses of this trench, so that I could overlook my men on both sides and shout orders to them, and cheer them up if they got hit. With wonderful luck none of us did get hit . . .[20]

Two days later, they were marching three miles under shellfire to billets, then on into Belgium. He described the German artillery:

> the big ones which we call Black Marias come along with a crooning whistle like pigeons and then you see a great outburst of black smoke and in due time hear the crash. But it is well to keep your head in cover in the hollowed out front of the trench, as splinters go a very long way and splinters have a song of their own like wasps. We got a good many bullets past us from the left and right, flying about round my head and shoulders and sometimes two seeming to meet with a smack in the air.[21]

There had been fierce fighting over the Messines Ridge for the past ten days since 21 October. Losses were heavy and the Germans outnumbered the British.[22] There were 48000 Germans and two British divisions of between 10000 and 15000. Charles arrived at Halloween, with plans to organise apple ducking with his friends, only to be met with a night of real horror and defeat. The little town of Messines had been a place of pilgrimage to the Virgin Mary since 933, and a century later Adèle, Countess of Flanders had founded a Benedictine Abbey for Noble Ladies. Hungry and tired, Charles and his men reached the village at 4 a.m. and found it in a ghastly state. Every house had been shelled, goats and pigs were wandering the streets. The medieval school had been occupied by the Germans five days before and it was Charles's company's job to clear any remaining Germans out of the convent with their bayonets.[23] The church had been burned, and was dead and empty with little shards of glass tinkling eerily as they fell against the bars on the windows. The eleventh-century abbey had been built with courtyards, stables, piggeries, and a moat, but now it was a ghostly scene:

> In one corner a subaltern of the 21st Lancers had been looking out over the wall with one of his men, when a shell caught the wall below them. I found them lying very waxen and stiff, in the

> moonlight (for the moon is full just now), the officer clasping the cord of his revolver in his hand . . . I walked round in the moonlight to look for a wounded trooper in the 5th Dragoon Guards, whom I had promised to shelter. The ground was dotted with dead Germans, young boys mostly. The living ones we took in, some wounded, others active prisoners. Part of the town was still held by Germans who sniped at us from windows. They killed one of our subalterns and four or five men who went up a wrong street by mistake.[24]

The regimental historian, Captain Stair Gillon, who was able to put the action into the perspective of the whole battle, fourteen years later described the same night in more heroic terms. The KOSB had joined the final phase of a three-week battle on the critical day when the Allies were close to losing their grip and letting the Germans pour through the gap.

> A detachment of cavalry, the 5th Dragoon Guards were hanging on also by a hair, to the village of Messines. They were on one side of the main street and the Germans on the other. It was the task of the KOSB to pass through the cavalry, clear half the village and push on into open country to the south. An advance of 800 men began at 1 p.m. It was desperate close fighting, sometimes only 50 yards or less separated the foes. House to house fighting is as difficult to describe as it is to conduct. It is the most nerve-stretching, surprising type of warfare, when death may threaten from above, below, at the side and behind. The KOSB took the convent and cleared out the houses near the church.[25]

Charles saw it from the ground and it appeared more like a defeat:

> On Sunday morning, we got very sudden orders to clear out and fight a rearguard action while the cavalry retired, which we did. I had my first wound. Part of a shell hit me on the thickest part of my large skull, just on the front point of my battered old Glengarry. It was not punctured, though absurdly enough, I was, and got the credit of being wounded as the blood ran down over my right eyebrow . . . I was only held up for 15 seconds or so

> and retired as vigorously as any of them . . . We must have lost about 100 from our already reduced numbers . . . and we gained nothing, as they (the Germans) were further forward when we left than when we entered it. We three slept under some straw on the pavement opposite the gate of the school. It was a very cold autumn night, and we awoke stiff and tired to stand to which we do from 5 to 6.30 morning and evening.[26]

There was one ironic aspect to that Halloween night. The German regiment, fighting hand-to-hand through the Messines church, sniping and generally overlapping British positions, was the 16th Bavarian Reserve Infantry Regiment. A private in this regiment named Adolf Hitler distinguished himself for a whole month at Messines and was given an Iron Cross and later promoted to corporal. During his time off from fighting he made several paintings of the ruined Messines church. It was noted by fellow soldiers that Private Hitler had strong views and ranted at his colleagues who seldom listened and kept their distance, whereupon he made clay models of soldiers, lined them up on the top of the trench and delivered his speeches to them.[27]

Charles thought this battle spelled the end of the 2nd KOSB. To cap it all, on the morning of 1 November, when the British had an advantage, they were ordered to retreat far behind the lines, as they were needed as reinforcements to a battalion several miles away at Hooge. They finally left the Bavarians, including their trench runner, Adolf Hitler, in possession of what was left of Messines.

The retreat was nonetheless picturesque. There were still some trees left and the ground was covered in damp leaves like golden pennies fallen through the late autumn air. It was unusually warm and to add to the colour, the French Army still wore cornflower-blue and red uniforms, and their chevaliers had shining breastplates. Charles felt the surge of hope after success, thrill and praise, writing four days after the retreat:

> I have a strong presentiment that I am going to come out of this war alright. We had a very high compliment paid to us and three other Battalions this week by a cavalry General Allenby for saving the situation here last Saturday. My regiment has been ordered off as a reserve several times, but always found itself in the firing

> line once again. I feel rather a beast to be so utterly happy and free from care, when everyone else at home is slaving away.[28]

That day the regiment received orders to join the 9th Infantry Brigade at Ypres. The blanket name later given to all battles in the area at the time was the First Battle of Ypres, which dates from 20 October to 22 November. The British success was due to their superior rapid rifle fire. In artillery they were outgunned two to one, in heavy artillery ten to one, but in musketry they prevailed – trained as they were to fire fifteen aimed rounds a minute. The attacking Germans, coming forward in closely ranked masses presented unmissable targets. The casualties were terrible on both sides: 24,000 British dead to 50,000 German.

The First Battle of Ypres stopped the Germans from moving up to the Channel ports. It consolidated the earlier Belgian action of opening the sluices that held out the sea and flooding their own country: 22 miles were flooded between Dixmude and Niewport, stopping the enemy in their tracks. But the Germans did not give up; they decided to come through Ypres from the Menin road and were met less than a mile outside the town at a tiny village called Hooge. The Prussian Guards broke through at first but were eventually held off by the 9th Infantry Brigade.

This was 17 November and the KOSB threw themselves into the intense fighting. C company took a heavy toll of the enemy, especially 'a group of five or six men who remained for the whole 13 days in a very wet part of the trench and declined relief in view of it being an exciting position. One of these men shot six Germans in rapid succession who had got into his trench.'[29] Adrenaline was running high for some of Charles's company, but, as their commanding officer, he could see the real toll, recording the numbers lost daily in the Unit Diary, and describing his first experience of a trench mortar – 'a large shell of high explosive comes over like a football. It has a demoralising effect because of its slow flight and terrible violence. Men are blown into several pieces.'[30]

The personal commentary in his letters was always less brutal, '*Quant à la guerre, rien à signaller,* except that this wood has an evil smell, and that shells hit the pine trees and bring them down on us. I cut off the tops and fill my dugout with them to counteract the pervading smell.'[31] The smell was made up of ammonium chloride, dirty bodies and reeking trench foot. They spent two weeks in trenches unwashed and unshaven, then there was the release of billets again, with food parcels and letters from home. Charles wrote 'Billeted' verses which vividly reflect his gaiety of spirit in the face of death with a sort of boy scout camaraderie, in rhymes intended to entertain.

> . . .
> We're feasting on chocolate, game pie, currant bun,
> To a faint German-band obligato of gun,
> For I've noticed, wherever the regiment go,
> That we always end up pretty close to the foe . . .
>
> Mustn't think we don't mind when a chap gets laid out,
> They've taken the best of us, never a doubt;
> But with life pretty busy, and death rather near
> We've no time for regret any more than for fear . . .
>
> You may go to the Ritz or the Curzon (Mayfair)
> And think they do things pretty well for you there;
> When you've lain for six weeks on a water-logged plain
> Here's the acme of luxury – billets again.

'Billeted' was published in full later in 1917, with another three of Charles's poems, in E. B. Osborn's *The Muse in Arms*, an anthology of over a hundred poems by men serving in all three forces during the war. Charles was not the only soldier expressing himself in verse; there were fifty-two contributors to this volume, all men, including the poets Robert Nichols, Osbert Sitwell, Siegfried Sassoon and Robert Graves, all of whom would come into Charles's life later on.

Billets meant the sudden luxury of warm water to wash in and Charles was relieved to shave off his beard; it had been a surprise to grow a black beard beneath an orange moustache, and the colours, he felt, did not mix well. He and five other officers lunched in a Flemish restaurant where he noticed the décor had the mark of good craftsmanship: mantelpieces, panelling, china, everything down to the cutlery was beautifully made:

> Belgium was and still is a delightful country. Like Gabriel Nash, I like to go about looking at things and there are such millions of

> little details here that one might easily overlook, but that one does, at some time or other, notice with delight. In Belgium the aristocracy has always been an aristocracy of craftsmen. The commonest tin spoons are perfectly proportioned, nothing to worry or offend one except dirt, but we are pretty dirty ourselves . . .[32]

As he was writing, the room was suddenly invaded by weeping women, 'which seemed to hint at a German advance', and signalled the end of the only holiday the regiment had had since landing. The break did mean he received piles of post. One family friend wrote Charles a letter addressed 'Charles Scott Moncrieff, the K.O.S.Borderers, Somewhere', and miraculously the letter got to him as fast as any other. Meg sent him a second air cushion which was useful when a Gordon Highlander was brought in badly wounded, and Charles was able to give him that and his waterproof because they could get no stretcher till sunset. 'The Belgians are far better than the French,' he wrote. 'The Flemish really are like us. I don't know what it is, but the Flemish women at every house door are like the unmarried daughters one expects to find when one pays calls in the country in Scotland, and they are simple, capable, friendly folk. I love them.'[33] Having read of the city of Ypres, which epitomised the Flemish craftsmanship, he was longing to see it. When he finally got the opportunity he was not allowed to enter but still felt that:

> the effect of the town, with its convents indented here and there by a heavy shell, and its broad moat with slabs of ice and its torpid swans, and all the spires and gables showing beyond, against a blue sky, with shells bursting high up, like a medieval Jerusalem, was very haunting. The Halles must be a wonderful building, and the mere fact that it is unsafe to approach by daylight adds to the glamour. I thought of the line in . . . 'Golden Wings' . . .
>
> The draggled swans do greedily eat the weeds that in the water float;
> Within the rotten leaky boat you see a slain man's stiffened feet.

> I took no books into our pinewood except the *Oxford Book of English Verse* . . . I used to spend the dark hours trying to piece together Keats' 'Nightingale', there are some lines in the middle that I can never remember, and I get the epithets all mixed, it is a drowsy pursuit. I have two colloquial novels from St Nazaire . . . but . . . one does not want to read much . . .[34]

Marching away from Ypres, they came to what he called 'an unpleasant little manufacturing town' near the frontier. Here his company occupied an old tile factory while Charles and six other officers were sent to '*le chateau du patron*, a curiously pretentious and humble villa opposite'. They had a confrontation with an old woman (who, he wrote, resembled Mrs Besant) who would give them a room as they had a billeting order but not let them use the kitchen. So they went to a grubby estaminet full of flies and private soldiers but no food, finally finding a café on the main square where they got steak and chips and watery beer made of straw and coffee.

Charles, however, was unwell. He was invalided out at the beginning of December with trench foot, which came from standing too long in high mud and never getting the feet dry. Numb feet turned blue or red as a result of poor circulation and had a decaying odour in the early stages of necrosis: if left untreated it led to gangrene and amputation. He had written home in late October asking for: 'Boot insoles, size 11, cork or loofah – two or three pairs – some small tins of Vaseline for the feet'.[35] But the parcel had gone astray.

He was sent first to the officers' convalescent hospital at Osborne on the Isle of Wight, a beautiful old house. Then, miraculously, he thought, he found himself at home at Edgemoor for Christmas. Three of the grandchildren were staying: Colin and Connie's children – Colin, George and Dorothy aged six, four and two. Instead of mud, bombs and decaying bodies, he was surrounded by firelight, a decorated tree and children with Christmas stockings. Young Colin solemnly asked his uncle Charles if, when soldiers were given swords to fight a battle, they were allowed to keep them afterwards.

CHAPTER 7
God in the Trenches

Christianity is a characteristic of our armies far more nearly universal than courage or cowardice, or drunkenness or sobriety or chastity or the love of plunder.

CKSM, *The New Witness*, 29 November 1917

By 6 January 1915 Charles was well again, stationed at Red Barracks, Weymouth with a written instruction to rejoin his regiment and very happy about it. However, his hopes of returning to France were dashed when he developed a bad fever. He was put in the Weymouth convalescent home, writing to his mother that he had influenza. He had not heard of trench fever, caused by body lice, which plagued the trenches. 'I probably shan't have my clothes off before Christmas,' he had written in a letter in late October. Trench fever took two weeks to incubate, starting with a sudden high fever, severe headache, pain on moving the eyeballs and pain in the legs. Charles suffered from bouts of trench fever for the rest of his life, and often complained to his correspondents that he had a bad flu.

He was made a captain on 2 February. Promotion among officers was fast, particularly at the beginning of the war, partly because professional competence increased quickly in such extreme conditions, also because replacements were urgently needed. One odd reason for such high casualties among officers was the fact that they were encouraged to grow moustaches to distinguish them from the men, but with enemy trenches at such short distance, the moustache also distinguished them for the Germans who were encouraged to aim for the men in jodhpurs with moustaches. Uniform changed slowly and so did the moustache ruling.

By 18 February, he was ordered back to his old stamping ground, stamping also with frustration – the Wireless Station at Portland Bill on the south coast of England. He was put in the old lighthouse again, furnished as summer quarters by an absent landlady called Mrs Melladew, with a good lamp at night and 'everything snug'. A letter had arrived from his mother with a quotation from *The Times* which detailed an inscription on the Berlin Town Hall ('inscription' was the Edwardian term for graffiti): *Peace brings Wealth. Wealth brings Pride. Pride brings War. War brings Poverty. Poverty brings Humility. Humility brings Peace*, the endless circle. He remarked later in a letter, 'There is an illogical idea that the Germans are especially wicked because they used gas before we did . . . and because their airmen drop bombs upon the just and the unjust.'[1] In spite of this fair view of war and lack of any hatred for Germans, he realised that what meant most to him was to be with his men in France at the front line – but he had to stay at Portland, training troops, until May.

He spent his Easter leave in Winchester, describing it as looking incredibly beautiful – but feeling that it would fade away as quickly as a dream. He got the key to Gunners Hole and bathed in the chill spring water all alone, as he had done with friends as a schoolboy. He saw all the school staff, dined with the chaplain, Trant Bramston, and walked up hills with Rendall, his former housemaster and now headmaster, in Rendall's inimitable style: very fast and loaded with a revolver and kit.

Finally on 22 May he arrived, with six brother officers, at Le Havre, excited by the prospect of real and what he called 'honourable' work at the front. Next day was spent at Rouen where he visited the cathedral and admired the rose window over the organ, which he compared to a Turkish carpet. He and ten colleagues camped outdoors in the heat and he set out with a few of them to find the river, needing to bathe. On the way they were confronted with a long and high asylum wall – 'Asyle des Aliénées' it was called on the map – where Charles got talking to an old and toothless inmate, explaining to her that the Scotch army had been with Jeanne d'Arc rather than against her. However she kept on hissing at him, 'Vi – i – i' like a goose, and finally told her fellow inmate that Charles had been a friend of Jeanne d'Arc – a thought he fully appreciated.

The May weather made life in the trenches a more summery, flowery experience than his last visit. Firstly the trenches themselves were superior to those from the winter before, the ground quite firm with more sandbags and planks, and dugouts in the trench wall large enough to crawl into. The time was also quieter; with four days fighting in 'fire' trenches, two in 'support' and two days in reserve in dugouts hollowed out of the canal embankment. 'Support' was a long street of huts, adorned with armchairs and marble consoles taken from the châteaux, of which there were six within easy distance. Seated in a gilt, upholstered chair, battered by many sitters moving it about, in the glow of the yellow dust Charles could see the towers of Ypres Cathedral and the Cloth Hall with smoke rising, and a great pink glare then a flame rolling over wafted by a slight breeze. He tried to smoke a pipe but found it hard to get going and instead set to writing a poem which encapsulated all his feelings of sadness at the desecration of such beauty, the desire to protect the buildings he loved in his own land and the call to arms that seemed to come from former Wykehamists long dead. He called it 'Domum'.

> . . .
> Who will fight for Flanders, who will set them free,
> The war-worn lowlands by the English sea?
> Who my young companions, will choose the way to war
> That Marlborough, Wellington, have trodden out before?
>
> Are those mere names? Then hear a solemn sound,
> The blood of our brothers is crying from the ground . . .

The poem continued to value the men he knew, recently killed,

> . . .
> And all the gold their futures hold in youth's abundant store
> They'd freely give to have you live in their midst once more.
>
> What was it that you fought for; Why was it that you died?
> Here is Ypres burning, and twenty towns beside.
> Where is the gain in all our pain when we have loved but now
> Is lying still on Sixty Hill, a bullet in his brow?[2]

The man 'lying still on Sixty Hill [with] a bullet in his brow' was Robert Gibson, who had shared his tent at St Nazaire less than a year before. On 5 May the Germans had retaken Hill 60 after a massive bombardment and gas attack. Two thousand British lay dead in an area the size of a large back garden. One of them was Gibson, the don from Oxford, loved by all his colleagues. 'And all the gold their futures hold in youth's abundant store/ They'd freely give to have you live in their midst once more.' There had to be some reason behind his sacrifice: that Gibson knew he was defending his country – preventing Oxford's dreaming spires becoming like the ruin of Ypres before him. The poem was printed in *The Wykehamist*. 'Domum', home, the title of the Winchester School anthem – was school and all it stood for. The core of the public-school ethos was self-denial (even self-effacement), duty to House, to School and by extension to country, fortitude or endurance, and physical courage. Pupils were being taught or trained as leaders: anyone making the ultimate sacrifice, therefore, would be honoured. So clearly did Rupert Brooke's famous poem embody all that was felt in 1915, that it was read out in St Paul's cathedral on his death:

> If I should die think only this of me,
> That there's some corner of a foreign field,
> That is for ever England . . .

Charles would have read Brooke's poem earlier that March when it was published in the *Times Literary Supplement*. It was a 'curious thing', Charles mused in a letter home, that all the people that he had lived with in camp for a long time past seemed to have been killed, naming ten. He seemed muffled from the real pain, almost anaesthetised by shock: 'How gentle a thing war is, that can let me stay out in front of the German army from 8.30 till 2 carrying white sandbags about, with rockets streaming overhead like Crystal Palace, and come to no harm beyond treading on my spectacles, and that only because I had taken them off.' He went into a frenzy of work, seeming oblivious to the carnage around him: in his descriptions he never dwelt on the horror, perhaps because he was in a curious way protected from it. 'I am very pleased to-night at having done more work than Anderson. My way lies through an ex-French trench, with ex-Frenchmen lurking in it, which are not wholly pleasant. But one gets quickly used to a lot.'[3]

Charles's chief protection from the horror of the trenches was reading books and writing poetry. He read *Sense and Sensibility* to himself and the *Oxford Book of English Verse* to his friend and lieutenant, Machin. 'We had a great excitement this afternoon. I was sitting writing verses for the Wykehamist, when I heard a loud whizzing, and found several large rockets of a civilian kind going off amid flame and smoke on the little wood on my left.'[4] His poetry was of supreme importance and, at this point, the war was secondary. He used poetry as an aid to endurance and encouraged others to do the same. He gave *A Shropshire Lad* by A. E. Housman, with its lyrical lines evoking the beauty of the English countryside and the growing-up of a young man, to an officer from New Zealand. Neil Macleod had come to study at Oxford at the outbreak of war and stayed. His widow wrote to Charles's nephew, years after his death, saying, 'Neil treasured the book all his days,' and that the book had been with him in Germany as a prisoner, later in the Sudan and India, even at Dunkirk.[5]

When his battalion came out of trenches on 6 June, Charles was billeted in the Château Rosendael. In its small park an Anglican service was held overlooking views of the surrounding countryside, green and full of flowers. He could still see the towers of Ypres, the cathedral spire fallen on the horizon. He sat to write under trees at the company mess table on which one soldier had placed a shrapnel case as a vase and filled it with columbine and mock-orange blossom. The château garden was in full bloom: roses, pansies, budding pinks and a great clump of rhododendrons. He declared that he would like to buy the plot, build a new villa on it and grow old there, taking people for thankfully boring Sunday walks to Hill 60, and other battlefields. (All the British battlefields fought on since Christmas were within a good walk of the château.) Several of the officers thought it a great idea and he proposed they club together to buy the wrecked land, likely cheap in Belgium after the war. These were optimistic plans for the future during a war when many had no future and large numbers were dying all around.

At Rosendael, the men had a pet parrot which 'imitated the whine of a spent bullet to the life'. Charles remarked that it was the only animal he had seen to take an interest in the war. He perceived that the little frogs were worried when they fell into a long, dry trench, so if they were dry and clean, he would pick them up and throw them over his shoulder like golf balls. The big frogs, he said, in the water, made a sound like a cable-car passing, while the songbirds were puzzled by the bullets. There was a nightingale that he passed going to and from the trenches, 'that sings all night to the bullets, wondering why they don't stop and join it on its bough. This spot is infested before sunset with midges, and after with bullets, which come down very gently at intervals till bedtime. They smack into the trees but none of us has yet been hit.'[6]

Again he was protected from real horror by his own poetic bubble, his ability to see the beauty around him and focus on that, excluding the ghastly aspects no matter what. At Rosendael, he read that Rupert Brooke's younger brother, Alfred, had been killed, Rupert himself had died in April. When, two weeks later, at the same place, Charles's friend Lieutenant Gordon Swinley was shot, he spent most of the day writing to the dead man's mother and as the sun went down he transplanted a clump of Madonna lilies to his grave, where he hoped they would flourish. Briefly, on the death of Swinley, the protective bubble burst. Full of unexpressed grief and anger, Charles put his name forward along with the coal miners in his company to form part of a Brigade tunnelling company, a deliberately dangerous choice.

A routine strategy in trench warfare was to undermine the enemy's trenches by digging a tunnel at considerable depth, ending directly below the enemy trench; then explosives would be set off at the end. Both sides dug such tunnels but neither side was able to counteract the other; the challenge was to locate the enemy's tunnel and dig one even deeper, or, dig your own trenches so deep that undermining them was impossible. His old commanding officer from Lanark days, Holden Mackenzie, brought up a megaphone to be used by listening posts to identify the whereabouts of German tunnelling. Charles reported that this was excessive as all you could hear, very loudly, were the rats scratching their whiskers from several yards distance, which drowned and confused any sound the enemy might make.

When torrential summer rains halted any more digging work, Charles and his company were ordered to leave. On 6 July, he finally made the long awaited trip to the falling spires of Ypres, and picked up a piece of stained glass and a scrap of bell metal.[7] He wrote home, 'We are on tiptoe for a flight. This should be an interesting week of trekking away among the towered cities of France.'[8]

It was not a flash of light on the road to Damascus that turned Charles towards Catholicism but a steady tramp through France and the dramatic appearance of a devastated world. France had something to do with it; his aesthetic and historical interests were in art and buildings inspired by the Catholic spirit – pre-Reformation churches and cathedrals in Britain, the towered cities of France and the steady stream of chapels and wayside monuments to the Madonna in the Low Countries. However it was more by observing other people that Charles was inspired to conversion.

The writer and publisher Guy Chapman expressed the difference of attitude between the churches in his autobiography:

> . . . These bluff Anglicans had nothing to offer but the consolation the next man would give you, and a less fortifying one. The Church of Rome sent a man into action mentally and spiritually cleaned. The Church of England could only offer you a cigarette. The Church of Rome, experienced in propaganda, sent its priests into line. The Church of England forbade theirs forward of Brigade Headquarters, and though many, realising the fatal blunder of such an order, came just the same, the publication of that injunction had its effect.[9]

In recounting the progress of his own conversion to his parents, Charles was also impressed by the behaviour of individuals: he was careful to emphasise that the attraction lay not in ritual and the allure of beauty, but from sharing trenches with other Catholics and from small, everyday experiences, not even the heroic or exceptional examples. There were about two hundred Catholics in his battalion and company and in the trenches about forty. On Easter Sunday at Winchester he had been to the cathedral before breakfast and to Holy Trinity Church afterwards. Then he visited what he called a 'hideous, drab' little RC chapel in Portland, on a dull road flanking convict quarries, with an old priest recovering from a stroke, so that he could not speak the words he wanted to, but brought them out in a little rush, with omissions and repetitions. There was a large congregation in the chapel, made up of men from his previous 3rd Battalion including his old quartermaster, Major Parkinson, for whom he had a great regard, the Major's nephew, Sergeant Parker, who was with him at St Nazaire and a fine man, Dr Munro, a naval doctor and Highlander, whom Charles had got to know in September when he lived on Chesil Beach.

In Portland, he discovered that all these men were Catholics and one or two others who seemed to have been driven across his path about the same time, notably a young officer in the Wiltshire Regiment at Weymouth called Brooke – a friend of Neil Macleod's. 'I found sooner or later that I was a Roman Catholic,' Charles wrote,

> It wasn't anything to do with the sensuous appeal of music, flowers, lights, vestments, etc., as at Portland we had not a note of music, nor anything else except that ragged old man in his frayed chasuble. But finally at Rouen Cathedral at Pentecost (the last service I have attended in church) I felt quite sure that I was at home, while in Winchester Cathedral on Easter morning I realised – in spite of my love and knowledge of it – that my place was not there . . .[10]

Rouen Cathedral could certainly rival Winchester; it was just as old, its site dating back to the fourth century, with thirteenth-century stained glass including a piercing cobalt blue known as bleu de Chartres. Until the 1880s, its tower, at nearly five hundred feet, made it the tallest building in the world. Monet painted the magnificent front over thirty times in 1893 in different lights. Charles would already have known the history of the Cathedral from his reading of Ruskin who had used it as one of his examples in the *Seven Lamps of Architecture*, saying that as a building it embodied Sacrifice, Truth, Power, Beauty, Life, Memory and Obedience. The book was illustrated with some of the earliest of photographs of details, some from Rouen Cathedral. Charles would have been familiar with these thanks to his mother who had read and discussed Ruskin with him from an early age. Later Ruskin and Rouen would strike a familiar note when Charles started translating Proust; the boy in *Du Côté de chez Swann* has a transforming experience while reading Ruskin's *The Lamp of Memory* in the garden at Combray. Proust himself translated some of Ruskin's work and later said that he knew *The Seven Lamps of Architecture* by heart.[11] When criticised for his imperfect translation, Proust said, 'I don't claim to know English, I claim to know Ruskin.'[12]

What Charles did not tell his parents at the time of his conversion was that he had also met and corresponded with the Anglican priest Ronald Knox, who later wrote to Meg regretting that he could not find Charles's letters as 'he was, among other things, such a splendid letter-writer'.[13] Knox, who had been ordained in 1912 and was the Chaplain at Trinity College, Oxford, was the third of four brilliant sons of an Anglican bishop, a scholar at Eton and King's College Oxford, a prolific novelist and the shining star of the English clergy, later tagged by the *Daily Mail* as the 'wittiest young man in England'. He was very close to Guy Lawrence, a friend of Charles's from Winchester, which attachment was, 'the strongest human affection of Ronald's early manhood'.[14] The other attachment was to Harold Macmillan to whom Knox was a tutor until Macmillan's mother advised him that he was influencing Harold towards Catholicism and must stop. As a Catholic Macmillan would not have been made Prime Minister, but he remained close friends with Knox till the end of his life.

Many converts from Anglicanism to Catholicism during the first part of the twentieth century were influenced by Hugh Benson, one of the brilliant sons of the Archbishop of Canterbury, an Anglican convert in 1903 and ordained as a Catholic priest in 1904. A talented writer, he gave an inspired series of sermons, attracting crowds wherever he preached. Benson's influence could be traced to the mid-nineteenth century Oxford Movement. These were High Church Anglicans, often associated with the University of Oxford, who argued for the reinstatement of lost Christian traditions of faith and their inclusion into Anglican liturgy and theology. They saw the Anglican Church as one of three branches of the Catholic Church. John Henry Newman, the eloquent Anglican clergyman who converted and became a Catholic Cardinal, argued that the doctrines of the Roman Catholic Church as defined by the Council of Trent were compatible with the Thirty-Nine Articles of the sixteenth-century Church of England. Newman's conversion in 1845, and his writings, followed by that of Henry Manning who also became a cardinal, in 1851, had a profound effect on a largely anti-Catholic England.

Ronald Knox simply called conversion 'poping'. Knox met Father Martindale, another Anglican convert, who was writing the biography of Benson, for advice on his own conversion. Martindale advised caution, not to 'shut his eyes and take a plunge'[15] into the Catholic Church as Knox was inclined to do, but rather to go in with his eyes open. It was well known by his family and friends that Knox was flirting with Rome. His father, the Bishop of Manchester, thoroughly disapproved. Guy Lawrence converted first, longing for Knox to do so.

When Charles first met him, Ronald Knox was an Anglican priest with whom Charles felt he could discuss his love of men. In 1913, Knox wrote a prayer:

> O God, I submit my affection to thee, beseeching thee to take from me all particular objects of my desire, all friendships and acquaintance, however harmless in themselves, which thou seest to be a distraction to my soul . . .[16]

Knox corresponded with Charles during the war and in a short story Knox wrote at this time he showed he understood the feelings of one young man for another, and the struggle for celibacy:

> In an agony of loneliness, he stretched out his arms as if to fling them round some warm protective body and when they closed upon air, he shook with sobbing. His whole body shook with the unquenchable thirst for human contact. Yet when his brain cleared, it cleared completely.[17]

The self-disciplined Knox had taken a vow of celibacy as a schoolboy, and had reached a point where he could help someone like Charles. Knox himself was received into the Catholic church two years after Charles on 22 September 1917. An account of his conversion is given in the autobiographical *Spiritual Aeneid*. Charles kept his copy of this book all his life, and into the page that describes the day of conversion he stuck with glue a postcard from Knox, sent the year before publication on the actual eve of Knox's conversion, 21 September 1917. It says, 'Thank you awfully, yours affect. Ronnie.'[18] It seems likely that Charles had a hand in Knox's conversion and vice versa.

After his visit to Rouen Cathedral in May 1915 and his encounter with a priest in June, Charles moved towards formal conversion. In July he was officially received into the Catholic Church at Steenvoorde, a French town with a Flemish name on the Western Front, which had a medieval church with an astonishingly high bell tower, 92 metres, untouched by the war. At Mass, the priest named from the pulpit one of his parishioners who had been recently killed in action, and then called out, '*à genoux*', whereupon all the elderly people, those left behind not fighting in the war, got down from their chairs and knelt on the floor. 'The humility, piety and devotion here, as it was in Rouen, and I believe all over France, is very moving,'[19] wrote Charles.

> On Friday morning, I caught our Brigade Chaplain, Father Evans. I walked down the road with him and told him what I had in mind. We turned back and went to the parish church, where he received me, and gave me conditional baptism (in case my former baptism might be in any way invalid) and heard my confession. So now I am a proper Papist. As we left, the Sacristan, who had been tidying up things, said very kindly, '*C'est un nouveau frère en Jesus Christ.*'[20]

That summer Charles bought a leather-bound *Order of the Mass* in English and Latin. Mass was still said in Latin, and the beautiful language, both poetic and economical with words, appealed to the linguist and classical scholar. Three of the readings are bookmarked with stained army parcel string. One runs, 'O lord I have loved the beauty of thy house and the place where thy glory dwelleth. Take not away my soul with the wicked nor my life with men of blood . . . But I have walked in mine innocence; redeem me and have mercy on me.'[21] These three sentences could sum up his experience at Rouen Cathedral, the war and his homosexuality – in that order. The contradiction remained. Charles wholeheartedly joined a religion that expected either celibacy or marriage, but had the gift of absolution; repentance for sin in the confessional and a release from its burden. At the back of his book Charles noted each place he attended Mass from July 1915, and each place he received Holy Communion. Catholics in 1915 did not receive Holy Communion each time they went to Mass, since Communion had always to be preceded by Confession. However Charles recorded that he received Communion about once a month from then on. Another piece of army parcel string bookmarked the page with the text of the Mass, 'Grant, O lord, that what we have taken with our mouth, we may receive with a clean mind, and that from a temporal gift, it may become for us an everlasting memory.' Writing down each location where he took communion created a map of his movements throughout the war: 'Ribemont-sur-Ancre, Bray-sur-Somme, Cathédrale Rouen, Cathédrale St-Raphaël, Nice, St Mary's Lanark . . .'

During a war, when people are faced with death on a daily basis, there are more conversions than in peacetime. At the front conversion was common and the Catholics gained more than the Anglicans; nearly everyone was already registered as C of E on their official papers and a genuine conversion, turning towards God, often prompted a move.

Converts talk about 'coming alive' and God suddenly 'being real' – the experience is one of intense wonder and joy.[22] The normally conflicting demands of sexual and spiritual appetites, of family, duty, friends, society and ambition, no longer cause strife: after conversion unity reigns. When Pascal underwent a conversion he wrote down his *Mémoire* and had it sewn into his clothes; part of it ran: 'Certainty, certainty, heartfelt joy. Peace.' Converts speak of conversion as receipt and acceptance of God, they feel that they are chosen and acted upon rather than taking the initiative themselves. But instead of becoming floppy and passive, they undertake an amount of active work that exceeds expectations and has to be seen to be believed. Dante said, 'In His will is our Peace.' But the belief in the will of God lent an energy that surpassed normal human energy. Basking in the wonder, energy and peace of the act of conversion, Charles next took a trip away from the war to an almost celestial town.

While most of his colleagues waited exasperated for the field cashier to arrive with their pay, knowing the man could be several hours, Charles decided to ride to Cassel, five miles away, perched on a high hill, 'like Edinburgh set on the top of Arthur's Seat in the middle of Norfolk'. He rode slowly up a zigzag path with the town in front and thirty miles of fields and hedges over his shoulder at every turn of his head. In the little square at the top, he was greeted like a knight of old, he said, by a group of small boys who insisted he visit the Castle while they held his mare. Charles told them that he had only two sous, but they declared that they did it for patriotism and the love of animals, and not for the love of money. 'Their names were Jean Naels, Albert Vermoulin, and Emile Georges, who doesn't go to school, and so cannot write, but his father rings the bells in the Church.'[23] The boys trotted round with the horse and fed it with water out of a petrol tin, and after exploring the town they parted under a gateway, where Charles gave the eldest boy his sous to buy sweets. He was impressed by their ability to speak French to him and Flemish to passers-by almost in one breath. Just before leaving he met two little girls whose father was a prisoner in Germany. Then he rode back through peaceful side lanes and small sunny villages. It was typical of Charles to remember and write home about all the details of such a visit, even the names of the children, which to most would seem totally irrelevant.

So entranced was Charles with Cassel that he went there four days running, both alone and with fellow soldiers. He walked there cross-country with his friends, Captain Lionel Machin, Lieutenant A. Anderson and Captain Alexander Herries. Herries, who became a close friend, was an only son of the family of Spottes Hall in East Lothian; an Etonian who rowed for Cambridge, he already had an Arts Degree and was about to study Medicine when war broke out. He was responsible, talented, spirited and epitomised a certain quality of manhood and leadership nurtured by generations of the very best upbringing. Charles wrote that Anderson said, 'This is one of the three finest views in the world, and I haven't seen the other two.'[24] Herries made out Dunkirk quite clearly and Machin, on a bright day, remarked to Charles that he saw the sea glittering through hollows in the dunes. It was as if Cassel embodied Charles's conversion and he wished to share the epiphany with his most valued friends.

On leaving Steenvoorde on 30 July, Charles was asked to command the whole Battalion for a few hours while they marched four miles to a train. The train journey from Flanders to Picardy took twelve hours – only marginally faster than walking the distance of 111 km. The troops were hot, tired, hungry and thirsty, but on their arrival Charles was well pleased: 'We take over trenches from the French, beautiful ones, with good dugouts, cut in chalk.' Here at Bray-sur-

Somme, he went to Mass again: 'a rather pleasant custom here is that they bring round little pieces of bread in baskets for the congregation. I ate mine on leaving the church, as I was probably meant to do . . .'[25] He did not realise that the 'pleasant custom' was sometimes a way of sharing bread in a starving population.

Two days later when he saw some men of the King's Own Yorkshire Light Infantry decked in flowers, he remembered that the KOSB shared the same privilege as the Yorkshires on the anniversary of the Battle of Minden in 1759. He had forgotten about the tradition until he saw the men wearing roses. He went over to the stationmaster's wife, who was tending her garden, and explained that his regiment had defeated the Germans (and, he knew but omitted, the French) on 1 August and had worn roses on that day ever since, but here he was without one. 'So very graciously (for a Picarde) she said that I might take one, which I did, and borrowed a pin from one of the Yorkshire officers.'[26]

Many letters from the Great War are about carnage and stinking trenches and lice and disease, but, although he experienced all of these, Charles wrote chiefly about friendships and flowers, and about the beauty of the French countryside and the idiosyncrasies of the French and Flemish people, especially at places where he was billeted. He had been protected by his passion for poetry. Beauty was his rescue from horror; but it also distanced him. Now out of a dark hole, as well as beauty, came peace. His faith, first dormant now flourishing, lifted him above the mundane and gave him insights into, and a bond with, other people. He was protected from cynicsm by the sacraments; he became patient and appreciative of seemingly mundane people and actions. This time they were billeted in a small farm within a village. The old owner was 'reported to be very fierce' but Charles spoke to him and heard his story: his son was married and settled in the village, and his wife was dead. They could do as they wished in the house, he told Charles. Charles granted himself a small bedroom and his next lieutenant, Machin, slept in the dining room, where there was room for eight at table, lots of chairs and some good old furniture. After discovering that the soldiers were careful with his belongings, the old man brought them eggs, which were very scarce, and milk and lettuce and told them stories. One evening, seeing Charles out on the steps, he brought out a chair for him and then more as the circle of soldiers grew. Cordially Charles asked him to join them but he said he was too old and solitary. The farmer preferred the company of the regimental servants who were billeted in his rooms and spoke to him in Scots, 'which seemed to comfort him'. He had fought at Bapaume in the Franco-Prussian war and knew about soldiers pillaging, and his grandson was fighting in this war. Living alone, he had, Charles thought, rather loosed his hold on life. It was hard to understand him, especially after the broad French of the border, but Charles thought he would get used to it, 'like Glasgow Scots after Dundee'. Yet as soon as he had learnt the dialect, they were moved on. Such was the transient nature of all these connections, but it did not make them meaningless, each was a part of the tapestry.

In Bray-sur-Somme, the officers of the French Army entertained Charles and his colleagues to lunch: 'The officers, of whom the French have fewer than we, have very fine dugouts with beds, stools, tables, etc. We sat down to lunch; a party of eight and were given tinned lobster, herring roe, hare, cheese, tinned apricots, red wine, coffee, and rum, and a deal of conversation and instruction. They took our photograph afterwards . . .'[27] In the photograph Charles is given place of honour, sitting in the middle with his moustache curled at the ends, his legs elegantly crossed and his cane across his knees. He looks as though he is enjoying the brief sophistication of a French lunch, but he realises it is a standard that cannot be upheld, 'The French have a wonderful system of cooking behind the trenches, but it will be hard to break our men of the habit of boiling tea and frying bacon at all hours, day and night . . .'[28]

A French officer stayed with them for twenty-four hours to act as a liaison, which was tiring for Charles who was the only person who could speak both languages. The French soldiers had a custom of making rings out of aluminium fuses from German shells, using files and penknives, and his French officers gave him one of the best. In return he gave them some of his scraps of stained glass from Ypres Cathedral to have set in other rings. Meanwhile Charles occupied himself with reconstructing old dugouts for surplus officers, and with making a little chapel for the soldiers. He now fully understood the importance of faith in the lives of his men. A road from Battalion Headquarters ran through the village, and on towards the Germans. Just above his dugout was a barricade, and above that in the ruined village, he fixed the figure from a big iron crucifix on logs of wood and he and the men worked at squaring-off and clearing-up the ground in front. The idea was that the men could go there and be alone, if they wanted to say their prayers.

At Mass in the village, he was called upon to serve, 'which frightened me rather, as I could not quite remember or find out from my book when to ring the bell, but I made up for that by the purity of my Latin.'[29] Later that day he took his company down to bathe in the Somme, and found it very cold. He was thinner than he'd ever been. That last week in August he was given leave and went home to Lanark for a brief stay with his family. After his mother was called upon to say goodbye she wrote in her diary that he, 'packed up his few things in his satchel and his father saw him off at the station where a number of his brother officers were waiting to give him a good send-off. He is very popular among them – so bright and handsome and full of humour.'[30] He left behind a special list entitled 'Useful Things for Parcels' which ran: '4 oz Three Nuns Tobacco, tin of matches, hankies, shortbread, sweets, chocolate, gingerbread, envelopes, writing pads, currant loaf, books and Blackwoods Magazine.'[31]

Returning to France, Charles was in time to celebrate his twenty-sixth birthday in September with the men of his company. He began the day by riding up the trenches on a 'strange horse of great strength' who galloped all the way and got him there far too early. 'We pottered about looking at German positions with a view to occupying them.' Then he and Aleck Herries came back in 'the heaviest rain I have seen for a long time, a thundering gallop downhill. Most exciting.'[32]

That night they had a dinner party mostly of hors d'oeuvres and vegetables as they had very little meat – although they eked it out by chopping it into mince and adding hardboiled eggs. Charles managed to get two bottles of Moët et Chandon at the local brasserie. Two of his subalterns rigged up a sort of candelabrum, and made a table-centre out of a disinfected shirt, on a turkey-red table cloth which belonged to the house they were billeted in. The Catholic chaplain Father Evans sat on Charles's right, then Lieutanant Lionel Rooke, an undergraduate from Oxford, a slim figure always immaculately turned out, known for his optimism. Even though badly wounded in the legs later in the war, he went on to win the Irish Grand National in 1919. Next to him sat 2nd Lieutenant J. Grant, the transport officer, then 2nd Lieutenant E. Giles at the foot of the table; Aleck Herries was on Giles's right in a pyjama jacket belonging to Charles as his clothes were still wet, then Captain Lionel Machin, who survived to become a lieutenant-colonel, then Lieutenant J. M. Challoner, who was asked at the last moment because the piper was in his company. They found a pretty aluminium cup to use in the evening as a quaigh (Scottish drinking cup) to toast the piper, which Herries then paid for, as he wanted to give Charles a present, and during dinner he engraved it neatly with CKSM and the date. The piper played their regimental march, 'All the Blue Bonnets are over the Border'. It was often the last tune his fellow Borderers heard.

Charles did not know that on the same day at the Battle of Loos a piper in the 7th Battalion of KOSB was making history. The regimental historian Stair Gillon wrote that the push forward would probably have been lost if the anxious new recruits had not heard a sound that 'pointed the path and steeled the will. It was the skirl of the pipes of Daniel Laidlaw, who with complete sang froid, strutted about on the parapet playing the "Blue Bonnets".'[33] He kept on playing till he was wounded and won the first VC awarded to a KOSB in the war. The Piper of Loos became the subject of a picture in *The War Illustrated*, a patriotic war magazine.

When they practised a battle formation on the downs behind Bray-sur-Somme, Charles was impressed to see three regiments, many thousands of men, rise out of the ground in a long single line and move forwards: it was a rehearsal for the structure of the Battle of the Somme the following year. As the autumn progressed they were moved to chalk dugouts which, although carved and decorated by stationed soldiers, were very cold. Officers kept falling ill and Charles was asked to command the whole battalion, but then became very ill himself. He turned yellow and was sent to the French Riviera to recover. Though still not named, this was the recurring trench fever.

'Cimiez which as its name suggests is on a hill above Nice' Charles began his next letter from the Red Cross Convalescent Home for British Officers. As a respite from the trenches, the light and air on the hill were delightful. 'My room is on the second floor with a view of palms and the sea.'[34] Charles, however, only wanted to get back to his men; it took so long to build a team that worked well together. He cared less for the officers as they changed so often.

Years later, after Charles's death, one of his men wrote of him,

> Captain Scott Moncrieff was adored and respected by every man, not only in his own Company but in the Battalion and it is curious indeed when I learn that he only possessed the MC when, if ever a man earned the VC, Captain Scott Moncrieff earned it over and over again . . . I can't help glorifying my own Company Commander, whose behaviour in the face of death helped us to keep our reason. His presence in the front line, under a severe strafe, imbued us with a strong feeling of safety and security.[35]

Lance-corporal William Buchanan said of him at the same time:

> I can see him strolling about No Man's Land as cool as if he were on the parade ground, seeking information and the position of the enemy . . . On one occasion he brought back, as a souvenir, a German sandbag . . . When we took over from the French it was he who reconnoitred and discovered the various enemy positions on our immediate front. Dangerous work was evidently his strong suit, not because he wanted military kudos but he felt it his duty to his men. Those who had the honour to soldier in his Company looked to him as a child would to its father.[36]

It was no wonder that he missed his men and wanted so much to get back to them, but he lay yellow and weak in bed and it was ten days before he was even able to get up and walk about.

Charles spent the whole of December recovering, being fed salt bean curds and told to fatten up. He even had a short holiday, motoring under a blanket to Les Antibes with old friends he encountered by chance. He said that the French *Daily Mail*, 'an even viler rag than the English', had reported that Cardinal Hartmann had arrived in Rome 'for the meditation of the Pope in favour of peace – a particularly happy misprint.'[37]

He was determined to get up and rehearse for the officers' Christmas concert. On Christmas Eve, he went to Midnight Mass at the cathedral in Nice where there was such an enormous crowd that he had to stand in the corner. He said that he had never seen so many communicants. Holy Communion went on for a full hour and when he got back at 2.30 a.m., he couldn't sleep much, nervous over his performance the next evening. For the concert he shaved off his moustache and gave himself a middle parting, trying to look as young and handsome as in the 1913 photo, but he was, he knew, thinned and aged by war.

It was the first Christmas he had ever spent away from his family, who were all together with the grandchildren. In November his brother Colin had become rector of Little Stanmore (or Whitchurch) in Middlesex. Charles was sad that the family had to leave Scotland and that the children wouldn't be brought up as Scots, but it was hard to find a patron who supported Colin's liberal, theosophical views. Muriel, Countess de la Warr, feminist and socialist, was one such and she provided the living at Whitchurch. The rectory was large enough for Colin's growing family and the garden ideal; they had found a home at last. The church itself was unusual, decorated by Italian artists in 1715, it contained the organ that Handel played upon when organist to the Duke of Chandos. When Meg arrived from Lanark that Christmas she decided that they would sell Edgemoor and move closer to the grandchildren. John, now an army vet, was married to Anna and living in Cyprus with a baby boy named David.

However much he may have wanted it, Charles was not well enough to rejoin his men, and at the very end of the year he was sent home. On the train from Nice to Paris he met his brother's new patron Muriel de la Warr who did not impress him, but epitomised the gulf of understanding that lay between soldiers and families back home in Britain. Stopping in Paris for the night, Charles dashed off a letter to his mother: 'Lady W. seemed deaf and stupid about the trenches, having first maintained that I had been on holiday since May, and then said, "Do tell me about the trenches, are they quite comfortable – do they feed you well?" (Who?) I said we feed ourselves. She said, "Haw! But I thought they did it with motors so wonderfully."'[38] This seemed to reinforce what he had remarked in a letter home a month earlier, 'The truth is that the English people haven't yet begun to dream of taking the war seriously.'[39]

CHAPTER 8

Critic at War

Without poets a nation cannot be great in war.

CKSM, *The New Witness*, 17 May 1917

Waiting on the steps of the Rectory at Whitchurch in the cold, sharp air were four little children: Colin, George, Sita and Dorothy. It was 19 January and they had already waited all day the day before and been told to come in and be patient. Finally, the watching paid off; there, through the gate and up the path, came brave Uncle Charlie in his war uniform, two days late. He was carrying his kit and a present of a heavy box. They opened it once they were inside the house – a great sculpture in chocolate from Rouen of a snail shell, its head being old Franz Josef of Austria with the Kaiser on the top of the shell driving him along, and the Sultan of Turkey pushing from behind. The snail was carefully broken, starting with the Kaiser, and a little was eaten, then the children showed their uncle around the new house and the garden in the dark.

Charles stayed for one night and then went north with his mother, who had decided at the last moment to go with him to spend the precious hours of the journey together, talking all the way. He went straight to Edinburgh that night to see his dentist the next morning. The trenches had taken a toll on his teeth: '8 badly decayed teeth require to be removed and artificial cases made.'[1] It would take three weeks, which he would spend at home.

He returned to Edgemoor to be with his father, smoking in the study in civilian clothes, browsing among the books and catching up. With Meg he went over his old letters from Winchester days and came across a poem anticipating death,

I pray that death may be,
No thing of pain to me,
No weary memory of long buried sin.
But may the low sound of thine angels' wings
And may the message each angel brings
Soothe all my fear.[2]

Charles attended both Catholic Mass and his father's Protestant services. He returned from Mass relaying a sermon on the war which had declared that the 'meaning of suffering was as inexplicable to us now as a surgical operation would seem to the observer quite ignorant of its purposes'.[3] Like everyone else, Charles was questioning the scale of brutality and loss. His mother wrote in her diary with steely calm, 'War is the most painful act of submission to the divine law that can be required of the human will. Soldiers are single-hearted: they do not argue, they act.'[4]

During his stay at Edgemoor, Gladys Dalyell came to stay for a night and she and Charles spent all day together walking. Then in the evening by the drawing room fire, Charles read a story of Saki's, and a story and a ballad of his own. No doubt Gladys was another possible match hoped for by his parents. They would not have been discouraged by the six-verse ballad Charles read that evening called 'The Willow Tree Bough' which included the lines:

He's got moustaches, a good natured rifleman,
Curl'd at each end like the fiery young moon.
Yes and he marches so deft and delightfully,
All the old streets here still echo the tune.

Now that he's given himself up for a soldier,
All over the world his brave body to show,
How can you wonder that I in my anxiousness
Weep with my eyes on the willow tree bough?[5]

Like the rifleman's, Charles's ginger moustache was curled at the ends. The ballad may have seemed romantic, except for the odd fact that it was written from the female point of view in admiration of the male rifleman, in appreciation of his bravery. It goes on to describe the infantry 'Fighting like seals in a lickerish estuary', and the speaker talks of her 'Children yet to be born to me'. The ballad was later set to flowery, baroque music by the musicologist Edward Dent.

After the reading that evening Charles travelled to London on the night train and was at 40 Half Moon Street for breakfast with Robert Ross on the morning of 20 January. There he discussed the recently published *Spoon River Anthology* by Edgar Lee Masters, a poetic exploration of a village community which Ross had recommended. Charles added it to his pile of books, with Dante (of which he had decided to read a canto daily before breakfast 'like a proper Papist'[6]), Browning and Hugh Walpole's new novel, *The Dark Forest*, about his experience on the Russian Front (Charles described it as full of 'lurking patriphobia'[7]). The successful and prolific novelist Hugh Walpole couldn't join up because of poor eyesight but worked heroically for the Red Cross on the Russian Front and saw the war from a totally different angle. Walpole was picking up the bodies, without the adrenaline of the fight; while Charles had not questioned his own patriotism.

He met Charles Bonar Law, his Scottish friend from school, now in the 2nd KOSB, and took him to lunch at the Reform Club and to the theatre to see Jean Cadell, the Scottish actress with flaming red hair, in *The Man Who Stayed at Home*, a patriotic war melodrama. They went on to Edwardes Square in Kensington to dine with Charles Bonar Law's father, Andrew, the Colonial Secretary in cabinet. He had been leader of the Conservative Party in opposition following Arthur Balfour from 1911 to 1915. At this point in 1916, however, as part of the Coalition Government, he was Secretary of State for the Colonies dealing with manpower for the war.

Charles noticed that the Bonar Laws did without servants; the eldest daughter kept house. Charles felt at home in this Scottish Presbyterian household, made slightly austere since Mrs Law had died seven years previously and her husband had thrown all his energy into his work. 'They were all very simple and pleasant. I was rather frightened of him before dinner in his sanctum with his scarlet dispatch box at his feet and Charlie saying silly things from the arm of a chair . . . I think they show great promise of our future Government after the stale lees of this Asquith regime are poured down the sink of Time.'[8]

Later in 1916, after the resignation of the Prime Minister and Liberal Party leader, Asquith, Andrew Bonar Law was invited by King George V to form a government, but, being a wise and humble man, he deferred to Lloyd George, Secretary of State for War and former Minister of Munitions, whom he believed was better placed to lead a coalition. He did, however, serve in Lloyd George's War Cabinet, first as Chancellor of the Exchequer and then as leader of the House of Commons. Law briefly became Prime Minister from Nov 1922 to May 1923. But his leadership was short-lived: he resigned, unable to speak, with terminal throat cancer.

Charles felt at ease with the Bonar Laws and what he called their 'healthily decent family life', while disapproving of the dissipation of the privileged Asquiths. He had been at school with the children of both leaders, and Charles Bonar Law with his hard-working Scottish background had become a friend while Cyril Asquith had not. While Prime Minister, Herbert Asquith was generally criticised as being weak and vacillating concerning the war, partly, it was later revealed, because so much of his time was spent writing love letters to the beautiful young socialite Venetia Stanley. By 1915 Asquith was writing three times a day, often during Cabinet meetings, and would even ask her advice on strategy. He was accused of muddle and delay that led to considerable loss of life.

From the Bonar Laws' house Charles went back to Half Moon Street. He was leading a double life and thinking double thoughts. His letters home extolled the ideal of family life, while in London he was drawn as by a magnet to the Ross establishment, the antithesis of family life. However, a change was happening in him, as the war changed everyone. The gulf between his professed beliefs and his actions was beginning to show: he felt the battle of good and ill, the confusion, within himself; he did not know where he stood, and he was tired and sore. This questioning was sensed by Robert Ross who wrote to Millard that Charles was becoming 'tiresome' and 'an amiable bore of some accomplishment'.[9]

Leaving Piccadilly that night, Charles arrived at the coast at midnight and boarded a boat bound for France; settling down to sleep in the malodorous dining room with many other officers, he finally felt at home. The men slept on deck and after his brief leave he was glad to be back in their company, but it was February and the weather bitterly cold. He chose to be billeted for the week with the priest of the village, with whom he could talk about why he felt at home in the chaos and uncertainty of war, and yet uncomfortable in the 'civilisation' of London. He was confident and happy as a soldier, yet how could anyone enjoy such a war? The priest suggested Aristotle's simple formula for happiness: 'Happiness is Virtue plus Action.' Courage and industry were the virtues that kept Charles happy. The priest's sister washed all his clothes, for which he offered her a five-franc note; she would only take 25 sous, so he suggested giving the rest for *l'oeuvre de l'église*, 'which loosed the tides of eloquence. They were very sweet and humble and gracious.'[10]

That freezing February he marched his company fifteen miles through biting wind, snow and hail to Doullens, twenty miles from the front. He had to send half of them back again to help push the transport up the hills. Horses were lighter than some of the heavy vehicles used to move food and medical supplies, but they too slid in the deep mud and the wagons got stuck. Men were needed to heave the wagons from behind and to carry extra loads. On arriving at the town they had to shovel snow off the roads as there was 'a great uproar of French motor transports going down, possibly to lend a hand at Verdun' and trying to get through the drifts. 'It is a great thing to get reasonable food in a hotel after a continuous diet of tinned salmon rissoles.'[11]

By March Charles had marched with his men to Arras, where secret tunnelling on a massive scale was going on beneath the seemingly quiet place. As an ancient town with Roman origins Arras had tunnels and sewers – known as *boves* – running beneath the streets, and the countryside between the British and German positions was full of underground caves, from where chalk had been quarried during the Middle Ages, some of which were cathedral-sized caverns. The Allied Command decided that if they could link these various subterranean holes in secret, an entire army would be able to move safely from the front to the rear of the German positions, and attack from behind.

Until then, tunnelling had merely been used by both sides to detonate explosives under enemy lines: here it would take on a different purpose. It was a hugely ambitious plan, and 500 men of the New Zealand Tunnelling Company – all professional miners – set to work with a battalion of 'Bantams', short Yorkshire miners below the Army's minimum height of 5 foot 3 inches. In a matter of months, they had created two interconnected labyrinths, 12 miles long, capable of hiding 25,000 troops, with electric lighting provided by its own small powerhouse, as well as kitchens, latrines, and a medical centre with a fully equipped operating theatre. It was here in the fledgling underground kingdom that Charles and his men made a brief stay. However, it was a full year before the Battle of Arras, when the cellars came to be used for their surprise attack. Charles wrote a poem called 'Summer Thunder', which was published much later, kindled by the underground city.

> . . . he was come into the King's Palace,
> And timidly walked through corridors, down flights
> Of echoing iron stairs that never ended;
> And moved, pressed hurrying on, through days and nights.
> And sometimes paused at spider-haunted windows
> To catch the blinding flare of beacon lights,
> And heard artillery grumble in the distance,
> For he knew that they warred against that Palace, when
> He saw the gnomes come chattering from their chambers,
> Well-armed for battle; little, dusky men
> Complaining, shrill, in the old early language,
> Conscious that Fate was falling upon them then,
> Suddenly, in the midst of the field of battle,
> He stood bewildered, with a roar in his ears
> As the two armies frantically crashed together.
> Men running forward and falling. Groans and cheers,
> And the sobbing breath of quiet men keenly fighting . . .[12]

Again he was transported to other wars, this time ancient ones from the Anglo-Saxon world, 'in the old early language', and was tapping the thread of soldiery through the ages. Thankful to be briefly free from these vivid sounds of struggle and death, and seeing it was quiet on 3 March 1916, Charles rose early from the cellars which, though deep and gloomy, were kitted out with beds and some carpets, except that the carpets were hung on the walls to keep them from getting dirty. With a guidebook he went around the city. Not all the citizens had fled and he estimated there were about 800 left out of a population of 26,000; some shopkeepers stayed in business furtively behind closed doors, replenishing their stocks from unnamed sources. 'Then there are all the oddities of shattered houses; in one place an iron spiral staircase, rising some 15 feet with all the masonry round it fallen. In others complete rooms with photographs on the mantelpiece, but the whole front wall unhinged as in a dolls house or a theatre, storeys with no stairs to them.' Most of the fine buildings described in his guidebook – the cathedral, palace, town hall and belfry – were now flattened or gutted, although the Grand Place with its gabled houses was intact. He and two colleagues drank coffee after lunch in a clean and smart little patisserie in the main street that ran down to the German lines. 'A determined-looking woman sold me a cake, or tart which she had baked that morning, very delicately and well.'[13]

As soon as he reached his dugout, Charles requested a table of his own on which to put his papers: copious correspondence, books and company reports as well as poems. There was no light and he 'consumed a disquieting number of candles'.

His aunt Kate sent him a new anthology of prose and poetry, ancient and modern, by Robert Bridges, chosen to strengthen and console both soldiers and civilians in wartime. Bridges, the Poet Laureate, wrote in his preface, 'man is above all a spiritual being and the proper work of his mind is to interpret the world according to his higher nature',[14] a sentiment that Charles agreed with, but Bridges was not at the front, and consistently trying to live through the higher nature while savagely killing with the lower nature was nervously exhausting and for many destabilising. The poems yet to be written by greater war poets would bear witness to this. Charles was critical of the volume, thinking it more a revelation of the author's tastes than a representative collection: Bridges had omitted Browning altogether, and quoted Rupert Brooke, Julian Grenfell and Lascelles Abercrombie, but not Walter de la Mare.

Meanwhile Charles's war letters were still entertaining; in fact there was a gaiety about his particular dance with death. On 22 March he described a new bomb to a friend:

> The chief amusement of our particular enemy there was daily at teatime, to launch aerial torpedoes on to my Company headquarters. They are things like turnips with their leaves clipped

> into wings, which are fired out of some kind of trap, like clay pigeons. You hear the click as they start, and then gaze out over the fields to see where exactly it came from, and then yell downstairs to someone at the telephone to get the guns going, and then one's voice is drowned by the torpedo arriving somewhere near the lobe of one's right ear, and so on till the box of torpedoes is emptied, and we and the Germans both stop for tea and in the middle a British shell comes sauntering overhead, hotly followed by a polite R.A. subaltern who asks (down the companionway) 'Was that all right, sir?'[15]

An able raconteur and good mimic, Charles also kept his fellow soldiers amused and the atmosphere optimistic. Charles Lunn, a cousin also at war, wrote home about him that March:

> Capt D. declared that Charles was the bravest officer he had ever seen, 'offensively brave' he added. Charles would light a pipe and stroll along a sap to see if there were any Bosches at the far end. In D.'s opinion Charles would be killed or court-martialled or else win the V.C. before the end of the war. He added that Charles ran the Company very well and seemed a very capable business man.[16]

Although the creative effort of reading and writing was an effective tool to distract him from the horror emotionally, it could not fend off the physical results of life in the trenches and by 29 March Charles was in hospital with trench fever again. This time the hospital was a rough-and-tumble place where his own servant seemed to do most of the work, and the other officers on the ward were 'Kitcheners', the all-volunteer army named after the then Secretary of State for War, Horatio Kitchener[17]. He appreciated the Scottish Territorial nurses, 'with gentle voices, and a habit of lingering for an indefinite while by one's bedside, making a very little conversation'.[18] Charles was homesick for his own company or at least his own 13th Field Ambulance where he would have had the chaplain Father Evans to talk to. The Kitchener's army men annoyed him with their genuine keenness to be away from the regiments in the field.

However, he could not get back to his men; he was sent home before Easter on sick leave. He remained in London until he was passed by the Medical Board for one month's light duty, to be followed by two months' home duty with the 3rd Battalion of his regiment at Duddingston Camp, near Edinburgh. This brought him near enough to Lanark for the occasional weekend with his parents who thought he looked older, grave and thin. In July he was ill again and was sent to Buxton for treatment.

The summer of 1916 was a time of significant events in the war, but Charles was out of action and could only read of them in disjointed reports back home. There was the inspiring victory of the Battle of Jutland, which ensured British control of the North Sea, allowing the continuing naval blockade of the German ports and stopping their food imports. The only naval routes for the Germans to the Atlantic were the Straits of Dover or the North Sea minefield which the British had laid between Orkney and Norway. On 31 May 1916, the Germans made for the latter but the British Grand Fleet, based in Orkney and Cromarty, intercepted a coded message and met them just off Jutland in Norway. It was a huge battle with 250 ships on both sides and ended in a German retreat to their blockaded harbours. Lack of food played a major part in the eventual German defeat.

Then there was the most infinitely depressing battle of all, on land: the Battle of the Somme. The KOSB, though not Charles's battalion, were present and were lined up along with General Haig's twenty-seven divisions, an astonishing 750,000 men, against 16 divisions of Germans. The idea was to break through the German lines by sheer power of bombardment. However, the trenches were impenetrable. The Germans had spent two years digging several lines of deep trenches, with bomb-proof shelters and connecting tunnels. In front were two belts of wire 'forty yards broad, built of iron stakes, interlaced with barbed wire often almost as thick as a man's finger'.[19] Haig sent over wave after wave of infantry, not moving fast and dodging and ducking as they were used to, but standing and marching relentlessly. This was supposed to over-power the enemy, but they were just machine-gunned down, the generals having refused to change their tactics. At the end of the first day, 1 July 1916, there were 58,000 casualties, making it the worst day in the history of the British Army. Yet the same tactics were employed for nearly five months, until 21 November when snow forced them to stop fighting. By then the British troops had captured twelve kilometres of ground and lost 420,000 men.

Charles, yellow and feverish with trench foot and trench fever, in and out of hospitals, lay in Britain reading of the battles his comrades were fighting, and having medical after medical in frustrated attempts to get back out there. On the last day of July, he heard to his dismay of the death of Aleck Herries, killed in action on 22 July on the Somme. Herries had been with him since the First Battle of Ypres, in the trenches in Flanders and France, and his spirited company had kept Charles buoyant; he was a great loss to his friends and the regiment. For the first time Charles wrote a poem about the horror, later published in the *Wykehamist* and the anthology *The Muse in Arms*:

The Field of Honour

Mud-stained and rain-sodden, a sport for flies and lice,
Out of this vilest life into vile death he goes;
His grave will soon be ready, where the grey rat knows
There is fresh meat slain for her; – our mortal bodies rise,
In those foul scampering bellies, quick – and yet, those eyes
That stare on life still out of death, and will not close,
Seeing in a flash the Crown of Honour, and the Rose
Of Glory wreathed about the Cross of Sacrifice,

Died radiant. May some English traveller to-day
Leaving his city cares behind him, journeying West
To the brief solace of a sporting holiday
Quicken again with boyish ardour, as he sees,
For a moment, Windsor castle towering on the crest
And Eton still enshrined among remembered trees.

Charles's faith in life after death was powerful and orthodox. Death through sacrifice for one's friends meant Glory, and Glory was an experience of God's presence. Charles never lost his belief that they were fighting and dying to protect the England evoked in the last verse of his poem (Aleck Herries was an Etonian). If he had no wife or child to protect, the protection of architecture and tradition was itself a passionate cause; but perhaps not enough to salve the loss of such a splendid friend, and make him forget that his body was a 'sport for flies and lice'.

While recuperating Charles turned his mind to his journalism and started writing for a new periodical. *The New Witness*, formerly *The Eye-Witness*, was a weekly magazine set up and edited by Cecil Chesterton in 1912; it was polemical and political with roots in Distributism. A split from Fabian Socialism, Distributism was a third-way economic theory which criticised both socialism (state ownership) and capitalism (ownership by the wealthy few) and said property should be owned by the general populace through the use of co-operatives and small family businesses. It argued that economic activity should be subordinate to human activity as a whole; our spiritual, intellectual and family life should come first. When the editor became fatally ill at the front in 1916, his famous brother G. K. Chesterton took over, and immediately brought in Charles as a contributor. Charles's brother Colin, the vicar, known for his unorthodox religious views, knew Chesterton well enough for an introduction. Chesterton himself was forty-two in 1916 and was described by Bernard Shaw as a 'man of colossal genius'. He was six-foot-four and weighed twenty-one stone, wore a cape with a squashed hat and carried a swordstick. Starting adult life as an artist, he was now famous as a poet, writer of fiction, essayist and journalist, and a larger-than-life public figure seen by many as a latter-day Dr Johnson.[20] His autobiographical *Orthodoxy* published in 1908 was a description of his own journey towards Christian belief, and his ultimate conviction that the world is good and meaningful and something to be grateful for. His humorous and optimistic attitude permeated his writing and he held no grudges, maintaining, 'The Bible tells us to love our neighbours and also to love our enemies; probably because they are generally the same people.' This humanity permeated the magazine, which became more balanced, but still supported Distributism. Another Chesterton epithet was, 'Tolerance is the virtue of a man without convictions', which ensured the magazine was not bland. Other contributors to *The New Witness* included E. Nesbit, Arthur Ransome, Conal O'Riordan, Desmond Macarthy, Maurice Baring, and, later, the young Eric Blair (George Orwell). One of Charles's close friends was the pioneering lawyer E. S. P. Haynes, who used the magazine as a continual battle-ground forum for his liberal reform of divorce law. Cecil Chesterton was against law reform to make divorce easier and the dispute was fierce, but Haynes was a seasoned lawyer and won every spat, conceding, 'I dislike divorce as heartily as I dislike surgery. But I am intellectually convinced that divorce on proper lines is as essential to social hygiene as I am that surgery on proper lines is essential to medical hygiene.'[21] He never had cause to divorce his wife, Oriana, although later she had reason to divorce him. She was to become one of Charles's closest friends.

Since the age of fifteen Charles had used four different *noms de plume*: Amos (A Man of Scotland) and A. L. (A Lowlander) or even A. L. H. (A Lowland Highlander), for his poetry. He now used 'Bramantip' or 'Allison' for his column in *The New Witness* (Allison was the name of the old servant his family had when he was a child at Weedingshall and Inverness), which was a continuing tale of a soldier, based on the character and experiences of one of the men in his company, containing the realism of life in the trenches, but sometimes from a comic angle,

> The frost had slipped away unnoticed in the darkness and a heavy rain was falling. Allison wore a Burberry over his greatcoat, and, on his Sam Browne belt, a revolver, fifty cartridges, field glasses, a prismatic compass, a water bottle, a haversack, and (mark you) a sword. It is difficult to believe it, that in those archaic days, and even on push bikes, people did wear swords, and with this bumping against him or sticking between the spokes of his back wheel, Allison paddled out along the dark and quite unknown road . . . And ran bump into a little gesticulating knot of Indians and recoiled into a shell hole. It was not a very deep one, luckily, and the Gurkhas bailed him out without difficulty.[22]

He only used his own name, C. K. Scott Moncrieff, for his reviews, which were long, rambling and opinionated, often more about the purpose of literature than the books under discussion. When critical he was devastating and the poets and writers did not always forgive him. After the twelve Bramantip articles which began in October 1916, he started a regular review column sometimes entitled 'From the Logrollers Cabin' which allowed him free rein on matters literary and was lively, ardent and relentless. He was also allowed to publish his own poetry on a regular basis.

The number of pseudonyms reflected his difficulty with his identity. Some early poems, to those who could decipher the meaning between the lines, were homoerotic. The vivid, even harsh descriptions of the Bramantip articles were at odds with his detached critical persona, but at the end of a long series of articles from the Bramantip pen, he admitted, 'Next morning Allison, with whose identity the present writer's has now become totally confused, was sent down the line with frozen feet, and found himself at home, after all, on Christmas morning.'[23]

Charles's articles were not at first political, but Chesterton had pet bugbears, one of them being Alfred Harmsworth, later Lord Northcliffe, the owner of the *Daily Mail* and *The Times*, whom *The New Witness* accused of whipping up war fever in 1913 and abusing his power throughout the war. Charles was not interested in such feuds: his passions were first and foremost literary. The other Chesterton obsession, which slowly developed after 1918, was with Jewish oligarchs, and could easily be seen as a growing anti-Semitism if his later published works had not contradicted that slur, and revealed a complex theory of what he called 'Jewish tragedy'. *The New Witness* certainly published clearly anti-Semitic letters in its letters page, but also replies from a Mr Rubinstein who suggested that Catholicism was not in keeping with the attractive and tolerant English spirit and that all Catholics should be encouraged to emigrate to Rome.[24] Charles became gradually politicised, but not in a blatant or dogmatic way – he preferred satire.

During October and November 1916 Charles stayed at Lanark with his parents, where to relax he worked on family genealogies with his father. Alongside his reviews for *The New Witness*, he wrote a series of Halloween stories for the magazine, based on his experiences in Messines in 1914. He also visited friends in Edinburgh, including Richard Ball, who was there on leave from the Russian Front working with the Society of Friends, the Quakers. Charles felt keenly that his dear friend Richard was pale and sensitive, loving and good and that this would be their last meeting. It was. Ball distinguished himself as a conscientious objector and pacifist and died bravely as a medical orderly on the Eastern Front two years later.

At the end of November, since the Battle of the Somme had reduced the Allied forces by over half a million, Charles was called up for a medical and passed fit for active service. He went straight to Duddingston on the outskirts of Edinburgh where he spent December retraining. At Christmas he met his parents in Edinburgh for tea at his mother's club, bringing with him a new friend called Douglas, the Episcopal Chaplain of the regiment. He then explained to his family that he had decided to make some provision in the camp for Roman Catholics for whom no church was provided. He told some of the men to let it be known that any who liked might parade voluntarily and he would march them down to the midnight Mass at the nearest Catholic church in Portobello. He felt a sense of awe when he found that over two hundred were waiting for him, one a wounded convalescent on crutches and in carpet slippers who kept up manfully with the others over a mile and a half of ice-covered roads. On Christmas Day again over a hundred went with him to church. He hoped that Major Herries, father of his friend Aleck, would arrange a monthly service for them. He kept murmuring, 'it was wonderful, so many turning up . . . it seemed almost a miracle.'[25] In France or Belgium it would seem normal, but given the intolerance towards Catholics in Scotland at the time it was a daring and indeed miraculous event. The war had already changed people.

On Boxing Day 1916 Charles set off for London to talk to his mother's cousin, known as the 'Father of the War Office', now Major-General Sir George Scott Moncrieff,[26] about helping to get a proper placement for his brother, Johnnie the vet. The next day, he sent his mother a telegram, 'George very affable will help to secure commission in the Remounts. Foresees no difficulty.'[27] The Army Remount Department was responsible for requisitioning 460,000 horses between 1914 and 1920, and was in dire need of vets. Ever the loving son, in the midst of seeing London friends, Charles didn't forget to send Meg a telegram for her fifty-ninth birthday.

After brief duty as a son and a brother he was back to being a soldier. On 10 January 1917 Charles left Victoria station early in the morning with nineteen KOSB subalterns to go to France, he believed in order to train troops at Etaples. The corps at Etaples was commanded, noted Charles the journalist, by Lord Bathurst, whose wife owned the *Morning Post*, and consisted of his men and another Scots regiment. Two days later Charles was on his way by train up the now familiar French valley to rejoin the KOSB, at the tail end of the Somme action. Snow concealed the usual hideousness of the ground, but the country was laid with miles of boards between and among shell holes. These boards were frozen stiff and as slippery as glass. 'On this plain we have among the mud, scarred with last summer's shell holes, mile upon mile of wooden pathways, boards placed end to end like dominoes, and zigzagging all over the country. The effect, especially lit by moonlight on the snow is extraordinary. I see how full of imagination Nevinson is.'[28] The gifted and volatile futurist painter Richard Nevinson had recently exhibited a series of striking paintings of the front. Charles may have seen the exhibition but photos were also published in newspapers, along with those of the other popular war artist Muirhead Bone.

In spite of deep frost, the action of 27 January 1917 at Soues was a great triumph when two battalions of Charles's brigade took nearly 400 prisoners. His own battalion relieved them the next day, consolidated the position and were congratulated. The only sad consequence was that his New Zealand friend Neil Macleod was taken prisoner by the Germans.[29] Later that day a German officer with twenty-one men strayed into KOSB territory and they were taken. Charles turned 'yellow as a guinea' with jaundice and was taken off to Amiens in a field ambulance. Five days later he was up and about with his guidebook and visited Amiens Cathedral, which he was glad to describe as 'perfect and harmonious', unaffected by the war; he walked the streets for a couple of hours and bought two leatherbound volumes of Guy de Maupassant's short stories. When he returned to the hospital he found to his childish excitement that his post had arrived with *The New Witness*, with his column documenting the continuing adventures of Allison, and his description of Ypres, on the eve of its destruction 'a city admirably defensible by archers';[30] the post also brought the *Wykehamist* with his poem 'Domum' printed and a copy of the *Daily Mail*. Charles was finally beginning to see himself in print as a writer and critic.

At Amiens he saw Vyvyan Holland, stationed with the Royal Field Artillery, whom he had not seen since long before the war. They arranged to meet at Amiens Cathedral to catch up on old times. Vyvyan was a changed and shattered man. He had been married in 1914 to Violet Craigie, the daughter of an army officer, then he had gone to war, as had his brother Cyril, already a soldier for eight years. Cyril had been killed by a sniper's bullet in 1915 and for Vyvyan, 'The last link with Tite Street and the spacious days had snapped.'[31] He later learned that his wife Violet was badly injured in a fire and before he could get home to her, she died. For Charles and Vyvyan it was a moving meeting and they were both glad to relive old memories, joke and tease as they used to before the war.

Returning to the regiment on 17 February 1917, Charles was put in command of a prisoner of war company. He was given a very comfortable little hut with tables and chairs, china plates and a lamp. Nearby was a 'large cage containing 500 Germans – who did an amazing amount of work' cleaning equipment, mending uniforms and boots, and seemed normal, unaggressive, 'clean and good and docile'. Beside this prison Charles wrote two long reviews for *The New Witness*. The first was of two slim poetry volumes by Claude Houghton and Robert Graves. He called the piece 'Lesboefs and Morval'[32], after two small destroyed towns on the Somme, the first still occupied by the invader, the second freed. He compared Graves's work in *Goliath and David* to the freed town, inspired by a muse who has shaken off her fetters; while Houghton's was like the town enslaved, writing that 'dates back to the school of Arthur O'Shaugnessy and the "poppied sleep" poetry of the seventies'.[33] He finished the second review, a critical one of the American Edgar Lee Masters' volume of poetry *The Great Valley* on Good Friday when he also heard the news that the Americans had entered the war. He wrote: 'the effect of this new adhesion on the War concerns me . . . for a nation can wax great in commerce without poets, and America is grown great. But without poets a nation cannot be great in war.'[34] As a critic he had swiftly taken to making statements on the state of poetry internationally and the war in general.

Six weeks later, on 2 April, Charles was near Arras, shivering under the heaviest snow he could remember for over ten years. He had just got his men into billets and late that night started a letter home which stated ominously, 'My hostess is very old and sunken and is crouching over the other side of the stove telling her beads and looking up dully over my shoulder at the snow.'[35] The Battle of Arras had already begun. Long columns of motor lorries arrived with supplies, along with several Scottish regiments. For three days their pipe bands playing in all the squares made 'the whole town full of life and rejoicing'[36] – then Charles and his men joined the 1st Battalion KOSB who had just been evacuated from Gallipoli. From Arras they marched ten kilometres across the frozen plain to the small town of Monchy-le-Preux, one of the keys to the northern end of the Hindenburg Line.

CHAPTER 9

Wounded Out

'I,
Like a pailful of water thrown from a high window, fell . . .
Alone . . .'

CKSM, 'The Face of Raphael', 1917

Monchy-le-Preux is a town built on a hundred-metre-high knoll on a fertile plain, with a road winding up and round the hill like a drawing in a fairy tale; the highest point for five miles all around. At the top is a château, a church, a town hall and houses for about six hundred people. It had been unchanged since 1200 and had seen many skirmishes at its foot, but none as violently destructive as this.

The Germans had taken Monchy in 1914 and held the vantage point until two weeks before Charles arrived. He and his men were lucky not to have been involved in the first British assault. On 11 April 1917 during a week of snow, twelve infantry battalions (nearly ten thousand men), four tanks and one cavalry regiment attacked and took the knoll with huge losses. The cavalry were the first to climb the two roads to the château, but were shot down from the air. When the Allies eventually entered Monchy, they found the main roads blocked by the carcasses of 196 horses and 91 cavalrymen. They spent so long flushing out the remaining snipers that the roads were still blocked by dead horses on the night of 22 April when Charles arrived.

This was the first day of thaw, and the reconnaissance officer tried to make his way down the east side of Monchy to look for a suitable trench location for the assault into the German lines. The enemy were only five hundred yards away and needed pushing further back if the town was to be held. The officer got his men to clear a path through the dead horses, and the digging party got under way constructing an assault trench only 100 metres east of Monchy in a flat field, wet and sludgy after the thaw.

Black, thick, fertile soil formed the cold walls of the KOSB's fortress that night, as they waited for the signal. At zero hour, 4.45 a.m., in darkness and mist, they left the trench, each man carrying in his pockets a bomb, a flare, a sandbag and rations for three days. The German trench was a short dash across a muddy field, a simple stroll in peacetime.

Shivering after a night in the mud and daunted by the likely outcome (losses averaged at 4000 a day on the Arras offensive), Charles's men may have shown some reluctance. Therefore he led them, something company commanders were not meant to do, out into the guns. Amid a roaring din, the high explosives pitched in the ground with a shaking thud, to explode a fraction of a second later with a bang like the slamming of a giant door, throwing up a huge column of earth and blowing men to pieces. Continually, too, came the high-explosive shrapnel: a big shell, known to the troops as a 'Woolly Bear', bursting with a fierce whipping 'crack' about one or two hundred feet from the ground, delivering hot shrapnel and portions of burst shell case like rain.

'Tomorrow is St George's Day, best of all for the armies of England,' Charles had written home the day before. Shakespeare's birthday and the day Rupert Brooke had died, 23 April, was the day Charles's life was cut in half by friendly fire. At 5 a.m. in the pitch dark a small British shell aimed at the German trench fell short and exploded in front of him. He fell, his left leg broken in two places with shrapnel in his right thigh. He lay on the battlefield for some time, successfully directing his men and urging them on until they overtook his position and claimed the German trench. He heard the sounds of men fighting, the rasp in their throats and the cough of the dying taken by surprise. He waited until well into daylight, thinking and imagining, wondering if he was going to be shot, to die, or to be found, until he was carried fainting and delirious back to the village. That German trench was never lost again to the other side for the duration of the war.

The road to the village followed an ancient red brick wall with trees leaning overhead along a path cleared as if through a snowdrift between banks of frozen dead horse flesh. Through this in the grey morning light Charles was carried on his stretcher to have his leg set in the château which served as a temporary dressing station.

There was a transcendental explanation, he thought, for being alive after the battle and carried safely back to a field hospital. Quoting the French poet Paul Claudel's poem 'Hymne à SS Agnès', he wrote, '*"l'amér commencement du ciel"* is a marvellous phrase, and the 2 lines are just what I felt that morning at Monchy; *"quand l'âme frémissante étudie l'amer commencement du ciel."*'[1] A literal translation of Claudel's lines might run: 'when the trembling soul studies the bitter beginnings of dawn . . .' But knowing that 'ciel' means both 'sky' and 'heaven', here, as later with Proust, Charles took liberties with his translation. His poetic rendering of those lines took a personal, interpretative, leap: 'In the dim hour of life and death, when the slow agony is begun,/ And the soul scans with faltering breath that hard road whereby Heaven is won.' He was acutely aware at this point of the other world; of the sense that this earthly battle at Monchy was mirrored by the battle on another level for each man's soul. He had his own poetic vision and that confidence gave him vigour. His own poem about his wounding, called 'The Face of Raphael', quoting Claudel, was published later in *The New Witness*. All the time alert to the other world, he described their march to battle, unaware of what was keeping step with them, 'Coelistis exercitus' – an army of angels.

I,
Like a pailful of water thrown from a high window, fell . . . Alone.

An hour or two I lay and dozed, my unattempting features
closed,
Or opened a reluctant eye to search the irresponsive sky,
Not speaking, while my dull ears heard many a
just-remembered word
Twine themselves into a song, tuneless
Here beginneth
That old lesson, earth to earth turns, and death regards birth,
Nothing of us but doth fade utterly . . .

. . . Ah, whose mind prayed
Through mine then? Whose quiet singing heard I from my
stretcher, swinging

Sorry, weary, sick, belated back to Arras? Who dictated
Strongly, clearly, till I sung these French words with my English tongue?

The poem was a forewarning of his vocation; an intuition of his inspiration as a translator. 'Who dictated strongly, clearly, till I sung these French words with my English tongue?' Sing was the right verb, as his future translations would show, starting with the *Song of Roland*, the ancient verses passed down by word of mouth from the time of Charlemagne when the jongleur 'sang' the troops into battle.

Charles's leg was set in Monchy, but then it shoogled unset again as he was driven in a field ambulance, bumping the long ten kilometres back to Arras. In the better equipped underground hospital in the cellars beneath the town, he was examined again and doctors wondered if it would not be a better idea to amputate. However, he was then sent to the seaside Base Hospital in Camiers, on the north coast of France, where doctors took more time debating whether the limb was worth saving, and decided to give it a chance. Seven weeks were spent stabilising the leg with much agony, both physical and mental. He wrote home on 1 May, lamenting 'this awful inability to control or co-ordinate my thoughts, which is, I suppose, a result of the shell shock'.[2] It was probably also the morphine.

Two of the first letters announcing his injury were written in wobbly pencil as he could not sit up or use a pen. The first was to his mother announcing his injury with a delirious 'Tell Susan Lunn that I love her very much'[3] scribbled wildly on the back. Susan Lunn was his mother's cousin who had just lost her own son, Charles's contemporary, in battle. Another letter was to the Warden of Winchester College with whom he had been staying when last on leave, in which he said that his legs 'gave way beneath me like a trayful of claret glasses'. Shattered as he was, the rest of the letter insisted that he felt 'entirely and solely uplifted by the hands of God'.[4] He was pleased that his priest brought him Holy Communion. However, there was a crane at the foot of his bed with a sandbag hanging from it to raise his leg and so many people bumped into it that he got into a state of panic whenever he saw someone coming up and down the busy ward. Finally, when 'a fat old parson who crusades around these wards ran full tilt into it', and Charles yelled in pain, 'He turned to see what he had done and said blandly, "Aha, you stick out too much." After this I could stand no more, and got my bed shifted across the ward.'[5]

Like so many active, fit young men he suddenly found himself dependent, inactive and bedridden, sure he would never walk properly again. It was a blow to his confidence that took a long time to recover from and changed his life for ever. He was, however, well aware of the fact that he did actually have his life and even his leg for the moment, and was luckier than the many men he had known who were already dead. He wrote another poem on the distortions caused by his dreams, later published in *The New Witness*.

> The queerest thing of all now, is the way the sizes shift, Johnny:
> Bracken Hill's no height now, no height at all.
> And the little dog Peter, was the weight I just could lift,
> He has grown to hide high mountains, but the great dog's
>   starved and small . . .[6]

In a letter to his Edinburgh friends, the Pyatts, he explained, 'I have been given one of the fourteen Military Crosses allotted to the 29th Division. No one else in the regiment, I am sorry to say, for most of them deserve it more than I do . . .'[7] Charles initially refused the award because he was injured by his own barrage, and because he did not think himself more deserving than anyone else. Lieutenant-Colonel Welch, commanding the Ist Battalion KOSB, wrote back to the Headquarters of the 87th Infantry Brigade, insisting, saying,

> Captain C. K. Scott Moncrieff is an officer with a distinct temperament, and of an intelligence far above the average, and in my opinion, whatever he says to the contrary, I shall still remain convinced that, not only on the date in question, but on one or two previous occasions also, he thoroughly earned the award which His Majesty has been pleased to bestow. This opinion would be borne out by the officers and men who were serving with him in this Battalion.[8]

Charles was given a copy of the letter, implying that he would be in trouble if he continued to object to his medals. They still belong to the family, framed in a box backed with his regimental tartan, enshrined by his mother after his death: a Military Cross, the 1914–15 Star, the British War Medal and the Victory Medal.

By June he had been conveyed, painfully in a stretcher, to the Lady Ridley Hospital, 10 Carlton House Terrace, London. Another semi-autobiographical article appeared in *The New Witness* on 12 July 1917 entitled 'On Being Wounded', subtle in its analysis of feeling and consciousness. He described the 'continuous, insensible shifting of the perspective from the moment that he feels the thud made by the arrival of the bullet' as being like the point of focus of a microscope, passing through successive layers of an object, each layer being the only one existing at any time. He talked of the 'abrupt transition from a life of incessant strain and action to one of complete inactivity. The engine is abruptly stopped – dead.' He longed for news of the front; he had seen artillery officers nearly weeping at the thought that while they lay impotent, their battery was at last, after months of waiting, moving forward in pursuit. Did the mine go off? Did they take the wood? But reality is a battered foot or shattered arm. Soon the realisation that this means a return to England hits the soldier and 'he whispers, *London*, almost reverently. It is a splendid moment.' It may be weeks before the wound is stable enough to move, but the moment comes then 'Another strand is interwoven; the insignificance of one wounded man when in the grip of a system which handles the unending stream of casualties with the indifference of a universal store.' With his large luggage label the soldier is pushed on and off stretchers, dumped in odd corners of draughty railway stations, stacked in rows on ambulance trains, but all the time nearing an increasingly vivid England. Then there was the pain and the morphine, which gave an alternation of depression and exultation, between enduring it and contemplating convalescence, 'it is as if one were changed suddenly from a black bishop, moving freely about the black squares of the chessboard, into a white one, for whom blackness does not exist.' Finally there was the welcome 'spectacle of taxicabs, parks, delightful old gentlemen who raise their hats at the sight of the ambulance'.

At Carlton House Terrace, the location, treatment and company could not have been better and Charles began to perk up. He was lucky to get a bed in a drawing room from where he could see the back of Downing Street and the Foreign Office. By mid-June his brother Colin was visiting with armfuls of roses, and Vyvyan Holland came with a huge and rare box of chocolates. Robert Ross arrived fresh from a weekend at the Asquiths with gossip, a novel and the latest poetry books. Charles asked Ross, also an art critic, to give his opinion on the portraits in the room, and discussed with him his surgeon who, he said, looked about fourteen.

A young officer called Broadway, also a patient, but a mobile one, would come down in his dressing gown after breakfast and again for messages before going out. He brought notepads for Charles and arranged visits from brother officers. In one notepad there is a pencil sketch satirically depicting Robert Ross as a devil-like figure. The idea of a decadent influence and 'bad' company still haunted Charles, however he could not ignore Ross's genuine compassion and kindness.

The same notepad contained two handwritten short stories, later published in *The New Witness*. The most striking, called 'Mortmain', was about the supernatural effect of shell shock. A wounded officer is taken to have an arm amputated in a field hospital in France, and while under anaesthetic he dimly sees an image of Shaftesbury Avenue in London from outside a theatre, and his wife, Claire, wearing the pearls he gave her. She is accompanied by a slick male acquaintance, aptly named Courtly. From his vantage point, semi-conscious, the soldier watches as his wife is accompanied home by Courtly, who enters their flat, reaches for the light and is mysteriously electrocuted by the action of an unknown hand (the right, like the narrator's own amputated hand). The maid enters early next morning to see a dead man sprawled on the sofa. Then outside on the balcony 'Claire sat, laughing unevenly. The string of her necklace had broken, and upon her lap was a little pool of pearls, which, from time to time, she flung at the sparrows, splashing, quarrelling and courting in the dust of the courtyard.'[9] Back in the field hospital in France, her husband, the officer with the amputated arm, is also found to be dead, just as a fellow patient lowers the gramophone needle on to a popular song titled 'Who were you with last night?'

Still haunted by ghoulish imaginings, Charles's poetry also expressed his physical and mental despondency. He was awarded the Silver Badge, which was given to all military personnel who were discharged as a result of sickness or wounds received during wartime but his reaction was cynical and negative; and he wrote:

Silver Badgeman

Houses I hate now, who have seen houses strewn,
A bitter matter for battle, by sun and by moon:
Stones crumbled, bricks broken, timbers charred and rotten,
And the smell of the ghost of a house; these are ill-forgotten.

Gardens too, I hate; for I have seen gardens going
Into green slime and brown swamp, no flowers growing
In pits where old rains linger, stale snows harden,
And only graves, where roses grew, still tell of the garden.

And I hate plowed lands, who have been set a-plowing
Crooked furrows to fight in, where the guns go sowing
Bodies of men in the trenches, and grey mud covers
Fools, philosophers, failures, labourers, lovers.[10]

Five stanzas were written in May 1917, when his dreams were still nightmares. But a year later, without as he himself said, 'justification or foundation', he added five more stanzas. The poem changed direction, citing not just ruined gardens and buildings, but a ruined people who had regressed to stone-age savagery.

I have gone to the woods where in ages before me
Grappling, my hairy ancestors got me and bore me;
I have sought out the caves where, pursued, my mothers
Whimpered, and turned to receive grunting lovers.

. . . Yet not these in their time loved peace nor knew it,
Who, scented afar their quarry, grew stiff to pursue it,
When a brown arm, shot from the bough, caught the bird for plunder,
Or limb on the ground tore the screaming rabbit asunder.

So no peace shall I find, in all the ages,
Short and harsh man's life is and death is its wages.
Life goes hot from the throat, by the cry made holy,
Or passes, bedded in towns, with unction, slowly.[11]

Charles's hospital locker was full of books to review. Through writing he felt stable, almost forgiving himself for not being out in the field fighting. Yet he was still angry and he turned his anger on other poets. Siegfried Sassoon was the first to come under fire. Sassoon, three years older than Charles, had a private income and was a man who could afford to be a poet. He had been to Cambridge, but left without a degree, he loved hunting, and was an officer in the Royal Welch Fusiliers. *The Old Huntsman and Other Poems,* published by William Heineman, was the first volume of Sassoon's poetry not published by himself. It was June and Charles was still suffering from nerves; the graphic war poems were too brutal for his worn sensibilities. In the review, Charles regretted Sassoon sang 'only in two keys, anger and cynicsm; anger with himself for being such a fool as to go soldiering . . . cynicism . . . turned like a flammenwerfer on officers and men alike'. The poem, 'One Legged Man', was 'too obvious to be effective'. 'I have saved a leg of my own from destruction; but in the other event, I think I should not have made a song about it.' He did however praise the lyrical poems at the end: 'Again and again in the short lyrics and the sonnets . . . he touches perfection.'[12] However, his conclusion was fairly damning: 'I dismiss then Mr Sassoon's war poems as a regrettable incident.' He wanted him instead to celebrate the return of peace.

The next book of poetry he reviewed while recuperating in Carlton House Terrace was Robert Nichols's *Ardours and Endurances.* His review contained more of his own confused inner dialogue than of Nichols's poetry, of which he wrote, 'It is not, can't you see? good enough.'[13] His reviews were essays on the state of poetry as a whole and little space was dedicated to the unfortunate poet in question. The next was on a clutch of four collections and Charles complained at the outset, 'the output of printed verse has reached a density unknown in days when the last word in poetry was recited among a thousand cliques too proud, too recondite or, it may be, too epicene to publish.' He gave a decent consideration to Helen Hamilton's long poem *The Compleat Schoolmarm,* about the only respectable career available to women as yet, that of a school mistress: 'Wrongly educated; underpaid and therefore ill-fed; overworked and therefore ill-rested, socially and sexually an outcast – she does indeed make a sacrifice to the higher education of women.' However, he could not help suggesting that it would have been better done in prose: Miss Hamilton's verse 'wanders about the page like a lost thing without rhyme or metre'.[14]

By August 1917, he could get around in a wheelchair. Still news came from the front: he was devastated to hear from Mrs Chisholm Batten that her son Jack, his fellow scholar and great schoolfriend, had been killed earlier that month. Slowly he became strong enough to be taken out in his chair to his club. On 12 September Gladys Dalyell and his mother Meg wheeled him to the RAC Club where he gave them lunch. They discussed a book by Ian Hay, a novelist and soldier, called *The Oppressed English,* which had something to say on the union: 'Today a Scot is leading the British army in France [Field Marshal Douglas Haig], another is commanding the British grand fleet at sea [Admiral David Beatty], while a third directs the Imperial General Staff at home [Sir William Robertson]. The Lord Chancellor is a Scot [Viscount Finlay]; so are the Chancellor of the Exchequer and the Foreign Secretary [Bonar Law and Arthur Balfour]. The Prime Minister is a Welshman [David Lloyd George], and the First Lord of the Admiralty is an Irishman [Lord Carson]. Yet no one has ever brought in a bill to give home rule to England.'[15] It was the sort of absurdist approach to politics that appealed to Charles and he was gradually changing and becoming interested in pointing out the irony in governance.

Being a gentleman and a man about town meant you had to belong to a club and Charles attended many clubs on a freelance basis. Officers during the war were more or less welcome everywhere. He had been officially a member of his father's club, the New Club in Edinburgh, since January. The only club of Scotland's ruling class, it had reciprocal rights with the London clubs White's, Boodle's and Brooks's.

The RAC Club in Pall Mall, where he went for lunch with Gladys and Meg, which had opened in 1897, was a mini-palace of opulence to compensate for the hardships suffered in war, almost becoming an officers' club, with, by 1919, over thirteen thousand officers registered as temporary members. Designed by the architects of the Ritz Hotels in London and Paris, it had a luxurious gilded interior, sauna and shooting range. Many of Charles's literary friends and associates belonged to the Reform Club, also in Pall Mall. Its library contained 50,000 books, mostly on political history and biography. At a time when many other clubs dished up school dinners, the Reform was famous for the artistry of its French chefs. When one head chef was found with a housemaid and dismissed, the members held a mass meeting to demand his reinstalment – with rights over all the housemaids. In spite of the war the spirit of hedonism was still alive. However a man's clubs said a lot about his character, and Charles was becoming less and less of a hedonist. After the free membership for officers during the war was over, he had to join a club officially, and the club attended historically by the Scottish writing intelligentsia was the Savile Club, then at 107 Piccadilly. R. L. Stevenson, Andrew Lang, Compton Mackenzie and George Saintsbury, Charles's own professor from Edinburgh, were members. Although he came here in a freelance manner during the war, Charles would be officially proposed in 1919 by the critic Sir Edmund Gosse, Sir J. C. Squire, the literary editor, and eight others.

Charles's reviewing was now coming in fast. E. B. Osborn, who was soon to kindly include Charles in his book of collected poetry, made the mistake of writing a novel. Charles sketched a description of a self-regarding Great Man writing in the trenches – 'sheet after sheet of neatly written but illegible gibberish . . . his book is, I regret to say, wholly unreadable.'[16]

The following week he was sent the nineteen-year-old Alec Waugh's *The Loom of Youth*, 'If I had been given the alternatives – to lie about in Flanders and, in mid-August, occupy Langemarck, or to return to England and, about the same time, criticise 'The Loom of Youth', I know not which of these adventures, alike so arduous and so gratifying, I should have chosen. But I had no choice . . .'[17] He dedicated a whole page of the periodical to Waugh who then wrote to him and formed a lifelong acquaintance. At the same time Charles in a letter to a friend described the book as the 'Doom of Youth' and called it 'a curiously boring book'.[18]

The book became a controversial bestseller, openly mentioning romantic love between schoolboys. However, the romance was all of two pages and the rest of the book chronicled mundane life at a boarding school.

Charles became interested in translations, reviewing some from the French – two novels and a collection of French war poetry. He was critical of *Under Fire* by Henri Barbusse; faced with French soldier slang the translator, Fitzwater Wray, rendered it word for word, making it neither English slang nor English literature. Although he gave the poetry plenty of space and discussion, Charles found its translation irritating. Translation in Britain did not occupy a significant place in literary culture, and reviews of translations were not common. On the other hand Charles knew the Balzac translation supervised by his professor Saintsbury and executed by Ellen Marriage, and had also read some of Constance Garnett's translations from Russian. He knew Ezra Pound's translation from Anglo-Saxon and Provençal, and it has been said that Charles's first translations 'are like some Pound in their challenging foreignness'.[19] What is beautiful in one language is often clumsy or sheer nonsense in another. Fidelity and transparency, dual ideals, were usually at odds in translation. A seventeenth-century French critic had coined the phrase, *les belles infidèles*, arguing that translations, like women, could be either beautiful or faithful but not both. Charles however thought the translation of Barbusse was neither. He had lofty ideals about translation as he did in other areas of life, seeing it as a vocation and a service to literature.

Meg came again to visit her son in hospital on 15 October and saw him huddled exhausted in a chair by the fire after having another operation to remove dead bone from his leg. He soon had a new splint, jointed at the ankle and knee with the promise that he could learn to walk again. Within a week Meg saw him on crutches taking a rapid walk through the wards. After six months in a seated or lying position, it was very exciting to be moving. 'I feel like a child on its birthday,'[20] he wrote. At the end of October she took him out to visit his tailor to get some much-needed civilian clothing that fitted his now slender frame.

Impatient to walk, Charles bought a bulldog called Molly as a companion, hoping to learn from her pugnacious spirit. In November his cousin Catherine[21] took him to visit the family at his brother's rectory at Edgware. There he hirpled round the garden and the library rearranging the books, always with Molly at his heels. He then went off in a taxi with Catherine, leaving his wheelchair and the dog at the rectory. The next day, Meg observed that Molly was a quiet beast and most gentle with the children. She was not however gentle with Connie, Charles's sister-in-law, jumping out on her during a game and butting her violently in the stomach, which caused an internal rupture that needed an operation. Molly also constantly ran away. In December Charles was sent to Eastbourne for convalescence, and when he rang at the end of the month, his voice sounded strong and cheerful. He told his mother that he had been promised work in the War Office at the end of January.

Ronald Knox had often visited Charles when he was in hospital in Carlton House Terrace. Charles informed one visiting priest, 'If you'd been here earlier you would have met Ronald Knox.' The priest replied that he would like to meet the man thought of as a 'second Benson'. Charles was indignant: 'A second Swift, you mean.' Knox was an ideal bedside visitor. It was later said of him, 'the incredibly brilliant and accomplished R. was always there, intermingled with the near-saint and incomparable expositor of alive religion. But in all that he was he *gave* with both hands – spiritual help, scholarship, entertainment.'[22] With his clever, ironical view of the world and immense knowledge, Knox also worked at the War Office, along with his brother Dillwyn the code-breaker, which made the prospect of Charles working there all the more appealing.

Charles could see the War Office from Carlton House Terrace. The new neo-Baroque building housed its largest staff ever, nearly seven thousand of them in one thousand rooms linked with two and a half miles of corridors. They had even erected a new storey of wooden huts on the roof, known unofficially as 'Zeppelin Terrace'. He started almost immediately in Section IV, Military Intelligence, under Major Claude Dansey. Military was the largest intelligence section, preparing reports and liaising with MI5 on counter-espionage and counter-revolutionary matters. Dansey himself was later described as a 'copy-book secret service man. Dapper, establishment, Boodle's [Club], poker-playing expression, bitterly cynical, but with unlimited and illogical charm available particularly for women.'[23] There must also have been some charm available for men, as he was said to have been seduced by Robert Ross while at a boys' school in Bruges, Belgium.[24] Dansey was in charge of Political Section V, dealing with agents who served in Athens, including Charles's cousin Louis Christie, and on liaison duties with the French.

Although he was physically wounded, it was a source of great succour to Charles that he could continue to fight with his mind, on a different front, but in the same war.

CHAPTER 10

In Love with Wilfred Owen

> It was in January, 1918, at the crowded wedding of another poet, that I first saw him . . .
>
> CKSM, *The New Witness*, 10 December 1920

At Robert Graves's wedding on 23 January 1918 Charles met Wilfred Owen, a man who would enrich his life for ever, and wrote retrospectively in 1920 in *The New Witness*:

> I had been provisionally released from hospital a few days earlier, and had spent all that day, ineffectively, at a Police Court [magistrates' court]. I was too sore at first, in mind and body, to regard very closely the quiet little person who stood beside me in a room from which I longed only to escape. But that evening I met him again after dinner and found that we had already become, in some way, intimate friends.[1]

They were both uncomfortable. Charles's leg still gave him great pain and remained in an iron truss, and he on crutches. He was also deeply uncomfortable because earlier that day, at considerable risk to himself, he had given evidence in support of bail for his old friend Christopher Millard. Millard, now forty-five, was admitted to court that January for 'committing an act of gross indecency with a male person and being party to the commission by other male persons of acts of gross indecency'.[2] Charles's application in support of bail was rejected; Millard pleaded guilty and was given twelve months in Wormwood Scrubs prison without home leave.

A man with a homosexual past, which he regretted,[3] Robert Graves was marrying the eighteen-year-old elfin feminist, Nancy Nicholson, sister of the painter Ben Nicholson, and an artist herself.[4] Graves had thick, dark, curly hair and a crooked nose, broken playing rugby at school at Charterhouse. He had been about to take up a classical exhibition at St John's College, Oxford when interrupted by the war, and had published his first volume of poetry, *Over the Brazier*, two years later, in 1916. After Charles gave it a good review, a friendship between them sprang up. Graves was six years younger than Charles and had been invalided out of France with shell shock. Another wedding guest, Wilfred Owen, a fragile and unknown poet, was also recovering from shell shock.

A three-tier wedding cake was brought into the room to shouts and cheers from the guests, but it was a casing made of plaster, and, due to rationing, the real cake underneath was pitifully small and not very sweet. However, twelve bottles of champagne made up for wartime shortcomings. Owen had brought as a wedding present a set of eleven apostle spoons – explaining to the groom that the twelfth had been court-martialled for cowardice and was awaiting execution.[5] Throughout the war, over two hundred soldiers were executed for cowardice or desertion when it was likely they were suffering from shell shock. The year before, Graves had written to Charles telling him of his proposed new book of poems, *Fairies and Fusiliers*; he had mentioned Charles's bad review of Siegfried Sassoon's book of poems, but admitted he agreed with Charles's criticism and that one bad review was healthy. In response to his own poems Graves begged Charles's criticism before publication, writing again, three weeks before the wedding,

> Rotten missing you the other day. A certain compensation in meeting the noble Bainbrigge to whom I took an immediate like. But I should have preferred you both. Want to talk poetry again with someone who understands . . . Look here, I'll be brave and trust you with a book of my poems to look at, they are all unfinished. You can therefore note in pencil on the side possible alternatives . . . Also dear Charles please say if you think any paper would want any of them to publish. I only want advice. Yours ever, Robert le Diable.[6]

Charles had persuaded William Heinemann to publish *Fairies and Fusiliers* and his review appeared in *The New Witness* the day after Graves's wedding. He wrote, 'Posterity will give the palm to Mr Nichols for inspiration, to Mr Sassoon for technique and to Mr Graves for a kind of fancy, the elfin equivalent of humanity . . .' and ended, 'I cannot do justice to this book.'[7]

In spite of such strong ties, Charles longed to escape from the wedding reception, partly because the room was full of other poets, critics and writers. He used his *New Witness* column as a kind of diary from where he could write at length about whatever he liked and whichever books he pleased. He was not always kind, and some of his targets were in the room. After he had called Sassoon's war poems 'a regrettable incident', Sassoon had written to complain and Charles apologised, saying that he had 'enjoyed your book much more than I have said'.[8] Charles's eyes searched the room, but Sassoon wasn't there, surprising as he was also a close friend of Graves. In fact Graves had intervened the year before to protect Sassoon from being court-martialled for publishing in *The Times* his letter of 'wilful defiance', accusing the British Government of prolonging the war. Instead Sassoon was sent to Craiglockhart War Hospital to be 'treated for shell shock', where he had met Owen. Although he had sessions with the psychiatrist Dr Rivers, his condition was not like that of Owen and the other inmates who were stammering, trembling and screaming at night.

Wilfred Owen was not at ease at the wedding. He was intensely shy and intimidated by the company, not used to grand surroundings or famous people. At Craiglockhart he had nervously shown Sassoon his poems, and Sassoon had thought Owen a 'rather ordinary young man, perceptibly provincial',[9] when he first met him, adding, 'He was embarrassing. He had a Grammer School accent.'[10] Sassoon considered Owen's poems old-fashioned, yet he helped and encouraged Owen who responded with an admiration of Sassoon and his poetry that was close to hero worship, 'I love you, dispassionately, so much, so *very* much, dear Fellow, that the blasting little smile you wear on reading this can't hurt me in the least.'[11]

Owen's father was a railway clerk, and the family had struggled financially in his childhood. Having been to the local school and never gone to university, he was in awe of men like Sassoon, educated at public schools, with a private income, who hunted at weekends. Charles, in spite of his Winchester background, had more of the common touch, being Scottish and understanding the necessity of having to earn his own living: there was a genuine compassion in his regard for Owen. For Owen, the wedding reception in St James's Square was full of impressive people. The writer and cartoonist Max Beerbohm was there, as were Edward Marsh, the publisher William Heinemann, Roderick Meiklejohn, a civil servant from the Treasury, and the poets E. V. Lucas and Robert Nichols. Although Charles had just reviewed Nichols's new book and called it 'this dreadful stuff', Nichols had a mature reaction to criticism and didn't take offence. Charles may have been in pain from his leg and frustrated by the earlier court case, but he could still impress the quiet but attractive, sensitive and intelligent 'little person', Wilfred Owen.

Owen went from Graves's wedding to dinner at the Reform Club as a guest of Roderick Meiklejohn, who then took him to see Robert Ross at 40 Half Moon Street for after-dinner conversation. There Owen was met by two critics, More Adey and Charles. Charles monopolised him and was excited to learn that on his return to Scarborough where he was stationed, Owen would be near to Philip Bainbrigge, his oldest and dearest friend. 'To make these two men acquainted was a pleasure almost as great as to share in their fellowship' for he knew 'no two men could be more complementary'.[12] Charles escorted Owen back to the Imperial Hotel in Southampton Row and left him at 2 a.m. Back in Scarborough Owen did become friends with Bainbrigge. Now that even physically unfit men were being called up, Philip had enlisted in the Lancashire Fusiliers, having tried and failed to get into the same regiment as Charles. Practically blind without his thick glasses, he had memorised the standard army eye test, and passed with full marks. He and Owen met in a Scarborough oyster bar, a stark contrast to the army café that Owen was running for the officers of the Manchester Regiment. They discussed the German advance on Petrograd, and Bainbrigge 'opined that the whole of civilisation is extremely liable to collapse'.[13]

While Owen recovered from his mental wounds, Charles was still being treated for his physical ones. He couldn't look after his bulldog, Molly, properly, so she lived at Edgware with his mother and his brother's large family. Charles was in and out of hospital having treatment for his leg. In February 1918 he stayed with his family, pottering about among his books, which Meg had moved to Edgware, with the adoring Molly at his heels. Meg saw him off at the station, as he limped with his two sticks to catch the train, and she noted in her diary: 'The war has left him old and lonely – so many young friends and companions gone – and he has suffered so much.'[14]

Charles was back in hospital again four days later on doctor's orders. Much dismayed, he had woken from the latest operation to see that they had removed his entire calf muscle. The calf muscle was often commonly known as the 'heart spring muscle'. When someone walks with a spring in their step it's easy to see the heart is happy; the spring is impossible without the calf muscle and the effect of its removal was emotional as well as physical. He was still in hospital ten days later, unable to walk, but given crutches and leg supports. Robert Graves was writing to him about his own problems, 'My dear Charles, Your letter has comforted me in an evil moment: my fit of the "horrors" that comes on every two months. You know; the bursting shell and the dead men in holes.'[15] Using his position at the War Office, Charles then helped Graves transfer from the 3rd Battalion to the 16th as a Cadet Trainer, which avoided his having to go back to the front. Graves wrote a letter of thanks on 14 March, 'Owing entirely to your kindness I am now posted to no.16 and a nicer lot of people I haven't met for a long time.' He wrote out on the letter a fresh poem for Charles, a 'mediaeval phantasy, automatically written by curacao',[16] entitled 'Manticor'. A manticor is a mythical man-eating beast,

> . . . Sing then of ringstraked manticor,
> Man-visaged tiger who of yore
> Held whole Arabian waste in fee
> With raging pride from sea to sea . . .

Still not recovered, Charles was sent by the War Office for three weeks to Deene Park, Hertfordshire, a medieval and Tudor manor house in a fine park with a large stream running lazily through it, then used as a convalescent home. He lay in an antique bed in a 'huge room with hand painted wallpaper of cruel looking birds chasing dragonflies', and drew back the curtains at night to watch Rockingham Forest in the moonlight. The house was built on a quadrangle leading

Charles had this photo taken when he was 23 on a visit to Winchester, before the war. He gave a copy to Wilfred Owen in 1918 and one to Louis Christie in 1926.

Charles's parents: Meg was a working writer who travelled, took opium for her cough, painted, carved and kept a diary. George was a Sherriff with interests in literature and philanthropy.

Charles's mother in one of her homemade dresses, reading with her mother, the Gaelic-speaking Katherine, whose portrait as a young woman hangs behind them.

Weedingshall House, near Polmont, Stirlingshire, where Charles was born in 1889.

The extended family at their annual seaside gathering at Elie on the Fife coast on the eve of war, 1914. Charles is standing in the back row (3rd from left), with Tony and Mary Ray on his right. His brothers, Colin and John (back row, 6th and 8th from left), are there with their wives, Anna (back row, 7th from left) and Connie (middle row, 5th from left). Meg and George are in the middle row (4th and 6th from left).

Charles looking mischievous, aged 20, with his father and brother John, in 1910.

Charles (back row, first left) in his first year at Winchester with other scholars, 1903.

Charles aged 16, when he first met Robbie Ross.

Christopher Millard, Robbie Ross's secretary, who greatly influenced the young Charles. Millard was 36 when he met the 16-year-old Charles.

Robert Ross, disciple of Oscar Wilde, whose house on Half Moon Street became home for a literary and homosexual coterie.

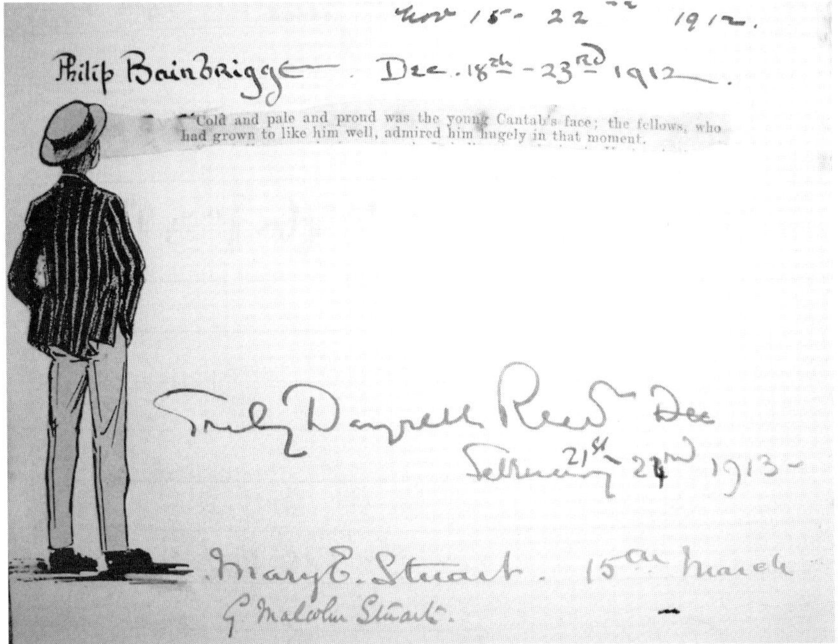

Philip Bainbrigge was a close friend of Charles's during his university years. This is his entry in the Edgemoor visitors' book.

Charles on a visit to Durie in 1916. He loved animals, dogs especially; later, in Italy, he kept a pet owl.

Charles surrounded by his first company in the KOSB at Portland Bill in 1914, before they set out for France. Charles was very attached to his men and hated leaving them whenever he got ill.

Robert Graves in 1920. Poet, writer, friend. Using his War Office contacts, Charles managed to get Graves a safe home posting in 1916, and as a critic he promoted Graves's poetry.

Wilfred Owen in 1916. Charles fell in love with Owen at Graves's wedding in 1918, subsequently writing him letters and sonnets.

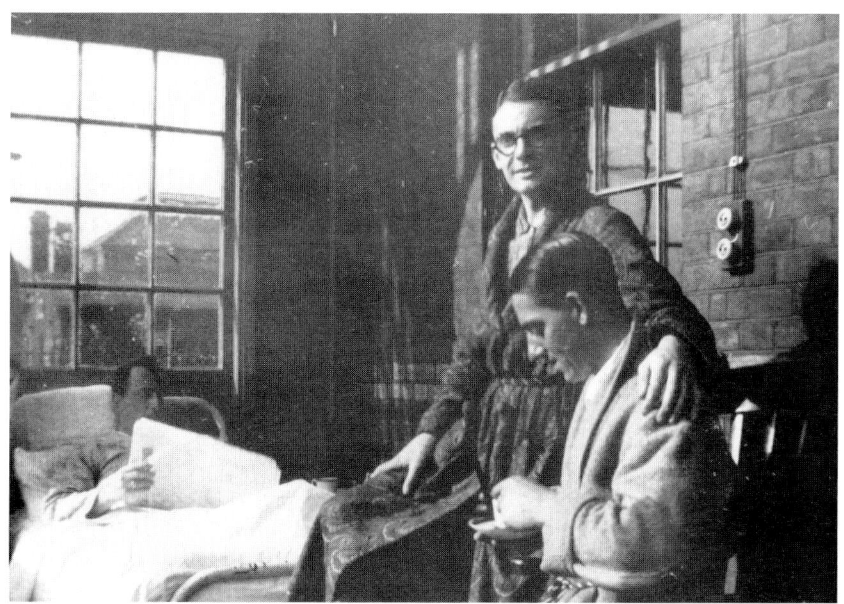

Charles (in spectacles) was badly wounded in the leg in 1917 and spent time in the Ducane Road specialist leg hospital.

1st August Ribemont sur l'Ancre Somme
22nd August. Bray sur Somme
29th – St Peter's Edinburgh.
5th Sept. Bray sur Somme
19th Sept. C Billon Wood & Bray
26th Sept. Bray sur Somme
17th Oct. Sailly-Laurette, Somme
31st Oct. Bray sur Somme (from Billon)
21st Nov. Cathedrale – Rouen. Sue [illegible]
Chapel – Grande Seminaire Rouen
28th Nov. Notre Dame Nice A.M.
5th, 8th Imm. Conc.
12th, 19th 25th Midnight C } Cathedral St Reparate
Mass, 25th High Mass, [illegible] } Nice.
2nd January 1916 } – Camp – Rouen
9th, 16th }
23rd 30th January } St Mary's, Lanark.
6th February }
20th February Saisseval par Picquigny
17th February Abbeville N-D. Somme
27th February Doullens, Somme.
12th March. Wanquetin. P. de C.
25th March (Lady Day) } Hospital St Jean
26th March } ARRAS
24th [illegible] ARRAS. P. de C.
16th April Palm Sunday)
Chapel (No 8 Hospital) Rouen
20th. M. Thursday. St Aloysius Oxford
21st Good Friday Cathedral Westminster
23rd C Easter Westminster Farm Street
Cathedral Westminster.
30th April } SS Peter & Edward Westminster
14th May }
11th June Whitsunday – St Mary's Cathedral Edinburgh
18th June Trinity. Cathedral Edinburgh

2nd July St Mary's Lanark
9th July St Peter's Edinburgh
16th July St Antony's Polmont
23rd July – St Mary's Cathedral Edinburgh
30th July – St John's Portobello
6th August. St Anne
13th 15th } Buxton
20th 27th }
3rd Sept. Westminster Cathedral
10th Sept. St Peter & St Edward Westminster & Cathedral
24th Cathedral W.
1st Oct. St Peter & Edward
8th }
15th } St Mary's Lanark
22nd }
27th Oct. St Peter's Edinburgh
All Saints St Mary's Lanark
5th Nov. St Peter's Edinburgh
12th Nov. St Mary's Lanark
15th (King Albert. Requiem for Belgians) Cathedral Edinburgh.
19th } St Mary's Lanark
26th }
30th Cathedral Edinburgh
3rd December " "
10th, 17th } St John's
24th C } Portobello
Midnight Mass C } St John's
3rd Mass Xmas } Portobello
31st Westminster

A page from Charles's Bible showing the places and dates he attended mass while in France from 1915 to 1916. He converted to Catholicism in 1915.

to a grand hall like a Cambridge college and was extraordinary by moonlight. He made friends with the owner, Bruno, who dressed for dinner in black silk knee-breeches and stockings and high white flannel waistcoat, like an engraving of a squire in a nineteenth-century novel. Bruno was desperate to marry . . .

> – only it will have to be an heiress as he can only just keep up the place . . . – and I think he feels that with his deafness, they might not exactly rush to marry him. He has lived there since September and it's begun to tell on him. These long passages and huge bedrooms on a winter's evening must be rather trying . . . No bathroom, no light but candles, no railway, delightfully secluded. I arrived when Bruno was out and found a wonderful equipage of tea, with butter which I literally have not seen since January the 7th.[17]

Charles returned to London refreshed and almost well, feeling that he had lived for a while in the borrowed beauty of a bygone age. He was full of energy for his new friendship with Owen. We do not know how often Charles saw him between January and May, but he later wrote, 'Over the next few months I saw Wilfred become happy again, though his dreams were still nightmares, and his thick hair was shot with white.'[18] He watched and encouraged Owen's fresh enthusiasm for the reading and writing of poetry.

On 16 May Owen got a long weekend leave, arriving in London on Thursday evening. Robert Ross let him use the flat above his at 40 Half Moon Street; Charles's lodgings were nearby in Arlington Street, round the corner from the Ritz Hotel on Piccadilly. Owen spent Friday with Charles at the War Office where they talked about the prospect of a home posting lecturing to a cadet battalion. They were both war shattered and mentally fragile. There was another reason for their excited discussion. Charles had recently 'found in the coolness of Hatchards on a hot afternoon' a copy of the *Chanson de Roland*. It was a school text showing both Old French and modern, done by M. Petit de Julleville; reading it married his training in ancient language and his current war experience in France; and, 'amid the distractions of that summer in London, where the sound of the olifant came so often and so direfully across the Channel, Roland was a constant solace'.[19]

In his free time he translated the first fourteen verses and showed them to Owen. He wanted to keep the feel of an ancient ballad, while still making it understandable in modern English. The key to this was *assonance,* the elusive repetition of vowel sounds to create internal rhyming; also *consonance* or the repetition of two or more consonant sounds. This took its cue from the original Old French, but was not common in English poetry:

> Li reis Marsilie esteit en Sarraguce.
> Alez en est en un verger suz l'umbre;
> Sur un perrun de marbre bloi se culchet,
> Envirun lui plus de vint milie humes.
> Il en apelet e ses dux e ses cuntes:
> «Oëz, seignurs, quel pecchet nus encumbret:
> Li emper[er]es Carles de France dulce
> En cest païs nos est venuz cunfundre.

Charles's translation reads:

> King Marsilies he lay in Sarraguce,
> Went he his way into an orchard cool;
> There on his throne he sate, of marble blue,
> Round him his men, full twenty thousand, stood.
> Called he forth then his counts, also his dukes:
> 'My Lords, give ear to our impending doom:
> That Emperour, Charlès of France the Douce,
> Into this land is come, us to confuse.

Owen's French was good; before the war he had lived in France and taught English at the Berlitz School in Bordeaux where the elderly symbolist poet Laurent Tailhade had encouraged him in his ambition to become a poet. Owen encouraged Charles to continue translating the Chanson using assonance – which he was also beginning to use in his own poetry, as well as pararhyme. They had discussions about the seemingly infinite scope of assonance and its effect on both the ear and the meaning. Pararhyme was half-rhyme vowel variation but the same consonant pattern: lover/liver, hall/hell, eyes/bless. They were explorers in poetic territory.

Owen spent Saturday with the aristocratic poet Osbert Sitwell and Sunday evening with Charles again. Slightly jealous of Owen's other friends, Charles showed Owen that he could pass judgement on Sitwell and Sassoon alike. He had just reviewed three anthologies of poetry for *The New Witness* the week before: *A Book of Verse on the Great War* edited by R. Wheeler, from the Yale University press, *Georgian Poetry 1916–17*, from The Poetry Bookshop and *The Muse in Arms*, edited by E. B. Osborn, which contained Charles's 'The Field of Honour', 'Domum', 'The Willow Tree Bough' and 'Back in Billets', along with poems by Rupert Brooke, Julian Grenfell, Nichols, Graves, Sassoon, Sitwell and Charles Sorley. He wrote, 'Captain Sitwell represents what might be called the Saki and Lawrence school of poetry – showing us the massive dignity of a Lawrence portrait peppered and salted with the wit of a Chronicle of Clovis.' He called Sassoon's 'Rear Guard' a 'singularly vivid and effective war-photograph'. However, he went on to write that Sassoon had obviously suffered in action with an effect easy to discern in his work, that his 'bitter cynicism contrasts harshly with the ingenuity of his earlier work'.[20] Impressed, Owen quoted several sentences from Charles's review in a letter home.

Owen was pleased that Charles had mentioned him in his criticism of the first American selection by Wheeler: 'Our younger fame seems not to have reached him: there is nothing in by Robert Nichols, Robert Graves, Siegfried Sassoon, W. J. Turner, Wilfred Owen, Osbert Sitwell . . .' Given that Owen had never published anything, it was a blast of advance publicity. Later that night Charles saw him off for his return to Ripon. It was a calm, clear, moonlit night as Charles limped back from the station to his lodgings – perfect for an air raid. He was woken from his sleep by cries in the street and the firing of guns – a large-scale German air attack, the sixth of the year was starting over London. It lasted less than an hour but over forty people were killed and two hundred wounded. Four planes were brought down as thousands of curious sightseers watched a pitched aerial battle. The next day Charles wrote a sonnet expressing his sadness at Owen leaving and his disappointment in returning to a 'lone bed', but relief at his safety,

All Clear

Last night into the night I saw thee go
And turned away; and heavy of heart I clambered
Up the steep causeway; weary, late and slow
By my lone bed arrived. But, I enchambered,
Out cried the sullen alert artillery;
Shrill watchmen; woke the slumbering streets in riot.
And I was sad for my night's swallowing thee,
Then was I glad because thy night was quiet.
But wer't thou near, I should not be afraid,
But, thou away, there is no harm to fear;
Thou not endangered, I am undismayed,
Yet must danger hide when thou art here.
So I am double saved and safe shall stay
Thine arms being close or all thyself away.[21]

It was a tender wish, with a physical longing for Owen, which Owen did not reciprocate. Like Graves, he started sending his poems to Charles, asking his technical advice and also hoping he would use his influence to get them published in literary magazines, like the *Fortnightly Review*, the *Westminster Gazette* or *The Nation*. When Charles wrote a draft dedication for *The Song of Roland* and gave it to Owen, Owen was flattered enough to keep it, along with a love sonnet from Charles and a photograph taken of him in 1913; in his golden youth looking handsome and unblemished by war. The dedication began 'To you, my master in assonance, I dedicate my part in this assonant poem . . .' He then wove in to this dedication his entire ethos as an officer, something he would significantly impress on Owen and that would influence Owen's return to the front:

> At this time lessons are to be found in the Song of Roland that all of us may profitably learn. To pursue chivalry, to avoid and punish treachery, to rely upon our own resources, and to fight uncomplainingly when support is withheld from us; to live, in fine, honourably and to die gallantly. So I have worked and written that the Song our Saxon forebears heard our Norman forebears shout at Hastings – may not be altogether unheard in their children's armies.[22]

Again he was linking himself with soldiers from the past, and taking their wisdom to pass on to soldiers of today. Early in their friendship, Owen had composed a ballad, which could describe a scene from the *Chanson de Roland*:

> Nay, light me no fire tonight,
> Page Eglantine;
> I have no desire tonight
> To drink or dine;
> I will suck no briar tonight,
> Nor read no line:
> An you be my quire tonight,
> And you my wine.

They both identified with soldiers in all time, past and present. When Owen wrote his poem

> I am the ghost of Shadwell Stair.
> Along the wharves by the water-house,
> And through the cavernous slaughter-house,
> I am the shadow that walks there.

the first person he sent it to was Charles, who, for fun, translated it into French. *'Je suis le petit revenant du Bassin; le long du quai, par l'abreuvoir, et dans l'immonde abattoir j'y piétine, ombre fantassin.'*[23]

Charles later said in a letter to Edward Marsh that Owen's reaction when he read the translation had been that the last word, *'fantassin'*, meaning infantry soldier, was the word which gave the key to its meaning: 'During the influenza epidemic in 1918, I tried to turn it into French prose, rhymed. I give the first verse, on account of the last word, which Owen welcomed rather as tho' it put the key in the lock of the whole.'[24] This was the ghost of an infantry soldier, perhaps one he himself had killed. Owen was also working on 'Strange Meeting', a poem that took several drafts and concerned the poet meeting his opponent soldier, or his own doppelgänger, in the underworld, talking to him, and accepting the truth of what he has done in killing him. It has a discomforting use of pararhyme throughout,

And by his smile, I knew that sullen hall;
By his dead smile, I knew we stood in Hell.

Meanwhile Charles, pursuing chivalry and dreaming of heaven, wrote a more explicit sonnet and gave it to Owen who kept and dated it 19 May. Written in turquoise ink on Half Moon Street paper, the first R is decorated and enlarged like an illuminated letter:

Remembering rather all my waste of days
Ere I had learned the wonders thou hast shewn
Blame not my tongue that did not speak thy praise
Having no language equal to thy own
Blame not my eyes that, from their high aim lowered
Yet saw there more than other eyes may see
Nor blame head heart hands feet, that overpowered
Fell at thy feet to draw thy heart to me.
Blame not me all that was found unworthy
But let me guard some fragment of thy merit,
That, though myself dissolve in the earth, being earthy,
In thy long fame some part I may inherit.
So through the ages while the bright stars dwindle
At thy fresh sun my moon's cold face I'll kindle.[25]

The sonnet was hurriedly dashed off, and restricted by the constraints of its genre. However its sentiment is full of hero worship, like the address of a medieval knight to his lady, written by a man who was mentally living the *Chanson de Roland*, and laying himself at the feet of the young man whose mind, soul and poetry he ardently admired. The poem was also visionary in its certainty of Owen's future fame. Because of the line, 'Blame not my eyes that, from their high aim lowered/ Yet saw there more than other eyes may see', the sonnet may have implied a failed seduction. Owen was not so enamoured of Charles, writing in a letter to his mother two days later, 'Scott Moncrieff is a lamed Captain, related to the General of that name known as the "Father of the War Office".'[26] He described him as a 'lamed Captain' not a poet or a critic, or an intimate friend, but someone with influence who could help him get a home posting.

Charles did start applications at the War Office that weekend to try to get Owen a position training troops in Britain as he had been able to for Graves. Slow negotiations followed between the General Staff, who were satisfied with Owen's competence, and the Adjutant-General's Department who had found it necessary to insist on the return of every fit man to the field. Charles pursued the work of both war and love with unequal energy. The sonnet was followed eight days later by the following letter,

> No sealing of the fount of passion is indicated by the cessation of the flow of sonnets – but simply an inflow of work here which will keep me busy till this damn pamphlet leaves the printers.

He was writing a propaganda pamphlet.

> Nichols turned up today and Graves's brother yesterday who wants to go and be a cadet at Oxford. We might send you to teach him.

Word was out that Charles saved poets from the front, and he dangled the power, but returned to his love for Owen,

> As to the sonnets – you mustn't take them too seriously. It's vivisection really – of both you and me – I want very much to add to the Shakespeare controversy[27] a conclusive word based on experience. I feel pretty certain Shakespeare selected some wight to whom he sent 'From Fairest Creatures' in a letter . . . He made use of the amazing free lines which as simple lines were always coming into his head . . . Bare ruined choirs where late the sweet birds sang, Rough winds do shake the darling buds of May etc etc Lines which had obviously come first like raisins on the kitchen table before the mince pies are mixed. Hurry up and send me Aliens. Either Aliens or Aliens of War you must call it. Alter that line about experience and I will try and get it into the Fortnightly.[28]

The letter is written hurriedly in the same turquoise ink used for both the sonnet and the *Chanson* dedication, on a page ripped from a jotter, yet Owen kept it carefully. Was Charles trying to say that he did not really mean this passion, was it passing, was it all just an experiment for the sake of poetry? Owen might have reacted differently if he had encountered love, rather than 'vivisection', but Charles was trying not to frighten Owen with the strength of his passion. We do not know if there were any letters from Owen to Charles at this point.[29]

On 7 June *The New Witness* published Charles's old sonnet to Alec Tonnochie, 'Thinking Love's Empire lay along that way/ Where the new-duggen grave of friendship gaped . . .' which indicated that a step too far over friendship had been attempted, that physical love might have spoilt the friendship. This time it was meant for Owen to read.

The pre-war Charles, the younger, healthier, carefree Charles would have been more likely to succeed at seduction. But the sick, limping, less handsome, careworn and Catholic Charles stopped short, or started then stopped, realising the ardour was one-sided. It is unlikely that the conservative and law-abiding Owen would have welcomed an advance: his poetry admired beauty in younger men, while Charles was aged by war wounds and covered in eczema.[30] He laid claim to a greater privilege as he wrote in his sonnet to Owen published with the *Chanson de Roland*; that of sharing with Owen the light of 'eternal day' in heaven, where their 'contented ghosts' would stay together for ever.

Graves had written to Charles on 24 March that year, 'You are splendid the way you look after the post-Georgians: may God requite your labours with one really good poet.'[31] But the poet Charles recognised at once as 'really good' was the man he had fallen in love with at Graves's wedding. Graves went on blithely to fantasise:

> I think a farm on the Downs would be great fun. You would manage the office. S.S. [Sassoon] the horses, Nancy and I the ploughing and sowing and spuds, Bob Nichols the sheep with an oaten pipe. Robbie Ross would hang the pictures and act as mess president – Alec Waugh perhaps the ducks and hens . . .[32]

Charles used his influence and two of Owen's poems were published in *The Nation* on 15 June. 'Hospital Barge' and 'Futility' both explored assonance, and the first also had an archaic feel:

> Budging the sluggard ripples of the Somme
> A barge round old Cerisy slowly slewed.

Softly her engines down the current screwed,
And chuckled softly with contented hum.[33]

Charles showed the poem he had advised Owen to retitle 'Aliens', but which Owen called 'The Deranged', to Osbert Sitwell, who wanted to include it in the next edition of *Wheels*. Owen, no doubt influenced by Charles's critical attitude to the Sitwells, wanted to read a copy of *Wheels* before agreeing to be part of it. 'I want to see the Sitwells' etc. works before I decide to co-appear in a book!'[34]

June was a month of intense public stress. The war was still raging, a flu epidemic was killing more people than the war, and amid the unrest came an extreme popular movement. Noel Pemberton Billing, an MP and aviator, alleged that the war was being lost because of corruption in high places. There were, he insisted, a band of homosexuals in prominent positions who passed secrets to the Germans, all named in a Black Book containing 47,000 names. Oscar Wilde's play *Salome* was in rehearsal for a production starring an actress called Maud Allan, whose erotic dancing evoked the character well. Billing alleged that Allan was part of a lesbian cult called the Cult of the Clitoris, linked, he claimed, to the colourful Margot Asquith, wife of the last Prime Minister. Allan took Billing to court for defamatory libel. The libel case stirred up the same sort of prurient public hysteria surrounding the trial of Oscar Wilde and Billing was acquitted to huge popular acclaim.

Charles at once used the only weapon at his disposal, his irony, in an article called 'The Moral Curfew', published on 21 June. 'How the nations, allied, neutral and enemy will laugh: they will laugh themselves almost into an armistice at the picture of Englishmen sitting urbanely down, the barbarian at their gates, to disapprove of one another's morals', 'let us line the grate, thoughout the coming winter, with the grimy pages of Wilde, Pater, Swinburne, Rossetti, Ruskin, Beddoes, Keats, Shelley, Congreve . . . and above all the unutterably slimy Shakespeare' . . . 'so we shall establish for all time on these islands an Intellectual Uniformity.'[35] He concluded that his fellow soldiers would rather fall and die in battle than return to find Mr Billing on the throne of justice. To Vyvyan Holland he wrote, 'I have not minced my words in my article and rather hope it will land me in the courts as I have wanted to do murder on a certain nobleman [undoubtedly Alfred

Douglas] for some time.'[36] He was trying to reassure Vyvyan, for the Billing trial reminded the papers of the Wilde trial and disinterred long-buried feelings of shame. He assured Vyvyan that it was a diversion, 'Everyone forgot the war here altogether, especially we who have taken a mild professional interest in it.' He said it would all pass quickly: 'You see, English people have barely heard of Salome and foreign people have never heard of Billing.' Then he made light of it, 'I am not really so sorry for you, though I am sorry for Miss Allan who is practically kicked off the earth, and for no fault whatever in this world save the exercise of her lawful profession.'[37]

Charles's relations with his family were close and good, although his intimate life had always been a secret and would remain so. Meg helped Charles to move from his expensive lodgings in Arlington Street to a cheaper but no less smart address in 70b Cadogan Square. 'A tiny cleverly contrived little house, looked as if it had been a cottage once, tiny, tiny rooms,'[38] noted the tall Meg. The house in Cadogan Square belonged to an elderly lady called Lady Augusta Fane whom Charles had met at Deene Park and who wanted a paying guest. They became great friends and a month later Charles invited Lady Augusta to meet his mother and the whole family at Edgware. He used the outing as an opportunity to pick up books and clothes, and Lady Augusta stayed to lunch. Meg noted that Charles looked much better and happier and she thought he seemed reconciled to never being fit for active service again. 'The lame leg is an inch shorter than the other but he has had a large thick boot made for it so that walking is easier. But he will always limp, I'm afraid,'[39] she ended.

At the War Office Charles was still struggling to get Owen a home posting. Given another medical, Owen was placed on a list for France on 11 August, then taken off it again. He was safe for a while until the Military Secretary's department claimed paradoxically that, having been returned home a year earlier in a condition that hinted at loss of morale under shell fire, he could only under shell fire be entrusted with the command of men. The case was put more briefly, but in words that Charles thought did not look well in print. Essentially he was accused of cowardice and would have to prove his valour in combat if he wanted to clear his name. By the end of the month of August Owen was back on a draft for France. Charles's last meeting with him was on the hot night of 30 August. Charles was, he admitted, 'irritable and ill', sickened by his failure to keep Owen in England and angry with himself for his unhealed wounds and the endless strain of working and living in London. Owen wrote to his mother the next morning: 'Arriving at Victoria I had to wheel my own baggage down the platform and through the streets to the hotel which was full. But I got a bed as I . . .'[40] The lower half of the page is missing. Charles's account continues: 'If I was harsh with him, may I be forgiven, as we tramped wearily round the overflowing hotels. In the end a bed was found in Eaton Square, and we sat down to a strange supper in the Queen Mary Hut, a cenotaph, now vanished, which covered many such last nights in England.'[41] Owen wrote, 'found no room in Hotels so got put up in an Officers' club thanks to S. Moncrieff's knowledge of the region.'[42]

From Eaton Square, Charles took Owen the half-mile to his own room in Cadogan Square to 'a few intense hours of books and talk in my lodging'. Then he accompanied him back to the Hut where Owen realised, Charles reported later, that he had, 'left his stick behind, but insisted that it was too late to return. I left him on the doorstep and went home to find not only the stick but his pocket-book with, I suppose, all his money on my table. I went back with them, but I hope he was already asleep. I never saw him again.'[43]

It was maintained by one of Owen's biographers, Dominic Hibberd, that a seduction of Owen by the older Charles took place at Cadogan Square. The fact that Owen's pocketbook was left behind, Hibberd said, would not have happened had he not removed his clothes.[44] But a pocketbook can be taken out and left behind for many reasons: to make notes or share photographs, or simply because the mind of a poet is on other things. We do not know where the landlady, Lady Augusta, was that night; if she was at home a seduction was unlikely. Charles was certainly romantically in love with Owen. It is more likely, considering the sonnet in turquoise ink, that an attempted seduction took place in May, and in spite of it the friendship continued, with Owen keeping Charles's letters and poems. Charles walked miles that night in August: first to Victoria, then to Eaton Square and round about looking for the hotel, then back to Cadogan Square. He escorted Owen back to his room then returned and made another trip later with the wallet and stick. Walking on his wounded leg was still slow and painful for Charles and he exerted himself well beyond endurance.

The two men had a profound effect on each other: on Charles, professionally, because he had met a poet so superior to him in his writing that he felt he should give up his own poetry for good; he called Owen 'a master of assonance'. The friendship set Charles on the course of ceasing to write poetry and turning to translation, which would also, unlike poetry, provide an income. Owen had relied on Charles to get him a posting in Britain and, although Charles failed to do this because he was, sadly, not the last word at the War Office, Owen himself felt he ought to return to the front. Charles's attitude to the war was well known; it appeared in his reviews: he was not against the war, did not think it was all folly and a waste of time, rather he believed that Britain was fighting to protect itself against invasion. He honoured its history and culture; also he held that as men together in the field, the soldiers were fighting for each other.

By 2 September Owen was in France in the Base Camp at Etaples: there was a YMCA rest hut there run by Conal O'Riordan, the Irish novelist with whom he had become friends. Charles was determined not to lose Owen and at once set about getting himself sent to France again. With his limp there was no hope of active service, but within his Military Intelligence Department at the War Office was the Press and Propaganda section, known as MI7,[45] and through that he applied for the position of Assistant Press Officer to the General Headquarters of the British Expeditionary Force in France. He failed his first medical, but with all his determination passed the second on 19 September 1918. The medical report ran: 'He states he can manage to walk for 9 or 10 miles a day. He cannot run at all. Degree of dis-ablement 30%.'[46]

He invited his mother to lunch with him at the Savile Club on his twenty-ninth birthday, 23 September, to say goodbye, but it was too crowded and they went to Jermyn Street instead. For Meg it was not so sad a leave-taking as the previous farewells; as a press officer with a bad limp he would not be in mortal danger as before. Charles found a new home for Molly, who required a tough master, with a retired army captain. On 11 October, Gladys Dalyell came to visit Meg, looking very pretty and told her, blushing, that Charles had taken her to dinner with friends and to the theatre afterwards. Gladys was in love with Charles who was in love with Owen who hero-worshipped Sassoon who was in love with someone else altogether.

That month, October 1918, Charles met E. J. Dent, the Cambridge musicologist who was part of the elite homosexual coterie that included Sassoon and the novelist E. M. Forster. He gave Dent the ballad he had written, the one he had read to Gladys two years before in front of the fire in Lanark. This time it represented the sentiment he felt for Owen, 'My heart is at war with a good-natured rifleman' and Dent set it to music.

Charles went to Edgware to deposit his boxes and pack the things he wanted to take to France. An evocative letter arrived from Richard Reginald Ball, a friend from Edinburgh days, and the original inspiration of the sonnet 'My Mistake'. Ball was working as a medical orderly on the Russian Front and described the funeral of a refugee in the snow, led by children holding icons and a woman carrying a wooden cross for the grave,

> shoulders hunched against the intense cold, followed by bearers carrying the body in its white grave clothes lying in the open coffin. The white linen seemed frozen like very thin white ice. It was half a mile walk from the church onto the open steppe behind the village. The children who were too small, very small people in diminutive sheepskins – passed by the body and blew a breath to it several times. Breath, in the church in front of the open west door is a very visible thing. When you open a door in going into a cottage, the cold air leaps into the room like a dragon across the floor in front of you, shooting out tongues of white steam.[47]

Charles and Meg both knew that with Russia in a turmoil of revolution and bloodshed, there was little chance that Ball was still alive. Then on the morning of 3 October, Charles read in *The Times* of the death of one of his closest friends, Philip Bainbrigge, killed instantly on 18 September as he was leading a patrol over a sunken road where the enemy were hiding.

Shocked and saddened, feeling stalked by death, Charles went out to the theatre then to Half Moon Street with a relatively new friend, the young, and as yet unknown, Noël Coward, whom he had met the year before. In his autobiography *Present Indicative*, Coward wrote, 'I will put on record that between 1917 and 1919, I knew . . .' then a list of eight people with whom he was 'intimate', including the actress Gertrude Lawrence and Charles Scott Moncrieff. He then listed those with whom he was on pleasant but not intimate terms, and finally those whom he could nod to and be nodded to by. He was therefore, on his own admission, intimate[48] with Charles. Coward was eighteen and announced himself as a 'boy actor'. Sassoon had chosen the same evening to drop in unannounced, having escaped from a loud Bloomsbury party after the ballet. Sassoon was still hurt by Charles's barbed review three months earlier. Charles was too caustic for him, too pedantic and scholarly and eager to criticise. That evening Sassoon was 'unpardonably petulant' and Charles guarded and morose. Seemingly oblivious to this atmosphere, Coward was delighted to meet Sassoon, who in turn found him 'gushing'.[49] Coward told Sassoon excitedly that he had just spent a holiday in Cornwall lying on a rock reading *Counter Attack* out loud to the female novelist G. B. Stern. He begged for his autograph and Sassoon reluctantly inscribed a copy of the poems from several lying on Ross's table. He was not in the mood for bubbling sociability; when he made to leave, Ross saw him to the door. He took his hand and Sassoon looked at Ross for a long moment, later writing: 'His worn face, grey with exhaustion and ill-health, was beatified by sympathy and affection.'[50] Two days later, at the age of fifty, Ross died suddenly of a heart attack.

After this strange evening, Charles spent the day with Philip Bainbrigge's father who showed him a letter from Philip's commanding officer – who had been in hospital with Charles the year before – and they consoled each other. Charles showed him Philip's own poem about the possibility of his death, which he had sent to Charles at the time of Brooke's 'If I should die', of which it was a parody:

> If I should die, be not concerned to know
> The manner of my ending, if I fell
> Leading a forlorn charge against the foe,
> Strangled by gas, or shattered by a shell.
> Nor seek to see me in this death-in-life
> Mid shrieks and curses, oaths and blood and sweat,
> Cold in the darkness, on the edge of strife,
> Bored and afraid, irresolute, and wet.

But if you think of me, remember one
Who loved good dinners, curious parody,
Swimming, lying naked in the sun,
Latin hexameters, and heraldry,
Athenian subtleties of δηζ and ποιζ,
Beethoven, Botticelli, beer, and boys.[51]

Charles crossed the Channel on a troopship the next day, and only heard that evening of the death of Robert Ross, his 'kindest of friends'. Immediately after the news of Bainbrigge, it doubled the pain. He wrote to Owen at once with the news. Owen, meanwhile, had led his company in a victorious attack on the Fonsomme line and having been immediately cited for gallantry, looked forward to a Military Cross. On 7 October he wrote Charles a letter that was 'big with his pride in his company who had fought well and with amusement that the War Office who had besmirched his character would have to announce the award of his military cross'.[52]

My dear Scott Moncrieff,
I received your note in a pill-box which I and my glorious little company had captured a few hours previously.

You may be able to inform yourself of the circumstances and Effects (in the Sassoonic sense) of our attack (2nd Man. Regt.) of Oct. 1st. I'm really glad to have been recommended, and hope an M.C. will come through – for the confidence it will give me in dealing with civilians.

I'm frightfully busy (as O.C.D.) and many glorious Cries of the blood still lying on my clothes will have to be stifled.

My Captain, wounded, was Somerville, M.C., of Edinburgh Univ. He thinks he knew you there. I find I never wrote a letter with so much difficulty as this. Perhaps I am tired after writing so many relations of casualties. Or perhaps from other causes.

I am far enough out of the line to feel the acute discomforts of Billets (ramshaks of corrugated iron.) Do write soon, with all the news you can spare of Peace Possibilities.

Yours ever W.O.[53]

He found he 'never wrote a letter with so much difficulty as this'. And thinks perhaps that he is tired, 'Or perhaps from other causes'. The unspoken question hangs in the air. Did he now, upon reflection of the shortness of life, find that he did in fact reciprocate Charles's feelings of romantic love?

But life sped on. From 8 October, in one of the greatest achievements of the war, the British Forces took three days to fight through the strongest section of the Hindenburg Line. So rapid were the advances that it was difficult to keep day-to-day records of the front. Charles experienced the exhilaration of travelling with the journalists William Beach Thomas and Philip Gibbs in a hooded car with a very low roof in the wake of the advancing troops. In a few hours they travelled the same distance they had crawled forward in three years of trench warfare and Charles hoped to whisk over to see Owen in the same car. However just at that moment Owen's battalion moved to Bohain, to Bussigny and then to St Souplet. The brilliant young poet, only twenty-five years old, was killed on the line west of Oise-Sambre Canal six days before the war ended. Charles did not hear of his death until weeks later.

After staying with the journalists at GHQ in Amiens, Charles then motored across five miles of destroyed country amid rumours that the Kaiser had abdicated, that there was revolution in Berlin, and so forth. He was in Lille when General Birdwood marched in with his troops and exchanged flags with the mayor, surrounded by rejoicing people.

On Armistice Day, 11 November, Charles was supervising a photographer and a cameraman capturing a series of momentous meetings:

> Sir Douglas Haig and the Army Commanders met in conference, duly photographed and filmed by two of my men, a historic scene, a small knot of troops outside, motor drivers, etc. When the chief came out they suddenly gave a ringing cheer, which you will see in the film by the row of opening mouths. After lunch, the Prince of Wales slipped up very quietly in an open car to congratulate the Chief on winning the war. Today's excitement is the repatriates, who are beginning to come through. There is much to do and so few of us to do it that I quite despair.[54]

Until Christmas, Charles was busy flying about France and Flanders with his photographers making records of great events. His base and flat were in Lille which had a theatre where he and his fellow officers staged the Christmas pantomime for the troops. As befitting his role in the Propaganda Department, he wrote a patriotic song on the back of the playbill. 'I fancy,' he wrote to his mother, 'I can retain some sort of job here as long as the Army lasts, and hope during that time to pick up enough health to face the struggle for existence at home. The prospect is not very bright, and I can easily understand that partly disabled men will be a drag in the market and command a very low wage. A profound apathy reigns everywhere except in the demob branches.'[55]

It was in Lille, that December, that he eventually heard of Owen's death, and he sat down in his cold but comfortable flat above a shop to write his last sonnet to the man he loved, later published as one of the three dedicatory poems in his *Chanson de Roland*. Certain of Owen's greatness, he wondered possessively whether he would form part of it in centuries to come.

> When in the centuries of time to come,
> Men shall be happy and rehearse thy fame,
> Shall I be spoken of then, or they grow dumb,
> Recall thy glory and forget thy shame?
> Part of thy praise, shall my dull verses live
> In thee, themselves – as life without thee – vain?
> So should I halt, oblivion's fugitive,
> Turn, stand, smile, know myself a man again.

The poem ends with the sort of sentiment a man would write on his wife's tombstone, that of longing for the day when they would meet again in heaven.

> I care not: not the glorious boasts of men
> Could wake my pride, were I in Heaven with thee;
> Nor any breath of envy touch me, when,
> Swept from the embrace of mortal memory
> Beyond the stars' light, in the eternal day,
> Our contented ghosts stay together.

In a school debate at Winchester in the spring of 1907, he had held that 'loyalty died after the Battle of Flodden. Courage and loyalty were pre-eminent in ancient warfare . . .'[56] But his innocent idealism had not been killed by the war. In fact he had tackled fiercely and rejected the attitude of futility and cynicism about war in books and poems he reviewed. Throughout the conflict Charles had produced a steady stream of criticism from trenches, base camps, rest areas and hospitals. He had reviewed many books on the war and been savagely critical of most. He suggested that war played a trick on English poets, distorting their perspective, confusing their roles and exiling their muses. He maintained that real poets did not improve through war, if anything they deteriorated. He attacked the emotion war inspired in poetry, its demolition of idealism, its degradation of human hope. Poetry for him was about truth and beauty and preserving these as shields for the human heart. This sentiment was expressed in Owen's last poem, 'Strange Meeting':

> Whatever hope is yours
> Was my life also; I went hunting wild
> After the beauty in the world,
> Which lies not calm in eyes, or braided hair,
> But mocks the steady running of the hour,
> And if it grieves, grieves richlier than here.

To say that the war was a futile exercise and a pointless cull of lives was a slur on the memory of his friends. Owen's death left a crater in Charles's life. Owen's poetry changed for ever the way we look at war. Charles recognised this, not distinguishing between his feeling for Owen's poetry and his love of Owen himself. Much later he wrote to Owen's mother, describing a passion based on a mutual love of poetry.

> Owen was during the last year of his life, one of my most intimate friends; and I may therefore (though I think not) be prejudiced in my opinion that in his death the war dealt the severest of all its blows on English Letters. He employed a very thorough knowledge of English poetry with exceptional taste, and, while eminently sound in his derivations, was equally daring in innovation.

Charles went on to discus Owen's use of assonance and to compare him to Pope, Swinburne, Keats and Milton, but ended the letter:

> As I read these passages over they seem to me terribly priggish and cold blooded as if I cared only for W's literary value, and not for the inestimable value of his friendship.[57]

After Owen's death, Charles was cold-shouldered by the group of war poets he had thought were his friends. The light and intimate correspondence between Charles and Graves stopped abruptly after Owen's death when a rumour went out from the Half Moon Street group that Charles had seduced Owen. This also stopped any communication from Sassoon and the Sitwells who had prepared Owen's first book of poetry for publication, even though Charles himself owned a number of Owen's first drafts. There was no proof anywhere of seduction, there were no witnesses and no confessions. However, the rumour later found its way into the first edition of *Goodbye to All That*, Graves's autobiographical novel of the First World War, published in 1929. Harold Owen, Wilfred's brother, started a libel suit and had the entire first edition pulped, and a second 'first edition' had to be issued three months later. Graves never spoke to Charles again, and continued to believe that he had seduced Owen. The whole incident was shrouded in gossip, half truths and hypocrisy.

CHAPTER II

Sniping in the Literary World

> The flash of one poet catching almost intuitively the emotion of another long dead . . .
>
> Richard Aldington, *Times Literary Supplement*
> 11 December 1919

After covering the first few months of the Paris Peace Conference Charles sailed back to England on 3 April 1919 looking very thin. He was a ghost of his former self. The war had taken in an ebullient and confident man and delivered home someone prematurely aged and weary – physically broken, in constant pain from his injuries and bereaved of his finest friends. At least he was alive.

Even finding lodgings was a trial. On his first visit to Edgware, he told his mother that he felt constantly tired; he had spent one night in a hotel near Piccadilly, but on going back the next night found they had sublet his room and thrown out all his things. He then passed a night in the Turkish Baths at the RAC club, there being no spare room in the club rooms, either. Luckily he bumped into an acquaintance, Lady Hill, who invited him to stay with her; relieved, he took the next day off and took his mother to lunch with Lady Hill in town. Charles made a habit of making good friends with genteel elderly landladies whom he always introduced to his mother. Lady Hill also owned a seaside cottage in Sandwich which Charles rented for a week in May as a present for his brother Colin's family.

Not yet demobilised, he was employed every day at the Imperial War Museum cataloguing the photographs he had supervised in France. The Army recommended him for a staff job if his health improved; a report advised he was 'possessed of initiative, quick-witted, a hard worker and good disciplinarian.'[1] His health, however, did not improve and though a permanent job would have been reassuring at the time, his ambitions were literary. The war had battered not only the physical but also the creative self and, after meeting Owen, he no longer saw himself as a poet. Criticism, satirical verse and translation – the minor, but no less important, writers' roles – all beckoned.

He continued writing weekly for *The New Witness*. After the war, its editorial policy, laid out in G. K. Chesterton's column 'At the Sign of the World's End', was to attack capitalism, inequality and hedonism. It was in favour of the ownership of small businesses and small properties and fair redistribution of wealth by means of liberal government reforms; both readers and contributors tended to belong to the Reform Club – the most effective being the divorce reformer E. S. P. Haynes. Osbert Sitwell called *The New Witness* a 'queer bastard Catholic-Socialist-ultra-Conservative paper'.[2] A public bicker about the war started between Charles and Osbert Sitwell. That October in the periodical *The Nation,* Sitwell delivered a scathing review of *Mr Punch's History of the Great War*, a fat anthology culled from the pages of *Punch,* Charles's favourite humorous magazine. One essay written by an officer killed in the war, was quoted out of context, 'Every public schoolboy is serving, and one in six gives up his life. They cannot be such bad places after all.' Sitwell extracted a perverse conclusion, 'We may suppose, then that if one in three had given up their lives the public schools would be just twice as good. Obviously, the ideal would be to have a train wreck, in which the engine-driver and all the guards and passengers hailed from the same public school and all perish in agony.'[3] He signed the review with his initials, which were the same as Sir Owen Seaman, the editor of *Punch*.

This enraged Charles who rushed to the defence of the dead essayist and reviewed the review two weeks later in *The New Witness*. He asked whether Mr O. S. and 'the little clique he dominates, are themselves going to show us any work of positive value . . . No, no, no this kind of an attempt to spread and to make universal an effete aristocracy will not do: for we cannot all be aristocrats and we cannot all be effete.'[4] Robert Nichols weighed in with a long peace-making letter to *The New Witness,* listing every important name in literary London as having been guests of the Sitwells or published in *Arts and Letters*: Strachey, Bell, Sassoon, Huxley, Eliot, Fry, Gide and also Charles himself. Nichols then suggested that Charles must be a little off-colour on account of his wounded leg. In his next letter Nichols apologised for mentioning the leg. Charles snapped back at once, 'Mr Robert Nichols having withdrawn his allusion to my club foot, I must suppress what I was minded to say about his block head.'[5] To follow that, in his review of Sitwell's *Argonaut and Juggernaut* Charles accused Osbert of plagiarism. Sacheverell Sitwell, Osbert's brother, leapt to his defence in the *New Witness* letter page, 'may I thank the last five years for one thing, that they have produced powers of percussion more potent than a pick-axe to let light into a Scotsman's brain.'[6] In November 1919, in a review of *Wheels,* Edith Sitwell's annual anthology of new verse, Charles lamented that their problem 'is, that they won't go round'.[7]

The jousting was more or less good-natured; the participants were kept informed privately of what was appearing so that Sitwell friends could raise objections at the same time as Charles replied to them. Charles's objections to their work were both moral and aesthetic, in fact they rested on the point where the moral and artistic met. He thought Edith's elegant arrangements of vowel sounds were largely devoid of meaning, and Osbert's rhymes fairly facile, yet their self-promotion was astounding, mainly because they had the private income to do it. The Sitwells regarded a failure to admire their poetry as an affront to their aristocratic status, so they were amusingly easy targets, and Charles let them have it with both barrels. Charles was not the only one to see them as ridiculous figures; writing to Ezra Pound, T. S. Eliot privately called them the 'Shitwells', while Noël Coward wrote parodies of their poems and satires of their lives; and much later the critic F. R. Leavis said that the Sitwells belonged to the history of publicity rather than the history of poetry.

Charles's attitude was in part a result of the same bitterness he had criticised in Sassoon.[8] In his next review of *Arts and Letters*, he began, 'In the Isles of Greece, Lord Byron reminds us, the arts of war and peace grew simultaneously. In these less fortunate islands the arts were (with all deference to the editor of *The Muse in Arms*) killed by war, and peace seems to express herself best by dancing on the hecatomb.'[9] 'Dancing on the hecatomb' was a metaphor for what would later be seen as Modernism. A hecatomb was an ancient Greek sacrifice, involving the slaughter of 100 oxen; the war was a vast slaughter, the only answer to which for these particular artists, however mad it seemed, was to dance. Edith Sitwell's strange verse did startle a weary world. In spite of his fierce criticism, Charles himself was to become a major player in the movement, as the translator of one of the greatest modernist writers. His spiky reactions expressed the pain of being dragged into the modern age, as well as grief at loss of his friends and hurt at the gossip surrounding himself and Owen. Charles saw Owen as heroic and war as an opportunity for heroism; heroism did not appeal to Modernists. Also Charles admired and emulated *Punch*: to reinforce his support of the magazine, he started a series of politically satirical verses for the *New Witness* entitled *The Child's Guide to an Understanding of the British Constitution,* one of which lampooned Sir Philip Sassoon, politician, host of celebrities and a cousin of the poet. The ten verses were not offensive but Charles's irony was often seen as too irreverent, particularly the endnote which said that the song could be sung in public to the tune of the 'Laird of Cockpen'.

Sir Philip Sassoon is the Member for Hythe;
He is opulent, generous, swarthy and lithe,
Obsequious, modest, informed and jejeune,
A man in a million's Sir Philip Sassoon.'[10]

This would have annoyed Siegfried Sassoon who may have seen the use of the word 'swarthy' as anti-Semitic. Charles did not stop at attacking those he knew personally. The whole post-war political scene was up for critique, particularly the 'hard-faced men who looked as if they had done well out of the war'.[11] Above all the press barons:

But everyone is not a crook
Of Bathurst, Burnham, Beaverbrook,
Cadbury, Northcliffe, Rothermere;
So everyone is not a Peer.
There are some commoners as well,
Notably Hulton and Dalziel . . .
'For I was led to understand,
King, Lords and Commons rule this land.'

'True in a sense but none the less,
They get their orders from the Press.'[12]

Or the following verse about Sir Edward Carson, the leader of the Ulster Unionists,

Say whose is that enormous jaw?
So grim a man I never saw.
His body glows with latent heat.
He seems some General in retreat,
Or else a Calvinistic Parson.
My child, that is Sir Edward Carson . . .
He loves to hear the Irish groan,
A people he has made his own.[13]

The situation in Ireland was extremely distressing to those who longed for peace. In 1919, after being ignored at the Paris Peace Conference, Sinn Fein declared an independent Ireland and set up a parliament in Dublin, the Dail. The British Government ruled both Sinn Fein and the Dail illegal and responded by sending in troops, ex-First World War soldiers known as The Black and Tans, who, in a bid to quash a tide of civil uproar, were involved in acts of extreme brutality against civilians. Carson dominated the Unionist cause in Ireland; but also on a personal level he was a man Charles would loathe as the pugilistic barrister who had been employed in 1895 by Queensberry to defeat Oscar Wilde.

Some of Charles's verses however were utterly cryptic, like this one in October 1919:

It is clear that you and I are
One a dupe and one a liar;
If the fault be proved in me,
Bullitt, where will England be?
Bullitt, had I guessed that you were
Just a Yankee interviewer,
Both your ears a-cock for tips;
I'd have locked, not licked my lips.[14]

William Bullitt was a US attaché at the Paris Peace Conference who was sent on a clandestine mission to Russia where he met Lenin and brokered a deal to withdraw Allied troops. Lloyd George was told nothing of this mission until after it had taken place, when it was repudiated by Western leaders. It is not clear in this verse who is the speaker, either Charles or Lloyd George. Charles probably met Bullitt in Paris in March 1919 where he let something slip that Bullitt used. Like a good civil servant Charles could not directly engage in politics or take political sides, except to be utterly loyal to his country. His verses likewise had to be cloaked in mystery. The verse continued:

> Lenin I believe to be
> Much the same as you or me;
> But had Winston Churchill heard,
> Shouldn't I have got the bird?[15]

Charles collected his satires into a book entitled *Snakes in the Grass* and presented them to the publishers Constable & Co. However they found them too topical and too cryptic; they would date fast and need copious notes for explanation. So on 22 October 1919 Charles made Constable another suggestion, 'a translation of Marcel Proust's *À la recherche du temps perdu*, now being published by the *Nouvelle Revue Française* . . . The rights are reserved in all countries by Gaston Gallimard: as you know the book is being widely read in France and England – but I have not heard of any proposal to translate it. If you entertain this idea formally I shall be glad to shew you a specimen of my translation in due course.'[16] This was Charles's first reference to Proust, but Constable had never heard of him; they replied that they did not see much use in publishing a translation of Prevost.

Marcel Proust was nearly fifty in 1919 and only just beginning to be published. Son of a Jewish mother and a provincial doctor who had become successful in Paris, he had suffered from asthma all his life and spent most of his time indoors being cosseted – reading, studying and writing. He also worked his way up the social ladder, and attended fashionable salons where he met aristocrats and famous writers like Anatole France. He published in literary magazines and in *Le Figaro* where in 1904 he wrote an article entitled '*La mort des cathédrales*', in which he argued that socialism posed a greater threat to France than the Church, whose cultural and educational tradition he valued. He started to translate Ruskin but found his English not good enough, then worked on an essay, *Contre Sainte-Beuve*, which argued that biography was not a good tool for understanding an author's work. From a very tight world of Parisian high society and visits to the Normandy coast, he observed and analysed people and developed an approach to memory and time that would transform European literature. A closet homosexual, he lived alone with faithful servants on the Boulevard Haussmann, a broad and lively avenue in the smart 9th arrondissement of Paris, and lined his room with cork to keep out noise and dust. From there he chronicled and satirised the decadent *fin-de-siècle* Paris. The first volume of *À la recherche du temps perdu* had been published in 1913 but, with the interruption of the war, the second much later in 1919.

At 1.2 million words Proust's is one of the longest novels in the world. Charles did not know that it would run to seven volumes, with 3200 pages and 2000 characters, but what he read was writing relevant to himself. In the first volume, *Du Côté de chez Swann,* Proust wrote openly about homosexuality, apparent even in a small French village before the turn of the twentieth century. He also, less surprisingly, wove Catholicism into the fabric of the prose. This blend spoke to Charles's heart, not to mention the sophistication of language, philosophy and art that appeared in the uncovering of the world of a sensitive young boy surrounded by adults who adored his mother. A mother who, when she read to her son, approached words with respect:

> She came to them with the tone that they required, with the cordial accent which existed before they were, which dictated them, but which is not to be found in the words themselves, and by these means she smoothed away, as she read on, any harshness there might be or discordance in the tenses of verbs, endowing the imperfect and the preterite with all the sweetness which there is in generosity, all the melancholy which there is in love; guided the sentence towards that

> which was waiting to begin, now hastening, now slackening the pace of the syllables so as to bring them, despite their difference of quantity, into a uniform rhythm, and breathed into this quite ordinary prose a kind of life, continuous and full of feeling.[17]

It was almost as if the mother breathed life and knowledge into her child through the act of reading. The detailed relationship of the word to the emotion struck a chord with both Charles's own memories of his mother reading to him and the *Chanson de Roland*, which was written to be read aloud. Finding that the great length and complexity of Proust's sentences presented an addictive challenge, Charles started translating his work privately in the autumn of 1919.

Until October he rented rooms in Chelsea and spent daylight hours in the studio of a painter, Edward Stanley Mercer,[18] who was painting his portrait in oils. Mercer also painted Compton Mackenzie, who did not like the results, and Vyvyan Holland, who did. The canvas, now in the National Portrait Gallery of Scotland, is lifesize and it shows all of Charles except his wounded leg. It is a handsome portrait in full KOSB mess kit with jacket, medal ribbons, military bonnet and tartan trews. He is holding his captain's cane in one hand, which displays a bloodstone signet ring, which the other rests on his knee. The head is slightly tilted and his eyes look thoughtful and dark. His mother said she never liked the picture as it made him look so deathly pale. However this is a portrait of a wounded man having to sit still for hours in some pain and who was still mourning his friends. On the other hand the banter with Mercer was jolly; he was a friend of Vyvyan Holland and knew many in his circle of friends around Robert Ross.

Charles had by now finished his translation of the *Chanson de Roland*, and it was soon to be published by Chapman and Hall, in December 1919. He inserted three dedicatory poems to dead friends, but the poem to Owen was changed slightly to make it less personal or inflammatory; the word 'shame' was cut out, so that there was no more reference to his supposed cowardice and the rhyming 'name' replaced it:

When in the centuries of time to come,
Men shall be happy and rehearse thy fame,
Shall I be spoken of then, or they grow dumb,
  these numbers this name
Recall ~~thy glory~~ and forget ~~thy shame~~?

His poem to Philip Bainbrigge was daring, 'mind of my intimate mind, I claim thee lover,' it proclaimed, and went on to absolve him of sins, 'the scrutinous Devil / Finds no gain in the faults of thy past behaviour'. Ian Mackenzie was the last of Charles's friends to die in the war, not on the battlefield but from pneumonia in an Edinburgh hospital on Armistice day. Charles remembered him: 'Like fire I saw thee / Smiling, running, leaping, glancing and consuming.' Ian Mackenzie was handsome and athletic, good at cricket and sent to Sandhurst by his military family, where he had met Alec Waugh in 1916. He had been stationed in Scotland during the war and never actually went to the front. Ian often visited the Waugh home in Hampstead and a volume of his poems, *Forgotten Places,* was published in 1919 by Arthur Waugh, Alec's father, to which Alec Waugh wrote a posthumous introduction.

Charles's dedication in the *Chanson* ran: 'To three men; scholars, poets, soldiers, who came to their Rencesvals in September, October and November Nineteen hundred and Eighteen, I dedicate my part in a book which their friendship quickened the beginning and their example has justified the ending.'[19] As Peter France wrote, 'it was precisely the translation of the *Chanson de Roland* that gave Charles the opportunity to write an utterly different kind of war poetry. In recreating an old epic, he was able to re-enact ancient ideals for modern times; his friends Owen, Bainbrigge, and Mackenzie had not just met pointless deaths as the war was ending, but had "met their Rencesvals".'[20] Charles sent Mrs Owen a copy of the *Song of Roland*, 'the whole book is full of thoughts of Wilfred and it is a great joy for me to be able to give you a copy of it, and to feel that you may see in it what I have put in it.'[21]

By November Charles had found a place to rent at 136 Ebury Street, SW1, a narrow house on five floors with three rooms on each, in bad condition but worth improving. He rented it with two friends known in his letters by their surnames only: Parkes and Ashton. The latter was a young Canadian singer who was 'thoroughly domesticated' and was to be the housekeeper, as he could cook and sew for the other two. Meg sewed through the last week of October making curtains and tracing a border of vine leaves on them. Then on the 30th Charles appeared at Edgware with Ashton in a lorry and took away his books, which he was at last to have around him in his own home. Parcels and boxes and furniture were heaved on to the lorry and driven back to Ebury Street where for the first time Charles really set up home himself with friends. Until now he had lived with soldiers or in hospital and this new home gave him a fresh start in his life.

The neighbours were fun: Noël Coward lived nearby with his parents who ran a boarding house at number 111 Ebury Street. George Moore, novelist and playwright, also lived on the street, and Charles visited both. Moore, the prolific Irish writer, held a strong belief that literature had a high moral role, while Coward the precocious actor who was already writing plays, believed that the primary aim of all the arts was entertainment. Coward shared Charles's views on the Sitwells and hilarious evenings were spent improvising spoof Sitwell poetry. Coward concocted a book of poems by Mrs Hernia Whittlebot (Edith) who had two adoring brothers, Gob and Sago. The introduction explained that the thin and angular Whittlebot was 'busy preparing for publication of her new books, *Gilded Sluts* and *Garbage*. She breakfasts on onions and Vichy water.'[22]

Visiting Noël with his exhilarating theatre friends was a shot in the arm for Charles. Next door to Noël was another boarding house, run by a Mrs Evans, whose daughter Edith was a budding actress. Noël was playing the part of Ralph in *The Knight of the Burning Pestle*[23] at the Kingsway Theatre and although everyone else received it tepidly, Charles gave the production a rave review. Thinking of Edith Evans, Charles decided to help revive a play he loved. Noël introduced him to a group of actors and writers and together they formed a society whose aim was to revive what were at that time forgotten plays. They called themselves 'The Phoenix Society', and Charles was its first Secretary; administration was his forte, and he could no longer move around a stage easily. They began rehearsing a production of John Webster's *The Duchess of Malfi*. Apart from Shakespeare, Elizabethan, Jacobean and Restoration plays were practically ignored by the theatre in the first two decades of the twentieth century. The Lyric Theatre in Hammersmith was engaged for two performances and Charles worked tirelessly with the actors, managing to play a supporting role himself as one of the executioners. The main players were famous actors: Cathleen Nesbitt as the duchess, Robert Farquarson as the cardinal and the young Edith Evans as Julia. Charles wrote to his friends the Pyatts in Edinburgh, 'I wish you were both coming to see it. Even if it is not a great play it is full of the most excellent lines in English poetry.'

The Duchess of Malfi was performed in a Sunday matinee on 23 November 1919 and again in the evening. It was not well reviewed: A. B. Walkely in *The Times* said the play was 'no longer a live classic but a museum classic, a curio for connoisseurs'.[24] T. S. Eliot argued that the production had failed to uncover the elements that made Webster a great dramatist – specifically his poetry. All of Charles's friends attended the performances, as did Osbert Sitwell who noted, 'Our worthy Scotsman was superb, in his favourite role of an iron-clad bourgeois flogging a madman and effete aristocrats and his appearance momentary though it was, served to dispel the whole atmosphere of the play and to recall a pleasant and familiar sense of harlequinade.'[25]

Meanwhile the Sitwell feud was still going strong. Aldous Huxley had tried to stop the fury by writing in *Arts and Letters*, 'If Mr Sitwell, like most intelligent men, finds *Punch* boring, snobbish and indifferently illustrated, he has quite as much right to say so as CKSM has to give utterance to his own opinion of Mr Sitwell. It is, we all know, great fun throwing high moral stones but then Safety First, one must beware the glass.'[26] Charles wanted the last word, though; and a week later replied that he was not responsible for *Punch* but that the Sitwells were for *Arts and Letters*, which he, like many intelligent men, found infinitely more boring, more snobbish and worse illustrated than *Punch*. 'I do not pretend to be a poet and he need not pretend to be a critic. I trust this correspondence may soon be closed, as in the words of the Duchess of Malfi, "I have not the leisure to attend so small a business."'[27]

Reviews of the *Song of Roland* were glorious and Charles inscribed a copy to his enchanting fellow actor Cathleen Nesbitt. Richard Aldington said in the *Times Literary Supplement*, 'the flash of one poet catching almost intuitively the emotion of another long dead, the thrill of reading an intelligent transcript of a great poem – these are the valuable things in this book.'[28] The reviewer in *Country Life* called it 'a version done divinely well'. Robert Nichols, feud now forgotton, wrote in the *Observer*, 'so adequate is Captain Scott Moncrieff's translation that it can but take its place with the classics of the sort . . . with Florio's "Montaigne", Fitzgerald's "Omar", Watts-cum-Pusey's "St Augustine", Urquhart's "Rabelais", and Burton's "Arabian Nights".' Joseph Conrad later wrote to express his 'profound and wondering appreciation of the difficulties overcome and captured beauty'. The *Song of Roland* was the exhortation to battle: Taillefer the jongleur went in front of the Norman Army throwing his song in the air, and Charles's use of assonance brought this vividly to life:

Marvellous is the battle in its speed,
The Franks there strike with vigour and with heat,
Cutting through wrists and ribs and chins indeed
Through garments to the lively flesh beneath
On the green grass the clear blood runs in streams.[29]

The battle is a bright picture, a scene of visual beauty; it is nothing like the horror expressed by Wilfred Owen. John Middleton Murry in his 1920 review of Owen's posthumous book of poems said that the poems 'record not what war did to men's bodies and senses, but what it did to their souls'. The *Chanson* by contrast glories in descriptions of its young warriors; it was a magnificent vision of a war against barbarians for the protection of sacred things – a view that Charles still held dear. His old housemaster from Winchester wrote and expressed what Charles had most intended for the *Chanson*: he said it was, 'a lovely book, so clean and wholesome, full of chivalry and the strength of battle'.[30] It described 'vassalage', the precursor to chivalry which it was honourable both to receive and to give.

G. K. Chesterton not only wrote the introduction to the *Song of Roland* but he also reviewed the book. In the former he said that he admired the 'abnegation of the translator, who is himself a very brilliant and individual writer, in having really translated the *Song of Roland*. It would have been easy for a man of his poetic gift to make out of it a modern poem . . . to deal with Roland as Tennyson dealt with Arthur.' But Charles was practising the honourable 'vassalage' in his approach to his translating. 'One of the most remarkable and valuable adventures and achievements of modern letters,' said Chesterton in his review. The translation scholar Peter France later commented, 'What Chesterton admired was the literalism that allowed the old text to speak with its own voice, to proclaim its own values. He singled out the notion of "vassalage", misunderstood by moderns as signifying subordination, but in fact implying a lofty ideal':[31]

> Now in this translation, merely because it is an honest translation, the reader will find the word 'vassalage' used again and again, on a note which is not only heroic but even haughty. The vassal is obviously as proud of being a vassal as anybody could be of being a lord. Indeed the feudal poet uses the word 'vassalage' where a modern poet would use the word 'chivalry.'[32]

Moreover Roland was a song and Charles was writing for the ear. 'Please read it aloud,' he wrote to the Pyatts. In his introduction he added, 'Scottish Presbyterian readers may like to be reminded that the whole poem can be sung, both in French and English, to the tune of their favourite metrical Psalm: 'Now Israel may say and that truly'. He was thinking of his training in 1914 on Lanark Moor with his superior officer banging out the rhythm on the table with his pipe. He wanted the work to be understood 'in the light of many of the aspirations, intentions and even the despairs of today'. In a letter to Henry Pyatt he gave his own ultimate statement about the art of translation:

> You must 'figure yourself' that I had never read a word of old French until I bought de Julleville's Roland . . . As someone, *The Times*, I think, said, it is a question of instinct; Turpin said the same thing when he offered to go and visit Marsilies. The question is to write a line that you know the original author would approve.[33]

He was also trying to write his own fiction. A short story by Charles was published in the 12 December issue of *The New Witness*. Entitled 'Ant', it was the story of a calm and ignored aunt living with her loud nephew and niece in a provincial town. Amid the bridge and tennis, Ant is befriended by a well-mannered young solicitor called Horsley

Bracton who listens to her. The innocuous-looking old lady nurses irritation at her position and longs to visit London, where she owns a flat in Hanover Square inhabited by a life-tenant. The tenant dies. Two weeks later Ant dies and at the funeral her brash nephew expresses disbelief that the flat has been left to the quiet, polite solicitor, 'in gratitude for the services he has rendered me'. More baffling is the fact that in the last two weeks of her life Ant spent time and money staying out all night in London. Bracton accepts the house and from then on takes a fortnight's annual leave in London, 'and drawing cheques upon her legacy, he consecrates twelve days and nights (reserving Sundays only for his own soul's benefit) to the poor old lady's memory, in a round of well-intended and exhausting but perfectly innocuous dissipation.' Charles hoped this would partly explain his own late-night tendencies to his family who saw little of him but would certainly read his stories wherever they appeared. Bouts of innocuous dissipation interspersed with long stretches of very hard work became the pattern for Charles's life. Another literary magazine was started that winter by Charles's friend, the poet and literary editor J. C. Squire. Like Charles, Squire favoured the Georgian poets over the modernist voices of the Sitwells. He called the magazine the *London Mercury*, and Charles would become a frequent contributer.

Amid the praise, Charles read a notice in *The Times* telling of the death of his friend from university, Richard Reynolds Ball, on 17 December of typhus in Warsaw. He had long suspected that he was dead. Ball's death was much on his mind when he started to translate another war epic, the early Anglo-Saxon *Beowulf*, giving full vent to his grasp of both consonance and assonance, and using metre and rhythm instead of rhyme. The lines are divided into two 'metrically equivalent halves', where 'at least one accented syllable in the first half-line is alliterated with one in the second', as in this description of the warrior's ship:

> There in the roads / ring-stemmed she stood,
> Icy, out-faring, / an atheling's craft:
> Laid they down / the lovely Prince,
> Bestower of bracelets, / in the breast of the ship,
> Their man by the mast. / There was a mass of wealth,
> Fretted gold ferried / from far away.

Nor heard I of a keel / more comely-wise garnished
With brave weapons / and battle-weeds,
With bills and byrnies[34]

Beowulf was one of the texts Charles had studied at Edinburgh, which made it relatively easy to translate. In the book he included the other Anglo-Saxon texts: *Widsith, Finnsburgh, Waldere* and *Deor*. The dedication ran: 'To Richard Reynolds Ball, who, like Beowulf, travelled fearlessly in a far country, risking his life to help the victims of war and oppression, until he died in Poland in December, 1919.' The dedicatory poem to Richard followed exactly the rhythm and metre used in his translation of the epic itself, expressing all the sorrow and anger of grief,

What! My loved companion, / in coldness liest thou,
Finished with life, / in a land afar?. . .

The long poem chronicled their life together and apart,

Summers and winters, / and four years following
Busily kept me / among killing banes.
Then thou wast with foreign races, / Russ-men and Frenchmen,
Serbs and Poles, /

And finished with a gentle memory:

In mood the mildest, / in mercy and pity
Best beloved, / most beautiful to remember
In the days / of this our life.[35]

In June 1920, still suffering from his war wound, Charles went to the Du Cane Road Special Surgical Hospital beside Wormwood Scrubs prison. It was a dedicated leg hospital as there were so many war leg injuries, amputations and the need for rehabilitation. He required orthopaedic treatment for his leg and foot and got a train to the nearest station, East Acton, which was half a mile from the hospital, too far away for amputees to hobble comfortably. 'The daily procession of out-patients along Du Cane Road is as harrowing as any I have seen in peace or war; nor is its pathos diminished by the background of empty trains flashing past the hospital every few minutes.'[36] Even in his reduced state he was still effective and dynamic. He later started a campaign in letters to *The Times* to move the station nearer the hospital for ease of access for the limping and legless patients. With advice from his cousin in the Royal Engineers, he even proposed a site, a timetable and a budget for the building of the new station. The Great Western rail company was stony and unhelpful, and with great lack of foresight the Director-General for Traffic Sir Philip Nash said that, 'however great our sympathy with limbless men might be, it is impossible on business lines to make it work.' What is now the vast and busy Hammersmith Hospital still has no adjacent station. However in 1920 the letter-reading public of *The Times* were generous and heartfelt in their response and sent cars and money to help the wounded patients. By the end of his short stay, he had established a fund and rota, which would help taxi patients from the station to the hospital free of charge.

While at Du Cane Road hospital he wrote to Vyvyan Holland asking if he might help an ex-War Office porter to find a job: 'he is in his own words as strong as an elephant',[37] realising that the only way in the post-war labour market was through influence. He also begged Vyvyan to visit and gave him directions saying he would have to walk past 'Wormwood Scrubs murmuring orate pro anima Xpoferi Millard',[38] also mentioning that they must do something about Millard's imminent fiftieth birthday. Christopher Millard meanwhile sent Charles a small box of chocolates.

As he was recovering from his leg operation, lying as he wrote, 'quiescent like a goldfish under a lily leaf',[39] he read in the personal column on the front page of *The Times*:

> Assistant Private Secretary wanted by well-known Public man, good war record, shorthand, typewriting, and excellent French essential: Etonian or Wykehamist preferred, full particulars in applicant's own handwriting, photograph, and copies of testimonials, with stamped and addressed envelope for return, to be enclosed. Age under 30, salary commencing at £600 per annum. The appointee will be of a secretariat of three, and his credentials, demeanour, and other qualifications will be

minutely examined by the other two. It will, therefore, be a waste of time for any but those exactly answering the description given here to apply.[40]

Alfred Harmsworth, by then Lord Northcliffe, was the proprietor of *The Times*, the once oblivious object of *New Witness* criticism. Northcliffe liked to have Scotsmen on his newspaper, favouring their exactitude and hard work and it was almost as if the rest of the advertisment had been written to fit Charles. Northcliffe was a self-made man, a gargantuan figure. He took people on as private secretaries for a year, then moved them on to the editorial board of *The Times* knowing that by then he had trained them by keeping them close to him.

Charles was hired immediately and took up duties as soon as he was released from hospital a week later, on 12 July. He told Henry Pyatt that he had 'emerged upon Northcliffe's right hand', with £600 per annum to rise to £800 in the autumn (in today's currency this gave him the purchasing power of over £100,000 a year). Although it was not as much as his father had earned, along with his journalism and royalties, it would mean that he could help both his brothers' families and at last feel secure.

The day after his appointment came a terrible blow. His brother Colin received a wire from Fort Jameson in Rhodesia, where John had gone to take up a new job. SCOTT MONCRIEF [*sic*] ACCIDENTALLY SHOT HIMSELF DEAD THIS MORNING [13th July]. INFORM WIFE SHE SAILS 16TH JULY. STOP HER.[41] Charles met Colin at Rhodesia House and they went at once to a church to pray. Charles had to attend a lunch party at Lord Northcliffe's that day. He felt that he could scarcely sit through it and told Northcliffe before they went in, who was to his surprise, 'extraordinarily kind and sympathetic'.[42] His brother John had gone out to Rhodesia to make a new home for his family having been engaged as the vet at Fort Jameson. Later a letter arrived, written on 15 July from the land agent who had arranged to take John to examine some oxen. 'He had got up and dressed and was waiting to be called to breakfast about 8am and had been working with a rifle and had accidentally touched the hair trigger with the result that he was shot near the heart.'[43] Subsequent generations questioned this account as there was no proper investigation; his grandson[44] still thinks it could have been suicide or homicide, since anyone trained to handle a gun cannot possibly shoot himself through the heart by accident; but at the time everyone believed the official report from Rhodesia House.

Charles wrote to his brother's widow, Anna, 'by the greatest good fortune, I have now arrived at a decent position in the world and I swear to you that as long as I live I will do all I possibly can to be a father to them [the children] and a helper to you.'[45] Everyone mourned the handsome, enthusiastic and generous John. Charles went on, 'I think I knew more about him, knew him more intimately than anyone else but you – and I wish I could be with you to dry your tears, or mingle them with my own.' Charles contributed to the family income until his death. He was able to ensure that David, his nephew, was privately educated, and he visited the family in Oxford regularly. Such was Charles's charm and the children's joy at his arrival that the young David hoped that his Uncle Charlie would one day marry his mother.[46]

Meg sought solace in spiritualism like many people after the war who had lost close relatives. She was convinced that she was in close communication with John and also soothed Anna with this idea. In her edited *Memories and Letters*, published by Chapman and Hall after Charles's death, Meg inserted a postscript to Charles's letters, 'intercourse with the next life is happily possible, and has, especially since the war, become common knowledge to those who will receive it'. For Charles this was simply not true; he wrote of his mother's amazing 'tolerance of evil' in allowing herself to be fleeced by unscrupulous clairvoyants. He did believe firmly in life after death as part of his Catholic faith, in the rejoicing of souls in Heaven, the Communion of Saints and the efficacy of prayers said for the departed. But this bore no resemblance to summoning by clairvoyants with crystals.

Northcliffe, though not in the best of health and with only two years to go before his death, took Charles under his wing. He took him to meet Joseph Conrad in Kent, and a friendship and correspondence sprang up. Charles would come and stay with the Conrad family for a day or two several times in the next two years. Charles's translation of *Beowulf* was published by Chapman and Hall in the autumn of 1921 as a companion volume to *Song of Roland*. There is only one dedicatory poem this time; to Richard Reynolds Ball, but the book was dedicated to three people, including his brother John and Gladys Dalyell, who also died in 1920. Lord Northcliffe wrote the introduction and asked, 'How many thousand Beowulfs have we not sent out in the last seven years from these islands to face subtleties of horror as incredible as Grendel, fire as scathing as the Worm's, sea-monsters against which no armament was proof?' Northcliffe's final sentence, 'But I welcome this version of Beowulf because I find in its hero what I lament in countless men who have fallen in the field, simple courage, untiring endurance, stainless honour', might well have drawn still more scorn from Charles's enemies, those who felt that the myth of heroism fed war, and that potentates like Northcliffe only benefited at the expense of the blood of innocent men. Although rightly accused of whipping up war fever at the beginning of the war, Northcliffe was also credited with helping bring it to a speedier end by being a major force in bringing in the Americans.

Edmund Gosse reviewed *Beowulf* positively in the *Times Literary Supplement* and wrote a letter to Charles, worrying about what he was to translate next, recommending another medieval text like the *Roman de la Rose*,

> I know no other man living who can retain the form of the middle age and yet not get wrecked in Wardour Street. Think of it seriously, as a duty. Since you told me you were translating Proust I have not felt happy. Not here, O son of Apollo, are haunts meet for thee.[47]

Rather like his old headmaster, Gosse thought of Charles in a fatherly way as being 'clean and wholesome and full of chivalry'. He warned against Proust, 'I grudge months of your best life spent shaking these French powders into your English box.'[48] Gosse was convinced of the superiority of the clean, protestant English ethos, as opposed to the decadence of the French. He did not know that Charles was not only homosexual but also Catholic, or that his more English and Apollonian interpretation of Proust might be all it needed to give it balance.

While translating *Beowulf*, Charles had continued to contribute to *The New Witness*. Of Lord Alfred Douglas's tenth book of poems, he said, 'The later work seems to lack whatever it was that charmed us, years ago, in the earlier.'[49] As the year turned from 1920 to 1921, he wrote four all-encompassing articles entitled 'The Poets There Are', about contemporary poets including Wilfrid Gibson, Walter de la Mare, Wilfred Owen, the Sitwell circle, John Masefield and Robert Graves. Of Edith Sitwell's *The Wooden Pegasus*, he said,

> . . . painted toys; the wooden toys of the nursery cupboard, the porcelain toys of the drawing room mantelpiece. Pretty but lifeless and therefore harmless; moving, thinking, and acting only when Miss Sitwell moves thinks and acts for them . . . her puppets are safe because they are lifeless; and because they are lifeless they are lasting. 'tout passe, tout casse, tout lasse'. . . whispers a voice in her ear. 'Does it?' mutters Miss Sitwell and smothers a doll with paint. 'Seulement l'amour dure' the voice goes on, 'It doesn't,' says Miss Sitwell, reaching for her scissors, and deftly snipping out the dolls heart.[50]

In the same article, he said of Robert Graves's new volume *Country Sentiment*, '. . . like the first growth of new leaves in a burned thicket. The wounds wrought by war on this poet's mind have healed . . .' His writing was self-referential; the wounds wrought by war on Charles's mind had barely healed. His love had not lasted, and Owen's death, Bainbrigge's death, Ball's death had deftly snipped out his own heart. He could look at his leg where there was a five-inch scar on the inside left thigh, a three-inch scar on the calf, the calf depressed and stuck to the bone, his ankle swollen and his left leg one inch shorter than the right. But looking into the mind was rarely done in 1919. His reaction to the mental wounds was a critic's strafing of other writers, a retreat into himself, a disillusionment in his poetry and creativity, satirical verse. What he needed was a shoulder to cry on.

CHAPTER 12

Translating Proust

> While, both at once or each in turn,
> Sharp-tongued but smooth, like buttered knives,
> We pared with studied unconcern,
> The problems of our private lives . . .
>
> CKSM, *Swann's Way*, dedication, 1922

Reading Proust, with its slow dissection of meaning, was the antithesis of the quick-fire mentality of life on the front line. Just as the translations of *Chanson de Roland* and *Beowulf* gave tongue to Charles's masculine exultation in war, so Proust was the opposite, giving him time to slow down and recover and explore the ebb and flow of human relationships. Charles's friendships became deeper and more of a lifeline:

> Those tiny problems, dense yet clear,
> Like ivory balls by Chinese craft
> Pierced (where each hole absorbed a tear)
> And rounded (where the assembly laughed).[1]

The process of translating Proust gave Charles two important female confidantes: Oriana Haynes and Eva Cooper, to whom the verses above were written. After work at *The Times* offices Charles would spend evenings at the home of Edmund and Oriana Haynes. Edmund was a fellow contributor on *The New Witness* and a member of the Reform Club, a pioneering lawyer and a warm man of formidable energy. He was tall and stout with a full head of brown hair and compassionate eyes. His wife Oriana was a beautiful and charming society hostess, welcoming musicians and writers to lavish soirées at their villa in St John's Wood Park, where Charles would entertain by reading aloud current works by Sinclair Lewis and Edgar Lee Masters in the panelled drawing room, or, in vivid Scots, his own satire, the further adventures of 'Mrs Jane Awlbruster Cramms' who wrote scandalised letters to Scottish newspapers.

The cultivated Oriana was excited by his translation work and offered to help, so when they were alone, Charles would read aloud Proust's novel as he translated it. His method was to read a passage silently, think on it, and scribble a version in English in a jotter which he would then test by reading aloud to a discerning ear. Later, as he got faster, he would ask Oriana, or another friend, to read the French aloud while he produced the English version, then read it back himself. Only after the oral test for rhythm would he begin to type it.

But there were also technical issues to grapple with. Proust's novel was published in France before, during and after the First World War.[2] There was a shortage of typesetters: many were dead and those who remained were overworked with under-trained assistants. The first volumes were printed with a lot of typesetter errors, far more than average because Proust was a complex writer and not all typesetters could follow the ideas or the sense of his sentences. Charles, however, did understand Proust. He also worked in a newspaper office and knew how typesetter errors occurred. In France the box of *e*'s and the box of *a*'s were adjacent to each other and to mistake *le* for *la* was a common error, but more so in Proustian compound sentences where the *le* or *la* is one of the many objects of the sentence, and could well be an idea. Much of the work in translating Proust was for Charles also a work of interpretation and instinct. He did not have access to the original manuscript (which was in longhand and extremely difficult to decipher anyway) and he still had a demanding day job.

In July 1921 Charles finished his year as personal secretary to the increasingly demented chief of *The Times* and was moved to the editorial offices. Northcliffe himself was preparing to go on a round-the-world cruise for his health, and his behaviour, always dictatorial, was becoming extreme. Charles was appointed as a foreign sub-editor at *The Times* which meant preparing foreign reports and articles; his work started at 5 p.m., when all copy had to be in, and ended at midnight. Translating, socialising and negotiating contracts had to be done in the few evenings he had to himself.

Charles had agreed a contract for the translation of the first volume of *À la recherche du temps perdu* with Chatto and Windus, one of the most respected publishers in Britain, offering £150 for exclusive UK rights – the equivalent of £20,000 in today's earnings. At the end of May, Chatto had agreed a deal with Proust's French publisher Gallimard, predicting that the translation would be released the following spring. In 1921 Chatto and Windus was run by Geoffrey Whitworth and Charles Harold Prentice. A Scotsman only a few years older than Charles, Prentice was to become an intimate friend. Charles's letters to his editor read like his own diaries would have done, had he kept them. As it was, he had no time for extra writing and all his descriptive and entertaining power went into his letters to friends. The novelist Richard Aldington described Prentice as 'gentle, almost hesitant in manner' and a good, generous man with benevolence shining from his pink, oval face behind gold-rimmed spectacles. He was both a scholar and a competent businessman. By education and taste devoted to classical Greek literature, he steered the firm of Chatto and Windus in the 1920s towards the great authors of his era, publishing Lytton Strachey, Aldous Huxley, Proust and Pirandello. He was a confirmed bachelor, living in a Kensington flat amid, what Aldington described as 'a chaos of books, boxes of cigars, wines, and pictures by Wyndham Lewis'.[3] His holidays were spent in the wilds of Scotland fishing and hiking. He had huge patience and forbearance, not only with Charles but with all his writers.

In September 1921 Charles met another important female confidante: Evangeline Astley Cooper, of Hambleton Hall in Rutland. It was Noël Coward who brought him to Hambleton for a birthday break and on the train told Charles of his history with the place. At fourteen Noël had become close friends with a painter called Philip Streatfield for whom he did some modelling. Philip took Noël on holiday with him to Cornwall where they made friends with Stephen Astley Cooper, walking the cliffs and beaches together. In 1915 when Philip was dying of TB, Mrs Astley Cooper had asked him if there was anything she could do for him, and he asked her if she would look after Noël and take him home with her because he needed taking care of. She agreed and took the charming fifteen-year-old home to Hambleton Hall. This was Noël's first experience of English country-house life and he took much of his high society banter in later plays from these early visits to Hambleton. Although a Catholic convert, Evangeline had a racy and unorthodox mind. It was said that she reappeared in his plays as a stock witty, upper-class lady of the Lady Bracknell variety, still part of Victorian England in terms of style and class, but far more liberated in life and opinions. Other visitors to Hambleton were the writers Hector Hugh Monro (Saki) and James Lees-Milne, who said Eva had 'a particular wry, no-nonsense kind of humour . . . She was just a tyrant with a heart of gold.' If her husband was unfaithful, she said, 'The children have good complexions, and one could not have everything.'[4] Charles benefited from the hospitality of the lady who loved to have what her grandchildren called a houseful of 'pansies up from London'.[5]

Until the 1930s, the aristocracy came to Rutland for the hunt. It was the classiest hunt in England, attended by royalty. Built in 1890, as a hunting box, Hambleton Hall's purpose was fun. The motto over the door said *Fay ce que voudras* from Rabelais, meaning 'Do as you please'. Even the architect had fun designing it, as a hotchpotch of styles – mock Tudor, Elizabethan, Georgian and Victorian, making it look as though it had grown organically, added to successively over the centuries. The substantial stables built in a quadrangle had a motto of their own, *Ride si sapis*, – laugh if you are wise – but a play on words makes it 'ride if you know how'.

Charles could no longer ride, but he could certainly laugh from the sidelines. The sundial in the garden said, *Nunc ora bibendi*, now it's time for drinks, *le temps passe, l'amitié reste, c'est l'heure de bien faire* – time passes, friendship remains, time to do what you like. There Charles would sit, translating the first volume of Proust which he dedicated to his hostess and friend, who became the next discerning ear to whom he read aloud his translations. Charles was unique as a translator who dared to preface the books he translated with long, personal poems or dedications of his own. He dedicated *Swann's Way* to Mrs Astley Cooper in the form of a six-verse poem which was an evocation of the atmosphere at Hambleton and the intimacy of their friendship.

> Here, Summer lingering, loiter I
> When I, with Summer, should be gone . . .

Where only London lights the sky
I go, and with me journeys 'Swann'

Whose pages dull, laborious woof
Covers a warp of working times,
Of firelit nights beneath your roof
And sunlit days beneath your limes . . .[6]

Evangeline Astley Cooper was four years older than Charles's mother, far less handsome or well-dressed, but thoroughly open-minded. Her husband was a vigorous member of hunting society, and Eva, too, needed a confidant. She said that Charles was 'the most intelligent person I ever knew', appreciating his mordant sense of humour. 'When he came to luncheon, he prepared all that he was going to say and then "let us have It".'[7] By 1921 her face was old and worn, but her eyes were young, large, blue and rather prominent. Aldous Huxley described her as 'one of these large handsome old-masterish women who look as though they had been built up from sections of two different people – such broad shoulders they have, so Junoian a form; and growing from between the shoulders such a slender neck, such a small, compact and childish head'.[8] During the war, Eva had turned Hambleton into a convalescent home for British soldiers and almost 600 wounded men had passed through. Noël would come down from London, sometimes only for Sunday night when he was acting, and sing and play for the invalids. 'I shall always say,' Eva maintained, 'the real cause of the war was the deep-seated jealousy of the Germans at the way the Englishmen wore their clothes – a sort of careless ease.'[9]

But Eva was also patient and generous. She sat with Charles under the lime trees in the garden, reading Proust in French out loud as he read his English translation so that he could get the rhythm of the prose. She later wrote in an unpublished autobiography, using a metaphor from her hunting life, 'I often used to look ahead and wonder how he was going to get over some of the fences, for what can be said in French without offence cannot be said in English. He surmounted them without a moment's hesitation.'[10]

What was it that made Charles such a superlative translator? Nearly a century later the scholar and translator Sian Reynolds compared the new Penguin translation with Charles's version and saw its approach as one of 'clarity of mind', while Scott Moncrieff had an approach of 'maturity': 'choosing to think about the text, to mull his sentences over, and wait until they were ripe for writing down'.[11] Reynolds takes a sample of text for comparison. Here, in the middle of the first volume, Swann is looking everywhere for Odette in a state of high anxiety:

> D'ailleurs on commençait à éteindre partout. Sous les arbres des boulevards, les passants plus rares erraient, dans une obscurité mystérieuse, à peine reconnaissables. Parfois l'ombre d'une femme qui s'approchait de lui, lui murmurant un mot à l'oreille, lui demandant de la ramener, fit tressaillir Swann. Il frôlait anxieusement tous ces corps comme si parmi les fantômes de morts, dans le royaume sombre, il eût cherché Eurydice.

Scott Moncrieff translated in a way that the new Penguin translator, Lydia Davis, found 'dressy':

> Meanwhile the restaurants were closing and their lights began to go out. Under the trees of the boulevards there were still a few people strolling to and fro, barely distinguishable in the gathering darkness. Now and then the ghost of a woman glided up to Swann, murmured a few words in his ear, asked him to take her home and left him shuddering. Anxiously he explored every one of these vaguely seen shapes, as though among the phantoms of the dead, in the realms of darkness, he had been searching for a lost Eurydice.

Davis translated a leaner version, shadowing the French text more closely,

> Lights were beginning to go out all round him. Under the trees on the boulevards, in a mysterious darkness, fewer people wandered past, barely recognisable. Now and then, the shadow of a woman coming up to him, murmuring a word in his ear, asking him to take her home, would make Swann start. He brushed anxiously against all those dim bodies as if, among the

> phantoms of the dead, in the kingdom of darkness, he were searching for Eurydice.

In Charles's version we can see his interpretative leap – he takes liberties, but he is there. We are on the Champs-Elysées, we can see the restaurant lights going out and these are prostitutes, soliciting, coming up to Swann and, because he is looking for a loved one, the suggestion that he take home a whore makes him shudder. Not 'start' as in fright, but 'shudder' with something deeper. He adds the word 'lost' to Eurydice, for better rhythm, and also because, as we learn, Odette is indeed a lost soul. Charles emphasises the Eurydice metaphor because if Swann wants Odette, and, later, Marcel wants Albertine, then they must be prepared to visit their own Hades.

The new Penguin translation is more literal, but Charles's version goes through the sieve of his soul; it involves his history, his education, and his experience in the trenches. The translation scholar, Peter France, made the point that translation . . .

> is not merely a technical task to be carried out with proper efficiency (as done ideally – though not so far in reality – by a machine). The sort of translation to be discussed here has to do with the values, the personality, the intention that underlie the original. In relation to these, the translator's duty is in part *ethical* (or even political).[12]

Ethics and duty were an essential part of Charles's make-up, both the soldier and the writer. Once he became a translator, he devoted himself solely to the task; he never owned a home, had no children, lived through his work. Susan Sontag described the roll of the translator in her St Jerome Lecture in 2002.[13] She agreed that translation was:

> an ethical task, and one that mirrors and duplicates the role of literature itself, which is to extend our sympathies; to educate the heart and mind; to create inwardness; to secure and deepen the awareness (with all its consequences) that other people, people different from us, really do exist.[14]

Proust was stylistically and morally foreign to a protestant English audience, and bridging that gap was part of Charles's role. He would have liked to meet the author and Gallimard had asked for Proust to read the translation before it went to press, so a near-finished portion was sent to Paris on 21 November but by February Proust still had not replied. Charles finished the volume and settled on a title without being able to consult him, writing to Whitworth at Chatto, 'M. Proust will probably have a word to say about the English title of the book and of each volume.' From *Beowulf* he took 'swans weg' – Swann's Way – as the title of the first volume, and decided that a line he had chosen from Shakespeare was rich enough in associations to cover the whole multi-volume novel. He knew he could not find an English equivalent, rich in ambiguity meaning time wasted and time lost, involving memory and still reflecting the beauty of what the novel contained, so he chose a line from Sonnet 30: 'When to the sessions of sweet silent thought/ I summon up remembrance of things past.'

They had still heard nothing from Proust by May, when the volume was at the printers. Charles, who had just moved from Ebury Street to a room on the Strand opposite the Courts of Justice, and whose things were in a state of chaos, received the first proofs. He was furious:

> The translation of Proust presents many difficulties, to which I have given a great deal of thought. Every comma was put there deliberately by me . . . Please tell the printer that if any of my copy is 'improved', I shall wash my hands of the book altogether . . . I felt like a gardener who has stooped all day over his beds, sticking little pegs with labels on them, and finding that a child or a dog or a hen has pulled them all up in the night.[15]

Proof sheets from Henry Holt, his American publisher, and from Chatto continued to arrive over the summer and he had to reinstate every deleted comma. There was still no word from Proust. It was exhausting, the commas took their toll on the fragile man and suddenly in July Charles was rushed into hospital with appendicitis, operated on and put in a worryingly expensive nursing home. He wrote to Whitworth to ask if Proust was coming to London as Gallimard had suggested, 'we should welcome him – you on foot, I on a stretcher – beneath the

Cavell Statue, and escort him to some of the secret haunts denounced in John Bull – ending in a reception in Seaport House.'[16] But the revels never took place. Proust was already far more unwell than Charles; he had only a few months to live.

That August Lord Northcliffe died of infected endocarditis and was buried in Westminster Abbey. Writing to Conal O'Riordan, Charles said, 'I am still living in hospital coming out for a moment or two to look at the world and read Northcliffe's obituaries.'[17] He was also reading the advance publicity for the translation. Sydney and Violet Schiff, who had become Proust's closest English friends since meeting him in 1919, were both protective and outraged by the Shakespearean title of the whole work. Sydney Schiff, who wrote semi-autobiographical novels under the name of Stephen Hudson, was the heir to a rich Jewish banking family and considered to be one of the best-dressed men in Europe. He had married an equally cultivated and wealthy woman, Violet Beddington, the niece of the novelist Ada Leverson who had corresponded with Oscar Wilde. It was the Schiffs who had arranged the famous Ritz supper party at which Picasso, Stravinsky, Proust and Joyce were brought together in May 1921, only to have Proust and Joyce talk briefly about their illnesses. Intensely loyal to Proust, the Schiffs were shocked at the liberties that had been taken with the translation of the title and wrote at once to Proust in protest. In spite of the fact that Gallimard had been sent the translation, it turned out that Proust, isolated and ill, had not been shown a copy. He was distressed by what the Schiffs wrote and considered stopping publication. 'I cherish my work,' he told Gallimard, who could have prevented the shock, 'and won't have it ruined by Englishmen.' However, the Schiffs bought an early copy of *Swann's Way*, sitting down to read it and telegraphing the same day to Proust that the translation was excellent. They then became as passionate and loyal and generous to the translator as they had been to Proust.

Charles was invited for most of September 1922 to Brahan Castle in Ross-shire, Scotland. His host was James Stewart Mackenzie, the colonel of the 9th Lancers whom he had known during the war. Mackenzie was what Charles described as 'the finest imaginable type of Highland Chief'. Exactly a year before, in September 1921, the Seaforth Mackenzies had acted as hosts when Lloyd George called the

Cabinet together in an emergency. The first Cabinet meeting ever to take place outside London was in Inverness Town Hall. Here the 'Inverness Formula' was agreed that would be the basis of negotiations over the next three months that led to the Anglo-Irish Treaty which established the Irish Free State. After two years' bitter conflict in Ireland, a truce was signed in June 1921 and the urgency was such that the unprecedented move of interrupting the Cabinet while hunting, shooting and fishing in Scotland was taken.

The seventy-four-year-old colonel had inherited not only a fine castle and estate but also an ancient and efficient curse. As a child in Inverness, Charles had heard of the Curse of the Brahan Seer. Kenneth Mackenzie, a labourer on the Brahan estate in the late seventeenth century, had been well known as a seer, or prophet, and when Lady Mackenzie asked him to tell her how her husband, the third Earl, was faring in France, he said he would not. She insisted, so he told her that her husband was in the arms of a Parisian courtesan. Furious, Lady Mackenzie ordered that the seer be burnt in a barrel of tar. Kenneth Mackenzie's last prophecy was a curse. 'No future chief of the Mackenzies shall bear rule at Brahan or Kintail.' Every direct male heir had died without issue since that date, and James Stewart Mackenzie himself was to die the following March without issue, and his barony become extinct. Brahan Castle itself was demolished in 1952 and its stones used as the foundation for the road to Dingwall.

The curse did not alarm or surprise Charles – he was used to the numinous activities of his mother, and this was yet another superstition to be ignored. Meanwhile he waited at a safe distance from London for the public reaction to his translation. He had already made good friends with Lady Seaforth; like many older, married women, she found him charming. She asked him to stay on to be part of her Northern Meeting party. Every year since 1788, the Northern Meeting Society had organised Highland balls to keep alive the tradition of dancing Scottish reels; they also ran a piping competition. Bagpipes, dancing and wearing kilts had been outlawed after the 1745 rebellion and this society, as well as the London based Highland Society, re-established and kept alive that part of Highland culture. Charles, though no piper, was a determined dancer of reels, in spite of his limp, and an entertaining addition to the party. There would be many old family friends and cousins at this Northern Ball, still hoping that he would finally fall in love and marry.

There was a great shortage of men after the First World War; Lady Diana Cooper famously wrote as early as 1916 that everyone she had ever danced with was dead.

Charles wrote to his publisher Prentice from Brahan Castle on 14 September advising him that he would like to send copies of the translation 'to certain people who have shown an interest and have allowed one to inflict long passages on them viva voce'.[18] To Oriana Haynes he sent a copy and later wrote to her: 'there is something great in Proust and in the book – not in the pretty bits at the beginning which are pure window dressing. I use it as a guide to word and action in myself and others, and am constantly explaining things to myself in terms of Proust.'[19]

To his relief the reviews were good. *The Times* critic A. B. Walkely said it was 'very close to the original, yet it is written in fastidious English'.[20] John Middleton Murry in the *Nation and Atheneum* declared, 'nothing less than amazing. Had it not been done, it would have seemed impossible. But it has been done . . . No English reader will get more out of reading *Du Côté de chez Swann* in French than he will out of reading *Swann's Way* in English.'

The praise boosted Charles's confidence and helped to heal old wounds, but his mother pricked a pre-war conscience when she wrote saying she was, 'rather depressed by Mlle Vinteuil and Swann's promiscuous love-making'.[21] Battles, bereavements, a new-found faith and his own physical decrepitude had changed his attitude to sex. He was quite celibate for the moment, though he never stopped being charming, and did not stop teasing Vyvyan, 'It was very kind of Stanley to come on Saturday. I enjoyed him immensely.'[22] Vyvyan was now living with Stanley Mercer, the painter, in a large rented house in Carlyle Square in Chelsea. They lived in a sometimes strained companionship: Vyvyan was an avidly practising ladies' man and Stanley was dedicated to his career as an artist, which meant he could not always cover the rent. Charles would end his letters to Vyvyan, 'Love to Stanley' as if they were a couple. For himself, he would channel his romantic frustration into a phenomenal period of work which would both distract and fulfil.

'You will let me know, won't you,' Charles asked Prentice, 'if Proust acknowledges receipt of his copy. He is a reticent devil.'[23] On 10 October, the desperately sick author wrote to thank his English translator:

Dear Sir,
I have been very flattered and touched by the trouble you have taken in translating my Swann. The miracle is that I can thank you at all. I am in fact so gravely ill (not contagiously) that I cannot reply to anyone, you are the only one of my translators in many languages to whom I have written, perhaps after seeing the fine talent with which you have done this translation (I have not yet read it all, but just to let you know that I do not leave my bed and take no food etc). Nonetheless, I have one or two criticisms for you. For example À la recherche du temps perdu cannot possibly mean what you say. The verses that you add, the dedication to your friends do not replace the intentional ambiguity of Lost Time/Wasted Time, which finds itself again at the end of the work in Time Regained. As for Swann's Way that can mean Du Côté de chez Swann, but also à la manière de Swann. If you had added the word 'to' you would have saved everything. I am sorry I have to write to you in French, but my English is so appalling, that no one understands it. 'How can you criticise,' I hear you say, 'when you hardly know one or two words of English if at all – in the face of all the praise for my translation?'

Please give my compliments to your editors for the remarkable way they have had the translation done and please believe in my good faith . . .[24]

As he struggled through, however, Proust was, according to his first biographer George Painter, more and more pleased by the beauty of the translation and even more so by the press-cuttings from the London reviews which 'tended to declare the translation superior to the original'.[25] Charles picked out Proust's phrase *'l'amphibologie voulue'*, intentional ambiguity, and used it afterwards in conversation or correspondence whenever it seemed apt.

Meanwhile, as Charles was basking in success, Proust died, emaciated and febrile, from pneumonia, holding the hand of his faithful servant Céleste on the evening of 18 November 1922. His final word was, 'Mother'. At his funeral with full military honours, as was due a chevalier of the Legion d'Honneur, were all the great and the good of the French literary world. However, the state of the remainder of his novel was shaky. Five parts had now been published: *Du Côté de chez Swann*, in 1913, *À l'ombre des jeunes filles en fleurs*, in 1919, *Le Côté de Guermantes I*, in 1920, *Le Côté de Guermantes II* and *Sodome et Gomorrhe I* in 1921 and *Sodome et Gomorrhe II* in 1922. The other three volumes were left in manuscript at his death.

Saddened at yet another death to add to his catalogue, of someone he sensed he knew intimately, though in fact not at all, Charles felt even more obliged to do him justice. In his chaotic room at 191 The Strand, opposite the Law Courts, he realised that he had made a real howler in the first translation. Rushing out to the theatre on the night of Monday the 27 November 1922 to see a production of Shelley's *The Cenci*, starring Sybil Thorndike, he wrote to Prentice from the back of the theatre. 'I made an absurd blunder over "chapeau melon" an expression which seems every day of the week to meet my eye . . . Luckily no reviewer seems to have reached that part of the story yet, but my howler is quite impossible, even if it means a "stub".'[26] It should have been 'bowler hat', but 'melon hat' remained to embarrass Charles until the second impression a year later.

Worried that the death of Proust might diminish future interest in the rest of the novel, Charles wrote to *The Times* five days later. He quoted from Proust's friend, de Pierrefus, in the *Journal des débats*: 'His work which is in the process of publication, is completely finished. He said many times that he had nothing to add to the series of volumes.' Charles expected the final three volumes *La Prisonnière, La Fugitive* or *Albertine disparue*, and *Le Temps retrouvé*, to be published some time in 1923, but they were not; the final volume of the French edition did not come out from Gallimard until 1927.

In December 1922, fifty illustrious French literary men assembled a 340-page double number of the *Nouvelle Revue française* to commemorate Proust; the tribute contained fragments of the unpublished volumes then called *La Mort de Bergotte* and *Sodome et Gomorrhe*. Charles wrote a review of this extended tribute which appeared in the *Times Literary Supplement* on 18 January 1923, quoting at length from the fragments and describing the whole with all the excitement of the discovery of new literature, seeing the volumes ahead as a 'kaleidoscope of ever shifting pieces of glass'.[27]

He had already written to Chatto to ask if he could edit a similar tribute in book form, asking for essays from the best-known English writers of the day. 'I want a collection of opinions that will make people in this country believe that Proust is worth reading.'[28] Prentice agreed, providing he approached Conrad first. In reply to his request Conrad said, 'It is clear you have done this for love . . . and there is no more to be said.' He went on to speak of his preference for the translation over the real thing.

> . . . I was more interested and fascinated by your rendering than by Proust's creation. One has revealed to me something and there is no revelation in the other. I am speaking of the sheer maitrise de langue; I mean how far it can be pushed – in your case of two languages – by a faculty akin to genius. For to think that such a result could be obtained by mere study and industry would be too depressing. And that is the revelation. As far as the maitrise de langue is concerned there is no revelation in Proust.[29]

Charles's translating did require his study and industry, but also confident inspiration, and an understanding that was similar to Proust's: an affinity with the same literature, a passion for genealogy and aesthetic appreciation. He had lived through the same events and, like Proust, had witnessed the end of the century's Victorian legacy, its literature, the dawn of the Edwardians, and he travelled often in Europe during that time. Pasternak was to say later in his *Notes of a Translator* that 'Translation must be the work of an author who has felt the influence of the original long before he begins his work. It must be the fruit of the original, its historical consequence . . .'[30]

For the book of tributes, Charles sought to recruit as many writers as possible. If the French could muster fifty, surely he could find twenty? He wrote to George Moore, who replied that he couldn't stomach Proust; Edmund Gosse, who deplored Charles wasting his talent translating the man he pronounced Prowst, would not contribute either. Saintsbury, his old professor, wrote that he had only read the first volume in Charles's translation and asked, 'Has anybody said that he partakes both of De Quincey and of Stendhal? He does to me and I'm shot if I ever expected to see such a blend.'[31] He did eventually contribute a very short piece.

Charles wrote to Alec Waugh, J.C. Squire, E.S.P. Haynes and Walkely. He was even prepared to approach those he did not know, including Lytton Strachey, Virginia Woolf, Arnold Bennett, Middleton Murry,

Desmond MacCarthy, Mme Bibesco and Arthur Symons (whom he was soon to meet at the Schiffs and who immediately sent him a copy of his biography of Aubrey Beardsley for review). The Schiffs persuaded Murry to contribute. Virginia Woolf wrote to Clive Bell in February 1923 with various boasts, 'Boast Three, Scott Moncrieff pesters for a few words.'[32] In the end she did not contribute although she co-signed a short letter to the *Times Literary Supplement* Charles had written with eighteen others, including E. M. Forster, lamenting Proust's death and thanking him for enriching our everyday experience with the 'alchemy of art'.[33] Woolf loved Proust, writing of his 'astonishing vibration and saturation and intensification'.[34] She first read Proust in the Scott Moncrieff translation, admitting to Roger Fry that reading the translation was akin to a sexual experience, and in her notebooks all her page references correspond to the translation.[35] In *To the Lighthouse* published in 1927, entire phrases are taken from the Scott Moncrieff translation.[36] Similarly there are two coinages in *Finnegans Wake*, which Joyce started working on in 1922, that can only come from the translation, not the original – 'swansway' and 'pities of the plain'. Proust's great influence, particularly on the stream-of-consciousness novel, stemmed from Charles's careful choice of words. In the eventual volume, *Marcel Proust – an English Tribute*, published by Chatto in 1922 and by Seltzer in New York in 1923, the critic Francis Birrell wrote the longest appreciation including the candid sentence, 'Proust is the first author to treat sexual inversion as a current and ordinary phenomenon, which he describes neither in the vein of tedious panegyric adopted by certain decadent writers, nor yet with the air of a show-man displaying to an agitated tourist abysses of unfathomable horror.'[37] Catherine Carswell said that he recreated 'the glamour in which for every one of us our own past is bathed.'[38] Conrad wrote that, 'He has pushed analysis to the point where it becomes creative.'[39]

In February 1923, T. S. Eliot, who was editing the ambitious literary periodical, *The Criterion,* founded the year before, wrote to Jacques Rivière, the editor of the *Nouvelle Revue française*, saying, *'J'ai causé avec Monsieur Scott Moncrieff qui s'est fait un succès éclatant par sa traduction de* Swann'[40] ('I have spoken to Mr Scott Moncrieff who has made a brilliant success of his translation of *Swann*'), and could the *Criterion* please have a morceau of unpublished copy and Scott Moncrieff would translate it. Eliot wrote to Charles saying that it would be a coup for *The*

Criterion to print something not yet printed even in French. Charles agreed but Rivière delayed sending the piece. Meanwhile Richard Aldington, Eliot's assistant, was given the task of dealing with Charles, but went to Italy, so Charles was left hanging, not knowing what was going on until Eliot sent him a courteous letter explaining the situation and insisting he would rather print the piece in French than have any translator other than Scott Moncrieff. The promised unpublished fragment, 'The Death of Albertine', eventually appeared in July 1924.

Charles also sent Eliot a short story, 'Cousin Fanny and Cousin Annie'. This was a 10,000 word story written from a child's point of view about a young boy who is left with an elderly cousin, her cook and her dog while his parents are in India. He loves the cook, Annie, and calls her 'cousin' too, to the amusement of his elderly relative. When he is sent to boarding school he still spends the odd holiday with his increasingly impoverished and ageing cousin whom he judges with all the callowness of youth. It is not until, having gone through the war, he becomes a man that he wonders what has become of the old servant Annie, who has left his Cousin Fanny. He goes to find her tenement in Glasgow and is called upstairs by a neighbour who knows who he is, because Annie spoke of him so much. He enters the bare, single room, 'frowsty with the smell of poverty' to discover she died the evening before.

> He had stood this way by many of his intimate friends during the last five years, had lain awake in hospital wards where someone or other died every night, had helped bury brother officers, and men of his own company, when the ground was frozen too hard for a pick to break it; but Annie dead; Annie to whom he had scarcely given a thought all that time, was different. He knelt by the bed, sobbing, felt for her hard little hand and kissed it again and again, then rose and stooped over her face and kissed her shining forehead . . .[41]

He recalled for the first time all the 'laborious, loving, ungrudging service of all those years, poured out for himself and other people without any question of their response to her'.[42]

The story was harsh, moving and very moral. What was striking was how unlike Proust's in every way was Charles's own voice. Eliot wrote to Alec Waugh saying how much he liked the story, and asked for Charles's address, as he wanted to publish it in the spring. He did not manage this until 1926 when *The Criterion* brought it out in two parts; the first in April covering the childhood, and the second in July, taking us through the boy's youth and manhood. It is the most autobiographical of Charles's writings, describing his Victorian childhood and the social hierarchies that were gradually crumbling with the levelling process of the war.

Two more of his short stories were printed in the *London Mercury* of August 1923, 'The Mouse in the Dovecote', a Saki-style story about a social climbing wife who has just acquired a country house to take guests from London, and 'The Victorians', a tale of a butler who discovers that he is in fact the son and heir to the stately home where he serves. Being born before marriage was regarded as a shame to the family and he was brought up as a servant. He must therefore remain a butler, although he is in fact the child of the lady he serves. Both stories were satires on bourgeois and aristocratic snobberies.

With regard to Proust, Charles was having trouble with the title of the second volume, *À l'ombre des jeunes filles en fleurs*, with its '*amphibologie voulue*' being that of young girls blossoming, or starting their period. He did not think that allusions to menstruation would go down well among the English, where the subject would prompt disgust, while for the French it was more poetic and the sensibility was one of productivity; flowering to bring forth fruit. He wanted to choose a line of poetry – Proust himself had borrowed the phrase from Baudelaire, '*Car Lesbos entre tous m'a choisi sur la terre/ Pour chanter le secret de ses vierges en fleurs*'[43] ('For Lesbos chose me among all the earth/ To sing the secret of its blossoming maidens') and Charles went to others for help. His demands were rhythm, brevity and association; he thought the title should be short enough to be printed on the spine of a book without cramping, admitting that his own name was a serious inconvenience to the binder. In early January he spent a day with Joseph Conrad at his house in Kent, and Conrad suggested 'In the shade of young girls in bloom' and 'In the shade of blossoming youth'. Too long for Charles. Conrad was by now the most famous living writer in Britain and America and his appreciation of Charles's writing and his company meant a great deal. George Moore came up with 'Under blossoming boughs'. Charles wrote to Geoffrey Whitworth at Chatto suggesting several: 'For many a rose lipt maiden' from Housman's *A Shropshire Lad*, 'Under bowers of embowering blossom' from Shelley's 'Sensitive Plant', 'A Rosebud garden of girls' from Tennyson and Marvell's 'To a green thought in a green shade'. He finally chose 'In a Budding Grove' from William Allingham's poem of that name.

Charles's social life still revolved around his old friends. He entertained them to dinner at the Savile Club and in January he invited Edmund Haynes, Alec Waugh, Beverley Nichols, Stanley Mercer and Vyvyan Holland. Charles's bawdy banter was reserved for his letters to Vyvyan, and in April he began, 'You dashed past me the other day in Lower Regent Street as I was putting my nephew into a Tube – which is, after all, better than putting one's tube into a nephew . . .'[44] Charles had a habit of reading his translations to Vyv, as he called him, who was not as tolerant as Oriana. For Vyv simple apologies would not do, Charles had to tease him about his women and say sorry for 'boring you so. It is as bad as a mistress showing you her miscarriage and asking for 2/6 a week on the strength of it . . . I always want to see you and promise not to read to you.'[45]

Charles longed for a discerning mind who felt as passionately about the translation of Proust as he did, and on 26 March 1923, he read in the *London Mercury* a letter from arts patron Edward Marsh about Proust. It was a plea, through the *Mercury*, to both French editors, Gallimard and Rivière, for 'a tolerable text of the masterpieces'. Complaining that Proust's novel was printed in a 'corrupt' form, even though he was venerated by all of literary France, Marsh went on to list the errors he found in the French version such as 'forme' for 'femme', and 'defend les ports' for 'devant les portes', alongside mistakes in punctuation. Proust's elaborate style put a strain on readers

> and the strain is wantonly increased when the comma, which can be such a useful little creature when under control, is allowed to gambol among the long paragraphs like an ignis fatuus. Proust himself seems to have taken but little interest in his commas, even when they were 'inverted'; but this makes it all the more incumbent on his Editors to keep them in their places.[46]

Marsh's passion for commas struck a note, especially when described as 'wanton' and 'inverted'. 'Invert' was the medical euphemism for homosexual, and this article started a lifetime of exchanging innuendo between Charles and Edward Marsh. Marsh was a sophisticated polymath, educated at Westminster School and Trinity College, Cambridge, and now a powerful civil servant. Private Secretary to a series of ministers, though mainly Winston Churchill, he was also an energetic patron of artists and poets. He had edited the five collections of *Georgian Poets*, had encouraged and corresponded with Rupert Brooke and Siegfried Sassoon, and knew all about Wilfred Owen. Charles could not hope for a more kindred spirit. He wrote a reply at once: sending him three pages of the 'worst howlers' that he had so far come across in *Jeunes Filles*. 'What worries me,' wrote Charles, 'is how far I am justified in tidying up the discrepancies when translating. You are the only person I have come across who is enough interested in the text of Proust to have noticed them, and almost the only one who has remarked on the misprints.'[47] This started a correspondence about the problems of translating particular sentences and Edward Marsh became the man to whom Charles submitted all his worst problems over translating Proust for the rest of his life. In the meantime the two men had much in common and Charles suggested a meeting.

> I have so long known you, as Bloch père knew Bergotte, sans le connaitre, that I am fully ready to bring that unsatisfactory state of mind to an end. Unfortunately my habit of spending the evening in Printing House Square makes it impossible for me to dine except on Saturdays when you, I imagine, are usually out of town.[48]

Marsh was an elegantly dressed, monocled bachelor, who was either out of town at important people's houses at weekends or attending first nights at the theatre. He did however arrange not to be out of town one Saturday and invited Charles to dine with him at Gray's Inn. Charles accepted the invitation from his desk at *The Times*: 'I look forward to April 7th as Proust looked forward across his *Giboulées de la Semaine Sainte* to Florence and Venice' – and then continued to discuss the errors in Proust's text.

> . . . extrêmement identique is so bad that even if P. wrote it it should not be made public. Exactement identique is otiose and

> a little better; but extrêmement identique is like a badly laced pair of stays.

He knew all about typographical errors from working on *The Times*, where compositors corrected as they went along,

> When he sets a line right and inadvertently repeats it, he discovers his mistake and fills up the second line with a 'pie' of odd letters, xs and so forth. If by an oversight they get into the paper, they are utilised next week to afford the readers of Punch a good hearty laugh. So I picture this printer setting up extrê realising his mistake, having to finish the line, and doing the next line correctly. Anyhow exactement is consolidated by the first edition.[49]

It was an intimate dinner, after which Charles no longer called him Mr Marsh but addressed his letters to 'Dearest Eddie'. Marsh showed him his famous art collection; he had specialised first in the English watercolourists, then in 1904 with the help of Robert Ross he had acquired a collection of drawings. In 1911, he first bought a painting by Duncan Grant, and gradually became a patron of contemporary British painting, adding John Currie, Mark Gertler, John and Paul Nash and Stanley Spencer to his collection: by 1914 he had brought together the nucleus of what became one of the most valuable collections of modern work in private hands. It covered every inch of the wall space in his apartments at 5 Raymond Buildings, Gray's Inn. Surrounded by colourful paintings, they had a lively and literary conversation, and Charles left at 2 a.m.[50]

Charles then went to stay for a week at Deene Park in Peterborough, where he had been before for convalescence, and wrote to Dearest Eddie from there, 'but I owe you many apologies for keeping you up so late – my consolation is that I am sure the delights of your conversation must have caused many similar offences'.[51] On his return, they met for dinner at Charles's Club, the Savile, which had the tradition of communal dining at long tables like at school, but Charles promised to sequester him away from bores. As it was, they dined with Street and Sedgewick, two 'discerning young Proustians'. He then sent Marsh a naughty limerick on a Savile Club postcard, which referred to Street's civil service licence job,

There was a young poet of Praed Street[52]
Who said: I am dreadfully afraid Street
Will refuse me a licence
For my play on the Nice Sense
Of the Smell of a Man as a Maid's Treat.

Charles also apologised for not being a good host as he had just come down with flu and was rather muddled, and thought he had done Marsh out of a cab fare by handing him coppers by mistake. Probably all Charles had at this point were coppers. He had now given up his job at *The Times* after a post-Northcliffe shake-up, and had decided to dedicate all his time to literature. As he explained to Prentice, though, he had 'others to provide for, nine hungry nieces and nephews'. He took a short-lived placement at an advertising firm, the London Association, which, though well-paid, was a job he found antipathetic. In the evenings he wrote occasional reviews for the periodical the *Saturday Review* with the hope of being appointed as its next drama critic. Judging by the names of its former incumbents, Bernard Shaw and Max Beerbohm, this was a prestigious post; but later that year the position was given to the critic James Agate.

Translating Proust took up more energy than Charles had anticipated. His letters to Prentice were full of gallantry: on 4 May he wrote, 'in the course of these afternoon conversations which emerge, in memory, the sole green islets in the troubled sea of the last six months, I have entire faith in the good will and loyalty of your firm, and therefore approach any offer that you may make me in a spirit of acceptance.'[53] He asked Prentice to deal with the complex details of the contracts with the American publisher, Seltzer, and with Gallimard, and laid out in painstaking pound signs what he needed to ensure that he and his 'heirs and ensigns' got a good deal.

> I have given you the lengths of the first three books of Proust, which are: Swann, 188,500 – Jeunes Filles 232,500 – Guermantes 257,500. Total 678,500 words. For translating these words (they are not all different words, of course), I am to receive, assuming Seltzer comes in level with you, £750, or a little more than a guinea per thousand words.

His health was not good: the 'flu' lasted for a long time, and was probably a recurrence of his trench fever. Lady Seaforth from Brahan Castle, newly widowed and in poor health herself, suggested in July that they go together to Germany for a rest cure. She was a Steinkopf by birth and knew of a good wateringhole at Bad Kissingen, and Charles was happy to accompany her. Despite being in her sixties, Lady Seaforth was adventurous and wanted to go to Germany by air. Air travel was still in its infancy – the first solo transatlantic flight would not take place until 1927 – there were no passenger terminals, and the trip meant flying from an open field in Croydon to Amsterdam and then on to Berlin. The party consisted of her ladyship, her doctor, her maid and a caged pet bullfinch as well as Charles, who wrote to Eddie Marsh about the flight on 19 July 1923,

> Never having recovered from that evening at the Savile I took an aeroplane from Croydon to Berlin (a safe but slow method – 36 hours from end to end) and duly arrived here where I am gradually growing stronger. I have never been in this country before, and wish I had been in it before all these hostilities came to exacerbate us. I cannot but feel that if Palamède de Charlus had been sent to the Pariser Platz ten years ago, all that might have been averted.[54]

Proust's character of the Baron de Charlus was a fiendish diplomat, one who, Charles felt, had he been real, might have helped avoid the war. As for Bad Kissingen, the rich and famous, crowned heads of Europe as well as Tolstoy, Bismarck and Shaw, had come to the resort for over a century to drink the waters tasting of sulphur, bathe in the waters smelling of sulphur, be attended by the doctors and be rested and cured. Lady Seaforth had her own German doctor who brought his sister and his nephew Erik to join the party. They all booked into the Kurhaus Fürstenberg. 'The only custom I cannot acclimatise myself to is that of people standing like seagulls round a liner and saying "Mahlzeit", [din-dins] as I go in to dinner. And that is chiefly because I do not know the "*mot juste*" to retort with. I usually say "granted" but I feel somehow that it is not right,'[55] Charles explained to Eddie. To Vyvyan he was more frank, 'After I got here I had a bad breakdown, more or less in connection with my brother's death at this time 3 years ago, and for two days could do nothing but weep.'[56] Erik, who had also been wounded at Monchy, came and discussed literature with Charles in his room; he thought Oscar Wilde the greatest writer who ever lived, which Charles conveyed to Vyvyan.

By 2 August they had moved to Oberhof in Thuringen, with Charles reporting to Eddie that since arriving in Germany, he had done one third of *Guermantes I*. Looking out of his balcony window, he continued,

> This place is almost 9000 feet above the railway station, and I walked up to spare the horses. All the male visitors wear knitted jumpers, bound with leather belts. The jumpers are the loveliest colours – but the women are more soberly dressed . . . I have pitched my German doctor through Sodome et Gomorrhe to his great edification. It takes our minds off the Ruhr. And he argues that there is no literary form like it in German.[57]

Lady Seaforth quarrelled with the hotel over a bill of several million Deutschmarks, and Charles quarrelled with her over the fact that inflation was out of control and they must give them what they asked. She left and Charles stayed on,

> when I, after a day of magic solitude in the woods, courted only by dragonflies, was standing naked in a wash hand basin preparatory to passer un smoking and go down to my 600,000 mark table d'hote – the door opened and a blushing post boy, chaperoned *luckily* by his hotel porter, who looks as if he had faced one in a trench, came in and said whatever the German is for 'sign please'. This is a beautiful place, marvellously beautiful . . .

Charles elaborated on his disagreement with Lady Seaforth:

> I know what you feel about Germany – as W's late hostess feels the exact opposite and gives me no peace, thank God she has left this hotel. Being very rich she always ordered the worst wine; now I, being alone, and very poor, can still afford and do prefer the best . . . She, de son etat, was a Miss Steinkopft – a fille unique of the man who made all the Apollonians water, and considerably

> rich. Widowhood has accentuated her hatred of the French, whom she chooses to personify in me. I say that so pigheaded a woman should have been nee Schweinkopft – and also that it is a pity that seeing that at her baptism the faeries denied her the power of thought, they should have let her have the gift of speech. The rest of the party is her personal doctor, from Berlin, a very good and intelligent man, who discussed with me his nephew's relations with the Hausdiener at the Kissingen hotel in the frankest manner conceivable as though it had been the weather . . .[58]

He asked about London gossip:

> Were you at the Chatsworth wedding last week? I hope you didn't give away the bridegroom. Is he still as radiantly beautiful as he was ten years ago? I haven't seen him since early in 1915 when he was one of the more ornamental subalterns of that very proud corps the 3rd Royal Scots.[59]

He also experienced at first hand the gargantuan inflation in post-war Germany.

> On Wednesday night I got a bottle of quite good Rhine champagne for about 1,500,000 marks including tax – the pound being next morning 21,000,000 – On Friday the pound fell to 13,000,000 ten minutes before I entered the Bank, and last night a bottle of wine cost 7,500,000 . . . I now have an outstanding debt of 30,000,000 marks and a horrible fear that the mark may return to par during the night! I am leaving here about the end of this week; it depends on whether I send my clothes to the wash tomorrow, as if so I must wait till Saturday – they wash them so badly poor souls. They have no soap, so they rub them with pine bark, of which there is an unlimited quantity; they are then strewn on the grass, and the pigs roll on them (this is *absolutely true*) till they are dry . . . And after *that* you expect Germany to pay reparations.[60]

This he threw out as a challenge to Marsh who would soon become Private Secretary to Churchill at the Treasury. He told Oriana another story of two men who went with a wheelbarrow to fetch money from the bank. On their way home they stopped to get a glass of beer and on leaving the bar, found the money lying on the ground and the wheelbarrow stolen. To Vyvyan, Charles wrote that he lived on pumpernickel bread and light beer for 39,000 marks a day.

On the last day of July, driving with Lady Seaforth in the rain from Bad Kissingen to Thuringen through dense and sodden pine forests, he wrote a dedication in the form of a poem to Katherine Shaw Stewart, sister of the poet Patrick Shaw Stewart. She lived in Scotland, knew Lady Seaforth and was part of their Highland party the year before. Charles had spoken to her about her brother who had died in 1917, and in general about the war and loss of friends. As he had explained to Eddie Marsh, he felt close to his dead friends here in Germany. In 1924 he dedicated *Within a Budding Grove,* to Katherine Shaw Stewart with a poem in memory of her brother Patrick. The poem described the fields in Germany, prescient of further war:

> That men in armour may be born
> With serpents teeth the field is sown;

Going on to talk of friends fallen,

> Their friendship was a finer thing
> Than fame, or wealth, or honoured age,

While he sent his poem to Katherine, he wrote to Marsh admitting, 'I don't write good poetry, and fortunately I know it.'[61]

CHAPTER 13

Writer and Spy in Fascist Italy

The whole point of the Secret Service is that it is secret.

Compton Mackenzie, *Water on the Brain, 1933*

Charles went straight from Germany to Scotland to stay with his cousins at Durie in Fife. Louis Christie was now working for the intelligence services in a position Charles had himself been partly responsible for creating. At the War Office, Charles had worked alongside Claude Dansey,[1] one of the men who came up with the idea of using the British passport offices as cover for intelligence gathering. It was not acceptable for diplomats to collect secret information from their host countries because as representatives of the sovereign, they must be above reproach. An intelligence officer or spy could not hold diplomatic rank, as it would compromise the Foreign Office. Even today they are merely 'attached' to the Foreign Office. The solution in 1920 was to create a Passport Control Department so that their real job was hidden beneath the mundane duties of stamping passports. They did however get some diplomatic perks – a travel budget, a certain accommodation budget and the use of the diplomatic mailbag.[2]

In 1923 there was a need for intelligence officers in Rome. Mussolini's rhetoric was expansionist; he wanted Rome to return to being 'the guiding light of civilisation throughout Western Europe'.[3] The fall of the Ottoman Empire and the First World War had given Britain control of much of the Middle East. Mussolini felt that, historically this was Italy's part of the globe, and intended to get it back. Britain needed to keep an eye on Italy's armaments, as well as its movements. A year before, in June 1922, an Italian delegation had steered into the Foreign Office in Whitehall with an agenda that worried the British administration. They demanded the cession to Italy of ten different British Protectorates: Coenaculum, Senoussi, Jubaland, Egypt, the Dodecanese, Abysinnia, Tangier and Palestine.[4] When British officials stalled or prevaricated, saying these places were too valuable to let go of – the Dodecanese could provide naval bases, Abyssinia provided the water for Egypt – the Italians just persisted with the same questions again. Documents on British foreign policy for 1922–23 are swamped by the question of Italian imperial expansion.

There had been one hundred intelligence agents based in Italy during the war, but since 1918 numbers had hugely decreased because officially Italy was politically friendly on the surface. However, it was apparent the country now needed watching again. The head of the service had set out guidelines in 1919 about the type of personnel they needed to recruit. No individual could set forth without '"cover", that is to say a fictitious cloak for his real activities – some open and legitimate pursuit, business, or calling under which he can operate without detection'. Journalism and translation were a good cover for agents. It was also stated that the best results were obtained by individuals where the 'sense of honour is as high an order as the courage, acumen, brains, audacity, and presence of mind which are the other essentials of success'.[5] Again the job description could have been written for Charles, his sense of honour was still paramount. Recruiting Charles was an enormous help to Louis, who was needed to travel in countries across the Mediterranean – Greece and Turkey, also Egypt, Yemen, Aden, Muscat, Iraq and Palestine.

Working as a gentleman writer abroad fluent in several languages, Charles could do a bit of reporting on the side, observe military manoeuvres and naval bases, and keep files on British nationals within the country who were possible Fascist sympathisers. Troops went through railway stations and sailors frequented ports. Wherever Charles travelled he could pick up local information on numbers of troops or destinations of ships and, if relevant, pass it on. He had regular briefings with Louis in order to know what to look for. Much of his reporting was mundane, and all the records were destroyed in 1932.[6] As Compton Mackenzie wrote in his satirical novel *Water on the Brain*, an agent's work did not consist entirely of meeting 'mysterious Polish countesses in old castles'. The 'greater part of the work was routine stuff. Card-indexing, filing, making out lists, putting agents' reports into proper

English'.[7] Charles had already got accustomed to living parallel lives; secrecy came naturally to him, he was always in control of conversations and never had prolonged romantic relationships.

Meanwhile the Christies were consistently hospitable and their house, Durie in Fife, felt like a second home. Charles's loyalty to them was as automatic as his loyalty to his country. Louis's father the Laird had a grand motorcar and there are photos of them sitting three abreast, well wrapped-up before a drive: Louis corpulent and relaxed, Charles rather emaciated, and a young man whose initials were AWN looking healthy and happy – he had clearly not gone through the war.

Charles travelled from Fife to London in early September 1923, to prepare for his move to Italy. He wrote to Edward Marsh asking him to lunch at the Royal Automobile Club where they would, 'celebrate 1 my birthday 2 my departure from England in a fortnight 3 Noel Coward and the success of *London Calling* – I hope to get Monty Mackenzie who speaks of being in London, but he hasn't turned up here yet – and a few other men – perhaps eight altogether, like M. Grévy's parties at the Elysée.'[8] *London Calling*, which had opened the week before, was Coward's first musical revue and starred Gertrude Lawrence. It included a sketch called 'The Swiss Family Whittlebot', which satirised the Sitwells.

Marsh replied by asking him at once to a dinner before the lunch at his home in Raymond Buildings. 'Many thanks for your charming hospitality,' Charles wrote afterwards, 'I felt at last that I had returned to London and that London was worth returning to.'[9] It is quite possible that Marsh alone of his friends, knew of his work with the Service, and how it affected his move to Italy.

Charles's farewell birthday lunch was attended by Edward Marsh, Compton Mackenzie, Reggie Turner and Noël Coward. They discussed the impossibility of publishing a book in Britain entitled 'Sodom and Gomorrah'. Of course fiction was something different; Coward was no coward and the following year Act Two of his play *Easy Virtue* opened with its heroine reading Proust's *Sodom and Gomorrah*. Coward later gave Charles a signed copy of his first draft of the play. He also mentioned he had named his cat Proust. Amid the birthday atmosphere, and the fuss surrounding Coward and his success, there was Compton Mackenzie, egotistical but exceedingly kind. He had the actor's gift of always knowing what his audience or friends needed or wanted. Marsh and Turner, Eddie and Reggie, were the modest and receptive foils to the boisterous pair. Charles announced to his friends his intention of going to live in Italy, possibly for good. The climate would be kinder to his injured leg, the exchange rate was kinder to his pocket and would enable him to live cheaply and still be a major support to his brothers' families, and there was already a community of English writers living in Italy. The impetus for this abrupt and unplanned move was not revealed, but not probed into either, because another unspoken but generally understood reason was that the legal climate in Italy was gentler on homosexuality. Although illegal and, certainly as far as the Church was concerned, immoral, a blind eye was turned. He would not have to constantly watch his back as he did at home, which in England made him not a little paranoid and also cynical. As he wrote more dramatically about a character in a short story in the *London Mercury* that year called 'Free Verse':

> He had now gone irreducibly abroad, though not so much with a fellow he knew, as to escape from fellows who claimed to know him and his address would not, for the present, be made public.[10]

He had so much 'cover' for moving to Italy that it was almost suspicious. September 1923 was a busy month; Charles visited his nephews and nieces in Edgware, bringing as presents a suitcase full of carved and painted wooden figures from Germany which were described by his mother, with a common antipathy to all things German, as 'hideous'. That month he also wrote the long introduction in the form of 'An open letter to a young Gentleman', for a new edition of Petronius's *Satyricon*. The young gentleman is probably William Armstrong (to whom he also dedicated his short story in the *London Mercury* called 'The Mouse in the Dovecote') who was about to launch his acting career in London. The introduction to Petronius's 2000-year-old romp and satire was also a blithe farewell to the fleshpots of London. The main character and narrator of the *Satyricon* is Encolpius, a former gladiator, who has a sixteen-year-old boy lover called Giton. In Charles's introduction he advises his young man: 'Quartilla [a nymphomaniac] you will hardly escape, or Tryphoena [infatuated with Giton] either; Fortunata [wife of a boastful millionaire] will pester you with her invitations, and, if you visit the National Gallery or the Turkish Baths, you must beware Eumolpus [a pedant who prides himself on his poetry which no one else can stand].' All these characters, he warned, were alive and kicking in contemporary London.

In discussing the translator Burnaby, he also revealed the qualities he valued in a translation. Being scholarly was not, he argued, as important as using colloquial English with common sense in interpretation. His view of translation was light-hearted. He had just written jokingly to Edward Marsh, 'My trouble is that I know comparatively few French words and no grammar – so when I come to the most frightful howler, like the German musician on whose score a fly alighted, I "play him."'[11] This agile method of skipping along a heavy text meant he could translate at great speed. However, the errors already printed in Proust's French text, like the fly, sometimes remained.

In the *Saturday Review*, Charles reviewed the ballet *Ajanta Frescoes*, Anna Pavlova's composition inspired by her recent visit to India. 'Frankly, a tedious spectacle copied with a wealth of superfluous accuracy from the dreary Buddhist art of India.'[12] It was the sort of thing his mother would have loved, and Pavlova was the darling of the nation, but it did not impress Charles. He was tired of London and 'when a man is tired of London, he is tired of life'.[13] His last short stories to be published were satirical about the lives he was leading: country house parties and literary London life; the small, small society of upper-class England.

His parents, George and Meg, were already in Venice and intended to spend the whole winter in northern Italy. He planned to join them in October 1923 and branch out from there. Winding through Lombardy on the train he came upon the American novelist Sinclair Lewis whom he had met not long before at the house of the writer Violet Hunt, a contributor to *Marcel Proust – an English Tribute*. Lewis, his wife Grace and six-year-old son Wells, were also on their way to Venice and Charles suggested they stop off at Padua to see Giotto's fourteenth-century frescos. With *Swann's Way* in hand, he took them round the chapel of the Madonna dell'Arena to gaze at Karitas, Invidia, Iustitia. Charles thought Giotto's frescos the most seductive things in the world, not so much as great and glorious works of art, but infinitely human and delightful. He read his version of Proust's descriptions aloud in the galleries. Grace Sinclair Lewis had been bored by Proust but her husband, Harry, was more appreciative, having had it recommended to him by Edith Wharton that summer. They looked for what his Baedeker described as the 'largest café in Europe', built in 1831. 'It is open all night like Paul Morand,'[14] commented Charles who had been reading Morand's 'quite unprintable' *Ouvert la nuit* on the train along with Andre Maurois's *Ariel*. They talked until the early hours, Harry Sinclair Lewis proving to be a champion drinker. In his enthusiasm Charles saw the family on to their train and pressed upon Mrs Sinclair Lewis his own last copy of *Swann*, which he later regretted, admitting to Prentice that 'their society has been rather a snare.'[15]

Charles had never been to Venice before, only read of it in Ruskin during his childhood and in Proust as an adult. He was amazed by what he saw. He went round San Marco with an old friend of his father, Dr Robertson, and was deeply touched by one of the early mosaics on the porch – 'Noah helping a lean and anxious-looking lion into the Ark through a small and high-up window.'[16] Dr Robertson, who had lived in Venice for many years, showed Charles his collection of curiosities, among which were white and blue majolica jars, medicines from old monasteries, one marked as the sinister *Pulv. Viporini* – the dust of dried and powdered vipers.

Beneath the beauty lay political unease, all through Italy. After the First World War, fearing that there might be a revolution inspired by events in Russia, the Italian government began to welcome association with Benito Mussolini's small fascist party. In 1920 Mussolini's Blackshirts (*Squadristi*) had been used to break a general strike started by trade unions at the Alfa Romeo factory in Milan. A year later in Naples, Mussolini declared his aim 'to rule Italy', and in October 1922, just over a year before Charles and his parents arrived, Mussolini organised a 'March on Rome' when thousands of fascist supporters, many armed with mere farm implements, marched on the city threatening to seize power. Fearing civil war, King Vittorio Emmanuelle III handed over power to Mussolini, who was supported by the military, the business class and right-wing voters. Mussolini formed his cabinet as 25,000 Blackshirts marched in triumph through the streets of Rome. There was still palpable tension in public places and although Charles would later discover it to be more disturbing, he described his perceptions of fascist government jauntily to Prentice almost as soon as he arrived.

> The Government of the country being done by soldiers, sailors and police who are superannuated at 19, it is rather like living in a Public School from which all the masters have been eliminated. The slightly older Fascisti seem to live principally on cocaine which makes them a trifle eccentric.[17]

From the moment he touched foot in Venice he was exhilarated by his new job and his new life. Italy was seen as a place of sexual liberation to those in Britain. Leaving his parents mid-meal one evening he embarked on a casual rendezvous in a back alley, writing to Millard, partly as a boast, partly because it was what Millard expected, 'I wish I dared put in writing my adventure on Sunday night with a drunken gondolier, but it might compromise you, so I abstain.'[18] Instead he described another adventure in another alleyway with a nineteen-year-old German sailor, a blow by blow account, in German and Italian with the compromising parts in German, to Vyvyan. In the middle of the encounter, a policeman was seen standing at the end of the alley, and Charles was fearful, until the sailor informed him that this was just another client waiting his turn.

Soon he moved with his parents to Florence, where they stayed in the Pensione Balestri on the Piazza Mentana, their bedroom windows overlooking the Arno, with an arched balcony and a view up to the green Belvedere Hill dotted with villas and cypresses. There, he thought, he could rest and catch up on work. He finished translating the first volume of Proust's *Le Côté de Guermantes* on Saturday, typed it on Sunday and got it 'sent in the diplomatic mail bag by one of the embassy people'.[19] From now on Charles would use the diplomatic mailbag for his manuscripts – even though he was only 'attached' to the British Passport Office. He would on many occasions in the next six years be found in the sort of luxury hotels that his family would not dream of using. It seems the accounts for the British Passport Office in Rome had a separate budget for translators.[20]

The occupation of professional translator was perfect for an undercover agent, writing occasional reports on the rapidly changing fascist regime; Charles was free to travel wherever he liked all over Italy with the excuse of research or journalism. He rented rooms in Pisa or Rome for periods of up to a year, but he never spent more than two weeks at a time in any one place. His letters bear the addresses of *pensioni*; up and down the country.

Meanwhile, he enjoyed the ex-pat literary life. D. H. Lawrence and his wife Frieda lived on and off in and around Florence – and the English Florentine colony of the 1920s was parodied in Lawrence's novel *Aaron's Rod*: original characters trying to live a stylish life on limited means. Among them were Norman Douglas and Reggie Turner, both writers, now in their mid-fifties and constantly searching for work. Douglas was a bohemian aristocrat with a scandalous past; he had been a diplomat, but was expelled from St Petersburg for having affairs with three Russian women at the same time. He moved to Capri, the setting for his most famous novel, *South Wind*, and there he married an Austrian cousin and had two children, but got divorced on the grounds of her adultery and obtained custody of the boys. Douglas had been prosecuted in London in both 1916 and 1917 for misdemeanours with young boys and jumped bail to Italy again. He had already published ten novels and travel books and was living on meagre royalties. Douglas had a fine head of white hair and good features, he was dominating, garrulous and liked a drink, yet when he wanted to ingratiate he had charming manners. His charm worked on Charles, who also rated his novels and tried to help get Douglas some work with his publishers. Suggesting to Guy Chapman that Douglas do a translation of Latin classics, he wrote, 'I think Eumolpus must have been rather like Norman Douglas.' (Eumolpus is the pedantic poet in the *Satyricon*.) Douglas lived on the Lungarno delle Grazie, near Charles's *pensione*, with Giuseppe (Pino) Orioli, the Italian bookseller who operated a small, private press and printed editions of his friends' works.[21] Orioli was small and chubby with a debonair manner and a gift for telling long, profane stories in the manner of Boccaccio. He maintained Charles's translating method was a casual part of daily life:

> He carried in his left hand the French volume he was translating, read a few lines of it, interrupted his reading in order to talk to me, and then took a notebook out of his pocket and

wrote in English the few lines he had just read, leaning against a pine tree.[22]

Douglas's friend, Reggie Turner, author and aesthete, had written twelve novels and was living frugally on their royalties. He had his own very neat and tidy flat at 35 Viale Giovanni Milton on the north-west side of the city. Douglas and Turner spent as much time as they could at other peoples' elaborate lunch and dinner parties where each was a demanding conversationalist. At the second party Charles attended, Douglas complained that he was unappreciated and would leave for Africa unless someone would rent him a flat. He was often escaping the police because of his pandering to young boys and his predilection for not paying debts, 'but I shall believe him gone when I have seen him go,' Charles told Prentice. Reggie Turner would regale dinner parties with his many personal anecdotes about his friendship with Oscar Wilde, including one about Wilde on his death bed, waking from a reverie, frightened, saying, 'I dreamt I was having dinner round a table with the dead,' and Turner consoling him by replying, 'I am sure you were the life and soul of the party.'

These three men were particularly good sources of useful information concerning the entire British ex-pat community, while Orioli knew all the Italian gossip. Another writer in the town was Ada Leverson, Violet Schiff's ageing aunt, also known for her connections and correspondence with Oscar Wilde. Ada spent her energy promoting the Sitwells. Sir George Sitwell, father of Osbert, Sacheverell and Edith, was currently renovating a fortress-like Baroque castle, Montegufoni, perched on a hilltop near Siena. Also part of this English-speaking community around Florence was the antique dealer Arthur Acton and his American wife who owned the Renaissance villa, La Pietra. Charles visited and made friends with their son Harold, then at Oxford. He would later be knighted as a diplomat, but at the age of nineteen was suitably impressed with the thirty-four-year-old translator, who presented him with a copy of his *Song of Roland* that Christmas, with a written dedication in the flyleaf, which is now in the library at La Pietra.[23]

Acton's parents had bought the fifteenth-century villa in the late 1890s. His mother Hortense had American banking money and his father a habit of collecting antiques: an eclectic selection of medieval religious statues and paintings, marble busts, gilt picture frames, chairs and tables. They collected obsessively until the villa was full, and designed a terraced garden which fell on four levels from the drawing-room window, full of white statues, walks and perspective views. Harold grew up there but went to school at Eton and then to Christ Church, Oxford, where his languid, flamboyant character attracted the admiration of Evelyn Waugh. Acton was the original student to declaim Eliot's *The Waste Land* over a microphone at a party, a feat that Waugh gave to his character Anthony Blanche, although later Waugh claimed Acton was not in fact the model for this character. In *Memoirs of an Aesthete*, published in 1948, Acton recalled entertaining Huxley, Lawrence, Aldington and Charles in Italy:

> Talking of Proust, I remembered that Paul Claudel had thundered against *Du Côté de chez Swann*, as 'that world of snobs and lackeys'. Were we snobs? Not according to Proust's definition or that of the Oxford Dictionary. We did not puff ourselves out or try to enhance our importance. I am only a snob in so far as I often want better company than my own.[24]

Charles may have mixed with aesthetes and read and written about them, but his personal habits were more ascetic. Frieda Lawrence described a tea party in 1924 at which Charles and Acton appeared together.[25] D. H. Lawrence had railed at Acton's snobbery and attacked their admiration for Henry James, whom Charles had defended. Prose style was the point where they parted company: James and Proust made an art of implicit suggestion, evocative description, fine discernment; while Lawrence, Charles felt, hammered a point home till you were sick of it with his use of repetitive prose style. Nor did Charles like his 'filthy' sexual diversions, equally explicit and repetitive. Lawrence did not warm to Charles either; in his autobiography he describes a tea party with Charles and Turner as 'old queens bickering round a teapot'. At that particular tea party, 'Douglas took Lawrence's side and the argument degenerated into a broadside against James's Americanness.'[26]

'This is Armistice day here, and the Carabinieri have got plumes in their hats, and the Neptune statue is sloshing all over the Signoria, most obscenely,'[27] Charles wrote on 4 November, the night he had dinner with Aldous Huxley and his wife Maria who were staying at the Schiffs' villa in Florence. For fun, they sat around the fire reading Huxley's *Antic Hay*, the alternate pages only of the uncut novel. Charles said he was now in a position to write a review of it for the English language newspaper the *Italian Mail* and in return Huxley agreed to write a review of *Marcel Proust – an English Tribute* for the same newspaper. Charles gave Huxley a copy of *The Satyricon*, with all the pages cut, in the hope that he would also review that. The *Times Literary Supplement* acknowledged this reprint of the lusty romp but gave Charles's name as C. E. Scott Moncrieff, 'which is my eminently respectable and married cousin the Revd. Canon D. D. Vicar of Buxton; he will be very cross, like the little rabbit.'[28] Prentice, who also published Huxley, sent encouraging cuttings of good reviews of the *Tribute* from the *Literary Review* and the *New Statesman* and Charles asked Prentice to send a copy of his *Tribute* to his friend Bruno at Deene Park, who had finally solved his financial problems by getting married.

Before moving on to *Guermantes II*, Charles asked Prentice if he could have a break from Proust. Instead, he proposed translating some Stendhal, which Compton Mackenzie, a Stendhal scholar (and director of the Aegean Intelligence service during the war) had suggested to Charles as a marked contrast to Proust's laborious style, offering to lend him his copy of *La Chartreuse de Parme*. Mackenzie had a copy of the 1846 edition, preceded by a letter of Balzac's; this letter he had never seen translated. Stendhal had chosen to settle in Italy in 1814 in preference to his own country, combining the activities of writing novels with spying for the Napoleonic regime. Stendhal's realist style was not appreciated in his lifetime, and he was only now beginning to be more widely read. Since Charles was living in northern Italy where the novel was set, it had a particular appeal, and, moreover, there were three volumes, meaning a future in Stendhal could be mapped out. Prentice first wanted to know if he would consider translating Proust's early works but Charles was not keen, calling Proust's *Pastiches et Mélanges* 'a series of parodies of French stylists which it would be utterly impossible to render even into Belgian'.[29]

A handwritten postscript to Prentice was Charles's final cajole regarding Stendhal, 'His body lays in Père Lachaise as someone said of HBV's father.'[30] HBV was their pet name for Vyvyan Holland – it was his initials backwards, and a reference to the Blessed Virgin. Charles constantly suggested works for him to translate, including at one stage Pittigrilli's *Cocaina*, 'the most amusing novel I have read for years; he has all the humour that Morand lacks.'[31] Guy Chapman at Chapman and Hall, however, looked at a few pages and said that he would be 'marched between two constables to Bow Street within three days of publication'.[32]

Vyvyan made numerous visits to Italy over the next seven years to see Charles. He wrote about touring a thirteenth-century church in Stazzema, Tuscany, with him during the empty siesta period, looking into one of the confessionals and seeing printed instructions on which sins had to be referred to a higher authority before absolution could be given:

> These consisted of five: murder, blasphemy, abstention from the sacraments for over a year (which implied excommunication), the seduction of minors and, finally, indulging in sorcery of any kind, and particularly gettatura.[33]

'*Gettatura*' was cursing on the scale of the Brahan Seer. 'The seduction of minors' brought to mind again Charles's short story, written at Winchester: 'he felt that a millstone round his neck might perhaps be less offensive than the picture of those small, startled features hung for all eternity before his eyes.' Prostitutes in Italy were often minors and Norman Douglas was often in trouble for his dealings with boys. The other Douglas, Lord Alfred, whose father had obtained evidence from rent boys for prosecuting Wilde, was now being prosecuted by the Crown for libelling Winston Churchill. Charles commented, 'It is nice to think of Alfred Douglas in gaol at last, but almost too much to hope that they'll keep him there.'[34]

On 23 November 1923 Charles was still in Florence at the Pensione Balestri with his parents where he had developed a 'sort of Proust reading circle among the guests'. From there he wrote to Chapman, who had published *Chanson* and *Beowulf*, proposing a translation of *The Letters of Abelard and Heloise* from medieval Latin. He had been told by George Moore, the writer and former neighbour in Ebury Street, who had just written a fictionalised version of the lovers' story, that no one had ever translated the letters from Latin to English.

Previous translations had been from a debased French text. Charles looked at the French one first and found it 'stodgy'. In the Florence City Library, he found the only Latin text readily available in the *Patrologiae Cursus Completus*, a collection of writings by the church fathers.

From December 1923 until March 1924 Charles's parents stayed to winter in the Italian Riviera, in the hope that the weather would be kinder on all three semi-invalids. 'I am sweating blood to finish vol v. of Proust before moving to Rapallo on the 10th. I did 3,500 words yesterday and have 2,500 today, mostly in a café with Italians roaring all round,'[35] Charles complained, having had to escape the hotel where his father was unable to move with flu and cough. Finally, in late December all together they made the train journey to Rapallo along the coast through tunnels under cliffs, often with arches cut out of the cliffside so that they could see glimpses of the glittering Mediterranean beyond the beautiful Cinque Terre. In Rapallo Charles had booked rooms for them at the Grand Hotel Savoia.

The Grand Hotel Savoia was sadly not as grand as its name. Rapallo was a picturesque seaside town with magnificent churches and elegant buildings right on the coast, but the hotel was inland near the railway station, in a valley with no views and moreover rather damp. To make matters worse, Charles immediately turned yellow with jaundice. Meg moved him to her larger room and tried to persuade him to see a doctor. Eventually he agreed and on 2 January 1924, a doctor who shouted his limited English in a staccato rhythm said, 'The colour! It will be for two weeks! It is not serious! He is safe!'[36]

Reggie Turner travelled from Florence to see Charles in Rapallo and decided to stay; he was introduced to Charles's parents as a novelist and aesthete. His mother thought he was 'a very pleasant little man, and good, easy, interesting talker'.[37] George thought him 'a sweet dog' – hardly complimentary, but he did spot Turner's great quality of loyalty to his friends. He came to Rapallo with the express purpose of visiting the sick Charles and cheering him up by taking him to visit another close friend, Max Beerbohm, with whom Turner had enjoyed a lifelong correspondence.[38] Beerbohm, essayist, caricaturist and parodist, lived in Rapallo with his wife, Florence Kahn, in a house overhanging the coastal road. He had known Wilde and Beardsley and told Charles that he did not like Proust and never had; but when Charles showed him a review of the *Tribute* from the *Nieuwe Rotterdamsche*, Max 'was rather braced at seeing all about it in a strange (MB's ancestral for that matter) tongue'.[39]

By now Meg had decided to move to a rented room overlooking the sea with its own balcony rather than spend so much on an expensive hotel with poor food. The new room was in a pleasant villa and had its own fireplace. She hoped that the sea air and the open fire would quicken George's recovery. One day Charles and Reggie Turner brought Max Beerbohm and his wife to tea with the parents at the villa. Beerbohm looked at Meg's sketches of sails and said very appreciative things, while she described him as, 'a little elderly man with sparse grey hair and round features – they live very simply'.[40]

Charles stayed on at the hotel, given it was where his considerable correspondence was directed for the moment; he did not stop working, jaundice or no. The British Passport Office had doubtless already paid for it, as Charles had explained to Prentice, 'I shall be there for about a month, and then probably at Rome, with one of the Embassy people.'[41] This done, he returned to Florence and took a room in a bohemian house on the left bank of the Arno at 54, Costa di san Giorgio, owned by an obscure British artist called Stephen Haweis. The two WCs were accessible only though Charles's bedroom and another, while the bathroom opened directly on to a woman's room, and from the noise above he suspected that there must have been some sort of sawmill on the roof, 'but it is all very jolly, and when warmer weather comes, I shall be able to work on the roof which commands a boundless view of Florence across the river.'[42]

Teddy Wolfe, an artist and another friend of Marsh's whom Charles had known in London, was also living in the house. He was a high-spirited South African who had been at the Slade, and a member of the Omega Workshops, founded by members of the Bloomsbury Group in 1913. He took Charles to visit the historian and art critic Bernard Berenson at his villa, I Tatti, outside Florence, and in return Charles read part of his translation of Proust to him and asked Prentice if Wolfe could do some wood-cut illustrations for the cover of *Within a Budding Grove*. One trial wrapper symbolised the Champs-Elysées or Gilberte or both, the other a seascape with girls lying on the cliff; but Prentice declined.

Charles had lost time through illness in Rapallo and through caring for his parents; but he was now finally ready to hand over the first one hundred folios of *Guermantes II*. He explained to Prentice, 'They are what diplomats call identic, so you can send either to Seltzer [his American publisher].'[43] On finishing the first volume of the *Guermantes Way*, he dedicated it to Oriana Haynes and composed an acrostic poem for her forty-first birthday. The first letters of each line spelled out Oriana Huxley Haynes and he prefaced the dedication, 'To Mrs H . . . on her birthday.'

As to the rest of *Recherche*, he told Prentice, there were still two tomes to appear, and the Anglo-American community could not understand the stalling on *Sodome et Gomorrhe*. In Britain the publication would cause scandal and possibly legal action against translator and publisher. Teddy Wolfe appeared one day with a well-bound copy of *Ulysses*, published the year before in Paris to escape strict British censorship laws. Also,

> Seltzer seems to have secured an important decision in the US courts, entitling him to publish pretty well what he likes. If *he* is to print the book, the risk from (*not* of) suppression in Britain should not be very great. Reading one of Firbank's books here this morning, I am sure that there is nothing in Proust so indecent as almost every page of Firbank.[44]

Charles finished the second part of *The Guermantes Way* in five months; the same amount of time as it had taken to complete the first half. 'It has taken far too long,' he remarked, while admitting that of all three parts, *The Guermantes Way* was easily the best translation, being 'not so "literary" as *Swann* – which is probably a good thing'.[45]

By now Prentice had met the Schiffs and become extremely fond of them, though he did not visit Cambridge Square very often. 'I dare say you find their atmosphere rather exhausting,' wrote Charles, 'like tuberoses in a bedroom: that awed reverence for what the Philistine would regard as a bawdy book.'[46] Reading Schiff's latest novel, *Richard, Myrtle and I*, written in the second person and based on the couple's relationship with Proust, Charles commented, 'a grisly array of family skeletons'.[47] He did however continue to send Mrs Schiff proof sheets of his translations, although he soon realised that the Schiffs would not be able to help much with the difficult job of correcting errors. It had become a mere formality to send them his work ever since he had left London, especially since Mrs Schiff was so 'modest and laudatory, she will not venture to correct any slips'.[48]

Now that he had settled permanently in Italy, Charles had to tackle the language. 'I read the *Corriere* prayerfully, and the *Stampa*, which has an admirable London correspondent. But I shall never speak the language, still less write it, which seems to be immensely difficult,'[49] he told Prentice. However, before long he was suggesting Italian authors to translate. First Mario Mariani, whose *Meditazioni d'un Pazzo*, (*A Madman's Meditations*) he thought 'not exactly deep but the sort of shallowness sprinkled with allusions to Kant, Schopenhauer, Oscar Wilde and all those johnnies, and a certain amount of rather mordant criticism of contemporary life'.[50] Then he suggested the dramatist Luigi Chearelli and the young novelist Guido Morselli – all of which came to nothing. Finally he saw a book called *Uno per l'anno*, on a stall in Viareggio. He bought it, read it excitedly and wrote to Prentice, 'he is the goods. Freeze onto him.'[51] The author was Pirandello. 'In a year or two,' Charles swore, he'll be booming in England, there is no doubt that he is going to be the big noise in drama in the next decade . . . Whether his Novelle will be modern enough – they are a bridge between Maupassant and Aldous Huxley – I can't say.'[52] Nor could Prentice, who would later have the problems of dealing with the copyright, and who decided to welcome Charles's translations of Stendhal first, before turning to 'Eyetalian' authors.

Charles was eager to start on Stendhal, but found it difficult to concentrate in Florence. There was a steady stream of tourists, friends of friends from Britain who expected him to be their tour guide; the general literary milieu was too dissolute and indisciplined and the house he lived in with Teddy Wolfe had a number of drug addicts. He wanted a different kind of life. Vyvyan Holland offered to help; he had a friend, whom they called Consul Evans, part of a network of 'friendships fostered on battlefields' who lived alone with only servants and dogs in an old villa outside Lucca in a village called Cerasomma, without electricity or modern conveniences. Evans liked Charles and was prepared to have him as a lodger, 'free of charge in return for my conversation'.[53] There was an advantage from an intelligence point of view of staying with Evans. He was also ex-military and lived conveniently equidistant between Viareggio and Pisa. In June Charles bought a bicycle so that he could continue his reporting: travelling around picking up information on the local military bases, air bases and railway stations. Agents were given a train-watchers' guide to identify military units by the silhouettes of the wagons. You could tell whether a train was carrying an infantry, artillery or cavalry unit by the shape of the transport and number of carriages.

With less social life and more time Charles went into a frenzy of translating. He would cycle into Lucca to buy more Pirandello texts, so that he would have a ready pile to work on. On 19 June 1924 he finished typing *Sodome et Gomorrhe I*, next he would start the *Chartreuse de Parme*, then do *Abelard and Heloise* for Chapman and then move back to the rest of Stendhal and Pirandello. All this he explained in long letters to his publishers. 'Your letter arrived this extremely hot morning. I should be in Viareggio but am confined to the house and garden because of sore throat and stomach ache probably because of bicycling in the dust from Pisa yesterday.'[54] Charles then summarised several of Pirandello's stories in detail to persuade Prentice that he must take them on. He suggested publishing them in line with the Chatto Chekov series: a book of fifteen short stories of 5000 words each.

Proust was the handbook for the urban haute bourgeois: neurotic, intellectual, tortured, decadent. But Pirandello, what a breath of fresh air – though by no means simple: he could do torture and neurosis just as well – but his insights seemed cleaner. Pirandello came from Sicily and wrote about small town society that stretched from peasants to petite bourgeoisie. Laced through his writing was a different sort of Catholicism – the prayers of the poor. His stories were unpredictable, full of untidy endings and unanswered questions. Like Proust with Ruskin, Pirandello had started his creative life as a translator, translating Goethe. Charles was so impassioned that he wrote to Vyvyan, 'I am going to translate the complete works of Pirandello, in two hundred and eighteen volumes; it will be very difficult, as I do not know any Italian.'[55]

That summer Oriana Haynes and her daughter Renée came to Italy. Starting at the mud baths at Abano, they moved to Lucca and Pisa where Charles acted as guide and companion. He took them round the seventeenth-century fortified walls of Lucca, planted with trees;

the church of San Michele and the little shops and cafés in the myriad narrow streets. In Pisa he related the history of the Piazza dei Miracoli, the astonishingly beautiful square with its marble cathedral dating back to the twelfth century. He limped up the three hundred steps of the Leaning Tower, without railings, faster than the teenage Renée, and took them to the cafés and restaurants in his favourite haunts. They stayed at the Hotel Nettuno, which Charles had discovered on a trip that February. It was an elegant, palatial hotel overlooking the Arno, built in the early nineteenth century with over a hundred bedrooms, a winter garden, a ballroom for three hundred, reading rooms, concert rooms and a restaurant. All the major literary and political figures stayed there. Before they left, Charles gave Oriana the carbon copy of *Guermantes II* and the first chapter of Stendhal's *Chartreuse* to take to Prentice at Chatto.

Charles made regular visits to Viareggio, for bathing, he explained, and they were always punctuated with a stop at his favourite restaurant at the side of the Burlamacco Canal, where Armando Cassini, restaurateur and citizen of the world, became his firm friend as well as his source for any sailors' gossip about the Italian Navy, where ships were going and what was on board. But on 9 July he was called to Viareggio for Cassini's funeral. Distracted by the event he sat down at another pier restaurant and accidentally dropped his typewriter case into the sea – in it were chapters six, seven and ten of *Chartreuse* – he had just finished chapter ten a few minutes earlier. With them went 'the French text of Chartreuse and 2 vols. of Pirandello – and the whole floated, or rather bobbed on the tide – two gay hotel labels on top reassuring me with their coloured smile, while an intrepid nude hauled a double sendaline [raft] into the water and finally swam for and rescued the whole.' He tipped the youth ten lire, 'which was cheap for the recovery of a month's work'.[56]

Not far south, the island of Capri, off the coast near Naples, was the summer haunt of many writers and home of Compton Mackenzie, who invited Charles to stay for a period to discuss Stendhal. 'Mackenzie says he can read no novels now except Jane Austen and Stendhal.'[57] With Compton Mackenzie's experience of working as a secret agent in Greece all during the war, there was more than literary know-how to exchange. But Charles took his chance, as Mackenzie always remembered,[58] to test his translations by reading them out loud for Mackenzie's judgement. After a week with Mackenzie, Charles moved to the Hotel La Palma for ten days where he just missed the novelist Louis Golding but 'caught the dust left behind him. He seems to have got Norman Douglas and the Brett-Youngs to lunch together – all most willingly by telling each party that the other had invited him/them. The bill is still circulating between Capri and Anacapri.'[59] While in a restaurant with other friends, Charles was locked in the toilet by the waiter, who explained that he had done it '*per ridere*' (just for a laugh). For Charles it was only funny in retrospect, but what he did find amusing was the fate of the volume of Stendhal he had borrowed from the London Library:

> A loyal but misguided servant brought it from Cerasomma on a bicycle, which has rather frayed the boards. I should say however that it is not in great demand at the Library and should hold out another fifty years in its present state.[60]

He had to move from Cerasomma at the end of July because living with Consul Evans became complicated. After two years in India, Charles thought, he had become insane as he saw all Italians as 'natives and himself as the only "white man" in a large jungle area'. So Charles moved into the Hotel Nettuno in Pisa, from where he sent the translations of Balzac's preface to the *Chartreuse de Parme*. He wrote to Vyvyan that he revelled in being back in Pisa: 'I have wild adventures every night under the leaning tower.' Vyvyan was now inspired to visit. 'Bring bathing drawers,' Charles urged, 'we will bathe in the rivers, of which there are two, one still and one sparkling.'[61]

A group of young Italian flying officers were staying at the Nettuno. Several of these would invite him to take wine with them every night. 'They are extremely intelligent like all intelligent Italians and entertaining, like all Italians.'[62] One young aviator, Captain Federico Frezzan, was impressed when he heard Charles was translating Stendhal but when he discovered he intended to translate Pirandello, his admiration knew no bounds, and he became a firm friend and a part of Charles's network. They were excited about the huge investment Mussolini was making in the Italian air force and the details of it expanding into Africa. When twelve Yemeni nobles arrived in Rome to undergo training as pilots, the flying fraternity knew about it.[63] By no accident,

Wing-Commander Fletcher, the British Air Attaché at Rome arrived at the Nettuno: 'He has been most useful to me, as I am now accepted as perfectly "orlri" by the local aeronauts.'[64]

As a further encouragement to Vyvyan to visit, Charles related 'an interval of disrespectability', where he went with the head waiter at the Nettuno, another waiter and a friend in a car to Pisa Marina, then on to Leghorn where they

> abducted the only woman left in a d:s:rd:rly h::s: and took her to Pisa with a 'fall out on the right of the road, boys' en route, in which I did <u>not</u> participate: I was a little revolted when the head-waiter, who took her off into the darkness and had previously served the Compagnie Internationale des Wagons-Lits, came back calling out, 'Seconda Serie!' But such is life.[65]

Vyvyan Holland promptly arrived and they spent a week in Florence where Charles got 'flu' again but luckily had Vyvyan to nurse him and help him back to the comforts of the Nettuno. Then they took off for a tour of Northern Italy, going first to Milan where they had a cinema flick book made of themselves seated at a table smoking and talking, then to Carrara and the Apuan Alps, which they climbed with two donkeys and pack men. Vyvyan took photos of Charles with the muleteers and standing proudly at the summit of Monte Forato. Charles busied himself with correcting Vyvyan's Baedeker and they both translated en route. Charles was working on Stendhal and they visited the original Charterhouse at Parma, a working monastery.

Returning to Pisa on 1 October he found a parcel from Prentice which he 'hoped was full of Budding Girls'.[66] But it was not until the 9th that the finished version of *Within a Budding Grove* arrived. When it came, he sent a list of those who would have to be sent free copies including some of the contributors to the *Tribute*, 'such as poor old Violet Hunt; she has so few pleasures, as Saint-Loup said of his mistress'.[67]

Charles enjoyed the Nettuno, which was where Pirandello's eponymous hero stayed in his novel *Il Fu Matteo Pascale*, but it was too expensive for permanent life and in September he moved to a flat almost next door. 'Pisa is a very charming place to stay in,' he told Prentice, '– lively and quiet if you know what I mean. I write in my bedroom window looking down the Arno waiting for a friend to arrive from Viareggio on a bicycle. He may have gone to Cerasomma instead which would be a pity.' Number 20 Lungarno Reggio was a convenient few doors away from the Hotel Nettuno, where Charles had his meals. His landlord, Signor Frascani, was a gynaecologist and Charles received a receipt for his weekly stream of black coffees on gynaecologist headed notepaper, which he kept, '*per ridere*', in his translating notebook. The rooms were on the first floor with high ceilings overlooking the main road along the busy Arno, and he could see a tiny marble church set on one of the bridges across the river. The light was fantastic, reflecting off the river and the yellow stucco houses on the opposite bank. On arrival he had thirteen consecutive days of sunshine; he would wake at dawn and lie until his pillow scorched his face, then sit on the balcony in his pyjamas and an old hat and read until breakfast time. His books finally arrived from England and a local carpenter constructed a library. For his intelligence work he covered the walls with maps of the area, large and small-scale, and began sticking them together, and on 21 November he told Vyvyan that he was going on a trip to Siena with one aviator, two infantry officers, and a chemical expert. No further details were given.

Charles's copies of his translation of Stendhal's *Armance* catalogue his journeys up and down the coast: Pisa, Viareggio, La Spezia and Rome, with dates, sometimes only three days in one place. It is likely he was also being sent to watch or report on naval and military activities. To explain the political picture it was necessary to know that the Suez Canal and the Red Sea were the jugular veins of the route between Britain and India, and this was the area of Mussolini's ambition. It was discovered that Italian arms were being used against the British Aden Protectorate in Arabia. Britain asked fascist Italy to take every possible step to prevent this export of arms to Arabia, but, although Mussolini agreed to stop the shipment of weapons, British intelligence continued to obtain incontrovertible evidence that arms, ammunition, cartridges and guns were continually being smuggled into Arabia under the supervision of Italian naval vessels.[68]

As autumn advanced Charles felt he needed a companion in his room and fell in love with the large, yellow eyes of a small owl being sold on the steps of San Michele in Borgo, 'of the kind called Civetta, which means coquette or pretty lady'.[69] He bought it for ten francs without a cage and put it, tethered with leather cuffs at the feet, on his balcony, 'looking drownfully at the Arno . . . It does not love me yet, but I hope it will,' he told Prentice, 'the look of hatred in its painted eyes diminishes my loneliness.'[70] His hours of solitude were self-enforced in order to finish his work; this was hard, as he was pathologically gregarious. His landlady suggested the owl should be taught to type, but it would sit and stare, as owls do, behind Charles on a sofa, and was particularly attracted, he noticed, to the emblem of the head of Pallas on Chatto and Windus envelopes. He wrote all about his owl to Vyvyan: one evening he heard a bang from his bedroom; 'I went in and found a very self-righteous little owl on the floor', looking like 'one of the older members of the Savile.' The owl was hungry, and Charles 'boldly got some raw meat from the Nettuno, at the sight of which she gave one of her infrequent yelps.' Eating raw meat left an ineradicable mess on the furniture.

> I find it very invigorating to have a strong character battling against my own. I can always quell her by wrapping her in a coloured cotton handkerchief. She tucks in her claws and pretends to be dead . . . another tip from Tenente-pilote Frezzan was: 'Don't liberate her at night, or she will excavate you the eyes.' A grim thought.[71]

CHAPTER 14

Discovering Pirandello

> The man, the writer, the instrument of the creation will die, but his creation does not die.
>
> Luigi Pirandello, *Six Characters in Search of an Author,* 1921

In settling in Italy and finding Pisa a 'calm but lively' place to live, Charles was embarking on the most prolific writing period of his life. In the next six years he would translate fifteen volumes, compile a genealogy, write countless articles and thousands of spirited, intimate letters. Most of the time he was in pain from his old wounds, from recurring trench fever, and from the beginnings of what with hindsight can be seen as stomach cancer, but he thought was indigestion.

He longed to write a book of his own and at the end of October proposed to Prentice 'a kind of meditative Reisebilder book' travel-writing, memoir, social criticism and literary debate:

> There would be Apuan Alps, Massa-Carrara, Parma, thoughts in Milan, Piacenza, Pisa (without the Tower), Lucca, San Miniato al Tedesco, odds and ends from a Lungarno window, the Church of San Piero a Grado, where I saw last Sunday the recently laid-bare walls of the 1st century church built after the Apostle Peter landed there on his way to Rome; also some remarks on Stendhal's Parma and the real, the Balbec sculptures and Giovanni's pulpit. Any amount of history and geography, mostly lifted from obscure Italian gazetteers, and of reminiscences, personal abuse and reflexions generally . . . It would be a relief, as at present I go to bed and start stringing sentences in my mind and get no sleep and scramble over the cement floor looking

> for a geography book of Tuscany, and awake next morning about 9.15 with the sun scorching the tip of my nose.[1]

Prentice was encouraging without promising an advance. It would have been an intriguing read; a blend of the vivacity of his letters and the intellectual rigour of his articles. However, he put all his spare energy after translation into his vast correspondence and restarted an affectionate bout with Edward Marsh at the end of November 1924.

> Dear, ubiquitous Eddie,
> You have been so many times on the verge of receiving a letter from me . . . opening Henry James's Letters, a book that fills the emptiest winter room with the warm breath of intimate communicative people, I was immediately taken slap into your company, so much that I felt it almost indecent not to cry out to you that I was there . . .[2]

We do not have Marsh's replies, but Charles wrote a day later: 'Our letters cross like sky rockets in the breeding season, ut ita dicam, as Abelard says when he is being particularly rude to Heloise.'[3]

Edward Marsh was now in a position of some power as Private Secretary to Winston Churchill, the Chancellor of the Exchequer, after his re-election in 1924. Marsh remained at the Treasury until 1929, and was also officially Private Secretary at the Colonial Office. Charles begged him:

> Write to me and tell me – not secrets, of course, – about the Treasury. Do you help to interfere with prosecutions? Will you stop them from prosecuting me if I translate Sodome et Gomorrhe. Do they give you an adding machine? It must be delightful.
>
> I am seriously delighted that Winston has returned to power, and hope to see him Prime Minister when I return to England. I suppose his difficulty will always be to secure followers; but what followers more can a man need who has the exquisite, endless and devoted service of yourself?[4]

Marsh was the intellectual Jeeves to Winston Churchill's Wooster, following him to every department until his retirement in 1937 when he was knighted. At the end of 1924 Marsh's own translation of *Forty-Two Fables of La Fontaine* was going to press. He sent Charles a complimentary copy and Charles replied with comparisons of La Fontaine's characters to key political figures who mingled daily with Marsh at Westminster, asking if the similarities were intentional.

Guy Chapman had asked Charles that year to begin work on the medieval Latin text of the letters of Abelard and Heloise, which Charles started as soon as he had received the £150 advance. The first page of his translating jotter[5] titles the book, *Letter the First which is a History of the ~~Misfortunes~~ Calamities of Abelard written to a Friend.* The 'l' in the word 'calamities' is crossed and the last 'i' omitted, making it read 'catamites'. Above it is a fine sketch of an ejaculating penis. The doodle is either a sympathetic gesture to the fate of Abelard who was castrated, or a representation of Charles's own activities. He told Marsh that he had been to Florence to visit, 'the fleshpots and fiaschi'[6], and on return, to his remorse, found that his owl had died from cold, hunger and neglect. He was mortified, and went into a flurry of work. He wrote a gloomy and confused letter to Prentice saying that he had inherited the family trait of 'accepting diametrically opposite advice and feeling the full importance of things that don't matter.'[7] The death of his owl did matter, and the fact that he had left her alone while he went off to seek sensual pleasure made him guilty on top; even more so, he was reminded of the death of his dog Dido when he was ten and many deaths of loved ones that he had mourned since then. To make matters worse, the post brought 'a horrid budget of American Proust "clippings" among which the American Nature proves what I had long suspected, that I know no French at all. I feel a proper idiot, as B. and Charlus say, "Je suis seul, je suis veuf, et sur moi la nuit tombe."'[8]

However, entertainment was always around the corner. That December, his favourite literary enemies, the Sitwells, turned up at the Hotel Nettuno as he gleefully told Marsh:

> After the Sitwells had left the other day, in what the Maitre d'Hotel called a 'magnifico Rolls-Roger' he told me that they had inquired about me, and my last name being little used here, were told that Signor Scott divided time in Pisa. They will probably send a report that I am living under a false name. He also

> asked me whether they were signori o scrittori which left me at a loss for an answer.[9]

Were they gentlemen or writers? Charles would have answered neither. There was not the same dilemma over Puccini, who had died suddenly in November at the age of sixty-seven, after a glorious and controversial career composing great operas. Charles had attended a gala performance the night before of *Manon Lescaut*, and the curtain had not come down until four minutes to one:

> . . . which would hardly have suited a London audience. We rose and stood for a moment in pitch darkness in homage to the soul of Puccini who walked from Lucca to see a performance of Aida when seventeen, with a bosom friend they took a single room in a hostelry outside the Lucca gate, in his friends name – Puccini entering through the window – it was then that he decided to be a Maestro.[10]

On Christmas Eve Charles went to midnight Mass at the Duomo, the 'most beautiful church in the world'[11] and stood at the chancel rail in front of a group of drunken students, one of whom shouted into the painted dome, 'Io faccio un discorso' ('I want to make a speech'), going on to protest that the students' study of obstetrics gave them a professional interest in the Virgin birth. His friend kept telling him to shut up, in French

> 'Tesez fou, je fous prie; l'église est la meson de Die' and a slim smart carabiniere who was with them, muffled in his cloak, kissed him from time to time in the hope of keeping him quiet. All very odd in an English duomo, I couldn't help thinking.[12]

The winter was cold and wet and Charles at last bought an oil-fuelled stove, finding the domestic heating inadequate. The New Year 1925 began with an all-night party in Charles's flat to celebrate his completion of *The Charterhouse of Parma*, which, with red wine spilt on the first page, was then dispatched to London. A few days later, Charles noticed that the post office was shut on the Feast of the Epiphany, remarking that the Italians were still outwardly religious, despite the offices of the local Catholic newspaper being completely destroyed the week before by supporters of the government.

Mussolini had always argued that violence was a necessary part of his regime. In January 1925 he declared that for the good of the country he was assuming dictatorial powers; opposition politicians were arrested and national newspapers handed over to fascist proprietors. The Catholic press had been professional in reporting violence by Blackshirts, and they were destroyed overnight – the presses smashed and the personnel disappeared. Mussolini cleverly fostered the church divide by wooing the Papacy, who already thought the Catholic press too liberal, with conservative proposals. Over the next year Mussolini banned contraceptives, put a tax on bachelors, and received the official backing of Pope Pius XI. A year later, in November 1926, all non-fascist political activity, whether in the press or public meetings, was prohibited. The Fascist Grand Council replaced parliament, they compiled a list of candidates for election and the electorate had the right only to accept or reject their entire list. Charles began to notice that he was sometimes being followed.

In spite of or because of the political situation that year, Charles hoped to work on *Abelard*, then Stendhal's *Abbess of Castro*, three short stories about appalling corruption among medieval Italian aristocracy, one of which dealt very squarely with incest. He gave up the idea of translating Stendhal's *Chroniques Italiennes* and decided to hand over Stendhal's volume on romantic love with women *De l'Amour* to Vyvyan Holland who, he explained to Prentice, was constantly falling in love with women: 'It is much more his line and gives no scope whatsoever for prose style which is generally considered to be my stunt.'[13] Next he lined up *Le Rouge et le Noir* and a collection of Pirandello short stories. Charles was on a mission to propagate Pirandello and was convinced the critics would compare his short stories to Tolstoy and de Maupassant, and his plays to Chekov. He was to be proved correct in forecasting the public's appreciation, for when the stories were published – brief, dynamic and full of tragic absurdity – the reviews poured in more copiously than they had even for his Proust. Short stories were more satisfying than a million-word novel, even in volume parts, it seemed.

As Charles worked furiously in Pisa, his parents came south again, like birds for the winter: George, old and ill, was taken by Meg to the French Riviera for some January sun. For Charles, duty called. He tore himself away from his lovingly reassembled library, fearful of the gloomy prospect which might await him by his father's bedside, arriving on 12 January in Eze-sur-Mer, at the ominously named Hotel Terminus. George, however, did not die. Instead he revelled in reading the copy of James Melville, the sixteenth-century Scots memoir-writer, which Charles had asked Chapman to send on. He did not think it wise to let his father read *Petronius*. The parental tour, organised by the indefatigable Meg continued and a week later they arrived at Beaulieu, still on the Riviera. His parents were blooming, but Charles, struggling with Abelard's letters vi and vii, fell victim to the 'treacherous dolls house climate',[14] and was too weak to type the rest of letter vii. There was the continual problem of which translation of the Bible to use, because what was familiar to the public was not necessarily appropriate to the text, so he had sometimes to translate straight from Abelard, who would have used his own Latin eleventh-century version.

He complained to Chapman that:

> There is not the least vestige of love in Abelard's last letters; in fact he obviously was tired of her when he sent her to Argenteuil, or at any rate when he lost his worker's dreadnoughts.[15]

As with his other books, Charles started to care about the characters. Before long he realised that George Moore had written his fictional romance based on the seventeenth-century French version of the letters, which differed almost entirely from the medieval Latin original. By the end of January he was only halfway through 'the insufferable Abelard'. Chapman encouraged him by saying the booksellers were expecting it. Any clamour from booksellers, Charles replied, was doubtless because of his name as the translator of Proust rather than any assumed erotic popularity Abelard might be expected to have, 'though I suppose people will read his letters as they go to see the Ermafrodoti at the Uffizi, with a comfortable sense of their own entirety'.[16] Abelard's castration continued to preoccupy him, as did any whiff of sex in the medieval latin,

> The passage about fornication at Argenteuil you will find on my folios 76-77. They did it in the refectory, apparently, in a smell of stale mutton fat and wine lees.[17]

Still with parents in tow on 11 February 1925, he took his typewriter to the Pensione Ginevra in Viareggio on the via Manin, opposite the sandy beach and near the Burlamacco Canal with its restaurants that cooked the catch directly off the boats. The beach had romantic if tragic associations, as the body of the shipwrecked Shelley was washed up at Viareggio in 1834, and was immediately cremated there on a pyre attended by his friend and fellow poet Byron. A string of English writers and poets came on pilgrimages to this beach at some point in their lives and a Protestant English church was built in Catholic Viareggio to accommodate the growing number of visitors, which increased as the town became a fashionable wintering place. Charles's parents were now staying in front of the beach at the other end of the straight, windswept promenade, and the daily walk to see them gave him both rheumatism and tonsillitis: 'It is cold and damp – I must abed and go on reading d'Annunzio's *Fuoco* which is longer even than Abelard's evasion of his conjugal duties.'[18]

At the end of February, he was hurriedly typing the last of letter vii in between visits from his parents. He had the idea of writing the introduction also in the form of letters; one from himself to George Moore, which he would make controversial, and then the reply from Moore. He wrote to Chapman on Abelard:

> Only the irrepressible young prig who insisted on lecturing impromptu upon the interpretation of Ezekiel, and expected his better instructed seniors then to sit under him, could have grown into the intolerable old egoist who could write to his wife (in the Fifth Letter) of his own emasculation: 'Neither grieve that thou wert the cause of so great a good, for which thou needst not doubt that thou wert principally created by God.'[19]

Charles did, however, admire Heloise; not many female scholars still call out from the twelfth century. Heloise unflinchingly describes her desires in her letters: Abelard may have been castrated, but she has not. Her letters are truly loving and she has a professional and conscientious interest in running her convent, whereas Abelard, Charles maintained, was motivated by lust and self-interest. In the introduction, George Moore defended Abelard, and identified with him and his life of lamentation, remembering that Abelard had to contend with the line from Deuteronomy 23:1, 'He that is wounded in the stones or hath his privy member cut off, shall not enter into the congregation of the Lord.' George Moore, like Abelard, saw Heloise as a sexual object and ended by fantasising, somewhat absurdly, about her sitting as his Muse at the end of his 'mahogany-rimmed bath', whispering words 'so shocking that I dare not repeat them.'[20] Whereas Moore could only see, and exploit, his erotic and romantic fantasy of Abelard and Heloise, Charles, the scholar, both worked from the original letters and tried to tease out the truth of their relationship. He saw Abelard's hurt pride and priggish ambition and realised that Abelard had not loved Heloise, while she did love and desire him.

Charles moved back and forth from Pisa, working in the intense cold of a north-facing room while wind was blowing off the snow in Viareggio. Fortified by whisky and Ellimans Embrocation he finally managed to finish the 'wretched stuff' – just in time, as Arthur Waugh senior, Chapman's colleague and managing director and chairman of publisher Chapman and Hall, was due to arrive in Italy, expecting to be entertained by Charles and taken on guided tours. They travelled to Florence, back to Pisa and then to Rome for five days. However Waugh's refusal to learn a word of Italian made him a very dependent traveller. They visited St Peter's, which for Charles was a great disappointment; he now admired St Paul's in London more than ever. The main reason for the trip to Rome was to meet Pirandello and discuss copyright. Charles took Arthur Waugh and Captain Frezzan, the literary aviator from the Nettuno, on a tour of the Roman theatres and eventually found Pirandello in the Metastasio, rehearsing his company for a summer tour of England. He invited Charles to his home the next day and they thrashed out the copyright problems. 'He is a most delightful simple old gent. With large eyes the colour of good coffee, like A. France.'[21] The geniality of the man and the excitement of the meeting overshadowed the business aspect, but finally he was there. In June Prentice wrote to say that the coast was clear for Charles to start translating two of Pirandello's novels, *Si Gira* and *I Vecchi e i Giovani*. His translation of the first paragraph of *Si Gira (Shoot!)* spoke comically to him about his own hectic life:

> I study people in their most ordinary occupations, to see if I can succeed in discovering in others what I feel that I myself lack in everything that I do: the certainty that they understand what they are doing.[22]

Shoot! is a novel about filming a captivating actress called the Nestroff, who trifles with the affections of two actors. It was peculiarly relevant to Charles, who was in the midst of his own fascination for a woman introduced to him by Vyvyan: 'Life without you is almost more intolerable than life with you,'[23] Charles complained. Vyvyan had become entangled with a Mrs Ruby Melville, a London society beauty. In the 1920 society portrait by William Orpen she has lively brown eyes, a sharp red bob, a daring lace décolleté showing off long white arms, hands on her hips, slender fingers splayed over a wasp waist. She looks unafraid of anything. She was now on the run from her wealthy ageing husband and vivaciously interested in other men in Italy. Vyvyan fled and Mrs Melville stayed behind, ringing Charles who gave excuses on Vyvyan's behalf, using it to tease him as usual, '. . . and told her that you had conceived a violent but wholly unnatural passion for the fascista who collects the tickets at the uscita at Pisa station . . . She much shocked, promised not to breathe a word to anybody about your sad laps [*sic*].'[24]

Five days later Charles, ever in love with Vyvyan's company, implored him by letter, 'I want you badly – will you come to Capri with me for a fortnight?'[25] He went to Florence in search of Vyvyan. Walking into Casoni's, the fashionable café on the via Tornabuoni, he saw Ruby presiding over a cake party. Consul Evans came up to Charles and said abruptly, 'I don't like your beard,' and Ruby rounded loudly, 'I like every bit of him.' He then had to escort her round the town and home and 'press my beard into her face . . . R. seems to like me because I am so utterly different to what she gets served up to her . . . and has even asked me to marry her, to protect her from honourable intentions.' Meaning Ruby did not want to settle down and if married to Charles would be free to move from man to man just as he did. 'My beard is lovely now . . . and eminently desirable by women.' Charles was mesmerised by Ruby, she was the only woman he had ever met who was as confidently promiscuous as he was. In fact she made off with one of Charles's nubile young Italian consorts named

Pippo. Charles consoled himself with another regular friend named Nello who was in need of finances for his sick sister, and whose brother and mother both arrived asking for money. At this point Charles's life read like a bedroom farce: escaping from women, getting postcards from young Italian men, consoling a man in love with Vyvyan who had briefly fled back to England, calming mothers of young upset lovers, and writing spontaneous limericks to Vyvyan, such as, 'There was a young man of Faenza, who had terribly bad influenza: he plugged his meatus with Kidd's apparatus and drank selz, non con cognac, ma senza.'[26]

He would often give Vyvyan advice about what to translate, advising him to take on Stendhal's *De l'Amour* as he himself found Stendhal easy. 'You can do it straight on to the typewriter without even stopping to masturbate, as in the case of Proust.'[27] Vyvyan meanwhile sent Charles shirt samples, asking if he could try and match them with Italian cotton. Charles replied with customary innuendo, 'I am extremely busy . . . I am not in the shirt trade: I prefer what lies, or occasionally stands behind.'[28] Charles had to go straight to Bologna for a few days on an intelligence exercise for Louis, during which he had time for all the local churches and sights and sent 'Vybs' a postcard.

Through the hectically social summer of 1925, Charles translated Stendhal's two-volume novel *Le Rouge et le Noir,* and *The Abbess of Castro,* Stendhal's collection of short stories. Proof sheets of *The Guermantes Way* came from Chatto and the *Letters of Abelard to Heloise* from Chapman to be corrected at the same time, while he continued translating *Si Gira*, Pirandello's novel about the film industry. He dedicated the translation 'To O.H.H. and V.B.H. who have seen and survived the Nestroff' (meaning Ruby Melville). In October the *Nouvelle Revue Française* published the fifth part of Proust's novel, originally titled *La Fugitive*, but retitled as *Albertine Disparue* by Gallimard, to prevent it being confused with Tagore's *La Fugitive* of 1921. There was still pressure on Charles from Proust's American publisher, however, to work on *Sodome et Gomorrhe*. Charles was dreading the moral onslaught this translation might bring. These two volumes of Proust's novel began with the introduction, 'Introducing the men-women, descendants of those of the inhabitants of Sodom who were spared by the fire from heaven.' The first volume concerned

Portrait of Charles painted in 1922 by Edward Stanley Mercer, who shared a house with Vyvyan Holland in Carlyle Square in Chelsea.

Marcel Proust in uniform in 1889. Charles and Proust never met, sadly. Proust died in 1922, the year Charles's translation of *Du Côté de chez Swann* was published by Chatto and Windus to great acclaim.

Charles Prentice in 1935, with Norman Douglas. Publisher, friend and correspondent, Prentice was senior partner at Chatto and Windus and published Charles's translations of Proust and Pirandello.

Edward Marsh, civil servant and patron of the arts, took a deep interest in both Charles and his translations of Proust. They became great friends and lifelong correspondents.

Luigi Pirandello, whom Charles first met after a performance of one of his plays in Pisa in 1925.

A sketch of Charles in 1925 by Estelle Nathan, an artist who spent time in Italy and whose daughter Pamela was one of Charles's friends in Rome.

Vyvyan Holland and Charles visited Milan together and had a cinematic flip book made of their dinner conversation. They had a loyal and flirtatious friendship and wrote to each other frequently about their intimate lives and gossip about mutual friends.

In between translating and spying, Charles (left) was a constant tour guide for his many friends who came to visit him in Italy.

A portrait of Charles's great friend and confidante Oriana Haynes as a young woman. She spent many hours listening to Charles read his translations viva voce.

Ruby Melville (second from left) in Italy in 1923. Vyvyan Holland (far left) said of her: 'What an idiot I made of myself to be sure, following her round Florence and Paris, and she surrounded by dowry-happy gigolos.'

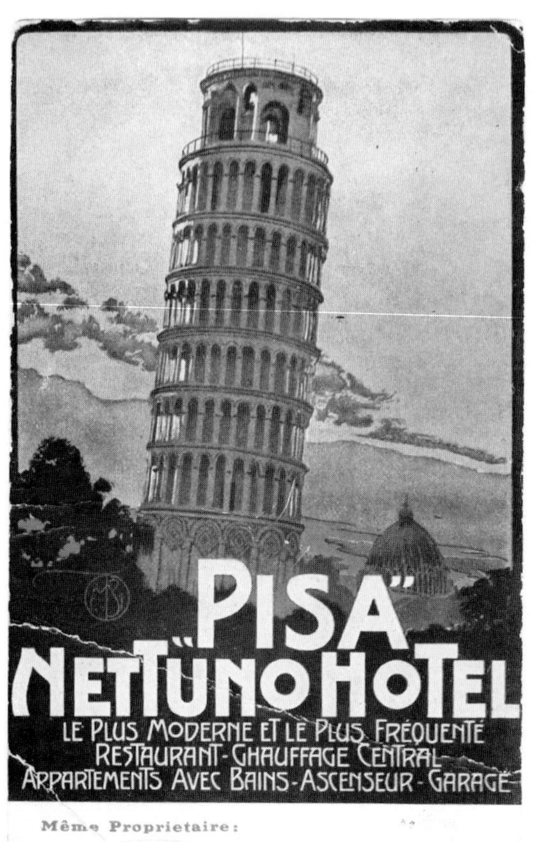

Charles was devoted to his nieces and nephews, especially after the death of his older brother John. To his young niece Sita, he would send postcards like this one of the Hotel Nettuno in Pisa, where he often stayed.

Alberghi proprietà Feroci:
PISA - HOTEL NETTUNO
VIAREGGIO - HOTEL EXCELSIOR
HOTEL REGINA

CARTE POSTALE

VISITATE ... E LA ... ESPOSIZIONE ... 1927

POSTE ITALIANE Cent. 75

15-3-27-

Miss Sita Scott Moncrieff
St Luke's Hostel
Fitzroy Square
LONDON W.1.
INGHILTERRA

Charles on holiday with Louis Christie at Durie in 1926. It was here in 1923 that Louis probably first broached the idea of Charles spying for him from Italy.

Claude Dansey, the spymaster. Charles knew him at the War Office in 1917 and Dansey was later head of station in Rome.

Charles on an Italian mountainside, taken by Vyvyan Holland in 1926. He looks noticeably ill here. He was to die four years later.

Some Part of the Descent

of

Charles Scott Moncrieff

(born on the 25th day of September in the Year of Grace 1889)

From divers persons of note both good and bad in the realms of the Scots and I-know-not-whom. With the names of many cadets of the lines, both those that be now alive and the blessed dead who are now alive for all time. Composed from no vain feelings of pride, but rather that the names and ages (if nothing more) of many members of families noble in God's sight and often in man's, might not altoge perish in the passage of time.

Like Proust, Charles was fascinated by genealogy, drawing family trees as a child and later compiling a complete history of the Moncrieffs with his cousin. This scrap is a dedication to his own ancestors.

the character of the Baron de Charlus, the ageing homosexual aristocrat, with his pot belly and make-up, seeking out the young hairdresser Jupien.

> Meanwhile Jupien, shedding at once the humble, honest expression which I had always associated with him, had – in perfect symmetry with the Baron – thrown up his head, given a becoming tilt to his body, placed his hand with a grotesque impertinence on his hip, stuck out his behind, posed himself with the coquetry that the orchid might have adopted on the providential arrival of the bee. I had not supposed that he could appear so repellent.

Charles thought that a light warning verse on the last page of *The Guermantes Way* might be a way of enticing the reader with what was to come next. On 6 June he sent this verse in the form of an acrostic poem to Prentice, the first letter of each line spelling ADIEU A MARCEL PROUST.

> A little chit who writes a lot
> Declares this book should be destroyed
> In fact, as Mister Lynam Dott
> Explains, it simply reeks of Freud,
> Ugly enough, he says, in Nature;
> Ah! But how foul when turned to literature . . .[29]

He carried on, teasing his editor about 'Love mentioned in connection with de Charlus'. Prentice found it funny, but not printable. He would have to read the translation himself then consult a lawyer versed in the Obscene Publications Act.

Accustomed as he was to writing really unprintable limericks to Vyvyan,[30] Charles thought his effort to Prentice was rather tasteful. During June, as the weather in Pisa got hotter, Charles lured Vyvyan back and they set off on a trip for fresher air up the Apuan Alps to escape the social chaos. After a climb of 6100 feet, Charles had to let the others go ahead. On the way back he found that his white linen summer trousers were covered in his own blood at the seat. Rectal bleeding is often the first sign of stomach cancer, but Charles did not know this. He still had a walk of twenty miles to the next railway station at Barga Gallicano. He spent the night at the inn there in considerable pain, 'where the daughters of the house are all speechless and coo like outraged doves'. And then with 'one hand at the back of my ruined trousers, picked my way through the chestnuts to Barga'.[31] Exerting himself to the point of bleeding, he typically remained stoical through the pain, and instead wrote up information from railway stations in reports for the Passport Office, and in letters as entertainment for his correspondents.

One of those correspondents was the young Alec Waugh, son of the publisher Charles had just taken around Rome, and brother of Evelyn, who in 1925 was working in a prep school. Alec, on Evelyn's behalf, asked Charles if he needed a secretary, seeing that life in Italy in the warmth and among expatriate writers was preferable to life in the cold in England, and Charles in conversation agreed. On the strength of this Evelyn threw in his job as a tutor and dreamed of 'a year abroad drinking Chianti under olive trees and listening to discussions of all the most iniquitous outcasts of Europe'.[32] Charles then wrote to say that he did not want a secretary after all, realising he could not afford one; he moved around too much for it to be practical and his work for the secret service made it all too complicated. He had a card index at Pisa with book research on one side and classified secrets on the back. Moreover at nineteen, Evelyn Waugh could speak no other languages and could not use a typewriter. Evelyn wrote, 'One night, soon after I got the news from Pisa, I went down alone to the beach with my thoughts full of death. I took off my clothes and began swimming out to sea.'[33] Fortunately he met a shoal of jellyfish and was stung back to reality and swam ashore.

That spring Oriana Haynes had come to northern Italy for a two-month rest cure, but instead caught rheumatic fever which was later complicated by pneumonia. Charles was very disturbed on hearing the news. He had earlier hoped 'to converge with Mrs Haynes and perhaps carry her off, Centaur and Lapith, to the hills'[34] where he planned to read her the proofs of *Chartreuse*. He leapt into action and had her moved immediately to Pisa, where he sat up all night with her. But there was no point in getting ill himself and nursing was not his calling, so at the Hayneses' expense he organised for her specific nursing needs a local nun who spoke no English. He also engaged a 'companion' – who turned out to be Mrs Ruby Melville – by way of some entertainment. With all three female charges he moved to the Palace Hotel in Livorno, the most luxurious hotel in the vicinity – a great, pompous yellow palace on the beach in the sea breeze. Charles began at once to read his translations to the bedridden Oriana, with the help of Ruby Melville, who could not quite take the pace, soon collapsing into bed herself. Not to waste a helper, Charles presented her with the entire translation of Proust so far, six volumes, for her entertainment and his observation. As he explained to Prentice, 'one needs to be bedridden to absorb them all; indeed, there might be a special edition with a red cross on the cover and a pocket for thermometers, syringes etc, inside the boards.'[35] Charles made Suora Agata laugh, but the nun had to turn him out when he stayed too long with her charge. On 2 August he read Pirandello's play *The Rules of the Game* to Oriana. In this drama on marital infidelity, the main character chooses not to feel angry and betrayed at his wife's affair, but instead empties himself of all emotion and talks to her lover.

Charles had to go down to dinner after the second act and when he came back Oriana was sitting up in bed, tense with excitement. The play did not have a happy ending, but explored a situation Oriana was living herself. She was to spend nearly five months being read to by Charles, being sickly and not eating much: 'A sumptuous meal, with the ribbons, is brought up twice a day, but eaten by nuns, with enormous relish.'[36] Meanwhile Ted Haynes wanted his wife back in England, 'Ted Haynes clamours at every post for his conjugal rights, which he cannot have for the moment.' Charles suggested to Vyvyan, 'I wish you would find him some easily assimilable substitute.'[37]

Life at the Palace Hotel Livorno held even more drama than Pirandello's plays. At dinner in a nearby castello, Harold Acton had introduced Charles and Ruby to a Livorno legend, Aldo Nadi, one of the greatest fencers of all time. He and his brother Nedo were Olympic gold medallists and came from a long line of fencers. Known as the 'bad boy' of fencing, he crushed his opponents and celebrated afterwards with champagne. Handsome, romantic, macho and deadly serious he fell at once for Ruby. Charles had hoped that 'the occupation of a sick room may take her mind off the omnipresent male organ'. However, that was too much to imagine for Ruby; she and

Nadi were romantically involved at once. They motored around between Livorno, Pisa and Florence. Charles suspected Ruby would emasculate Nadi: 'Mrs M seems thoroughly sick of Leghorn, and I fancy her fancy man is rather coming to the end of his social resources. He has a fight or match or display at Forte de'Marmi on the 21st, and when he's lost that, I expect his father will tell him to keep off the Punch and Judy show for a bit.'[38] In fact, the twenty-four-year-old Nadi was not disempowered; he was at his zenith and Ruby was a match for him. They stayed in the Palace Hotel and dined regularly with Charles, who later called Nadi, the man 'who put the L in Leg horn'.[39] On 17 August Aldo proposed to Ruby, who accepted and asked Charles to act as witness at the wedding planned for 20 August. 'I am to be her witness and shall invalidate the proceedings if possible.' He doubted her wisdom, and was, it seems, slightly jealous, but she 'has rather let herself in for it as A. N. intends to outrage himself with a revolver if she doesn't – and she is too tender-hearted to cause his suffering.'[40] Charles noticed that her temper kept Nadi in check, but suspected she might miss being able to mix with other men; however, he thought marriage might be more steady for her this time round. Ruby went with the Nadi family to the Palio at Siena and saw her ex-husband, Harry, in the crowd and bolted. 'I hope to God he doesn't turn up here,'[41] wrote Charles to Vyvyan. Ruby was in financial difficulties and Charles tried to help by introducing her to Douglas Fenzi, of the Fenzi banking family, 'But I shall make her clean off the paint from her mouth and the jewels from her person before entering the house, which will be a lesson to her.'[42]

Charles continued to enjoy himself at the hotel; when the waiters went on strike on the grounds of overwork and underpay, 'they all came up to my room instead, and we played tiddlywinks, to the envy of the other unmarried visitors.' The Nadi wedding was imminent, tensions were high and Charles was concerned that Aldo had run his fiancée through with 'the wrong weapon' and escaped with her jewels. Going to the hotel bar late one night he saw, Ruby, Nadi and 'Pippo in a blaze of erectile tissue'. Pippo made a noise like a steam train whistle when he was being naughty. At one point Ruby found a letter from Vyvyan to Charles which read, 'Is the A. N. affair really drawing to a languid close? Who is the sobraspaliente de espada if any?'[43] Charles had great physical difficulty in preventing her showing the letter to Nadi, who in turn burst into tears because he could not see it. However the marriage was duly celebrated on its appointed date, but was to be kept secret in England. Somehow through the haze of gossip, news arrived in London which made Ted Haynes believe that Charles had married an Italian actress.

Meanwile, 'we have all the plagues of Egypt here including crabs on the lift-boy',[44] wrote Charles of the hotel. Oriana was ill in bed, Ruby was now, post marriage, ill in bed, and a friend of Ruby's called Valerie Churchill arrived with a small dog named Pronto. Charles was circulating between sick women, when who should enter but Harry Melville, Ruby's ex-husband, 'as fresh as paint could make his senile form. He really is unbearably disgusting, more so than last year, though his voice is quieter.'[45] Ruby stayed in her room and fortunately Aldo Nadi was away in Rome for another fencing competition. Charles was left to deal with Harry Melville, whom he managed to dispatch to Siena.

All this time, Charles was doing a chapter of Stendhal by day and a chapter of Pirandello by night. He was also picking up intelligence information for Louis Christie. Livorno was a major naval base, and Charles gleaned facts from restaurants and sailors. British intelligence in 1925 discovered the extent of Mussolini's shipping of arms to the Arabian Peninsula where Italy was supplying Arab potentates hostile to Britain.[46] Italy wanted to claim the Farasan Islands, strategically positioned in the Red Sea, which was Britain's route to India. On one side of the islands was Eritrea, already colonised by the Italians, and on the other lay Yemen, a British protectorate. Mussolini wanted both and was by now infiltrating Yemen with weapons, diplomats, spies and industry.

Oriana's sympathetic company encouraged Charles's satirical wit, and while reading to his captive audience, he also wrote *The Strange and Striking Adventures of Four Authors in Search of a Character*. He told Chapman, 'I have written a highly diverting pastiche about the Sitwells in the manner of Edward Lear's Story of the Four Little Children (Guy, Violet, Lionel and Slingsby) which I want to have illustrated with woodcuts and issued as a Christmas book.'[47] Chapman recommended the new, private Cayme Press in Kensington where books could be published in limited editions for private circulation. The booklet appeared in 1926 with woodcuts in the style of Edward Lear, done by Charles's nephew George who was then sixteen. It was signed by 'P. G. Lear and L. O.' (P. G. Learandello).

The story began: 'Once upon a time there were four dear little children whose names were Frogbert, Sacharissa, Zerubbabel and Lincruston, inhabiting a stately home in the country entirely surrounded by every attention that natural affection could prompt or luxury afford.' It brought up their quarrel with the Georgian Poets: describing trees on a desert island 'the branches of which were peopled with Georgian poets of an unimaginable rusticity . . .' Towards the beginning of November they arrived opposite a chemist's shop, where with the utmost prodigality they purchased 'four ounces of delectable lozenges and a demijohn of London Mercury, prepared in the stillroom of the adjoining Squire'. They reached the 'edge of a monocular Marsh', set foot upon the 'shores of Ross', where they learnt thirty-seven languages, then were 'wafted into the Alimentary Canal, which speedily bore them to a dinner table in South Belgravia . . .'

Sitting down outside a place of refreshment on the 'Square of the Hypotenuse', they had a 'comforting cup of rococo'. It was all in the tradition of nonsense prose, with recognisable satire. No one minded except the Sitwells, whom he had ruthlessly lampooned. On the other hand, Charles had just read Osbert's first work of fiction, *Triple Fugue*, and identified himself in a character called 'Clubfoot the Avenger'.

By the end of August Oriana was well enough to go back to the Hotel Nettuno in Pisa and a few days of motoring followed, as Charles and she took sunny drives. Charles asked Chapman to pay his final *Abelard* cheque into Cox and Co. on Pall Mall, as he wanted to use the money to pay the school fees for his niece and goddaughter, Dorothy, who was now nearly fourteen. Proudly, he later sent her to a finishing school in Paris run by a connection of Mrs Haynes who had given him a reduction in school fees. Dorothy[48] always remembered that her wealthy classmates wore new Paris fashions while she bravely sported lengthened and patched hand-me-downs. Chapman was told, 'Your forty pounds have at last been dispensed already to my yowling dependents, for the noblest of all causes, education. Cura ut valeas, as Heloise would say.'[49] Charles was by 1925 a renowned and much in demand translator, continually being asked to take on different works. Chapman suggested the French poet Villon, which Charles maintained could only be satisfactorily translated into fifteenth-century Scots, and 'it would not be worth my while to do it on contract, though I might take it up as a subsidiary recreation of my old age, should your firm last as long, which I doubt.'

Meanwhile, that October 1925, Dr Robert Proust, Marcel's brother, visited Chatto and Windus in London. As Prentice described it the visitor was 'squat but tremendously broad, with black ringleted hair slightly streaked with grey, moustache, and a hand-grip of iron.'[50] Robert Proust spoke of the editing he was doing on his brother's novel, saying that the last part *Le Temps retrouvé* would appear within a year – which Prentice thought highly doubtful. He seemed really genuinely impressed with Charles's translations, but he did not ask any questions about its continuation. The meeting lasted less than ten minutes, after which Dr Proust 'drove off in a vast Luxus automobile'. Prentice was left with the memory of his referring to the novels 'of my brother Marcel' and his black-edged, mourning, visiting card.

On 15 October finished copies of *Abelard* arrived in Pisa. Charles said he would have preferred the tops cut and gilt: 'I hate the nonsense of unopened copies which fetch fancy prices, and merely prove that their former owners have been illiterate.'[51] His work did not stop. He returned to Prentice the corrected proofs of *The Abbess of Castro* and the text of *Scarlet and Black*, while continuing the translation of Pirandello's *Si Gira*. All of these he worked on whilst still reading to Mrs Haynes in bed as she made suggestions, helping as the listening ear. He complained to Oriana and Prentice that he had left his pen behind on the Palace Hotel bus, which he was determined to retrieve, having used it since he joined Northcliffe in 1920 and written out six volumes of his Proust translation with it. This was true, but in reality he also had to return to Livorno to see Montgomery Carmichael, who as former British Consul at Leghorn, was a colleague in work for the Passport Office, and they had business there. Although he said he spent a pleasant time with Carmichael and his wife, who both loved and admired him, Charles did not manage to find his pen and he was irritated at having lost the tool of his trade, one which had been with him for so long.

That autumn Charles met a young Italian named Ugo Bassi. Charles took him up the mountains, gave him English lessons and briefly paid for painting lessons which did not last as the money was instead used to help the legion of sick relatives of his young friend. It was not a new occurrence: he had also paid expenses for former lovers, many of whom still kept turning up and asking for money. By and large, he gave cheerfully. As he explained to Vyvyan by way of discussing Stendhal's *De l'Amour*,

> Amour-gouter is of course five o' clock love, as in the Kosy Khorner Tea-dive. Amour-physique I should be tempted to render as *bodily* or *sensual* love rather than *physical*. But it is a thorny problem. I have never felt any myself except l'amore deici-lire, which is pretty boring if done more than five times in an afternoon, anche costoso.[52]

Since arriving in Italy two years before, Charles had resorted to casual contacts for his sex life, but Ugo lasted longer. To take the short trip up the mountains with his young lover, Charles had guiltily abandoned the long-suffering Mrs Haynes. By 17 November, he wrote to Prentice: 'Mrs Haynes is now doomed to remain here at least a month. A bore for her but a great help to me having to go over these dreary typescripts. Only I can no longer say "this is my own unaided work" . . . Every word weighed in her admirable mind. The improvement in style should be at once remarked.'[53]

Two days later Alan Cobham, the aviation pioneer, flew to Pisa and booked into the Nettuno. Cobham had been in the Royal Flying Corps during the war and was now undertaking the Imperial Airway Survey Flight with the purpose of investigating aviation in Africa. He was also attached to the Air Ministry. It was essential at that point to ascertain the position of Italian military, naval and air bases in Africa, and Cobham was flying with a professional photographer. Charles explained to his mother that it was only a social call and that this was the first of twenty-two legs on the journey to the Cape. Given that Cobham had never met Charles before, and that Pisa was not an obvious first leg of such a mission from the Air Ministry, it is likely that this meeting was the last part of the link involving the Italian flying fraternity, Wing-Commander Fletcher, the British Air Attaché at Rome and the Passport Office intelligence network. They planned to ask Cobham to take aerial photographs of Italian bases in Africa. Charles gallantly took charge of 'entertaining' the party all evening, then did two hours work until 2 a.m., and saw them off at 8 a.m. Cobham was knighted the following year for services rendered.[54]

Mrs Haynes finally left Pisa just before Christmas 1925, after five months away from her husband and his affair. In his Christmas greeting-card to Prentice, Charles acknowledged how many other lives depended on his employment with Chatto. Montgomery Carmichael wrote in his memoir of Charles: 'Undeserving waifs, more helpless by far than waifs at home, found him out somehow, and to them all he behaved like an elder and good-natured brother, indeed we used chaffingly to call him Brother Charles.'[55]

Charles ended 1925 as he had begun it, with midnight Mass at the Cathedral in Pisa. He was now far more excited by his translations of Stendhal and Pirandello than Proust; but in January 1926 Proust's *Albertine Disparue* finally appeared from Gallimard and Charles immediately bought a copy in via Tourabuoni, a street of bookstalls in Florence, and began to read. 'It seems relatively harmless, though I see that Saint-Loup is to take the wrong turning at last in Vol. II.'[55] As Charles had guessed, Saint-Loup was to marry Gilberte, which he thought was a bad move.

His American publisher, Thomas Seltzer, was eager to go ahead with the previous volume *Sodome et Gomorrhe.* 'Please continue translation letter follows,' he had cabled in September and in December he had asked for the goods: 'I believe it is best to go ahead publishing at least 4 volumes a year . . . we must not allow interest in him to flag.' He also relayed that Edith Wharton had written about Proust in *Yale Review*, and 'she carries great weight with the book buying public'.[57]

Charles sent him the first part of *Sodome et Gomorrhe*, which he said was the most explicit, to see if Seltzer could stomach it. Seltzer wrote back saying he was a little troubled – he suggested, 'leave the worst passages in French, untranslated, and then, probably, our censors would not interfere'.[58] Charles replied that he did not like the idea of the worst passages left in French: 'We seem to be groping gradually towards a little more liberty here in England.'[59] Both publishers and translator agreed that the word 'Sodom' should not appear on the cover. Charles chose the allusive 'Cities of the Plain', the biblical reference to the cities of Sodom and Gomorrah. Sydney Schiff accepted his request to dedicate the volume to 'Richard and Myrtle Kurt and Their Creator'. However, Charles joked: 'They will both have to give evidence at our trial. The last name is an amphibologie voulue for 1. The Padre Eterno and 2. Schiff himself.'[60]

In February, he went to the Pisa carnival with Pisan friends. For his disguise he got a three times lifesize mask of a skull, which along with 'some soiled bedsheets and a pair of white carabiniere gloves, should succeed in putting the devil in hell',[61] which was the object of the carnival, rather like the Scottish Halloween he had grown up celebrating. Removing the outfit, he later dined at the Nettuno with the Prince Borghese, telling him a story he recounted to Vyvyan; it was of a man who went to the carnival ball 'totally naked save for a blue riband round one testicle. When they said: "But you can't possibly come in like that. This is a fancy ball," he replied, "Yes, I know. This is it . . ."'[62]

The Prince had been twice to visit Charles since January; this time he 'unlike most people had gone to Paris and bought the books I asked him to buy',[63] by this meaning the correct edition of Maupassant; the Conard, not the Flammarion. He also invited Charles to Florence to meet the Duchesse de Clermont-Tonerre who had been a friend and sometime critic of Proust since 1903. She embodied the world Proust described, and the meeting promised to be absorbing, but it never actually took place. These explanations of the Prince's visits were camouflage again for his political work. Prince Borghese was a serious man; as a politician he had been deputy of the Partitio Radicale, a far left party, now out of power. He was an abstemious man of great self-control and had also been a diplomat. Again the meeting would have been to discuss intelligence matters.

Towards the end of February, Arnold Bennett, with his heavily pregnant lover, Dorothy Cheston, arrived at the Nettuno Hotel and Charles acted as guide. Bennett surprised Charles by being more pro-Proust than he was himself, loudly praising everything Charles had translated and promising excellent reviews of all the Stendhal translations in his regular column in the *Evening Standard*. Bennett was not only a prolific novelist and dramatist, but the highest paid literary journalist in Britain.

Pirandello was putting on several plays in Florence in mid-March and Charles went immediately. He attended the Politeana Theatre seven times in eight nights; during a performance of *Cosi e*, where a girl in the audience stood up and shouted 'Pirandello', Charles saw the 'old boy appear, looking like some curious caged rodent coming out of the sleeping apartment into the outer cage'.[62] He rushed backstage and was greeted warmly by the dramatist, far more so than a year ago in Rome. After the 1925 summer tour in England, which went almost unnoticed by London drama critics, Pirandello must have been aware that Charles had written to London papers to counteract the poor reception: 'He quite made me feel that I was worthy to enter his room and begged me to look in every evening.'[65] Charles again tackled the copyright issue and had Pirandello assure him that in July when the last contract expired, the English rights to his works would go to Chatto and Windus. 'And before the end of this season, I hope that we shall be eating out of one another's hand.'[66]

As he was walking beside the Arno in Florence one day, a small Fiat skidded to a halt ahead of him, then reversed at speed. It was Ruby. Aldo emerged gesticulating and the happy couple drove Charles off to admire their new flat. He presented the two Nadis to Pirandello that night and, 'Aldo preened all his feathers and beamed.' The next day at a lunch given for Pirandello in the Palace Hotel, Aldo Nadi 'speedily outshone the guest of the day'.[67]

Charles continued to see Pirandello after each performance and the playwright, then fifty-eight years old, introduced him to Marta Abba, with whom he was deeply in love and who played leading roles in most of his plays. 'She goes from strength to strength and is already at twenty-four a very great actress indeed,'[68] Charles noted. The three never spoke of Pirandello's wife, who was clinically insane and in an institution. In March he could write to Prentice with the news that 'spiritually I have not been too idle and have built up a pretty fair degree of intimacy with Pirandello',[69] even adding that he was 'a little excited, a little warm from P's embraces'.[70] He found the man attractive. Pirandello looked rather like his own father: the same neatly coiffed beard and immaculate suits. He was also full of the vigour of creativity, alive with electric current. The plays and stories hit a switch in Charles – Pirandello tackled appearance and reality with a twist. Human situations are rarely as they seem from the outside, there is often a secret story, sometimes a sombre, sexual one. Pirandello's plays touched incest, adultery, prostitution, with a keen and compassionate eye, unveiling dark stories from the inside. Now, here was Charles in the stimulating company of genius. As he had with Wilfred Owen, he felt inspired to offer all his talents in service to this man.

Charles impressed both Pirandello and his agents by compiling a bibliography of the author's works, which had never been done before, hoping this would entice Chatto to buy the English rights. But he still had to fully persuade Prentice. He bought Chatto's *Tales of Chekhov* to show Pirandello what might be done with his tales if he would consent to a cheap issue which would only produce a small advance but would sell better in the long run. He warned Prentice: 'I wish I could make you feel the same. Three years ago I was suggesting that it might be a good idea to secure Noël Coward's plays: Benn now has them.'[71] Losing Coward was something Prentice would regret and he did take Charles's advice about Pirandello.

Meanwhile, social life was buzzing. Charles had bought a tartan waistcoat in Florence which was 'the joy of all Pisa'.[72] He also bought a gaberdine coat for Ugo Bassi as a late Christmas present. But his relationship though close, was loose; he invited a previous casual lover, a Danish opera singer called Jorlund, to stay. Jorlund in his turn picked up Prince Borghese and three companions while walking along by the Arno and they all came back to Charles's rooms to consume whisky. Following such excesses, the young Jorlund was sick in Charles's dressing room, while Prince Borghese and friends were entertained by Charles theatrically reading a Latin dialogue by Philip Bainbrigge about two schoolboys on a Sunday walk. On the subject of sex, the guests informed Charles that there had been raids on the dance clubs in Florence with a view to extracting minors. Laws differed from region to region on the regulation of brothels and the age of consent; in some places it was twelve and others fourteen. Part of Mussolini's reforms aimed to regulate this and raise the age of consent.

Charles knew he would have to go back to England to visit his ailing father, now seventy-nine and very ill. First, though, he had been commissioned to write an extended article for *The Times* on Pisa Cathedral by the thirteenth-century sculptor Giovanni Pisano: 'More consistently undervalued than any other great monument in existence'.[73] Created in the thirteenth century and scattered in the sixteenth, parts of the pulpit had found their way to the Kaiser Frederick Museum in Berlin, 'Innocently bought but negligently sold'.[74] In May 1926 after years of scholarly research, enterprise and patience these were being restored to the original pulpit and Charles described the gentle and compassionate biblical scenes carved in marble relief. He recognised two figures that Proust had put into the sculptures of the church at Balbec: the nurse in the nativity who is dipping her hand into the bath to see if the water is too hot, and the wife at the resurrection who is putting her hand on her husband's heart to see whether it is beating. Mussolini was to unveil the masterpiece. Il Duce, with great pomp and circumstance, booked into the Hotel Nettuno. He now travelled like a king with a vast retinue as there had been an assassination attempt in April by the Hon. Violet Gibson, the eccentric daughter of the Lord Chancellor of Ireland. Mussolini had pardoned her but she was deported and spent the rest of her life in an asylum.[75] The Italian leader's reaction to the pulpit restoration was also recorded in *The Times*; he called it a 'resurrection' and stated, 'Italy is moving towards a time of power and glory.'[76] Power certainly, for when there was a second attempt at assassination in October, allegedly by a sixteen-year-old Italian boy, the teenager was instantly ripped to pieces by the fascist guards and his body spread around the town. Even in Pisa, which Charles called in his article 'the loveliest and most loveable of Italian cities', sinister things were beginning to happen. Before leaving for London, Charles was asked to make a final intelligence gathering trip to Livorno, where his tiny pieces of gossip fitted into the jigsaw of active Italian relations in the Middle East: it was revealed that twenty Persian naval cadets had been accepted into the Livorno naval academy.

Arriving in London, Charles was thrown into the middle of the General Strike. He volunteered to work for ten days on *The Times*, and met Richard Aldington, another strike breaker. Although Charles had come across Aldington before, they had never been friends. Aldington had edited the imagist periodical *Egoist*, married the poet Hilda Doolittle in 1913, and served in the war. He was close to D. H. Lawrence, had been T. S. Eliot's assistant on *The Criterion* and wrote for the *Times Literary Supplement*. At this point Aldington was a troubled man: still suffering from his war experience, he was also disillusioned by his open marriage. He wrote reviews, novels and critical studies of French literature and was about to edit a series of translations of seventeenth-century French literature, one of which he commissioned from Charles.

Lodging was a problem: Charles's family at Edgware was too far away; Vyvyan and Stanley, together, could not have him to stay for long. At last, Noël Coward's mother, still a landlady herself, helped him find a room. 'I wish I'd stayed at Pisa where one is one's own master, and Ugo Bassi is one's mistress.'[77] He ate at the Savile Club, meeting friends for dinners, parties and theatre. At the back of a theatre, during the interval, Charles spotted Osbert Sitwell, and felt it was time to make peace. He asked a mutual friend to take him to Sitwell and explain to Osbert that an old friend would like to shake his hand. An angry Sitwell refused the proffered hand, 'because I have for a long time disliked you, and because you have been impertinent'. Charles was puzzled at the use of the word impertinent, more usually used of a child by a teacher, or a lackey by a duke – the old Sitwell snobbery was still in its place – and Charles replied in a way he thought diplomatic, 'I am sure I don't know why: I am older than you.'[78] Osbert admitted in his account that the encounter shook his nerves, and he was piqued beyond endurance when Charles's satire on the Sitwells, *Four Authors in Search of a Character*, came out the following week. He suspected Charles had gone off immediately and written the 'colossal piece of impudence'. Osbert at once published his response in 'A Few Days in an Author's Life', a chapter of the book *All at Sea* in which he attacked Charles as Mr X. Mr X had once, he wrote, had the temerity to call him, Osbert Sitwell, an 'effete aristocrat'. Well, he called Charles's wit 'thistle-nurtured braying', and said he was descended from 'long and repetitive lines of tedious literary clergy, as so evidently culminate in poor Mr X – a living argument for the celibacy of the priest, if ever there was one.'[79] He went on more menacingly to point out that Mr X was involved in a ghoulish cult of the dead, because of his interest in history and genealogy, and that his translation was as good as 'body-snatching', both unoriginal and uncreative. 'Mr X announced his intention of translating into Scotch the works of a great living French author, who died during the early part of this apparently vampiric and voodoo process',[80] implying that the mere act of Charles translating the first volume of *À la recherche du temps perdu* had been enough to kill Proust off.

The Sitwell knives must have hurt Charles, but there were distractions enough. At the Savile club he met an Italian, Professor Foligno, who presented him with the thesis that Pirandello had written while at Bonn University, in German, about the Italian dialects in Grigenti. He also met Marcel Boulestin, a French chef and author who wanted to write his next article for *Vogue* on Proust. Charles 'urged him to get up a Proust dinner, the dishes culled from P's pages'.[81] The Restaurant Boulestin, known as the most expensive in London, opened the following year and Charles had a vision of holding the fantastical Proust dinner in 1928 when the complete translation would be finished, and they could 'conceal subscription orders in the napkins'.[82] Instead, he was invited to dinner by friends: Arnold Bennet, Francis Birrell and Edmund Haynes.

He moved from the Savile Club to the Hayneses's country house, Tortworth Rectory in Gloucestershire, for a week where the twenty-year-old Renée Haynes, Oriana's daughter, read for him the proofs of *Shoot!*, his translation of Pirandello's *Si Gira,* and found 'nothing changeworthy'.[83] He also completed *The Abbess of Castro*, which he dedicated to Edward Marsh, and *Scarlet and Black*, whose dedication reads, 'To O.H.H., who had every word of both volumes read to her when she was powerless to resist. C.K.S.M.' He pointed out to Oriana at once that should she ever need grounds for divorcing Edmund, she need only scratch out the full stop before Charles's initials. However, Oriana, or Ria as he called her affectionately, informed him that her husband had already taken her back to his bosom.

By September he was staying at the Christies' house at Durie in Fife, while Louis was home for some fishing and walking. 'It is perishingly cold here and I am shivering in my Italian summer clothes,' Charles wrote to Prentice. Charles gave Louis a photograph of himself, taken long ago on a visit to Winchester in 1913 before the war when he was at his most handsome.[84] At the foot of the photo is Charles's signature with '1913–1926 *semper fidelis*' written above in different, turquoise ink. Presumably he had signed it in 1913 and added the later date on this visit in 1926, ever faithful to the cousins he had known and visited since childhood, and now also worked with. The dates could either point to the duration of a love affair, or the duration of Charles's work for HMS. On 6 September the diplomatic bag arrived for Louis. It contained for Charles the proofs of *Shoot!* and for Louis vital communiqués on what was happening in Italy that month. Charles was the only person in Durie with whom Louis could discuss the issues.

Relations between Italy and Britain were by now very strained, so much so that an immediate meeting was secretly arranged between the Secretary of State for Foreign Affairs, Austen Chamberlain, and Mussolini on a British boat off the coast of Livorno. Chamberlain was now worried about Mussolini's stated aim to supplant British influence in the Yemen by creating a core of Italian influence. First, Mussolini had backed the Yemeni rebels hostile to Britain by giving them arms, then he had provided engineers, doctors, telegraph operators and a spy network. He had now made economic and political penetration into Yemen a fait accompli and possessed considerable influence with which he could bargain. He proposed partitioning the Arabian peninsula into two zones of influence, British and Italian. Chamberlain realised that beneath supposed peace with Italy there was a covert war in the Arabian peninsula and the Red Sea. He had to decide to hold an official discussion over the question of handing over influence of certain territories to Italian control. They agreed to hold a conference on this in Rome in January 1927, by which time Louis and Charles planned to be in Rome.

While in Scotland Charles visited old friends like the Mackenzies and the Pyatts, and stayed with his distant cousin William Moncrieff of Easter Moncrieffe in Perthshire who was compiling a huge family history, with which Charles agreed to help.

Back in England he visited Anna, his brother John's widow, and her two children in north Oxford, and also spent time with Renée Haynes, now a student at St Hugh's College. On 8 November he took her and a friend for coffee. Observing a man with a full beard who came in and sat nearby, Charles asked the girls in an undertone whether they knew the distinguished-looking man. They didn't and lowering his voice even more, he whispered, 'He holds the Chair of Applied Sin'[85], teasing them over their reverence for academics, and remembering his own youthful visit to Oxford and encounter with the 'Public Man'.

Charles's six month stay in Britain ended with his return to London and a series of dinner parties, all very demanding. 'I don't think I shall ever dine out again,' he told Prentice. Christmas was spent with his family at Whitchurch Rectory. Although his visit to Britain was principally to visit his sick father, he could not stay long in any one place. He and Louis Christie both needed to get back to Italy before the New Year, taking the boat train and stopping at the Gare de Lyon to change trains, where he picked up a copy of Dreyfus's memoir of Proust. He was comfortably back in Pisa on New Year's Day 1927 and wrote to his father:

> I am enjoying the soothing air, and the sight of my own possessions, and the sound of the bells, each ringing in its own time for some undiscoverable purpose of its own. But the whole lot were ringing in the Tower this afternoon as I approached it, as though to welcome me back.[86]

CHAPTER 15

A Death and Eviction

> 'I shall pass though Pisa in a train without stopping tomorrow night as I don't want to stop a bullet.'
>
> CKSM, letter to Charles Prentice, 1927

The bells of Pisa were tolling for Charles: three days into January he received the news of his father's death. On 2 January 1927, a Sunday afternoon, George had fallen asleep and quietly died. Charles did not hear until the Monday about his father's death: the funeral was set for Tuesday that week: 'This much to explain why I am not in England,' he wrote to Prentice. 'Of course I am bitterly sorry that I was so petulant and impatient during those last months – but we had a long private conversation and mutual explanation after Christmas, which did us both good.'[1] Charles had to explain why he could not stay for long by the sick man's bed. He was busy, busy, busy: partly work, partly inability to sit still. Perhaps the upright and respected judge had finally seemed less distressed about his son's private life and, also controversial, his chosen religion.

Charles wrote daily to his mother that January, very long letters, less full of his own grief than comforting her in hers:

> I hope and believe you feel that there is no parting but that a long period of physical servitude – lightly as it lay upon you – is at an end – Certainly no man ever had a better wife or could have – it is marvellous to think of all those long years of loving companionship unbroken by the trials and difficulties and hardships of life.[2]

He invited her to come and live with him in Italy, unless she found it boring or uncomfortable: 'But what about Assisi at Easter – I will go anywhere within say a radius of 300 miles of Pisa without a moment's consideration.'[3] His father had been cremated at Golders Green crematorium, but Charles reminded Meg of a conversation a few weeks before where his father had asked for his ashes to be laid at his mother's grave in the Dean Cemetery in Edinburgh, next to Uncle John Irving the explorer's grave, and he suggested that they ought to commemorate their own John Irving in the same graveyard: 'I shall go out now in your fur slippers and post this.'[4]

The waiters at the Hotel Nettuno, where he still took his meals, were kind and tactful, remembering his father from his visits. Camillo Pellizzi, a professor from the university, who told him once, 'I am no judge of English writing but you seem to have put into good English the mediocre Italian of Pirandello,'[5] came to visit, gently and often, taking him out to meals, making sure he was not eating alone, and was eating properly. He invited Charles to his home, where, uneasy one evening, Charles jumped up from the table suddenly on hearing a noise in the street and cut his head on a low-hanging chandelier. Fascism was drawing in its net and those intellectuals who did not toe the line were on edge.

The obituary of Charles's father in *The Times*, written by an ex-colleague, was impersonal, taken from *Who's Who* and the *Landed Gentry:* there went the honoured judge, good citizen, model father and devoted husband. Charles knew he had not exactly followed in his father's footsteps, and tender memories flooded back. He wrote to his mother:

> What you said about two men carrying him so quietly down the stair reminded me that I had helped and almost carried him up that stair the last time he went up it – with a feeling of parting at the top – and night after night and stood below and watched him go up until he turned the corner – No more now.[6]

His mother asked if there were any things of his father's that he might want: 'As for wanting "Things" – I have long been conscious of having too many.'[7] He suggested that the gold signet ring should go to Colin's eldest son, also called Colin. Charles himself wore his brother John's signet, which he planned to give to John's eldest son David when he left school. He did, however, want some of his father's books, mentioning Ovid's *Fasti* and the *Scots Peerage*.

In the meantime diversion arrived at the Nettuno in the form of a young American family called Creal, with a three-year-old boy: 'They are so sweet and beautiful and innocent as only Americans can be (he asked me if there was anything worth seeing in Rome . . .) and also rather hard up.'[8] Charles took them round Pisa and off to Viareggio where he booked the cheaper rooms with the Pelagi family that his parents had taken two years before. He bought them lunch, gave them a majolica teaset and took them to bookshops and churches, including a tour of the Pisano pulpit. Mr Creal thought,

> . . . that none of the folk round about the world would know what the scenes meant. I assured him that every brat in the streets of Pisa would know the whole story. I ventured that every child in Europe would know . . .[9]

Their child had been born with club feet which were gradually straightening, and the family and Charles walked the length of the promenade in Viareggio, with the child calling him 'Mr Concrete'. 'Not bad for a club-footed child of three,' Charles concluded, 'and a little tiring for a club-footed man of thirty-seven.'[10]

For the meeting with Louis Christie in Rome he booked into the Hotel des Princes on the Piazza di Spagna, now bought by the owner of the Nettuno. Christie was also in the hotel and they dined that night with Mackenzie, the former Chief Passport Officer, whom Louis had now officially supplanted in the Rome office. Mackenzie arrived the following day at Charles's hotel, ostensibly to take him to a bookshop he thought Charles would like, but in reality for matters to do with the Rome Conference. Charles complained to his mother that the 'bookshop visit' was merely another irritating diversion from work.

Charles's mother, meanwhile, was staying in Oxford with her daughter-in-law, Anna, and wrote to her son saying that David was doing very well at Lynams, the prep school that Charles was paying for. Charles wrote telling him to 'work <u>hard</u> this term and have no more diseases',[11] and to try for a scholarship to Winchester where Charles had just founded a yearly Prize for Idiomatic Translation: it was only £5 but he thought that would mean something to a schoolboy. After his father's death, he now felt the call of family responsibility: Colin was ill and John dead. He had to be a leader.

He made suggestions about the future of Anna's house in north Oxford. It had belonged to his father and Charles suggested it be transferred into Anna's name, as he did not think she would marry again; no one who was not well-to-do would think of marrying a penniless widow with two children, he observed rather heartlessly. The house could, on the other hand, be transferred to him, and he would give it to them rent free and would not mind eventually living in north Oxford. Anna and the children were very excited by this idea and Charles spent the rest of 1927 dithering over the decision to move back to England. When Anna wrote to Prentice, thanking him for transferring money from Charles, she noted 'Charlie changes his mind so much.'[12]

While in Rome, another likely secret service man, Michael Parker, 'an expert on Roman antiquities', had dinner with Charles at Aragno's where they bumped into Renato Mucci, governor of the Bank of Rome, who had translated some Proust into Italian and whom Charles had visited on his last trip to Rome. After dinner, Charles and Michael visited the Colosseum, 'under a full moon – an amazing spectacle – I don't want ever to see it again by daylight. In the moonlight the gaps are softly covered over and the sloping lines of a wall have a curious, mossy effect.'[13] But the ruin was also cold and damp; Michael got flu and was put to bed. To his mother Charles complained, 'I feel rather tired here always and am not doing enough work. Rome is certainly a charming place . . . but I feel that I shall have to lead a more and more sedentary life in the future.'[14] To Prentice the same evening he admitted 'When humanity left me in my room, insomnia entered to derange me yet further.' He also revealed his exhaustion: 'I am too battered by fate and disease to be capable of feeling anxious.'[15]

Beneath the bravura was an exhausted man with far too much on his plate and no one to look after him. He found in Pirandello's chaotic world the irony he saw in his own life; that the appearance is rarely the reality and the layers of subterfuge people erect to present a face to family, friends or the public is excellent material for drama. Charles sympathised with Pirandello's themes intimately: his plays dealt with necessary lies and secrecy. In his early play, *Liola*, where a young labourer cuckolds the impotent landowner for his wife to bear a child, the lie turned out to be more true, or better, than the truth. The short stories waived the simple mask which hid the seething mass of contradictions, forced beliefs, half-held beliefs, and strange history, which formed the real person beneath. Pretence to others was almost second nature to Charles, but now he was guilty of masking things even to himself. His body's warnings of recurrent illnesses were passed off with a note about flu. He had never consulted a doctor about his stomach-aches, and he carried on eating badly and ignoring all signs of serious ailments.

He returned to Pisa with Louis Christie, who booked one of the Nettuno's new bedrooms with a bathroom, and who 'has kindly offered me a bath at 7.15'.[16] Charles took Louis round the Campo Santo and gave him a running commentary on all its treasures, before limping fast up the Leaning Tower with the overweight Louis puffing behind him.

Financial pressure was again bothering Charles. With his father's death he felt responsible for his mother. He renewed the offer to buy her a house in Italy for them to enjoy together; whilst also toying with the idea of moving to Oxford. For the moment he wanted her to travel south in comfort. Mrs Haynes was coming out again, heading for Sicily; could she accompany his mother? Even in Italy, life was becoming more expensive, with the drop in the value of the pound and the beginning of a worldwide economic depression. He decided to stop being so discerning about the literary merit of the texts he translated and offered up his skills for whatever job was suggested.

Nevertheless his plans for Stendhal were completed that year when he finished translating *Armance*, which he dedicated to Richard Aldington. The preface is an open letter to Aldington, outlining his difficulties in translating the quotations that Stendhal used to start each chapter. Stendhal often got the quotation wrong or attributed it to the wrong author. Charles had decided to give the correct author and work; including Stendhal's version in a footnote.[17] He had now translated a significant body of Stendhal: *Charterhouse of Parma*, *Scarlet and Black*, the *Abbess of Castro* collection and *Armance*. Orlo Williams, a clerk at the House of Commons, who had also worked for intelligence, wrote for the *Times Literary Supplement* that Charles's translations of Stendhal were 'accurate, faithful, yet smooth . . . Stendhal is easier to translate than Proust, since his effects do not depend on suggestion.'[18] Charles was glad of this ease, the simple and direct approach. He also enjoyed Stendhal's illustration of the Italian power of rising to noble or tragic intensity under the influence of love, wounded honour or the desire for vengeance; reckoning it was better to be wicked in a transport of passion than coldly correct through vanity or love of money. Transports of passion were his own speciality.

Pirandello delved even further into the Italian soul, and Charles kept outlining whole stories to Prentice to inspire his enthusiasm. Although *Shoot!* was now published in Britain, copyright agreements had still not been secured for any of the plays or short stories, despite Charles's best efforts. Charles had gone ahead and translated many of them; they remain still unpublished today, while his Stendhal and Proust translations continue to sell.

Richard Aldington had recently been commissioned by Routledge to be the general editor of a series of French memoirs to make up an eighteenth-century French Library. Aldington asked Charles to translate two of these: *Mémoires du duc de Lauzun* and *Les Aventures de Zeloïde et Amanzarifdin. Mémoires* was written in 1789 and published in 1822; Lauzun was the ultimate French aristocrat: 'witty, rich, brave, free and superbly insolent'.[19] Charles chronicled Lauzun's adventures after the memoirs until he was sentenced to the guillotine in 1794, 'When the headsman comes for him, he is sitting down to a dish of oysters, "Citizen," he says, "allow me to finish;" and offering the man a glass: "take this wine, you must have need of courage, in your calling."'[20] François-Augustin Paradis de Moncrif's fantasy, *Les Aventures de Zeloïde et Amanzarifdine*, was written in 1727. Paradis de Moncrif was a distant kinsman and the introduction was an opportunity for Charles to elaborate on his own bloodline. He discovered that Paradis de Moncrif's mother, whose Christian name was unrecorded, was described as 'A Lowland Scot, born Moncrieff, of a Presbyterian family which had provided the Cause with several ministers and theologians, she had not inherited the heavy austerity nor the rigid virtue of her lineage, in fact she was quite the opposite.'[21] Paradis de Moncrif's mother was a soulmate from another time, but Charles had little time to study or contemplate her history: the world outside his ivory tower was beginning to shatter his peace.

> The air here is still full of war with France. I am being harassed by a dreary attempt at blackmail, which a fascist friend kindly

'deals with' but it keeps cropping up again . . . not on Mr Piggins scale fortunately, nor do I pay the slightest heed, but it is boring and on top of this my mother arrives in little more than a fortnight.[22]

The 'fascist friend' was his landlord, the gynaecologist Signor Frascani, who had been a mayor of Pisa three times and had powerful connections in the fascist hierarchy. He died not long after Charles wrote this, leaving both Charles and Signora Frascani without a protector, so to speak. It is not clear whether the blackmail was connected to Charles's private life or to his secret service activities, or whether he himself even knew which. Random violence and threats of eviction were not uncommon; the entire regime used blackmail as routine behaviour. The Signora and her lodger were given three months to leave the house. Charles decided to board a train at once and:

> . . . offer the bulk of my library to the British Institute in Florence. What a woundily long book Proust is. I met D. H. Lawrence yesterday for the first time. An odd spectacle: also his German wife. I must go out now and take a bath with some verbena salts, spoils of Florence, which may *oter le cafard*, but I doubt it.[23]

Charles knew that Prentice was one of the few people to whom he could 'unbosom' himself. The other was Oriana Haynes, but she was too busy at that point unbosoming *herself* to Charles, since one of her reasons for escaping to Italy again was to be away while her husband was 'hobnobbing with Miss Lily Wallows'.[24] Vyvyan Holland was the man he was closest to, and to him alone he gave vent to all iniquitous thoughts: 'My mother proposes to arrive about Easter and speaks darkly of staying at least two years.'[25] He also wrote to Vyvyan about the other women in his life. He had seen Ruby, now Mrs Nadi, in Florence in Casoni's with Pippo, she being 'packed in manpower'. He had had difficulty assuring her that the dedication in *Shoot* did not refer to herself, Vyvyan and Oriana; to Vyvyan he wrote a wicked limerick about Ruby's sexual proclivities.[26] He concluded to Vyv, 'I long for your company and the elfin comfort you sometimes afford.'[27]

Charles was then asked to write the regimental history of the King's

Own Scottish Borderers and seriously considered it. The fee was £400 plus the opportunity to live at the KOSB depot in Berwick-upon-Tweed. But the climate of the Scottish town appealed even less than Oxford, accustomed as he now was to Italian sunshine, food and entertainment. He suggested that his old regiment ask his former colleague Captain Stair Gillon, who did end up writing the official history. In March Charles indexed the Moncrieff genealogy for his cousin, William, and started to sell his large personal library to the British Institute and 'an illiterate and degenerate millionaire'.[28] He wanted to unburden himself and needed the money; some of his books fetched as much as £50 – these were by far his most valuable possessions.

Disposing of his books was perhaps an intuition about the nearness of death. One night he had a sharp fever for which he took ammonium quinine which swelled his lips and nose and discoloured a large patch of skin on his wounded leg where a blood vessel had broken. The next morning he was given the order to leave his flat within two days, by 30 June. He wrote in exasperation to Prentice that he had just 'reawakened to the life of external facts on a rather hot morning'. He had earnestly hoped to finish the translation of *Sodome et Gomorrhe* in his flat, seated at his desk, and to do it well – but please could he know by the end of June whether it was worth going on with Proust? Could Chatto publish without contravening the obscenity laws?

> There are people here who would even give me houseroom, but I feel that it is better to cut adrift altogether and not risk another eviction later on. It is a sudden blow because my landlady had assurances from the Podesta that she would not be turned out.[29]

The Podesta were the rulers of the city council who were by now overwhelmingly fascist and could not be relied upon to keep promises. It was no longer possible for him to live in Pisa without a protector.

With an almost comical ignorance of Italian politics, many of Charles's friends had converged on Pisa by Easter 1927. Charles organised rooms at the Nettuno for Mrs Haynes and her daughter Celia as well as for Meg who arrived with Miss Stephen, and an elderly man with a pink face and a spade beard called James Bertrand de Vinceles Payen de Payne, with his wife and son. Payen de Payne was ten years younger than Meg but 'empathetic to the point of being gaga'[30] as he sat beside her and talked to her for a whole meal about asparagus. He was a member of the Savile Club and an expert on Proust.

Charles took the whole party to Lucca for a few days before they separated to different parts of Italy on their tours; all but his mother, whom he took back to Pisa to the cherished rooms he was about to lose. Meg was now seventy; she was never strong and had always been thin, but, apart from still suffering from grief and bereavement, she was much herself. The death of her husband had pushed her further into her obsession with spiritualism: her diaries of 1926, 1927 and 1928 were so full of automatic writing and communication with the dead that her frightened granddaughters later destroyed them.

Pisa was too hot, and Meg's séances made Charles uncomfortable, so he sent her to the Pelagi boarding house by the sea in Viareggio while he cleared up his room at Lungarno Reggio and finished translating *Cities of the Plain*. On 17 June 1927 this last part of the translation of *Sodome et Gomorrhe* was sent to America. He sold the American rights for the next six volumes to Albert and Charles Boni, in New York, for $3000, and wrote,

> I believe I am the only person in the world who has taken the trouble to correct the text of this book. It was published shortly before Proust's death, and the proofs never seem to have been corrected by anyone. An earlier volume appeared in French with a list of over 200 corrigenda; and that list was neither complete nor accurate.[31]

He added that he was in the midst of correcting half a million words in two weeks. To Prentice he expressed his difficulties with the names and places that varied their spelling,

> M. de Chevregny is alternately that and Chevrigny; Harambouville is Harembouville and Arambouville, and at one time its attributes seem to be given to Hermenonville, which at another place is mentioned as coexisting with it. All this is very trivial . . . but I do rather aim at a corrected text.[32]

It was a terrible rush trying to leave his rooms before he was evicted. He decided to destroy anything incriminating, including letters from

Vyvyan: 'I have already destroyed all of your letters and others even more precious.'[33] He was all ready to go and the packing cases had still not arrived: ever resilient, he considered making them himself, but before having to test his carpentry skills, they turned up.

His advance for the next volume of Proust was overdue from Chatto. He was due £150 upon their receipt of *Cities of the Plain*; he was still anxious about its publication, glad in a way that his father would not see it, yet knowing that there were other family members whom it would no doubt offend. He was well aware that the active and promiscuous homosexual world described by Proust was offensive to most people, so in his translation he had tried to soften the blow by not being as direct as Proust could be in French, using euphemism and hidden innuendo where he could. On the other hand this was the world in which he himself lived, but had always had to hide. Every visit to the bank was a visit to Florence where he also saw Orioli, Turner, Douglas and indulged in their decadent world. That July he also caught gonnorrhea and he described the visits to the doctor and costs of the treatment to Vyvyan.

Charles managed to move out of his flat with no time to spare on the afternoon of 30 June, with the sorry sight of his landlady, in the same state of fear, having her furniture pushed out into a horsewagon on the broad and bright Lungarno Reggio: 'As she never wears anything but a wrapper without buttons which was pink until her husband died, it will be difficult to evict her with dignity.'[34] She had already confessed to Charles that she was keen on taking the morphine in her late husband's professional supplies. 'Pisa I have now definitely left,' he told Prentice on 6 July. He explained that a young man had been watching him from the Arno below his window for some time, to whom the police all nodded as they passed. 'But I shall pass though Pisa in a train without stopping tomorrow night as I don't want to stop a bullet.'[35]

He was advised to leave Italy for a spell at once after his eviction. At Viareggio, he hired a car and drove with his mother to the twelfth-century town of Cuneo near the French border, 'but she didn't get much of an orgasmo,'[36] he observed to Vyvyan. For Louis he had to report on what he saw and there outside Cuneo was the Italian army on summer manoeuvres, hundreds of troops under canvas. An urgent summons from the Passport Office had him getting on a train to Rome for a weekend, leaving his oblivious mother in Cuneo. On return the guests at the Grand Hotel Ormea kept asking for the newspapers and

Charles found himself evading them and covering his tracks because of his 'mother's habit of taking the Daily Mail quite unconsciously up to her bedroom and lining drawers with it, like a swallow'.[37]

Meg needed to move on. Too much stagnation meant too much communicating with the dead and Charles preferred to avoid that. To blow away the cobwebs, he drove her for a thrill through the Tenda Tunnel from Italy to France, at that time the longest road tunnel in existence, two miles long and 4000 feet above sea level. The journey in their open-topped car gave him a severe cold and they had to stay in Nice until he was well again, which kept Meg busy for long enough before Charles had to go back to Cuneo to check again on the army, to collect his post and then move on, he was advised by Louis, to Switzerland. The post also contained an offer from Howe, a publisher in Soho Square, to publish *Cities of the Plain* if no one else was doing so and to take on the other volumes of Proust. Chatto was still stuck taking advice from counsel about the legality of publishing as they were sure to be prosecuted under the Obscene Publications Act. Charles replied that the ball was in the Chatto court and informed Prentice of the offer from Howe.

As for Pirandello, *I vecci e I giovanni* which Charles had translated as *Generations of Men* was to be published both in America and in Britain in by Dutton. Charles wrote an angry letter to the American firm for liberties taken in changing the text before printing and received the following robust reply, from John Macrae of Dutton and Co.

> Quite frankly you must not be too hard on us Americans; you must not expect us to be quite as civilised as you Britishers. The fact is that you have some 400 years of advantage in general culture. You must bear in mind that America is made up of a metropolitan people, a conglomeration of all races. As a matter of plain unadulterated fact, some of the best ability, brain and moral force that ever came out of the groins of the British have come to America . . . on the whole, man for man and woman for woman, we are about as good as you are.[38]

To John Macrae in reply Charles wrote long and thorough letters about spelling, columns, typeface and grammar, insisting that his corrected proofs be adhered to, concluding, 'I am glad you are not offended by my pugnacious spirit. It is largely inherited; my grandmother's two grandmothers were Macraes, daughters of Farquar Macrae of Inverinate: and the Macraes, as you know, were always the foremost fighters in Scotland.'[39] This formed a firm bond with John Macrae who promised to stick faithfully to every comma and spelling no matter how peculiar.

The summer was taken up with entertaining his mother with sightseeing as well as covering his own agenda for Louis: Interlaken, then Lucerne, then Bern. Only then could he return to Italy. They descended to the lush climate of Stresa on Lago Maggiore and booked into the most luxurious hotel they could find. But before long, Meg decided to go back to England, Colin was so unwell that he was considering giving up his duties as a clergyman and with seven children, five of them dependent, that was serious news. Meg returned to England in the company of her niece, Lucy Pearson, stopping in Locarno for a break on the way.

With his mother gone, peace descended and Charles could finish the eighteenth-century French memoirs for Aldington. The Introduction to *Zeloïde and Amanzarifdine* provided a great excuse for delving into his genealogy, about which he now knew everything, thanks to a lifetime of research and its culmination in William Moncrieff's family history. Stresa was beautiful – another world entirely from the rough send-off from Pisa. The Regina Palace Hotel was a relatively new building, started in 1908 and finished after the war; it was a monster of a hotel, glittering with chandeliers and gilt stucco amidst botanic gardens which flourished in the semi-tropical atmosphere. Snowy-capped alpine peaks surrounded the deep lake, and to escape the humid air, there were the fresh waters of the lake to bathe in. Bathing – at Nairn and Fife as a child, in the Channel and the Somme as a soldier, and all down the Italian coast now – was a constant pleasure in his life.

There were 100 guest rooms, and the two top floors had full-time staff who outnumbered the guests two to one. The stables were full of horses for the hotel buggies, bumping luggage from the station up the hill, and there was a library on the ground floor with writing desks and armchairs. It was so different from his monastic rented rooms that he did not feel at home. To Vyvyan he called it the 'Vagina Phallus Hotel', continuing, 'I am translating the memoirs of the Duc de Lauzun which are mainly a catalogue raisonée of the ladies who yielded and/or offered him the custody of their pussies, some of them, I regret to say, English.'[40]

Stresa was famous for its literary visitors: Stendhal had finished the *Charterhouse of Parma* here and Dickens and Hemingway were both inspired by the place. George Bernard Shaw had just left the Regina Palace hotel that September after a month's recuperation with his wife Charlotte. He had been entertained by an American couple, the Tompkinses, who had rented the Isola san Giovanni, a private island with a large villa opposite Pallenza. Molly Tompkins was a wealthy American woman who had everything: youth, beauty, education and a handsome and adoring husband. But she was bored and found writers fascinating. She had spent weeks romancing the seventy-year-old Shaw, trying in vain to draw him into a fully-fledged affair. It had not worked, and she discovered she was pregnant by her own husband. She then took off to Milan for an abortion – being in love with Shaw did not accord with the desire for a child from her husband – and Shaw wisely decided to leave Stresa.

Unaware of any of this, Charles was asked to lunch by another American, a William Kraut who lived in a villa above Pallenza which Charles compared to a museum, with a huge art collection that included a da Vinci. There he met Molly and Laurence Tompkins and, on being asked at the large lunch party 'What do you do?', he replied, 'I *bite rooks* – I mean, I translate books.' Then a voice from somewhere around the table asked, 'Didn't you translate Marcel Proust?' Molly suddenly came to life. She had read all his translations and enthusiastically launched into a lengthy and obscure discussion on Proust. She explained that she had just been to Milan for an operation and wished that she had had Proust with her to aid her recovery, but she had left her volumes in the 'Paris stoodio'. 'Poor old Kraut got left behind in the passion of the conversation,' said Charles, 'until we played croquet on a very rough bit of grass and he came into his own winning by several hoops.'[41]

There was another guest, a Polignac aristocrat, who had known Proust and felt she had to explain to Charles that she was not the template for the Duchess de Guermantes, '*Ni Madame de Verdurin non plus, j'espère*,'[42] replied Charles. In Proust's novel Madame Verdurin was the expert social climber and poseur who ran her own salon.

Molly Tompkins invited Charles to the Isola san Giovanni and then welcomed him to stay for as long as he wanted. The Tompkinses said that Bernard Shaw was much interested in the fascist experiment. 'I always thought he would, with his keen disciplinarian instincts, be,'[43] commented Charles to Prentice.

The island, which was large enough for a villa and a garden, nestled near Pallenza, but was entirely private, sheltered by its own border of trees and gardens. During the sojourn Molly slowly began to realise that if she was looking for a literary affair, she would have even less success with Charles than she had had with Shaw. Charles spent a happy four days on the island and thought if not Molly, then Laurence Tompkins was charming. He offered to send them a set of Proust but they declined and then he offered to send a copy of *The Charterhouse of Parma*, 'because it is a lot about the lake', but they protested, 'don't you have to pay for them?' and said they would order the books themselves from Hatchards. They were, he commented:

> . . . both very good looking and charming. It is an adorable little island; just their villa and a rambling garden with paths down to the lake and little balconies at the ends, and a gardener's cottage. The gardener belongs to Prince Borromeo and is rather distrustful of them, but the other servants appear devoted.[44]

On 14 October he left all his luggage with them to go on to Locarno to see his Pearson cousins and see Charlie Chaplin at the Kursaal. Charles was still worried about whether *Cities of the Plain* would be banned and suggested T. S. Eliot at *The Criterion* to Prentice, 'as they are meant to be fearless'.[45] However in October he received two money orders, one from Chatto for the English rights for £150 and one from Boni for the American rights for £200. Soon enough, in November, a letter from Hatchards arrived, c/o Chatto, asking when *Sodome et Gomorrhe* would be published and, if privately, how could they get copies as many clients wanted it.

As well as a literary history, Stresa had a great religious and spiritual legacy, being the death place of Antonio Rosmini, the priest, theologian and philosopher whose villa and garden sat a few houses away from the Regina Palace. It was a museum to his memory and housed some twenty thousand of his books as well as the originals of the 100 works on politics, philosophy and theology that he wrote in the course of his reforming life. He was credited as one of the great reformers of the Catholic Church in the nineteenth century, tackling the ignorance of the priests and the political greed of the cardinals. On his deathbed his three words of advice to his great friend, the writer Manzoni, were 'Adorare, godere, tacere' (Adore (God), Enjoy (Your talents), and Be silent.) Being naturally garrulous in company, Charles thought this worthwhile advice. He shut himself away and managed to finish translating the *Duc de Lauzun* and the story by Paradis de Moncrif. He was aware that his fame and recognition and this brief period of being lionised by the wealthy was only due to hard work.

The visit to Stresa was cut short on 24 October when Charles was required by intelligence to spend a few days in Bellinzona; he wrote cryptically to Vyvyan, 'I am here on a secret mission to sound the political bottoms of the Ticinese with a view to roping them in next year.'[46] He then had to travel to Rome. Florence was, as always, a halfway house, and here he spent a fortnight with old friends. Again, he met D. H. Lawrence. Reggie Turner, Orioli, Harold Acton and he hired a car and drove to call on the Lawrences at the Villa Mirenda outside Florence. Lawrence, recovering from a haemorrhage, was working on *Lady Chatterley's Lover*, and was not in a lively conversational mood, telling Aldous Huxley, 'Reggie and Orioli and Scott Moncrieff came en quatre – I poured tea, they poured the rest.'[47]

Charles thought *Lady Chatterley's Lover*, 'indescribably filthy'. Lawrence had a similar view of Charles. He wrote to Richard Aldington, 'Scott Moncrieff said he'd write to you. He has a nice side to him – but really an obscene mind like a lavatory.'[48] In January, when Lawrence was asked by Curtis Brown to review Viani's *Parigi*, he said that Brown should rather try Scott Moncrieff, as he himself doubted he could 'face the unending squalor'.[49]

Two years later Charles was still sniping at Lawrence. In a letter to T. S. Eliot he said, 'He will write about the sexual act as if he on some historic occasion performed it. Why doesn't he say frankly: I am a eunuch myself, but I admire sex in others. If he ever does die, Frieda's memoirs should be quaint reading.'[50] Meanwhile, Lawrence was being more sympathetic than Charles would ever know. Lawrence had appreciated his witty conversation, and asked Orioli late in 1929: 'Poor Scott

Moncrieff, I hope its not cancer.'[51] Two weeks later he asked again, 'How is Scott Moncrieff?'[52]

Nineteen-twenty-seven had been a tough year for Charles's health; he realised he was rapidly ageing. On top of a huge workload and a lot of travel had come the death of his father, his eviction from Pisa, and his taking responsibility for his mother only to realise that he was not up to it. At the end of the year he received a further blow, news of the death of Christopher Millard. Charles felt that he had neglected him, but that he was part of an irrevocable past and had indelibly influenced his own path in life. He wrote an obituary for *The Times* which praised the man and noted his achievements. It was published in the early edition, but then the editor took it out on the grounds of Millard's imprisonments for gross indecency. Charles did not fail to protest, writing to the editor that a paper with such an interest in the Cunard family could not afford to be so prudish.

CHAPTER 16

Rome

> The Scots are quite as capable of governing themselves as the Swiss – and have as much right as they to do so.
>
> CKSM, letter to Helen Stephen, 1929

The door at number 67 via della Croce in Rome was of studded wood, high enough for a man on a horse to pass into the courtyard. Charles limped through the long entrance corridor of stone mosaics, past wooden pigeon-holes, to a marble stairwell with polished brass balls and a lift cage in the middle; the lift, which had been there since 1900, was a blessing as his leg was troubling him much more now. The high ceiling on the second floor was of painted wooden panels and the floor tiles were of polished clay; his own door was ten foot high with brass handles and metal studs to stop it being kicked in, which was as much a risk under fascism as it had been in the centuries before. His flat was a high-ceiling room overlooking the narrow street; sombre, because the window was narrow and only half as high as the room which rose into the darkness. The shutters had to be half-closed against the cold – or the heat, the flies and the noise. Via della Croce was full of hawkers, horses and lively voices. Opposite were walls of faded pink tempera, peeling artistically but not dangerously, and painted wooden shutters on metal hinges. It was a literary neighbourhood: in the next street was a stone plaque on the house where Elizabeth and Robert Browning had stayed, put up by the municipality of Rome on the centenary of Robert Browning's birth, 7 May 1912.

The street was paved with black cobbles of a hard stone, like granite but smoother. Looking out of the window gave a view of all of life: small shops belonging to artisans with whom Charles became friendly;

a framemaker goldleafing a frame; fishmongers scaling red mullet on trestles set up in the street; market traders pushing barrows of Sicilian oranges, shouting as they made their way through the crowds of lingering men. Across the street was an artisan who repaired chair seats, reworking the basketry or cane. The place was heaped high with broken chairs; he had done it since childhood, he was an expert, weaving and repairing without looking while the room filled with company, bantering and gossiping.

Any couple on honeymoon in Rome on the way to the Spanish Steps would be side-stepped every few paces by a young boy selling roses to lovers: 'Bella Signorina', 'Signora', 'Ah, bella Signora, bellissima Signora', foisting a red rose on them, which had just been rejuvenated from the day before by the boy's removing its outer, faded petals. Early in the morning Charles could see the boys reviving their roses and the black cobbles would be spotted with the bright red petals. In one tiny front room a pasta maker shifted his sheets of pasta from a drying rack, where they hung like pillow cases to dry, to the scored wooden counter where they were cut into shapes for the varieties he sold; here for ravioli, rigatoni, tagliatelli, farfalle; next door for spaghetti, penne and linguini. The salami shop owner would be instructing his assistants in the art of sausagery; slicing and packaging, laying it beautifully on sheets of greaseproof paper. The cheese shop sold tiny cheeses made from cows', sheep's and goats' milk from small farmers outside Rome. A poor person could buy a small goats' cheese, a few slices of salami and then go to the bakers for one panini. The market two streets away sold every fruit, mushroom and vegetable imaginable; chestnuts, porcini, peaches, tomatoes, lettuce . . .

The British Passport Office was nearby and Charles would walk east along the via della Croce to the Piazza di Spagna, climb the Spanish Steps to the Piazza della Trinità dei Monti and turn left into via Gregoriana which descended as steeply as the steps had ascended. It was all good exercise for his leg, which he used as much as he could. Every evening Charles would eat at the office with Louis Christie and Lucy Lunn who was the secretary at the organisation. Petite and determined, with a chestnut bob, Lucy appealed greatly to Charles who said that she was so charming that she must be related in some way to Constance Lunn, his sister-in-law, 'with a touch of strangeness due to an upbringing in Moscow'.[1] English was her mother tongue, but she had fluent French, German and Russian and was currently tackling Italian. She would become his secretary and amanuensis in his final years. As they became close, Charles read her whole Pirandello stories in Italian for hours in the evening, and in his later letters he spoke of 'we' to Prentice when he received proofs. He would often head his letters to Prentice, 'Rome SW7', to indicate the Office, because London SW7, or Knightsbridge, was the headquarters of secret service operations and the British Passport Office. Charles was proud of the fact that while at the War Office he helped promote the whole idea of the Passport Office as a cover for spying, writing in March 1928 to Oriana about Louis Christie: 'His career was to some extent invented by myself ten years ago – and by Sir Denison R.'[2]

His enthusiasm in being involved in intelligence work was given an abrupt shock in late spring 1928. Louis was now also the King's Messenger in Rome, employed by the Foreign Office to hand-carry secret and important messages to embassies and consulates. The briefcase was often chained to his wrist. King's Messengers were usually retired army personnel, like Louis, travelled first class in plain clothes, and were covered by diplomatic immunity. A troubling story was reported in the *New Statesman* on 16 June 1928, under the heading 'Why Palliate Fascism?' It began, 'A few weeks ago an Official of the British Embassy at Rome was sent to Milan on official business . . .' This was the burly Louis who stopped to watch two bullies confronting a third person; they then turned on him and demanded his papers; he refused. A policeman arrived and Louis demanded to be taken to the police station where his identity and his connection with the Diplomatic Service were established, as were the identities of the bullies as two members of the plainclothes fascist police. They were all allowed to leave, but later in the day Louis was knocked down in the street by a blow to the head from behind. He was then kicked and beaten, his body was heavily bruised and his face deeply cut. If there were passers-by, they knew better than to interfere. He recognised his assailants as the two plainclothes fascist policeman he had met earlier that day. The *New Statesman* questioned why this had been hushed up, both in Italy and in Britain, when it was so clearly symptomatic of the behaviour of fascist Italy. It concluded that Il Duce was a popular despot who made the trains run on time and that Mussolini's vast energy atoned in some way for the Italians' 'delightful habit of letting things slide'[3]. (As late as 1934 the head of SIS was to give the apparently untroubled admission that 'the activities of our Passport Control Office all over the world are perfectly well known'.[4])

Louis was so badly hurt that he had to take an extended holiday to recover. He went to Castle Eerde in Holland, a Theosophy community, 'where he is in charge of the bees, etc. and will have to register 3000 people for next summer's camp. He is now on retired pay amplified by disability for a few years.'[5]

Another reason for Charles moving to Rome was to be near Pirandello. He wanted to translate all his novels, short stories and plays; the complete works. But Pirandello's agent – who spoke no English and answered no letters – would not part with the English rights, or so it seemed. *Shoot!* and *The Old and the Young* had only been acquired by Prentice from the American copyright holder. There were several hundred short stories, dozens of dramas and more novels, not counting what Pirandello might produce now that he had settled down to full-time writing after disbanding his troupe of actors in July 1927. Charles wanted to be the only English translator; Prentice thought this ambitious, if not greedy.

'Poor old Pirandello,' Charles wrote to Oriana. 'People go about saying he should take a rest, except for some elderly spinsters, who were sorry for Marta Abba and said: "Poor girl, she should have a younger lover." I realise with a start – that I am reckoned too old!'[6] Charles was nearly thirty-nine and Marta Abba now twenty-seven, while Pirandello himself was sixty. The couple were tortured by gossip about their supposed affair, while in fact it was more of an obsession; the elderly dramatist was dependent on Abba for, he claimed, his sanity: 'I am petrified to be left alone with myself. All the beasts of my cage wake up to tear me to pieces. And I do not know how to placate them.'[7] Charles introduced Pirandello to Ruth Draper, the American wit and monologuist, who was at the end of a season's tour in Rome. After the first act of *Sei personaggi in cerca d'autore*, in Abba's dressing room, Miss Draper recited one of her pieces: 'Marta with her back to the door keeping out the call boy, shouting, "But you must begin the second act, it's cheap seats tonight."'[8]

Charles gave a lunch party at Caffè Aragno for Draper and Pirandello, to which, as with all his parties, he invited everyone he came across, and filled up the restaurant completely. Pirandello became so excited by Charles's plans and so frustrated with his agent that he 'virtually said print and be damned'. This was reported at once to Prentice at Chatto, who unfortunately had other considerations. The last two Pirandello translations were selling poorly in England. Whitworth, who had worked hard to sell Proust, was not as keen on Pirandello's works. Charles's reply was full of righteous indignation; he had got more press clippings about Pirandello in the last six months of 1926 than he had received about Proust in five years.

> It is beyond question that he is better known to the public than Proust and Stendhal put together. It is a little hard that the highbrows should be saying his philosophy is balls, before lowbrows have had time to say, 'Well, I mayn't know much about philosophy, but I know what I like.' Italians dislike him because he has not enough philosophy. English people (esp. women of the rabbit-bottomed breed, who dust bookshelves casually with their once snowy scuts) because he has too much, is too difficult, as they used to say about Browning. The trouble is that English people won't read a book that requires the slightest effort.[9]

The irony for all but Charles was that less than six years later Pirandello would be awarded a Nobel Prize for Literature. Charles's letters to Prentice throughout 1928 re-echo his plea, but sales figures were against him. He became more determined than ever to continue translating Pirandello, even if he had to fund it himself, so he set out to get the English speaking rights from the man himself. In September Richard Aldington was staying and wanted Charles to take him to see Pirandello, but the dramatist was in his home town in Sicily. At the end of September, with Aldington gone, Charles called alone on Pirandello in Rome, and waited for an hour in his salon in the sole company of his pet praying mantis. When Pirandello did finally arrive, he asked Charles to kiss him on both cheeks ('from which I gather his Venus was no longer *toute entière a sa proie attachée*, as kisses were rather a drug in the market when I was dancing attendance on him in March'[10]). Pirandello had found that Abba could not return the ferocity of his passion in equal measure. In fact Pirandello's life was frequently one of painful despair, and he clung to anyone who showed him warmth and affection: he warmly assured Charles that he would be his official Anglo-Saxon translator. He said he would send a typescript of a new play, *Lazzarro*, straight to Charles, missing out agent or theatre, so it could be freshly translated with no compromise. Charles realised that it must be printed and he must also find an English supporter, so he asked Prentice if Noël Coward's producer, Charles B. Cochran, was still in London.[11] But a week later he told Prentice, 'Pirandello has slipped off into the blue, and has not sent me the typescript play he promised. Yesterday at lunch Frezzan drafted a magnificent letter for me to P's agent at Milan, which I must copy and send tomorrow.'[12]

Since he had moved to the capital Charles had also been enjoying the amateur theatricals of the students at the Scots College in Rome. Under the management of Mgr William Clapperton, who soon became a good friend, it was 'no mean establishment'. When not at via Gregoriana, Charles would dine with the Monsignor, drink much wine and slope off home to sleep it off. He was drinking more, as a respite from the gnawing stomach pain and continual fevers. However, to gladden his heart, the student clergymen at the college staged a production of the *Pirates of Penzance*. Nuns lived in the basement of the Scots College and came to dress the female impersonators in sumptuous paper costumes, lavishly trimmed with cut-out, coloured flowers. The Major-Domo had a blue frock coat with an Italian officer's splendid sash and carabiniere trousers, and a paper cocked hat. Both comic and comforting was the fact that, 'He was surrounded by five daughters with deep voices from which strange Lanarkshire sounds issued.'[13]

Charles always conveyed his entertainment to his mother, who was by now living in a mansion block in Maida Vale, not far from the Hayneses,' who said it was amazing that she had found a haven in such a busy thoroughfare, 'which makes it sound as though you live in a cabman's shelter'.[14] Renée Haynes had just written her first novel called *Neapolitan Ice* which Charles told Prentice he found disappointing, but had not yet the courage to tell her so. He wrote Renée a glowing appreciation, however; and mentioned the book in a letter to Edward Marsh. Charles was still teasing Marsh and wrote to him about an incident at 67, via della Croce, 'We have a male undergraduate living in this house, from Catanzaro, in the warm south, who (as I wrote to Miss H.) looks as if Neapolitan Ice woudn't half melt in his mouth; last night, going home, I unlocked my letter box and out tumbled a picture postcard inscribed 'Baci ed abbracci cari. Edoardo' I was puzzled and thought myself Piers Gaveston[15] until I observed that the postmark Catanzaro covered my younger gentleman's name.'[16]

Meanwhile Charles was asked by the American firm Simon and Schuster to translate 'Jean Richard Bloch's masterpiece Et Cie'. From their punctuation, Charles originally thought the title of the book must be Masterpiece and Company as he judged *Et Cie* to be certainly no masterpiece when he finally got round to reading it. 'A long and (to my mind) tedious book,'[17] he told the publishers. Simon and Schuster were not after his literary appraisal, however, only his translation. In September 1928, he accepted a $250 advance in the expectation of another $500 when finished. It was the only time he admitted to having been bought, and having translated what he judged as something less than literature. It was not in the rank of Proust and Pirandello.

Jean Richard Bloch was a French essayist and novelist, and the novel *Et Cie* with its penetrating insights into Jewish psychology was about a family of cloth manufacturers who moved from Alsace to Normandy in 1870. Halfway through translating *Et Cie*, Charles wrote to Simon and Schuster, 'I must say that I find the book extremely dull, and I cannot believe that it will have a very large sale. I don't think the Jewish community will enjoy it particularly as Bloch seems to dwell upon all their minor faults in turn. It may appeal to textile manufacturers, but I doubt whether they form a large enough public.'[18] But he had already spent the advance and had no choice but to continue.

At the same time he had a friend 'staying indefinitely'. Iacopi Frascani, the son of Charles's old landlady, had come from Pisa to settle the matter of his mother's pension. He discovered he would get only 12 lire a day, so Charles decided to add the Frascanis to his list of beneficiaries, which was by this time extensive. Iacopi had a doglike devotion and 'creeps about polishing my shoes until I tell him to go out until dinner time with some pocket money'. Lucy, who was by now Charles's secretary, helped by taking Iacopi out occasionally – on one day they all went round six churches and on another they went on a trip to Ostia together to swim. 'I am very old and weak and exhausted and likely to become so increasingly as time goes on,' Charles complained, noting that he was bathed in sweat every time he moved. It was a hot summer, and his illness was beginning to take its toll.

By October 1928 twelve boxes of his books had arrived from Pisa and he filled his bookcase with six of them. He pulled the bookshelf out three feet from the wall, making a passage behind and filling in the back of the shelves with the rest of his books, which had been stored in the packing cases long enough to breed a colony of black beetles. He had been given a second room which meant he could have guests. Sebastian Sprott, the professor of Psychology at Nottingham University, came to visit, on the advice of his close friend, E. M. Forster. Forster had written advising Sprott that 'Scott Moncrieff is reported as being entertaining, but unentertainable.'[19] No doubt Sprott needed to work out for himself what that meant. They went out to dinner in Rome and had come back with friends to Charles's rooms to play *scopa*, an Italian card game. Charles then wrote inviting him to return and stay in his study where he had a 'quite comfortable bed'. Sprott had connections in the London literary world, a scene Charles felt no longer part of, being cloistered in Rome. Charles explained to him: 'I linger on here, hoping to earn enough money to be able to go away at some very remote date. My eldest nephew has got a job, and a paying job, at Singapore, which may perhaps diminish my responsibilities, otherwise I am tied hand and foot by the claims of nepotism.'[20]

Charles was still in the middle of indexing the Moncrieff genealogy, to be published privately in two folio volumes the following year. He had got to 'F: Flodden; Battle of'. The reason it was taking so long was because, although he had now brought all his books from Pisa to Rome, he had left the cards for the Moncrieff index with a friend in Pisa, 'which I shall bring down one letter at a time, and take back, when copied, to be destroyed there, as they have all sorts of secrets on the reverse side'.[21] After Louis's beating in Milan, and in the general climate of fear, he carefully destroyed them. He told his mother that he kept

> one rather superior one, with the photograph signature etc of the Dowager Lady Crawford and Balcarres . . . retained as a bookmark . . . from where she continues to protest that she did not, when she came out to Italy in 1919, know how difficult the British would make it to get back to England! It does seem absurd as I think Crawford was in the Government at the time, and the

younger son, Sir Ronald, who is now at the Foreign Office after being Ambassador in Berlin must even then have been high up in the diplomatic service.[22]

Having friends in high places was not always enough, though, even in a cultural context. That autumn, the Home Office in Britain banned Radclyffe Hall's *Well of Loneliness*, a novel about love between women: it portrayed lesbianism as a natural state and made the plea, 'Give us also the right to our existence.' To Prentice Charles was indignant,

> In 1921 or 22 the House of Lords led by the Archbishop of Canterbury and Lord Chancellor (Birkenhead) indignantly rejected a proposal to make these practices illegal; in which case I don't see how a book dealing with the tendencies underlying them can be illegal. I should like to take it into court and subpoena Davidson, Birkenhead and Co, and examine them on the Hansard report of their speeches.[23]

In November 1928 Faith Mackenzie, the wife of Compton, came to visit Charles and told him that Compton's novel about the lesbians on Capri, *Extraordinary Women*, had also been banned, and that Radclyffe Hall, who had suffered over her book was now enduring a long and disabling illness. Charles told Prentice that he hoped Sir Joyson Hicks – the authoritarian Home Secretary – might also have a long and disabling illness. Faith said that the *Sunday Times* had rebuked Evelyn Waugh for making jokes about the white slave trade in *Decline and Fall*. Charles had enjoyed the novel, 'the most profoundly immoral book I have ever read, but immense fun – don't you agree?'

This literary gossip all had a bearing on his future as a translator. His translation of *Sodome et Gomorrhe*, even euphemistically renamed 'Cities of the Plain' or, as Charles quipped, 'Cissies of the Plain', still could not be published. On the advice of Counsel, experts on the Obscene Publications Act 1857, Chatto could not take the risk. Charles felt distressed that Prentice was £400 out of pocket on his behalf, having paid him for a translation he could not publish, and now having to go to private publishers to see if they would take it. On 11 April 1928 Prentice wrote to Charles that Chatto had taken advice from two counsel and that they both advised against publication, and suggested they approach Sylvia Beach at the Shakespeare and Co. bookshop in Paris who had published Joyce's *Ulysses*.

America, on the other hand was not flustered. Boni Inc. had already published *Cities of the Plain* and were sending copies by post to England to those clamouring for the next, stalled, instalment of Proust. They were paying Charles generously, without a murmur, £500 per volume, with six volumes to go. Charles offered Chatto an option of the English rights of the future volumes and for them to continue only to pay £75 per volume as before. He felt flush with American money and dearly loved his English publisher, confidant and friend, Charles Prentice, to whom he wrote, 'I am expected to complete the whole work by the end of June 1930, which should be quite feasible, though boring.' *Albertine* bored him because there was so much grammatical footwork: Proust had died before he had the chance to correct his proofs. On the other hand, he enjoyed working with Proust's style, which he thought superior to Joyce's *Ulysses*, and could not see why they were compared as similar by critics. That Christmas he wrote to Prentice saying that his association with him had been one of the pleasantest things in his whole life.

Albert Boni realised that Charles worked fast and sold fast, and suggested in December 1928 that he translate the whole of Boccacio's works, without investigating their length. Charles discovered the job ran to 17 volumes, much of it in medieval Latin. He proposed to take it on as a full-time job after he had finished Proust at the rate of $450 a month, telling Boni that he had to clear £1000 a year because he was still paying for the education of many of his nieces and nephews. The only possible barrier to this was that he had also agreed to translate the whole of Pirandello.

He was working hard and keeping irregular hours; 'I work nightly til 4 a.m,' he told Vyvyan, 'read Balzac for 2 hours, wake at 1.30 p.m. and go out as little as possible.'[24] When asked in December 1928 by society hostess Mrs Strong to go and meet a German scholar of Proust who was in Rome on a visit, Charles refused and replied with two quotations from Balzac written on scraps of jotter: *'le temps est le seul capital des gens qui n'ont que leur intelligence pour la fortune'* ('time is the only capital owned by people who have to live by their wits'), and *'les succès littéraires ne se conquierent que dans la solitude et par d'obstines travaux'* ('literary success is only achieved in solitude and by dogged hard work'). This only intrigued the German scholar further, and that winter he was determined to meet Charles. When Ernst Curtius, critic and professor at Bonn University, was eventually introduced to Charles, a friendship blossomed. Curtius was four years older, sensitive, literary and a lot of fun. Ernst later wrote that he found Charles

> enchantingly original. I had imagined the translator of Proust to be an aesthete. He was something much better: an individual character . . . He was a Roman body and soul. It was not an antiquarian or artistic interest that drew him to Rome, but the everyday life of the city. The via della Croce was for him a complete universe in which all human wants could be satisfied . . . By the dim light of a little lamp, and the smell . . . of a reluctantly burning oil stove, he sat at a table buried under books and papers, leaving just enough room for a half emptied fiasco of Chianti. He generally received me with some strong abuse of Albertine, whose moods and vicious habits were at that time keeping him very busy: he was translating one of the last volumes of Proust. The world of Proust was to him as familiar as the Via della Croce, and he roamed in it with the same enjoyment, though with a sarcastic want of respect . . . A dominating, brilliantly humorous mood was his usual attitude, whether it was a question of Proust, the latest newspaper rumour, or social events.[25]

Charles returned his admiration and affection and dedicated to him the volume about Albertine, which he titled *The Sweet Cheat Gone*. He wrote to de la Mare to ask if he could use this last line of a poem published in the 1916–17 anthology of Georgian poets, 'All the grey night/ In chaos of vacancy shone; Nought but vast sorrow was there . . . The sweet cheat gone.' Walter de la Mare agreed to the use so long as he was not mentioned himself, as a family man he did not want to be publicly connected to Proust. Curtius had no such worries and welcomed the dedication which ran – '*Ernst Robert Curtius, zugeeignet, obwohl die arme Albertine verschwunden ist, haben die Brüder Albreche gut gewusst wie uns zu trösten*' ('As Ernst Robert Curtius said, although poor Albertine has gone, the Albreche brothers knew how to comfort us well').

The brothers Albreche ran a beer house in via Rasella near the Trevi fountains where a small circle of friends met over a beer and sausage with sauerkraut nearly every evening. It was the gaiety of these evenings that Charles referred to as consoling them for the loss of Albertine. As Ernst knew, Charles did not need consolation, he was glad to be rid of Albertine; but the evenings were full of jokes and allusions to Albertine's coquettish behaviour which could also be seen in the men and women of their café life. Charles would illustrate the conversation as it flowed with pen drawings on the marble table tops, 'he was always a congenial companion, a laughing philosopher, a satirical censor, a bubbling fountain of wit'.[26]

This wit was widely appreciated among the expatrate social life of Rome. William Rossetti's daughter Helen, whom he called 'the little Angeli,' sought Charles out on a visit, and he said of her, 'she looks exactly the same, like a newly washed kitten in a blanket'.[27] In October he went to a party given by Estelle Nathan, a Jewish painter whom he had met with Marcel Boulestin and who had done a pencil portrait of him in London two years earlier. He went with Lucy and met Antonio Scarfoglio, son of the great Neapolitan journalist, as well as several 'pleasant and intelligent people including Pamela, who is 22 and the Prix de Rome Scholar. In about half an hour I must go to a farewell party at the British School. There is a very sympathetic lot there: painters, sculptors, architects, archaeologists, historians, embryo dons, and what not.' His letter ended, 'I must stop now and go up to the passport office as it is the night the Kings Messenger goes north and we dine at 7:30 and it is now 7:40.'[28] He was still networking and reporting for the Passport Office.

A week later he gave a lunch party for Macartney of *The Times* to meet Alec Randall, Britain's unofficial diplomatic agent at the Vatican, who also worked in intelligence. Randall was a writer who contributed to *The Criterion* and reviewed German books for the *Times Literary Supplement*. Randall and his wife, whose children were ill, arrived in deepest black . . .

> oozing black silk handkerchiefs from every pocket; I met them in the pend outside the restaurant assuming that all their children had died but that they were being brave about it; so I squeezed their hands hard and said nothing. Late in the evening I realised

that they were in court mourning for the Empress Marie. Randall is in charge of his ministry until the new Minister arrives so I suppose they have to be extra strict. I think they might have told me however.[29]

Another dinner companion was Father Mather, one of the priests at the Scots College, with whom he went on a trip during the following summer to Pisa and stayed with the monks at Calci. In Rome he sometimes dined with him at his clerical hotel which on one occasion was full of Irish policemen on a trip to the Vatican. Mather said that they had just been to the Pope's Mass and received Holy Communion from him. Afterwards their general gave the Pope a thank-you offering of fifty pounds, and one of them told Mather that the Pope was so excited at the sight of fifty pounds that he 'simply fell on the general's neck! Italians not being used to large sums of money.'

Charles was working hard between interruptions and had neither the time not the energy for a holiday, unless Pisa for Christmas. 'Tired in brain and body but things are looking up and I do hope to be enormously rich next year and provide for all the children.'[30] He did reach Pisa for midnight Mass at the cathedral and on Christmas morning recited Milton's Nativity Ode from memory, as he had every year on Christmas morning since the age of six.

In the end it was the Americans who were 'fearless' about the British obscenity laws. In the spring of 1929, *Cities of the Plain* in two volumes was at last published in England, by the American Alfred Knopf, who took over the rights from the still fearful Chatto as well as the rights to the rest of the series, paying Charles another £480. The review in the *Times Literary Supplement* by Orlo Williams on 21 March stated, 'There is no object in disguising the fact that a large part of this section is concerned with the observation of homo-sexuality in men and women: but Proust must be taken whole or not at all.'[31]

Charles also managed to persuade Chatto to reprint Frederic Rolfe's *Hadrian VII*, because, he teased, he had lost his own 1904 edition. He was at last becoming a man of influence. Finally, after all these years, the literary agents Curtis Brown offered 'unusually remunerative arrangements' for his first novel. 'What does that mean? They don't say. Fifty pounds I suppose, less ten per cent for them. Are they any use at all? They involve me in endless correspondence and make me give them opinions on books I have to go out and buy . . .' He was too old in spirit, cantankerous and otherwise well-paid to take the offer.

As Lent came, Charles began fasting, no food but bread and water on Friday and Saturday, and no meat on weekdays. His landlady, who carried a lorgnette in one hand while she did the rooms with the other, and said she was a photographer and a Russian aristocrat, was impressed with this regime. In April he wrote to Aldington, 'Rome has suddenly turned warm: the sun has, indeed, in the ram his halfe course yrun; two swallows fell down the kitchen chimney on Saturday – in the passport office, a most suitable place for swallows to call at. Smoked spectacles are invading the Piazza di Spagna.'

He was thinking nostalgically of home, 'I often dream that I am back in Lanark, usually with Johnnie, and in that commonplace house we discover all sorts of rooms and contrivances that never existed before, nor will again.'[32] He still felt close to his family and his governess Helen Stephen with whom he had always corresponded,

> About the death of your mother, you know that everything that touches you, touches me, only with regard to mothers we must all face the moment when we have to survive them, and I think that moment is worse for sons than for daughters, as sons must often feel that they have not been good sons.[33]

He was still guilty about his homosexual life and even, at this late stage, still considered the idea of marriage. 'I am thinking earnestly of getting married . . . to Miss Lunn,'[34] he confessed to Vyvyan, but then made it into a joke by asking Vyv to invite her for cocktails while still on her London visit, followed by a game of 'hearth rugger after dinner. Do you prefer full back or centre forward by the way?' But he ended seriously, 'I should very much like your advice on the subject.'[35] He also mentioned his nephew George who had just moved round the corner in Sydney Street. 'My only friends in Chelsea are Jacqueline Hope and yourself. One will corrupt his body, but the other his soul; so that I don't think I shall give him any introductions. He is a bright lad, much cleverer than myself, perhaps because he has had less education.'[36]

An article he wrote for *Country Life* about Carrara in April made him nostalgic for Pisa, especially the description of a 'synod of lawnsleeved clouds assembling on the Apuan Alps'. His mind was turned towards the religious, or at least the aesthetic parts of religion, though it was rarely reflected in his reading. He did not read many holy books, having all the latest novels sent by Prentice upon which he would comment, and reading all his friends' novels out of curiosity. He spent the summer evenings outdoors with friends by the Tivoli swimming pool where he could still impress as a fine swimmer and high diver. Ion Monro, a freelance journalist, described him as 'the elusive, swift-minded, and faun-like leader of evenings in trattorias, nights among books . . .'[37] The Pirandello battles continued: both in persuading Chatto to publish a complete works, and in trying to wrest the rights from the Italian agent, as well as trying to track down the elusive writer himself. In June the search paid off,

> Pirandello came to dinner on Friday. He was 23½ hours late, as he had fixed Thursday evening at 8.30 and came on Friday at about 8 while I was down here changing my coat. I got up to 12 via Gregoriana and found him having a tête-à-tête with Lucy, she addressing him in German and he replying in Italian.[38]

Pirandello had at last appointed an agent in London and Charles was in the middle of translating his unpublished play, *Lazzaro*, which was to be produced in fourteen days' time. Charles's sheer perseverance ensured that *Lazzaro* became unique in Pirandello's repertoire as the only play to be premiered in English, on 9 July 1929 (while the Italian premiere was on 7 December that year in Turin). Charles translated the title, as *Though One Rose*, from Luke 10: 'Though one rose from the dead . . .' A challenging play with numerous characters all shouting at once, tackling difficult ideas about faith and the afterlife, it was produced at the Theatre Royal in Huddersfield by the dauntless impresario Alfred Wareing. Wareing was a theatre producer of boundless energy who had known Charles's friends, the actors Frank Benson and William Armstrong. He had written the famous manifesto of the Glasgow Repertory Theatre in 1909, declaring it Glasgow's own theatre, a citizens' theatre in the fullest sense of the term and making it no longer dependent on plays from London.

Wareing had now bought the Theatre Royal in Huddersfield. His bracing letters include one advising Charles on a cure for his terrible stomach pain, 'immediately after waking in the morning and before anything else, a tablespoonful of rum with a raw egg in it, not beaten up but in the yolk like an oyster, swallowed whole!' ending the letter, 'Cheer-up! Yours sincerely, Alfred Wareing.'

Charles was far beyond the egg-yolk cure. He wrote to Prentice, 'I am very unwell just now, and creeping gradually into my grave. I shall be 40 tomorrow and feel already more like 80. I can neither eat nor sleep, nor indeed work, but I can read novels.'[39] He read seven novels of Balzac one after the other, maintaining that *Lost Illusions* was the greatest novel ever written, 'There is no other novelist really worth reading, and never will be.'[40] Lucy, now back in Rome, was worried about his health and wrote a long, exasperated letter to Vyvyan to ask him to help advise Charles to go to hospital and see the doctors recommended by his family. Vyvyan duly did and an X-ray showed a growth round Charles's oesophagus for which he was prescribed radium treatment. 'No sympathy, please,' he ordered Vyvyan. 'I am quite hardened to it. Probably due to excessive s.a.w.'[41] Fond of grim irony himself, Charles appreciated that the particular sexual act begun in his childhood, written about in his infamous story at Winchester, and practised so much in the playground of liberal Italy, should be his nemesis.

In spite of regular radium treatments, he took himself to Naples on 9 December to see his nephew Colin off by boat to Singapore. Death concentrated the mind and Charles thought of family and home and Scotland. That month his cousin Lucy Pearson sent him a copy of the *Scots Observer*, where he learnt of the early days of the Scottish National Party which the paper called 'proud and narrow'. His retort was,

> Granted that we are proud, is it not well that we should be taught to have something to be proud of? Granted that we are narrow, should we not be widened? The Scots are quite as capable of governing themselves as the Swiss – and have as much right as they to do so. Representative government may be a good or a bad thing, but it should be representative . . . I would cheerfully see all Parliaments abolished as they are most mischievous

> institutions, but so long as they exist Scotland ought to have one, and so ought England . . .[42]

It was probably the most political statement he ever made. But he was back to work on 2 December 1929, correcting the proofs of *Albertine*. That day he wrote to T. S. Eliot. A section called 'The Death of Albertine' had been published by *The Criterion* in 1924. He realised that the text had already been changed. 'In several passages my Criterion version does not conform to the French text afterwards published by Gallimard,' he told Eliot . He was convinced the Gallimard text was wrong. 'But how did it come to be falsified?'[43] He once had the original but had given it to Mucci, who translated it into Italian; Mucci, however, had now become the Governor of Rome and was entirely inaccessible.

In the meantime his critic friend Payen de Payne wrote to Charles complaining of the flu, to which Charles replied with a play on his friend's unusual name,

> Payen-Payne,
> What's this you say?
> You're an invalid again?
> Grim the tidings you convey, Payen-Payne!
> Much against my usual vein
> I indite this roundelay
> In a melancholic strain:
> Nearer draws the reckoning day;
> And for every cup we drain
> We must soon – ah, wellaway! Pay, in pain.[44]

He had drained many cups. Writing to Oriana in a similar melancholy strain he wondered, 'I begin to wonder if our driven barks will ever rub sides again in the same harbour.'[45] She and Vyvyan travelled to Rome to drain more cups, but after only one night's revelry Charles took himself off to hospital with what he described as gastric ulcers. 'You must not think that I am running away from you, but it is not that, I am fearfully weak, and the two delightful evenings with you and V. just tipped the beam and made it impossible for me to stay at home any longer. Lucy is unpacking at this moment in a double-bedded room which the nuns seem to want her to share.'[46] Another X-ray showed 'a foreign body exercising a stranglehold round the foot of the oesophagus which', he told Oriana, 'kept going up and down like the service lift in a block of mansions, thus obviating the necessity of more than one meal a fortnight.'[47]

It was finally confirmed as terminal cancer. He felt fear, certitude and peace. He needed to finish his work, to write some important letters and to read the books he had been meaning to read all his life; also to put his affairs in order: his nephew George, who wanted to be a writer, would inherit his library and his royalties, so that he could be free to spend time in creative writing – a luxury denied Charles.

Via della Croce could be translated as Cross Street or The Way of the Cross and it is no accident that Charles chose to live there. He had translated *Du Côté de chez Swann*, as *Swann's Way*, meaning Swann's life, the route he took, his journey; he had a copy of *The Way of the Cross* by Thomas à Kempis and in his own 'way' accepted the challenge of trying to live it. It is striking that he went from the via della Croce to the Calvary hospital, for this slow death was his Calvary.

The Calvary hospital had been set up in 1908 by a nun called Sister Mary Potter who had been told by the Pope that her mission was to found a hospital for British tourists in Rome. It is still called the British Hospital although it now caters for all, and there is still a portrait of Sister Mary with her blue veil in the entrance hall. She started the nursing order that came to be known as the Blue Nuns, and the order quickly started hospitals all over Europe. The building is on the Coelian Hill, which was then outside the city of Rome, but was only an hour's walk from the Spanish Steps and Charles's flat and a few hundred metres from the Colosseum. A cylindrical church with a lead dome formed an integral part of the hospital, with balconies perched up the cylinder so that invalids from the wards on the two floors above could go to Mass for as long as they could stand or sit or bear to be out of bed.

The windows at the front look out on to the medieval church of San Stefano Rotondo, also a circular church, unusual because of the extreme portrayal of suffering in its sixteenth-century frescos. There are twenty-five larger-than-life size frescos in brilliant colours depicting the martyrdom of the saints: mauled by lions, having their tongues pulled out, hands cut off, being crushed under a slab of stone, chopped to bits with a knife on a slab, boiled in oil, having breasts ripped off with a large sharpened fork, crucified upside down, flayed alive, flung out of a window, St Catherine broken on a wheel . . . an orgy of torture.

Slow death by stomach cancer with the help of morphine was by comparison an easier option, not that Charles had a choice. San Stefano Rotondo was near enough for the occasional Mass, and there was the alternative choice of Mass in the hospital church. Going to meet his Maker was a serious journey for Charles and one he approached with all the faith he had accumulated in his life; for most, a short life, but for him, whose friends had died in their twenties in the war, a long and exciting one. He had revelled in the gift of life. He was thankful for the sacrament of confession which meant he could wipe clean the murk accumulated on his soul. His last letters were written happily about his greatest love: literature. To T. S. Eliot on 12 December 1929 he wrote

> I am expecting a long spell of reduced life with these Blue Sisters, with little opportunity for work and much drowsy opportunity for mild reading. I begin by finishing up all the longish books that I have never before finished and have managed so far: *Moby Dick, I promessi sposi, the Dynasts, Les Possédés, The Wings of the Dove, War and Peace.*
>
> But for the difficulty of having books located in and fetched from my study at the other end of Rome, and kept here under the disapproving eye of a sister who thinks reading foolish, books untidy, and has never received a telegram in her life, I should have gathered a fair-sized library around me even here. But each volume has to come in and go out by stealth, like Nicodemus, swaddled in cast off pyjamas.[48]

Eliot offered to send out more books and mournfully asked: 'Is there ever any hope of seeing you in London again?'[49] They began a discussion about Shelley's 'Skylark' which had gone through Charles's mind over and over again in the trenches. Now at this hour, again close to death, the same poem re-emerged. Eliot asked, '. . . the real question is: are not all or most of Shelley's comparisons in that poem irrelevancies? Surely Dante would have shuddered at such a far-fetched simile to express "keenness".'[50] Charles replied,

> Shelley lived in a Jazz Age, like our own, when everything had been upset by 20 years of war, the language most of all . . . turning to *Adonais*, whom does he mean by 'a pardlike spirit, beautiful and swift'? I used to maintain that this was Byron, until I was forced to admit that Byron is suited elsewhere with a 'brow, branded like Cain's or Christ's'. Well then, is Shelley referring to himself? It outrages my sense of decorum that any man should call himself, or even his spirit, swift.[51]

Charles doubted that his own spirit would soon move swiftly on. Turner, Orioli, Aldington and Douglas, his friends from Florence, took the train to Rome to say farewell. Later Orioli remembered the numerous saints' medallions around his neck which he fingered as he spoke to them. Douglas assumed that the nuns, being Catholic and schooled in the benefits of suffering, would not give him enough morphine to deal with the pain. Vyvyan Holland recalled that Charles had a final, bitter, Sitwell moment, saying that it was all very well for them to sneer and call him a body snatcher, 'But my way was forced on me: I had to earn my own living.' At which point he threw back the blankets to reveal a wraithe-like body.[52]

He was in pain, 'Heroin is no good. Laudanum is a little more effective, and they won't even allow me to vomit, which I can do rather well.'[53] He could barely eat and lost 20 kilos rapidly. Richard Aldington and G. K. Chesterton visited on separate occasions; Chesterton read Virgil's *Aeneid* in Latin to him. Then he was 'sent to bed like a whipped dog because I vomited again. But a man must have some outlet for his passions.'[54]

His mother came to stay in the hospital for the last few weeks of his life and he shared with her his letters to Eliot, to whom on the 29 January, with only a month to live, he still managed a long letter, suggesting a short essay competition about the point in *The Turn of the Screw* where the little boy is dying and says, suddenly looking out of the window, 'Peter Quint: you devil.' Charles's interpretation being that the little boy is calling his governess 'you devil' or that at this point of heightened spiritual awareness, he could see the devil in her. Charles still maintained that his mother's conversations with the dead were evil, but she continued, mesmerised. He finished his last letter to Eliot, 'I am iller at the moment than I should have thought it possible for a man to be without being seriously ill, so to speak. Quite incredibly weak and as a rule unable to swallow any nourishment though for the last 2 hours I have been trifling with a cup of tea.'[55]

To his cousin William Moncrieffe he wrote, 'I should be perfectly happy to end my days in this room – looking out at a very pleasant mezzotint landscape . . .'[56] Then came his final literary visit on 14 February when Evelyn Waugh arrived and gave him 'the first blissful evening I've had for months'.[57]

A special blessing from the Pope was requested and given. While he was still mentally alert, Charles received the Last Sacraments of Confession, Viaticum and Extreme Unction. He died on the evening of the last day of February 1930. His funeral Mass was held by Monsignor Clapperton in the Baptistry of San Giovanni Laterano, the vast basilica and seat of the Popes before St Peter's. The baptistry itself dated back to the thirteenth century when it was built for a Pope Hilarious – a detail Charles would not have missed in his funeral instructions. The procession wound its way from the nearby Calvary Hospital round the ancient Roman wall that lines via Rotondo, to the mass at the basilica and from there on, a half-hour walk to the Verano Cemetery. Ion Monro, his journalist friend attached to the *Glasgow Herald*, was present and wrote: 'To the little group of friends who followed on foot his funeral car, there joined in with reverend furtiveness here and there along the route humble, weeping Italian workmen and women, folk hitherto unknown to us, but who had cause to bless his memory.'[58]

Epilogue

> That poetic, but positive and staccato soul . . . the supercilious curl of his moustached lip, and the fierce, straight look in his eyes.
>
> J. C. Squire, Obituary of CKSM[1], 1931

This picture, drawn by one friend after Charles's death, conjures up the elusive and attractive spirit. Charles had a tough, discerning mind which disciplined his own life into several compartments: the literary man to Prentice, Marsh and most of the world; the family man to his mother, brother and relatives; the spy to Louis Christie and the Secret Intelligence Service; and the Rabelaisian homosexual to Vyvyan Holland alone.

He was a man who on one day could write a metaphysical religious poem of great depth, and on the next a filthy, funny limerick. Charles would write limericks spontaneously onto his typewriter one after another without line breaks. Even dirty stories were written with characteristic wit, 'Reggie Turner thinks the jewels are concealed in Mrs Otway's bottom which is highly probable, and therefore should be probed.'[2] In the same letter he thanked Vyvyan for sending an *Anthology of Catholic Poets.*

A Catholic convert, he was also a family man, military man, a manly poet. A homosexual who flirted with women and had lasting emotional relationships with a number of close female friends: Eva, Oriana, Ruby and Lucy – and did not feel defined or confined by his sexuality. You could say that his conversion to Catholicism freed his spirit. He discovered the sacrament of Confession, where man is reconciled with himself and with God, not trapped in guilt, and this gave his spirit flight. The door was always open to be someone else: he noticed with delight during his last illness that the nuns in the convent hospital expected him to share a bedroom with his secretary Lucy.

Controversially, he enjoyed the war; his wounding in the leg jolted him for ever into a world of pain, but saved his life by getting him out of France. Healing came with his love for Wilfred Owen, combined with immersion in military intelligence at the War Office. Threaded through his war experience was his career as a journalist and critic, failed poet and fledgling short-story writer. Realising that his judgement of others' work was more valuable than his own, he recognised and helped bring to fame Owen, Proust and Pirandello. During the fruitful post-war years, he formed friendships with great literary figures of the day including Graves, Coward, Gosse, Waugh, Conrad, Eliot and many others less famous. He mixed with aesthetes and read and wrote about them, but his own habits were ascetic and restrained, living in rented rooms amid piles of books and papers, never having a proper home.

He lived much of his life under great threat and was bound by honour and secrecy; during the war he never became cynical of his reasons for fighting; later he defended Millard in court and collected from others for Millard's court fines. Arranging transport to the Du Cane Road hospital for the wounded was a point of honour. Finally, Charles's sense of honour is evident in his intelligence-gathering exertions all over Italy for the Passport Control Office. Today we often regard honour as fustiness or foolishness, misguided jingoism or false bravado, but for Charles honour meant integrity, nobility of character, distinction, dignity and, above all, self-sacrifice.

He may have developed a Catholic soul, but he always had what we understand as a Protestant work ethic, the legacy from his father and the Church of Scotland. He worked as hard as possible for two reasons: to support his family and out of a deep love and knowledge of literature. He championed Proust and Pirandello when they were still almost unknown to English-speaking readers and constantly nagged his British and American publishers to support their books.

He wrote thousands of letters and was a great entertainer to all of his correspondents, as he was to his friends, having a manifest enjoyment of life and people, 'he had a vivid pen, and a power of stripping superfluities from things and people and exposing their nakedness.'[3]

Even his only letter to Proust, to sort out their differences over the title, is full of grace:

> My dear Sir, I beg that you will allow me to thank you for your very gratifying letter in English as my knowledge of French – as you have shown me, with regard to your titles – is too imperfect, too stunted a growth for me to weave from it the chapelet that I would fain offer you. Are you still suffering – which I am very sorry to hear, and wish that my real sympathy could bring you some relief – I am making my reply to your critiques on another sheet, and by the aid of a machine which I hope you do not abominate: it is the machine on which Swann and one-third of the Jeunes Filles have been translated. Thus you can throw away this sheet unread, or keep it, or inflict it upon M. Gallimard. Charles Scott Moncrieff.

Charles not only breaks down our assumptions of stereotypes, he was also a perfect example of a man of his time. A masculine, muscular leader; and at the same time a great pansy. Fact is often more extreme and unexpected than fiction. Fiction orders things, gives them a structure and makes them palatable and understandable, but real life can be extraordinary. His life was tragic, but he managed to stave off the worst through arduous toil and the gift of humour.

Charles is recognised as having made a considerable contribution to English literature. Proust owes him a debt, as does everyone who discovers Proust in English for the first time, such as Scott Fitzgerald, who said of his translation, 'Scott Moncrieff's Proust is a masterpiece in itself.'[4]

Over thirty years after Proust's death his brother and publisher put together a new French edition, re-edited and lengthened by 300,000 words. This edition was retranslated into English in 1981. There are now enough new translations to provide material for arguments on their merits and faults for critics for centuries to come. However, it is generally agreed that if you want to read a translation from one hand, which understands the time of Proust, and which was taken from the French script that Proust personally approved and saw to publication, then that is Scott Moncrieff's. This was the translation that influenced Woolf, Joyce and the modernist generation. 'Any translation that appears now will inevitably – whatever its brilliance, whatever its concern to be faithful to the original – bear the imprint of our own age,' wrote the critic and Proust expert Jerry Farber in 1997.[5] Similarly, the critic Robert Douglas-Fairhurst wrote in 2002 in *The Observer*, when reviewing the new Penguin edition:

> Scott Moncrieff, for all his occasional carelessness and prissiness, was probably temperamentally better suited than many later translators to making sense of a style, which Montesquiou once described memorably as 'a mixture of litanies and sperm' . . . For the Penguin translators, one feels, this version of Proust is a job well done; for Scott Moncrieff, it was a labour of love.[6]

Charles understood Proust's 'mixture of litanies and sperm': that the sacred and the profane create an invigorating blend and thereby embrace the whole of life. Just as Proust's 'Jeunes filles en fleurs,' or young girls starting their period, were understood as an element of creation rather than objects of disgust, so it was with 'litanies and sperm'. You could say that the heady cocktail inspired his life. Charles's translation was indeed a 'labour of love', one production of a man who worked tirelessly for the good of literature as a whole, and cared as fiercely about the written word as he did about family and friends. Charles and Proust were linked by the inspiration of Ruskin who said, 'No true disciple of mine will ever be a "Ruskinian". He will follow, not me, but the instincts of his own soul and the guidance of its Creator.'[7]

Family Postscript

After the First World War, there must have been many families and unmarried uncles who cobbled together to support the children of those killed in action – theirs was a fatherless generation. As the only war-wounded member of his family to survive, Charles supported and assisted in the education of his nine nephews and nieces, after John's early death and Colin's long illness.

His entry in *Who's Who* under 'Recreation' cited only 'Nepotism'. His brother John had two children, David and Jean, who had three and four children of their own. Of Colin's large family, sons Colin and Charles died in the Second World War, with Colin leaving one six-month-old daughter. Elizabeth had two sons and Joanna one daughter. George, the would-be writer who inherited Charles's royalties, fathered seven children, one of them my mother. All the first generation retained their Christian faith, with George following Charles into the Catholic Church. In turn these great nieces and nephews have had their children and now grandchildren.

It is touching to think that Charles, who took such an interest in his ancestors, should by his providence have had an extended responsibility for eighty-three of his family's descendants.

Sources

I was given many of the primary sources for this book. The suitcase of unread letters from my great-aunt's attic contained also diaries and notebooks belonging to Charles, backs of envelopes, scribbled genealogies and poems, doodles, limericks and interesting receipts, correspondence with publishers and wrangles with Pirandello's agent. The most revealing was his notebook of poems (Findlay Collection, FC). Then my cousin Christina Scott Moncrieff gave me forty-four volumes of diaries of Charles's mother (JMSM.) These furnished the details of his childhood and the fabric of the family background, and also dates, times, places and people up until his death. *Memories and Letters* (M&L), published in 1931, was the collection of his letters edited by his mother and his secretary Lucy Lunn, after Charles's death. For those who question the reliability of letters edited posthumously by a relative, I have many of the original autograph war letters, in purple pencil, and although they have been edited for length, none were changed for content. My cousin Kate Moberly has boxes of letters and family papers which I foraged through over the last seven years, finding birth certificates, articles, and vital family information. Likewise my cousins Christina Scott Moncrieff and John Scott Moncrieff allowed me to go through their collections of family letters.

For information on the lives of the many literary associates and friends of Charles, I have used the *Oxford Dictionary of National Biography Online*.

Another useful guide was *Charles Scott Moncrieff: A Biography*, Charles Gale's thesis, published by Ann Arbor University Microfilms, 1969. Gale had access to letters not seen before, especially those from Charles to Oriana Haynes. Charles Gale's thesis can be obtained from the National Library of Scotland (NLS) in Edinburgh which also houses a collection of Charles's letters.

Family Sources

FC Findlay Collection
JMSM Diaries of Jessie Margaret Scott Moncrieff
M&L *Memories and Letters*, published in 1931 by Chapman Hall, edited by K. M. Scott Moncrieff and L.W. Lunn

Archive Sources

AC William Andrews Clerk Memorial Library University of California, Los Angeles
Berg Berg Collection, New York Public Library
BC John J. Burns Library, Boston College
BL British Library
BLN British Library Newspaper Archive
CA Chatto and Windus Archive, Reading University
EFL English Faculty Library, Oxford
FF Faber & Faber Archive
HRC Harry Ransom Centre, University of Texas at Austin
KC Charleston Papers, Kings College, Cambridge
IWM Imperial War Museum
NA National Archives, Kew
NLS National Library of Scotland, Edinburgh
WU Olin Library, University of Washington, St Louis
SAC South Asia Department, Cambridge University
WC Welland Collection, John Rylands Library, Manchester University
WCA Winchester College Archive

Periodicals and Broadsheets

Academy
The Athenæum
The Bookman
The Criterion
Daily Mail
London Mercury
The Nation
New Field
New Statesman
The New Witness

The Times
Times Literary Supplement
Westminster Gazette
The Wykehamist

List of Published Works by C. K. Scott Moncrieff

The Song of Roland (trans.), Chapman & Hall, (London, 1919)

Beowulf, Widsith, Finnsburgh, Waldere, Deor (trans.), Chapman & Hall, (London, 1921)

Petrus Abaelardus, *The Letters of Abelard and Heloise* (trans.), Guy Chapman (London, 1925)

Petronius Arbiter, *The Satyricon* (Burnaby's 1694 translation) (Introd.), Chapman & Dodd (London, 1923)

Jean-Richard Bloch, *— & Co* (trans.), Gollanz (London, 1929)

Armand-Louis de Gontaut, Duke de Biron, *Memoirs of the Duc de Lauzun* (trans.), Routledge & Sons (London, 1928)

P. G. Lear and L. O., *The Strange and Striking Adventures of Four Authors in Search of a Character* (trans.), Cayme Press (London, 1926)

Luigi Pirandello, *Shoot!* (trans.), Chatto and Windus (London, 1926)

—— *The Old and the Young, vols I* and *II* (trans.), E. P. Dutton & Co. (London and New York, 1928)

Marcel Proust, *Remembrance of Things Past, vol. I: Swann's Way* (trans.), Chatto and Windus (London, 1922)

—— *Remembrance of Things Past, vol. II: Within a Budding Grove* (trans.), Chatto and Windus (London, 1924)

—— *Remembrance of Things Past, vol. III: The Guermantes Way* (trans.), Chatto and Windus (London, 1925)

—— *Remembrance of Things Past, vols IV* and *V: Cities of the Plain* (trans.), Chatto and Windus (London, 1929)

—— *Remembrance of Things Past, vol. VI: The Captive* (trans.), Chatto and Windus (London, 1929)

—— *Remembrance of Things Past, vol. VII: The Sweet Cheat Gone* (trans.), Chatto and Windus (London, 1930)

François-Augustin Paradis de Moncrif, *The Adventures of Zeloide and Amanzarifdine* (ed. and trans.), Routledge & Sons (London, 1929)

C. K. Scott Moncrieff, *Memories and Letters* (eds J. M. Scott Moncrieff and L. W. Lunn), Chapman & Hall (London, 1931)

Stendhal, *The Abbess of Castro and Other Tales* (trans.), Chapman & Hall (London, 1926)

—— *The Red and the Black* (trans.), Chapman & Hall (London, 1926)

—— *The Charterhouse of Parma* (trans.), Chapman & Hall (London, 1926)

—— *Armance* (trans.), Chapman & Hall (London, 1928)

Various, *Marcel Proust: An English Tribute* (ed.), Chatto and Windus (London, 1923)

Published Sources

Acton, Harold, *Memoirs of an Aesthete* (London, 1948)

Aldington, Richard, *Pinorman: personal recollections of Norman Douglas, Pino Orioli and Charles Prentice* (London, 1954)

Amory, Mark, *Collected Letters of Evelyn Waugh* (London, 1980)

Arthur, Max, *The Faces of the First World War* (London, 2007)

Batini, Giorgio, *La Versilia Com'era* (Florence, 2007)

Bell, Anne Olivier, *Diary of Virginia Woolf, Vol. III 1925–1930* (London, 1980)

Borland, Maureen, *Wilde's Devoted Friend* (London, 1990)

Boulton, James T., and Vasey, Lindeth (eds.), *The Letters of D. H. Lawrence*, Vol. V March 1924–March 1927 (Cambridge, 1989)

—— and Boulton, Margaret H. (eds.), *The Letters of D. H. Lawrence*, vol. VI March 1927–Nov. 1928 (Cambridge, 1991)

Bridges, Robert (ed.), *The Spirit of Man* (London, 1916)

Burkes Peerage

Byrne, Janet, *A Genius for Living: The Life of Frieda Lawrence* (London, 1995)

Chapman, Guy, *A Passionate Prodigality: Fragments of Autobiography* (New York, 1966)

Cave, Nigel, *Hill 60: Ypres* (London, 1997)

—— *Polygon Wood: Ypres* (London, 1998)

—— *Sanctuary Wood and Hooge* (London, 1993)

Cecil, Robert, *Life in Edwardian England* (London, 1969)

Coward, Noël, *Autobiography* (London, 1986)

—— *Easy Virtue* (London, 1926)

Egremont, Max, *Siegfried Sassoon* (London, 2005)

Eliot, Valerie, and Haughton, Hugh (eds.), *The Letters of T. S. Eliot, vol. 2: 1923–1925* (London, 2009)

—— and Haffenden, John (eds.), *The Letters of T. S. Eliot vol. 3: 1926–1927* (London, 2012)

Ellman, Richard, *Oscar Wilde* (London, 1988)
Fiore, Massimiliano, *Anglo-Italian Relations in the Middle East 1922–1940* (Farnham, 2010)
Firth, J. D'E., *Rendall of Winchester: the Life and Witness of a Teacher* (Oxford, 1954)
Fratelli Alinari, Archivi Alinari, *Firenze: Immagini del XIX secolo* (Florence, 1996)
Fussell, Paul, *The Great War and Modern Memory* (Oxford, 1975)
Fitzgerald, Penelope, *The Knox Brothers* (London, 1977)
Fox, Colin, *Monchy le Preux: Arras* (London, 2000)
Gillon, Stair, *The KOSB in the Great War* (London, 1930)
Graves, Robert, *Goodbye to All That* (London, 1929)
Hart-Davies, Rupert, *Siegfried Sassoon: Diaries 1915–1918* (London, 1981)
—— *Siegfried Sassoon: Diaries 1920–1922* (London, 1985)
—— *Siegfried Sassoon: Diaries 1923–1925* (London, 1985)
Hassall, Christopher, *Edward Marsh, Patron of the Arts* (London, 1959)
Hay, Ian, *The Oppressed English* (London, 1917)
Haycock, David Boyd, *A Crisis of Brilliance* (London, 2010)
Hibberd, Dominic, *Wilfred Owen* (London, 2002)
—— *Wilfred Owen: The Last Year* (London, 1992)
HMSO *Documents on British Foreign Policy, vol. XXIV* (1922–23)
Hoare, Philip, *Noël Coward: A Biography* (London, 1995)
—— *Wilde's Last Stand* (London, 1997)
Holland, Vyvyan, *Son of Oscar Wilde* (London, 1954)
Hollings, Mary A., *The Life of Sir Colin Scott Moncrieff* (1917)
Hollis, Matthew, *Now All Roads Lead to France: The Last Years of Edward Thomas* (London, 2011)
Holmes, Richard, *Acts of War: The Behaviour of Men in Battle* (London, 2003)
—— *Tommy: The British Soldier on the Western Front* (London, 2004)
Holroyd, Michael, *Bernard Shaw* (London, 1997)
Huxley, Aldous, *Those Barren Leaves* (1925)
Hyde, H. Montgomery, *Christopher Sclater Millard* (New York, 1990)
Jeffrey, Keith, *MI6: The History of the Secret Intelligence Service 1909–1949* (London, 2010)
Karl, Frederick and Davies, Laurence, *Collected Letters of Joseph Conrad* (Cambridge, 2008)
Keegan, John, *The First World War* (London, 1998)

Knox, Ronald, *A Spiritual Aeneid* (1918)
Lejeune, Anthony, *The Gentlemen's Clubs of London* (London, 1979)
Linklater, Andro, *Compton Mackenzie: A Life* (London, 1987)
Marsh, Edward (ed.), *Georgian Poets* (1911–1918)
Masson, Rosaline, *I Can Remember Robert Louis Stevenson* (Edinburgh, 1922)
Moncrieffe, Frederick and William, *The Moncrieffs and the Moncrieffes* (1929)
Moorcroft Wilson, Jean, *Siegfried Sassoon: The Journey from the Trenches* (London, 2003)
Neville, Peter, *Mussolini* (London, 2004)
Nimmo, James, *Narrative of Mr James Nimmo Written for His Own Satisfaction to Keep in Some Remembrance the Lord's Way Dealing and Kindness Towards Him, 1654–1709* (Edinburgh, 1889)
Oldham, Peter, *Messines Ridge: Ypres* (London, 1998)
Orioli, Giuseppe ('Pino'), *Adventures of a Bookseller* (London, 1938)
Ortolani, Benito (ed. and trans.), *Pirandello's Love Letters to Marta Abba* (Princeton, 1994)
Osborn, E. B., *The Muse in Arms* (London, 1917)
Owen, Harold, and Bell, John (eds), *Wilfred Owen: Collected Letters* (Oxford, 1967)
Painter, George, *Marcel Proust: A Biography, vols I* and *II* (London, 1959)
Paradis de Moncrif, François-Augustin, *The Adventures of Zeloïde and Amanzarfidine*, translated by and with an introduction by C. K. Scott Moncrieff (London, 1929)
Pasternak, Boris, *Selected Poems*, (trans. Jon Stallworthy and Peter France) (London, 1970)
Pearce, Joseph, *The Unmasking of Oscar Wilde* (London, 2000)
Powell, Anthony, *Memoirs vol. I: Infants of the Spring* (London, 1976)
Raine, Kathleen, *The Inner Journey of the Poet* (New York, 1982)
Ricketts, Harry, *Strange Meetings: The Poets of the Great War* (London, 2010)
Robb, Graham, *Strangers: Homosexual Love in the Nineteenth Century* (London, 2003)
Royle, Trevor, *The Flowers of the Forest: Scotland and the First World War* (Edinburgh, 2007)
Ruskin, John, *The Seven Lamps of Architecture* (1849)
Sabben-Clare, James, *Winchester College* (Southampton, 1981)

Scott Moncrieff, Mary Ann, *Our Forefathers* (Edinburgh, 1895)
Scott Moncrieff, Robert, *The Branch and the Branches. With an Historical Outline of Persecutions Under which the Jews Have Suffered from Century to Century, Since the Beginning of the Christian Era* (Selkirk, 1900)
Seymour, Miranda, *Robert Graves: Life on the Edge* (London, 1995)
Shepherd, Ben, *A War of Nerves: Soldiers and Psychiatrists, 1914–1994* (London, 2002)
Shone, Richard, *Bloomsbury Portraits: Vanessa Bell, Duncan Grant and Their Circle* (London, 1976)
Sitwell, Osbert and Sacheverell, *All at Sea: a Social Tragedy in Three Acts for First-Class Passengers Only* (London, 1927)
Stallworthy, Jon, *Anthem for Doomed Youth* (London, 2002)
—— *Survivors' Songs: From Maldon to the Somme* (Cambridge, 2008)
—— *Wilfred Owen: A Biography* (Oxford, 1974)
Symons, A. J. A., *The Quest for Corvo: An Experiment in Biography* (New York, 1934)
Tadié, Jean-Yves, *Marcel Proust : A Life,* trans. Euan Cameron (London, 2000)
Thompson, David, *Nairn in Darkness and Light* (London, 1987)
Thompson, J. Lee, *Northcliffe: Press Baron in Politics* (London, 2000)
Waugh, Evelyn, *Ronald Knox* (London, 1959)
—— *A Little Learning* (London, 1964)
West, Nigel, *MI6: British Secret Intelligence Service Operations, 1909–45* (London, 1983)

Notes

If not listed in Sources above, publication details are given in full on first citation; thereafter a short reference is used.

Chapter 1: Bloodline

1 *Remembrance of Things Past: Swann's Way,* 15 (Chatto & Windus, 1957)
2 Mary Ann Scott Moncrieff, *Our Forefathers*, 16
3 *The Moncrieffs and the Moncrieffes*, 9
4 Forster to Sprott, 15.9.28. Charleston Papers, King's College, Cambridge
5 *Cities of the Plain*, vol. 1, chap. 1
6 Covenanters in Scotland were those who opposed the interference of the Stuart kings in the Presbyterian Church of Scotland. Kings upheld the Divine Right, while the Covenanters maintained only Christ could be head of the Church – the conflict fuelled uprisings, persecutions and imprisonments.
7 *Nimmo's Narrative*, 1654–1709, xiii
8 Paradis de Moncrif, intro., xl
9 Hollings, *Life of Sir Colin Scott Moncrieff*, 3
10 'And much I miss those sportive boys,
Companions of my mountain joys,
Just at the age 'twixt boy and youth,
When thought is speech, and speech is truth.'
(Walter Scott, *Marmion*, Canto 2, introduction)
11 Hollings, 17
12 MASM, *Our Forefathers*
13 Alan Scott Moncrieff, *Family Memoir*
14 http://www.s-asian.cam.ac.uk/Handlist_S.htm http://archive.is/2Sws (scroll down to Scott Moncrieff)
15 Rosaline Masson, *I Can Remember Robert Louis Stevenson*, 76

16 The purpose of the Franklin Expedition 1845–59 was to map out the Northwest Passage from North America to Asia. Under Sir John Franklin, 150 men set out with supplies to last five years, including 8,000 tins of early canned food. The expedition failed terribly, all the men dying from cold and starvation, and possibly lead poisoning from the lead in the tinned food.
17 *Blackwood's*, published in Edinburgh, was the most influential literary magazine of the nineteenth century, including among its contributors Coleridge, Shelley, George Eliot, De Quincey, James Hogg and Joseph Conrad.
18 JMSM, Diary, 6.11.1883
19 JMSM, Diary, 1.10.1885
20 JMSM, Diary, 13.11.1885
21 JMSM, Diary, 21.11.1885
22 For Colin SM's role read the ebook on *Modern Egypt* by the Earl of Cromer; also his own letters in *Life of Sir Colin Scott Moncrieff*, also published online, which show that the knighthood was awarded as a direct response to his taking the lead in abolishing the corvée.
23 JMSM, Diary, 1883
24 Scottish Record Office GD18/4968 Walker of Weedingshall 1791 – payment of £10 for a plan by Robert Adam.
25 JMSM, Diary, 25.9.1889
26 JMSM, Diary, 1889
27 JMSM, Diary, 1.11.1889
28 JMSM, Diary, 1891
29 Memories and Letters (M&L), 2
30 JMSM, Diary, 25.12.1895
31 Desk, Findlay Collection (FC)

Chapter 2: Childhood

1 JMSM, Diary, 5.1.1895
2 Ibid., 25.4.1895
3 Ibid., 24.6.1895
4 Ibid., 1.8.1895
5 Ibid., 25.9.1895
6 Ibid., 30.4.1896
7 Ibid., 20.8.1896
8 Ibid., 10.2.1897
9 Ibid.

10 M&L, 3
11 JMSM, Diary, 19.4.1898
12 Ibid., 11.8.99
13 David Thompson, *Nairn*, 86
14 JMSM, Diary, 6.7.1900
15 Ibid., 13.8.00
16 Prep school letter, undated. FC
17 CKSM to mother, undated. FC
18 From his father, 27.6.02. FC

Chapter 3: Winchester

1 JMSM, Diary, 7.7.03
2 From George to Meg, 16.9.03. Christina Scott Moncrieff
3 To his mother, undated, 1903. M&L, 13
4 To his mother, Winchester, undated. M&L, 21
5 To his father, 'Moberly Library, Wednesday afternoon'. Christina Scott Moncrieff
6 To his mother, 1904. M&L, 14
7 To his mother, 30.4.05. M&L, 19
8 To his mother, 1905. M&L, 20
9 JMSM, Diary, 1904
10 CKSM, letters. FC
11 Rendall to JMSM, 1904. M&L, 16
12 To his mother, undated. M&L, 21–2
13 CKSM, notebooks. FC
14 CKSM, letters. FC
15 M&L, 19
16 To mother, 30.4.05. M&L, 18
17 To mother, 1905. M&L, 17
18 CKSM, poetry notebook, 6, 1906. FC
19 Ibid.
20 CKSM to Colin, 18.11.07. FC

Chapter 4: First Love Affairs

1 M&L, 19
2 CKSM, poetry notebook, 12. FC
3 Ibid., 13
4 CKSM undated letter, Winchester. FC
5 CKSM undated story. FC

6 CKSM, poetry notebook. FC
7 M&L, 25
8 M&L, 21
9 Fussell, *The Great War and Modern Memory*, 284
10 Corvo was a talented writer and artist, thief, liar and pederast. A. J. A. Symons's *Quest for Corvo* is a masterly exercise in redemption through biography.
11 Ross continued to be a good friend to Wilde after the latter's imprisonment, working to have his writings endorsed, collected and legally published, ensuring the money went to Wilde's two sons. He tracked down and bought the rights to texts of Wilde's that had been sold off and scattered, and he fought the traffic in black-market copies of Wilde's books and of bogus erotic books under Wilde's name.
12 *Wykehamist*, no. 439, Nov. 1906. *Academy* 10.8.07
13 Joseph Pearce, *The Unmasking of Oscar Wilde*
14 Ross to Millard, 27.5.07. AC (UCLA)
15 Ross to Millard, 5.5.07. AC (UCLA)
16 Ibid.
17 A. J. A. Symons, *Quest for Corvo*
18 Monthly academic journal covering the decorative arts, established 1903. The editors were Roger Fry and More Adey.
19 C. J. Hope-Johnstone. Powell, *Memoirs*, 95
20 FC
21 National Archives, HO 140/346
22 'Gross indecency' was the criminal term used for acts where sodomy could not be proven. The penalty for sodomy was life imprisonment.
23 CKSM to VBH, 27.11.27. HRC
24 JMSM, Diary, 15.4.07
25 CKSM to VBH, 27.11.27. HRC
26 To mother, undated. FC
27 *New Field*, March 1908
28 *New Field*, April 1908
29 Plato, *Symposium*
30 Poetry notebook, Nov. 1907. *New Field*, March 1908
31 From the 1923 Francis Murray limited edition. FC
32 Burge to Charles's father, 7.4.08. Christina Scott Moncrieff

Chapter 5: To Edinburgh

1 To mother, Sept. 1908. M&L, 20
2 JMSM, Diary, 25.3.09
3 JMSM, Diary, 4.4.09
4 JMSM, Diary, 6.4.09
5 CKSM, poetry notebook, 'Lanark April 1909', 40. FC
6 Ibid. 'May 1909', 39. FC
7 'To a Public Man', poetry notebook, 17.8.09. FC
8 Ross to Millard, 6.1.09. AC (UCLA)
9 CKSM, poetry notebook, 45. FC
10 Francis was a journalist and critic and his father, Sir Augustine Birrell, was Chief Secretary for Ireland from 1907–1916. Cecil Spring Rice was a diplomat and poet; he wrote the hymn 'I Vow to Thee, My Country' while ambassador in Stockholm. It is not known whether this meeting was with him or one of his brothers.
11 To mother, July 1910. M&L, 30
12 Gale, 84. 'Long ago, there was an admirable series dealing with the Roman Emperors written, I believe, by Charles Scott Moncrieff, whom I never met,' wrote E. Clerihew Bentley in his autobiography, *Those Days*. Authorship of the clerihew quoted is now in dispute. According to C. D. Broad it is by F. W. Haskins. *Book Collector* (1980) vol. 29, p. 26
13 Gale, 67
14 Dedicatory poem in *Chanson de Roland*, written Christmas 1918
15 Holland, *Son of Oscar Wilde*, 126
16 CKSM to VBH, undated. HRC
17 (Lister House) CKSM to VBH, undated. HRC
18 (Edgemoor Lanark) CKSM to VBH, undated. HRC
19 (Lister House) CKSM to VBH, undated. HRC
20 CKSM to VBH, undated. HRC
21 (Argyll) CKSM to VBH, undated. HRC
22 To mother, 28.1.10. M&L, 29
23 To mother, 24.5.11. M&L, 33
24 Poetry notebook, 39. Dated Edinburgh, 1909. FC
25 JMSM, Diary, 9.4.09
26 Saintsbury, *A History of Criticism and Literary Taste in Europe from the Earliest Texts to the Present Day*, Vol. 3, 611
27 To mother, 19 to 29 Aug, 1912. M&L, 34–40
28 *Westminster Gazette*, no. 4684, May 1908

29 It was never published but Charles's typescript still exists in possession of Eileen Scott Moncrieff.
30 To mother, Oct. 1913. M&L, 41
31 JMSM, Diary, 8.8.13
32 CKSM letter. Collection of Malcolm Gibbs
33 H. R. Pyatt, reminiscence written for M&L, 43

Chapter 6: Lightness in War

1 CKSM original diary, 24.7.14. FC
2 CKSM diary, 25.7.14
3 Ibid.
4 To mother, July 1914. M&L, 45
5 CKSM diary, 25.7.14. FC
6 CKSM diary, 26.7.14. FC
7 CKSM diary, 27.7.14
8 CKSM diary, 2.8.14
9 CKSM diary, 8.8.14
10 CKSM diary, 20.8.14
11 To his mother, 18.9.14. M&L, 47
12 Ibid.
13 General information from Royle, *Flowers of the Forest*
14 Royle, 51
15 CKSM diary, 25.8.14. FC
16 'Does Sir reside in the hotel?' 'No, I reside in the dust.'
17 To mother, 13.10.14. FC
18 Unit Diary, National Archives, WO 95 1552
19 To mother, 26.10.14. M&L, 55
20 To mother, 27.10.14. M&L, 57
21 Ibid.
22 There were 48,000 Germans and two British divisions of between 10,000 and 15,000
23 Unit Diary: '31st October Messines 11am. Great-coats left in village as bayonet charge from east side ordered (coats badly wanted at night. They will never be left again). A and C Coys in firing line. C Coy pushed the line half by the cavalry to the East edge of the village, clearing the Germans out of the convent with the bayonet. House to house fighting ensued. Position south of the village taken by A Coy.'
24 To mother, 2.11.14. M&L, 61. The official casualty list and CWGC database record two subalterns of the 21st Lancers killed in action

on the 30th October 1914: Lieutenants Philip Francis Payne-Gallwey and John Herbert Butler Hollings. The subaltern killed was Lieutenant George Henry Cox 3 KOSB att. 2 KOSB. Both the CWGC and official casualty list give the date of death as 30th October (and record one man killed on that day). According to the war diary (and Stair Gillon) the action commenced on the 31st.

25 Gillon, *The KOSB in the Great War*, 52
26 To mother, 2.11.14. M&L, 62
27 Oldham, *Messines Ridge*, 24
28 To mother, 5.11.14. M&L, 65
29 Unit Diary, National Archives, WO 95 1552
30 Ibid.
31 To mother, 9.11.14. M&L, 68
32 To mother, 5.11.14. M&L, 65
33 To mother, 20.11.14. M&L, 76
34 To mother. M&L, 77. The lines in William Morris's poem to which CKSM was referring read:
'The draggled swans most eagerly eat
The green weeds trailing in the moat;
Inside the rotting leaky boat
You see a slain man's stiffened feet.'
35 To mother, 20.10.14. FC

Chapter 7: God in the Trenches

1 JMSM and CKSM letters. FC
2 E. B. Osborn, *The Muse in Arms*, 1917
3 To mother, 2.6.15. M&L, 86
4 To mother, 6.6.15. M&L, 86
5 From Mrs Macleod to David Scott Moncrieff, 5.6.52. FC
6 Ibid. M&L, 87
7 Which he kept all his life, left to his mother among his things, and which I now have – when the book is published, I will give the fragment back to Ypres Cathedral with a copy of the book.
8 To mother, 18.7.15. M&L, 91
9 Chapman, *A Passionate Prodigality*
10 To mother, 22.7.15. M&L, 93
11 Tadié, *Marcel Proust*, 350
12 Tadié, 326
13 From Knox to JMSM, 12.12.30. FC

14 Evelyn Waugh, *Knox*, 125
15 *Knox*, 201
16 Fitzgerald, *The Knox Brothers*, 121
17 Ibid.
18 Postcard from Knox to CKSM, 21.9.17. FC
19 To mother, 25.7.15. M&L, 94
20 To mother, 1.8.15. M&L, 98
21 Psalm 26, Douay-Rheims translation
22 J. Dalrymple, 'Conversion' CTS 1985
23 To mother, 25.7.15. M&L, 94
24 To mother, 1.8.15. M&L, 96
25 Ibid.
26 Ibid.
27 To mother, 3.1.15. M&L, 99
28 Ibid.
29 To mother, 7.8.15. M&L, 100
30 JMSM, Diary, 1916
31 Ibid.
32 To mother, 27.9.15. M&L, 103
33 Gillon, 390
34 To mother, 25.11.15. FC
35 Private Patrick Beattie, 2nd Bn., KOSB, to Charles's mother, May 1930. M&L, 107
36 Lance-Corporal William Buchanan, 2nd Bn, KOSB, to Charles's mother, May 1930. M&L, 107
37 To mother, 29.11.15. FC
38 To parents, 29.12.15. M&L, 109
39 To parents, November 1915. M&L, 108

Chapter 8: Critic at War

1 National Archives, WO 339/53655
2 JMSM, Diary, 7.2.16
3 JMSM, Diary, 6.2.16
4 JMSM, Diary, 12.2.16
5 Papers of E. J. Dent, King's College, Cambridge. Dent composed music for the ballad.
6 To H. R. Pyatt, 19.2.16
7 To the Pyatts, 19.2.16. M&L, 112
8 To mother, 13.2.16. M&L, 110

9 Ross to Millard, 4.9.16. AC (UCLA)
10 To mother, 24.2.16 M&L, 113
11 To mother, 26.2.16. M&L, 114
12 *London Mercury*, Oct. 1922
13 To mother, 3.3.16. M&L, 116
14 Bridges, *Spirit of Man*, ii
15 To a friend, 22.3.16. M&L, 118
16 Herbert Charles Lunn to his sister Constance Scott Moncrieff, 20.4.16. FC
17 Lord Kitchener, whose bewhiskered face famously adorned recruiting posters, had been criticised for not organising the supply of necessary munitions and had his responsibilities diminished until he was in charge only of recruitment and manpower by 1916. He was sent on a diplomatic mission to Russia in June 1916 and his armoured cruiser was sunk by a mine from a German U-boat west of Orkney.
18 To mother, 29.4.16. M&L, 119
19 Gillon, 179
20 *ODNB*
21 *The New Witness* (*NW*), 26.8.15
22 *NW*, 26.10.16
23 *NW*, 8.2.17
24 *NW*, 15.11.18
25 JMSM, Diary, 26.12.16
26 Major-General Sir George Kenneth Scott Moncrieff, 1855–1924, was a Royal Engineer serving in India, Afghanistan and China, and then in the War Office 1911–18.
27 Telegram to mother, 27.12.16. FC
28 To mother, 28.1.17. M&L, 122
29 Gillon, 188
30 *NW*, 8.2.17
31 Holland
32 *NW*, 12.4.17
33 Ibid.
34 Ibid.
35 To mother, 2.4.17. M&L, 126
36 To mother, 22.4.17. M&L, 127

Chapter 9: Wounded Out

1 To mother, 26.4.17. M&L, 130

2 To mother, 1.5.17. M&L, 128
3 To mother, 28.4.17. FC
4 To Trant, 4.5.17. Winchester College Archives
5 To mother, 14.5.17. M&L, 129
6 *NW*, 20.9.18
7 To the Pyatts, May 1917. M&L, 133
8 From Lt-Col. Welch to 87th Infantry Brigade headquarters. FC
9 CKSM notebook. FC. Also *NW*, 8.12.22
10 *Westminster Gazette*, 30.11.18
11 *New Statesman*, 30.11.19
12 *NW*, 28.6.17
13 *NW*, 2.8.17
14 *NW*, 6.9.17
15 Ian Hay, *The Oppressed English*, 30
16 *NW*, 20.9.17
17 *NW*, 27.9.17
18 CKSM to Burdell, 23.10.17. NLS
19 Professor Peter France, email to author
20 Ibid.
21 Catherine was the first of four daughters of Major-General Sir George Scott Moncrieff and grew up at Elie Castle. Charles was very close to Catherine all his life and later helped her get work in the Intelligence Services.
22 Sassoon quoted in Joseph Pearce, *Literary Converts* (San Francisco, 2006), 319
23 Cohen quoted by Jeffrey, *MI6*, 314
24 Jeffrey, 58

Chapter 10: In Love with Wilfred Owen

1 CKSM, *NW*, 10.12.20
2 National Archives, HO 140/346
3 'In English preparatory and public schools, romance is necessarily homosexual. The opposite sex is despised and treated as something obscene. Many boys never recover from this perversion. For everyone born homosexual, at least ten permanent pseudo-homosexuals are made by the public school system: nine of these ten as honourable, chaste and sentimental as I was.' Robert Graves, *Goodbye to All That*, ch. 3
4 Ross had tried to discourage Graves from marrying by hinting

that there was 'negro' blood in the Nicholson family and that one of their children might revert to coal-black (*Goodbye to All That*).

5 Owen, *Collected Letters*, 499
6 Graves to CKSM, 1.1.18. NLS
7 *NW*, 14.2.18
8 Moorcroft Wilson, 361 (Letter in Sassoon's press cuttings book in William Reese Collection, New Haven, USA)
9 Moorcroft Wilson, 399
10 Ibid., 400
11 Owen, *Collected Letters*, 5.10.17
12 *NW*, 10.12.20
13 Owen, *Collected Letters*
14 JMSM, Diary, 11.2.18
15 Graves to CKSM, 11.2.18. NLS Acc. 7243
16 Ibid.
17 To mother, copied into diary, 26.4.18
18 *NW*, 10.12.20
19 *Song of Roland*, Translator's Note, xiii
20 *NW*, 10.5.18
21 *NW*, 27.9.18
22 EFL, Oxford, dated May 1918. This was not used as the final dedication; instead there were three dedicatory poems to three dead friends, only one of which was Owen.
23 To Marsh, undated. Berg Collection, NYPL
24 Ibid.
25 CKSM to Owen, 19.5.18. EFL, Oxford
26 Owen to his mother, 21.5.18
27 Wilde had argued that Shakespeare had been in love with his sonnet's 'onlie begetter', 'Mr WH', and Charles felt he was in the same predicament with 'Mr WO'. Shakespeare's alleged aim had been to immortalise his young friend even though they could not be lovers. Charles was more modest, hoping his sonnet would live by basking in Owen's reflected glory.
28 CKSM to Owen 27.5.18
29 George Scott Moncrieff, the nephew to whom Charles left all his papers, had a bonfire just after the Second World War and after his wife's death. He later confessed to his daughter that he had then burnt things that he never should have destroyed.

30 NA, WO 339/53655
31 Graves to CKSM, 24.5.18. NLS Acc. 7243
32 Ibid.
33 *The Nation*, 15.6.18
34 *NW*, 21.6.18
35 To mother, 2.4.17 M&L, 126
36 CKSM to VBH, 14.6.18. HRC
37 Ibid.
38 JMSM, Diary, 18.6.18
39 JMSM, Diary, 18.7.18
40 Owen to mother, 31.8.18. CL
41 *NW*, 10.12.1920
42 Owen to mother, 31.8.18. CL
43 *NW*, 10.12.20
44 Conversation with author, Oxford, 5.5.2009
45 War Office file, 339/53655
46 NA, WO 339/53655
47 JMSM, Diary, 1918
48 'Intimate' in 1918 did not necessarily mean physical intimacy.
49 Moorcroft Wilson, 512
50 Sassoon, Diary, Oct. 1918
51 Gale. Also http://www.poetropical.co.uk/4.html
52 CKSM, *NW*, 10.12.20
53 Owen to CKSM. Dennis Welland Collection, John Rylands Library, Manchester University, DSW/1/1/1/23
54 To mother, 12.11.18. M&L, 142
55 To mother, 29.1.19. M&L, 143
56 *Wykehamist*, 1907. Winchester College Archives
57 CKSM to Susan Owen, 11.2.21. EFL Oxford

Chapter 11: Sniping in the Literary World

1 Major Neville Lytton, 25.12.18, Service Book. FC
2 Sitwell, 22
3 *The Nation*, 11.10.19
4 *NW*, 24.10.19
5 *NW*, 28.11.19
6 Ibid.
7 *NW*, 14.11.19

8 It is touching that Sassoon, this one-time enemy of Charles, at odds politically and poetically, and so hurt by Charles's criticism, would later come to embrace the same Catholic faith as Charles and choose the same priestly mentor and friend, Ronald Knox. In fact he asked to be buried near Knox in Mells, Somerset.

9 *NW*, 21.10.19

10 *NW*, 9.1.20

11 Stanley Baldwin of the new MPs elected in 1918; quoted by J. M. Keynes in *Economic Consequences of the Peace*, ch. 5.

12 *NW*, 24.10.19

13 *NW*, 12.09.19

14 *NW*, 26.09.19

15 Ibid.

16 Gale, 202

17 *Swann's Way*, 55

18 Mercer (1889–19??) studied at the Slade, then in Holland, Italy and Spain. A classical realist painter, he held his first exhibition in 1912. He exhibited at the Royal Academy and was a member of the Royal Society of Portrait Painters and the Royal Institute of Oil Painters.

19 *Song of Roland*, dedication

20 Peter France, 'Scott Moncrieff's First Translation', *Translation and Literature* 21 (2012), pp. 364–82.

21 To Susan Owen, 11.2.21. EFL, Oxford

22 The Whittlebot family first appeared in *London Calling*, 1923. *Chelsea Buns,* the spoof poetry book, was published in 1925; it included Noël Coward's 'Contours':

23 Written by Francis Beaumont, this is a seventeenth-century satire on chivalric romance, the burning pestle itself used as a heraldic symbol implying sexual bravado on the one hand and syphilis on the other.

24 *The Times*, 25.11.19

25 *NW*, 5.12.19

26 *NW*, 28.11.19

27 *NW*, 5.12.19

28 *TLS*, 11.12.19

29 *Chanson de Roland*, line 1610

30 From Rendall to CKSM, 25.11.19. FC

31 Peter France, *Literature and Translation,* Oct 2012

32 *Roland*, ix

33 To H. Pyatt, 30.12.19. M&L, 148
34 *Beowulf, Widsith, Finnsburgh, Waldere, Deor*, trans. CKSM, 8.
35 *London Mercury*, Sept. 1920
36 *The Times*, 28.10.20
37 CKSM to VBH, July 1922. HRC
38 CKSM to VBH, 31.7.22. HRC
39 M&L, 145
40 *The Times*, 5.7.20
41 JMSM, Diary, 14.7.20
42 CKSM to Anna SM, 14.7.20 . Letter courtesy of John Scott Moncrieff
43 From Charterland Agent to JMSM, 15.7.20, copied into diary 25.8.20
44 Conversations with J. K. Scott Moncrieff 2008–2011.
45 CKSM to Anna Scott Moncrieff, 14.7.20. Letter courtesy of John Scott Moncrieff
46 Conversation with David's widow, Anne Scott Moncrieff, 2008
47 Gosse to CKSM, 18.9.21. M&L, 150
48 Ibid.
49 *NW*, 28.10.20
50 *NW*, 11.02.1921

Chapter 12: Translating Proust

1 Dedication to Eva Cooper in *Swann's Way*
2 Proust paid for the costs of the first volume, published in 1913; it was successful, then war intervened. The publisher Grasset went into Military Service after the second volume and in 1919 Gallimard took up the rest.
3 Aldington, 88
4 Gale, 259
5 Hoare, *Coward*, 40
6 Dedicatory poem to EJC in *Swann's Way*, dated Michaelmas 1921
7 Gale, 256
8 Huxley, *Those Barren Leaves*, 14, 15
9 Gale, 262
10 Gale, 256
11 *Translation and Literature*, vol. 13, no. 1 (Spring 2004), pp. 124–30
12 Peter France, 'The Serva Padrona', *Art in Translation*, vol. 2, no. 2, July 2010 , pp. 119–30 (12)

13 This lecture, 'The World as India', reprinted in Sontag, *At the Same Time: Essays and Speeches* (New York, 2007).

14 Peter France, 'The Serva Padrona', *Art in Translation*, vol. 2, no. 2, July 2010, pp. 119–30 (12)

15 To Whitworth, 5.5.22. Chatto Archive

16 To Whitworth, undated (Feb. 1922). CA

17 Letters to Conal O'Riordan, Boston Public Library. Gale, 266

18 To Prentice, 14.9.22. CA

19 Gale, 270

20 *The Times*, 21.9.22

21 CKSM to Prentice, 26.9.22. CA

22 To VBH, Aug. 1922. HRC

23 Ibid.

24 Proust to CKSM, 10.10.22. NLS. Translation by Jean Findlay. Proust's letter read:

Monsieur,

J'ai été très flatté et touché de la peine que vous avez prise de traduire mon Swann. Le miracle est que je puisse vous en remercier. Je suis on effet si gravement malade (pas contagieusement) que je ne puis répondre à personne, et en tous cas vous êtes le seul de mes traducteurs en diverses langues, à qui j'ai écrit, peut être en voyant le beau talent avec lequel vous avez fait cette traduction (je n'ai pas encore tout lu, mais songez que je ne quitte pas mon lit, ne prends aucune nourriture, etc.) J'aurais bien une ou deux critiques à vous faire. Par example À la recherche du temps perdu ne peut nullement dire cela. Les vers que vous ajoutez, la dédicace à vos amis, ne remplacent pas l'amphibologie voulue de Temps perdu qui se retrouve à la fin de l'ouvrage, Le Temps retrouvé. Quant à Swann's Way cela peut signifier Du côté de chez Swann, mais tout aussi bien 'la maniére de Swann'. En ajoutant to vous auriez tout sauvé. Je vous demande pardon de vous écrire en français mais mon anglais serait si pitoyable que personne ne le comprendrait. 'Comment,' me diriez-vous, 'vous savez à peine – du moins actuellement – un mot ou deux d'anglais, et vous permettez délivrer certains critiques – inspirés de beaucoup d'éloges sur mon traduction!'

Présentez je vous prie à vos editeurs mes compliments pour la façon remarquable dont ils ont fait traduire Swann et croyez je vous prie à mes sentiments les plus sincères.

25 Painter, *Marcel Proust*, 668
26 To Prentice, 27.11.22. CA
27 *TLS*, 18.1.23
28 Chatto Archive, 8.12.22
29 Joseph Conrad, *Collected Letters*, vol. 7, 623
30 Pasternak, 165–66
31 CKSM to Prentice, undated (Dec 1922).CA
32 Woolf diaries, Jan. 1923
33 *TLS*, 4.1.23
34 To Roger Fry, 6.5.22
35 Berg Collection, NYPL
36 E. A. Macarthur, 'Following *Swann's Way*: To the Lighthouse', *Comparative Literature* 2004, 56(4): 331–336
37 *Tribute*, 26
38 *Tribute*, 67
39 *Tribute*, 126
40 T. S. Eliot, Feb. 1923, *Collected Letters*
41 *The Criterion*, April and July 1926
42 Ibid.
43 Charles Baudelaire, 'Lesbos', *Fleurs du Mal*, 1857
44 CKSM to VBH, 26.4.23. HRC, Austin Texas
45 Ibid.
46 *London Mercury*, 26.3.23
47 To Marsh, 20.3.23. Berg
48 To Marsh, 22.3.23. Berg
49 To Marsh, 25.4.23. Berg
50 According to Harry Ricketts, Marsh was a latent but not active homosexual. The nearest he came to physical contact was to ask a young man if he might take off his shoe or boot (Sassoon and his hunting boots come to mind) as erotic stimulation. However, Charles was no longer a young god in that department and one suspects that his deformed foot and iron calliper had less aesthetic appeal.
51 To Marsh, undated. Berg
52 Aubrey Beardsley lived on Praed Street.
53 Prentice, 4.5.23
54 To Marsh, 19.7.23. Berg
55 Ibid.

56 CKSM to VBH, dated 'Mary Magdalen V(?) &M.' (22 July) 1923. HRC
57 To Marsh, 2.8.23. Berg
58 To Marsh, 7.8.23. Berg
59 Ibid.
60 To Marsh, undated, but obviously from Germany, summer 1923. The writing is crushed all around the edge of the letter, every margin is used and crammed with Proust references and queries.
61 To Marsh, undated. Berg

Chapter 13: Writer and Spy in Fascist Italy

1 Dansey went on to become Assistant Chief of the Secret Intelligence Services from 1939 for the duration of the Second World War.
2 Jeffery, 154, 314
3 Mussolini, 1921, quoted in Massimilio Fiore, *Anglo Italian Relations in the Middle East.*
4 Documents on British Foreign Policy, HMSO vol. XXIV, 11
5 Boyle Somerville, post-war review, 1919, quoted in Jeffrey, 63
6 His War Office file states that files 1, 4, 5, 7 and 8 were removed and destroyed in 1932. The rest of the file relates to his wound and his pension.
7 Mackenzie, quoted in Jeffrey, 242, 243. Mackenzie was prosecuted under the official secrets act for revealing in *Greek Memories* that passport control was part of SIS.
8 To Marsh, 20.9.23. Berg
9 To Marsh, undated. Berg
10 *London Mercury*, Sept. 1923
11 To Marsh, 25.4.23. Berg
12 *Saturday Review*, Sept. 1923
13 Samuel Johnson quoted in Boswell's *Life of Johnson*. The conversation took place on 20 September 1777.
14 To Prentice, 22.10.23. CA
15 Ibid.
16 M&L, 151
17 To Prentice, 22.10.23. CA
18 CKSM to Millard, 30.10.23. HRC
19 Ibid.
20 West, *MI6*, 34
21 In 1928 Giuseppe Orioli was the first publisher in English of *Lady*

Chatterley's Lover, which could not be published openly in England until 1960.

22 Orioli, *Adventures of a Bookseller*, 228
23 La Pietra was left by Acton to New York University.
24 Acton, 365
25 Byrne, *A Genius for Living*, 320
26 Byrne, 321
27 To Prentice, 4.11.23. CA
28 To Chapman, 8.12.23. WU
29 To Prentice, 10.4.24. CA
30 Ibid.
31 To Chapman, undated (Dec. 1924). WU
32 From Chapman, 25.11.24. WU
33 Holland, 120
34 To Chapman, 14.11.23. WU
35 To Chapman, 29.11.23. WU
36 JMSM, Diary, 2.1.24. FC
37 JMSM, Diary, 9.1.24. FC
38 Edited by Rupert Hart-Davis.
39 To Prentice, 29.1.24. CA
40 JMSM, Diary, 13.1.24. FC
41 To Prentice, 12.12.23. CA
42 To Prentice, 29.1.24. CA
43 Ibid.
44 To Prentice, 26.2.24. CA. Ronald Firbank (1886–1926) wrote camp, witty novels, full of homosexual innuendo. He was also a Roman Catholic convert and lived in Rome.
45 To Prentice, 3.10.24. CA
46 To Prentice, 5.11.25. CA
47 To Prentice, 10.3.24. CA
48 To Prentice, 22.10.24. CA
49 To Prentice, 29.1.24. CA
50 To Prentice, 17.4.24. CA
51 To Prentice, 12.6.24. CA
52 Ibid.
53 To Prentice, April 1924. CA
54 To Prentice, 4.6.24. CA
55 CKSM to VBH, 22.6.24. HRC

56 To Prentice, 9.7.24. CA
57 To Prentice, 26.5.24. CA
58 Lesley Scott Moncrieff remembers conversations with Mackenzie in 1963.
59 To Prentice, 26.5.24. CA
60 To Prentice, 22.8.24. CA
61 CKSM to VBH, 14.7.24. HRC
62 To Prentice, 29.7.24. CA
63 Fiore, 24
64 CKSM to VBH, 4.8.24. HRC
65 CKSM to VBH, 4.8.24. HRC
66 To Prentice, 1.10.24. CA
67 To Prentice, 9.10.24. CA
68 Fiore, 18
69 To VBH, 21.11.24
70 To Prentice, 21.11.24. CA
71 To VBH, 28.11.24. HRC

Chapter 14 Discovering Pirandello

1 To Prentice, 22.10.24
2 To Marsh, 28.11.24. Berg
3 To Marsh, 18.12.24. Berg
4 To Marsh, 28.11.24. Berg
5 The jotter is in the NLS
6 To Marsh, 16.12.24. Berg
7 To Prentice, 17.12.24. CA
8 'I am alone, I am widowed, and the night falls on me.'
9 To Marsh, 16.12.24. Berg
10 To Marsh, 26.12.24. Berg
11 To Prentice. CA
12 To Marsh, 26.12.24. Berg
13 To Prentice, June 1925. CA
14 To Prentice, 25.1.25. CA
15 To Chapman, 21.1.25. WU
16 To Prentice, 9.1.24. CA
17 To Chapman, 11.2.25. WU
18 Ibid.
19 *Letters of A&H*, Intro, x

20 *Letters of A&H*, Intro, xviii
21 To Prentice, 8.3.25. CA
22 *Shoot!* Trans. CKSM, 1926
23 To VBH, 9.4.25. HRC
24 Ibid.
25 To VBH, 14.4.25. HRC
26 To VBH, 30.5.25. HRC
27 To VBH, 18.6.25. HRC
28 To VBH, 29.6.25. HRC
29 To Prentice, 8.6.25. CA
30 'There was a young woman of Modena, Whose priest put the fear of God in her, They found in her c---, The results of his s----, And the button-hook with which he'd been proddin' her.' (28.12.25. HRC) 'There was an old girl from Judea, Who gave her pet goat gonorrhea. She said that is one, Up the carpenter's son, Why she said that I've no idea.' (To VBH, 18.6.25. HRC)
31 To Prentice, 2.6.25. CA
32 Waugh diaries, 1.7.25
33 Waugh, *A Little Learning*, 229
34 To Prentice, 12.6.25. CA
35 To Prentice, 9.9.25. CA
36 To VBH, 29.7.25. HRC
37 Ibid.
38 To VBH, 16.7.25. HRC
39 To VBH, 8.8.25. HRC
40 To VBH, 17.8.25. HRC
41 Ibid.
42 Ibid.
43 Quoted back to VBH, 27.12.25. HRC
44 To VBH, 4.9.25. HRC
45 Ibid.
46 Fiore, 18
47 To Chapman, 7.8.25. WU
48 After her finishing, Dorothy married well and continued her godfather's legacy of educating nieces and nephews. I was one of these fortunate relations.
49 To Chapman, 25.9.25. WU
50 Prentice to CKSM. Gale, 389

51 To Prentice, 15.10.25. CA
52 To VBH, 7.2.26. HRC
53 To Prentice, 8.12.25. CA
54 Charles got a little black leather passport calling him *The Times* Special Correspondent in Tuscany for his services on this mission.
55 M&L, 162
56 To Prentice, Jan. 1926. CA
57 From Seltzer, 10.12.25. Copy in CA
58 From Seltzer, 18.12.25. Copy in CA
59 To Seltzer, 18.1.26. CA
60 Schiff had written a novel based on his and his wife's relationship with Proust in which the main protagonists were the Kurts: *Richard, Myrtle and I* (1926)
61 To Prentice, 5.2.26. CA
62 To VBH, 7.2.26. HRC
63 To VBH, 5.2.26 HRC
64 To Prentice, 9–10.3.26. CA
65 Ibid.
66 Ibid.
67 To VBH, 15.3.26. HRC
68 To Prentice, 6.3.19. CA
69 To Prentice, 26.3.26. CA
70 To Prentice, 26.3.26. CA
71 To Prentice, 23.3.26. CA
72 To VBH, 30.1.26. HRC
73 CKSM in *The Times*, 26.5.26
74 Ibid.
75 See Frances Stonor Saunders, *The Woman who Shot Mussolini* (London, 2010).
76 *The Times*, 26.5.26
77 To VBH, 22.4.26. HRC
78 Sitwell, *All at Sea*, 30
79 Ibid., 23
80 Ibid., 26
81 To Prentice, 7.7.26. CA
82 To Prentice, 17.8.26. CA
83 Ibid.
84 Another copy is in the English Faculty Library at Oxford among the Wilfred Owen papers and is published in Jon Stallworthy's

biography of Owen, where the given date (1918) is not correct. The photograph was taken in 1913.

85 Gale, from conversations with R. Haynes.

86 To father, 1.1.27. FC

Chapter 15: A Death and Eviction

1 To Prentice, 8.1.27. CA

2 To mother, 4.1.27. FC

3 Ibid.

4 Ibid.

5 To Prentice, 4.2.27. CA

6 To mother, 8.1.27. FC

7 Ibid.

8 To mother, 10.1.27. FC

9 Ibid.

10 Ibid.

11 To mother, 23.1.27. FC

12 Anna Scott Moncrieff to Prentice, Jan. 1927. CA

13 To mother, 25.1.27. FC

14 Ibid.

15 To Prentice, 25.1.27. CA

16 To mother, 27.1.27. FC

17 For example the epigraph to Chapter 18 quotes a French motto attributed to Schiller, which Charles rendered in English and attributed correctly to Pope.

18 *TLS*, 18.3.26

19 Aldington in Intro, xii

20 Appendix to *Memoirs*, 224

21 Paradis de Moncrif, *The Adventures of Zeloïde and Amanzarifdine*, trans. CKSM, ed. Richard Aldington, Introduction by CKSM, p.xxiii

22 To Prentice, 21.3.27. CA

23 To Prentice, 4.5.27. CA

24 To Prentice, 27.5.27. CA

25 To VBH, 17.2.27. HRC

26 'There was a young lady of Stroud, Whose head was unbloody but bowed, She said "I'm not ducking, My head I'm just sucking, the c---- of the boys in the crowd."' To VBH, 3.6.27. HRC

27 To VBH, 3.6.27. HRC

28 To Prentice, 27.5.27. CA
29 To Prentice, 27.3.27. CA
30 To Prentice, 15.5.27. CA
31 To Charles Boni, 17.6.27. Copy in FC
32 To Prentice, 13.6.27. CA
33 To VBH, 3.6.27. HRC
34 To Prentice, 2.6.27. CA
35 To Prentice, 6.7.27. CA
36 To VBH, 3.6.27. HRC
37 To Prentice, 28.7.27. CA
38 From Macrae, 26.8.27. CA
39 To Macrae, 5.9.27. CA
40 To VBH, 14.9.27. HRC
41 To Prentice, 7.10.27. CA
42 Ibid.
43 Ibid.
44 To mother, 5.10.27. M&L, 172
45 To Prentice, 14.10.27. CA
46 To VBH, 24.10.27. HRC
47 *Letters of D. H. Lawrence* 14.11.27
48 To Aldington, 18.11.27. *Letters of DHL*
49 To Brown, 6.1.28. *Letters of DHL*
50 To Eliot, Jan. 1930. FF
51 To Orioli, 11.11.29. *Letters of DHL*
52 To Orioli, 27.11.29. *Letters of DHL*

Chapter 16: Rome

1 To mother, 29.10.28. FC
2 To Oriana, 28.3.28. Gale, 452. Sir Denison Ross (1871–1940), Orientalist, was said to know 49 languages and speak 30. During the First World War he worked in military intelligence at the War Office. Later he became the first director of the School of Oriental and African Studies.
3 *New Statesman*, 16.6.28
4 Jeffrey, 739
5 To mother, Oct. 1928. FC
6 Gale, 438
7 Pirandello to Abba, 5.7.28. Ortolani, 18
8 To Mrs Pearson, 29.3.28. M&L, 178

9 To Prentice, 27.2.27. CA
10 To Prentice, 5.10.28. CA
11 To Prentice, 24.9.28. CA
12 To Prentice, 1.10.28. CA
13 To Mrs Pearson, 15.2.29. M&L, 186
14 To mother, 20.1.27. FC
15 Piers Gaveston (1284–1312) was the favourite of Edward II, and possibly his lover.
16 To Marsh, 28.9.28. Berg
17 To Schuster, 5.11.28. Copy in FC
18 To Schuster, 19.6.29. Copy in FC
19 Forster to Sprott, 15.9.28. King's College Archive
20 To Sprott, 13.10.28. King's College Archive
21 To mother, 19.9.28. FC
22 To mother, 19.9.28. FC
23 To Prentice, March 1928. CA
24 To VBH, 21.2.29. HRC
25 Ernst Curtius to JMSM, 1931. M&L
26 Ibid.
27 To mother, 20.10.28. FC
28 To mother, 12.10.28. FC
29 To mother, 20.10.28. FC
30 To mother, 29.10.28. FC
31 *TLS*, 21.3.29
32 To Helen Stephen, 17.3.29. M&L, 189
33 Ibid.
34 To VBH, Aug. 1929. HRC
35 Ibid.
36 Ibid.
37 *Glasgow Herald*, 4.1.32
38 To mother, 9.6.29. M&L, 191
39 To Prentice, 24.9.28. CA
40 To Mrs Pearson, Oct. 1928. M&L, 182
41 To VBH, 5.9.29. HRC (s.a.w. was their code for oral sex. There are now medical links between oral sex and oesophageal cancer.)
42 To Helen Stephen, Dec. 1929. M&L, 195
43 To Eliot, 2.12.29. FF
44 Inscribed in a copy of *The Captive* published by Knopf in 1929,

given to Payen de Payne. From CKSM, Calvary Hospital, Rome, St Andrew's Day.

45 Gale, 458
46 Ibid.
47 Ibid.
48 To Eliot, 2.12.29. FF
49 From Eliot, 12.12.29. *Letters* vol. IV
50 Ibid.
51 To Eliot, 26.12.29. FF
52 *London Mercury*, May 1930
53 To VBH, 14.11.29. HRC
54 To VBH, 14.2.30. HRC
55 To Eliot, 29.1.30. FF
56 Dec. 1929. M&L, 196
57 To VBH, 14.2.30. HRC
58 M&L, 202

Epilogue

1 *Daily Telegraph*, 15.12.31
2 To VBH, 24.12.25, HRC
3 M&L, 25
4 F. Scott Fitzgerald, in a letter to his daughter, Scottie, 1939
5 Jerry Farber, *Scott Moncrieff's Way: Proust in Translation*, March 1997
6 Robert Douglas-Fairhurst, *Observer*, 2002
7 John Ruskin, *The Works of John Ruskin*, vol. 24, 371

Index